Global Corruption Report 2001

Global Corruption Report 2001

Transparency International

Edited by Robin Hodess,
with Jessie Banfield and Toby Wolfe

First published 2001
Transparency International
Otto-Suhr-Allee 97–99
D-10585 Berlin
Germany
<http://www.globalcorruptionreport.org>

Designed by Iris Farnschläder and Jörg Mahlstedt, Hamburg
Printing and binding by Medialis, Berlin
ISBN 3-935711-00-X

Contents

Regional reports

Global issues

Data and research

Contributors

This list does not include TI chapters, institutional contributors, or authors for the data and research section of this volume.

Sa'eda al-Kilani is Director of the Arab Archives Institute in Jordan and a journalist with *La Croix* and Reporters Sans Frontières. She is a contributing writer for the French weekly *L'Express* and the *Financial Times*, and a founding member both of the Euro-Mediterranean Human Rights Network and of TI-Jordan.

Luke Allnutt writes commentaries on Eastern European affairs for various publications, including the *Wall Street Journal*. His articles have also appeared in *Industry Standard*, Canada's *Globe and Mail* and at CNN.com. He is currently deputy editor at Transitions Online, the Prague-based news agency.

Maria Antonenko is a journalist in Russia.

Dima Bit-Suleiman is a journalist in Georgia.

Rowan Callick is Asia-Pacific editor for the *Australian Financial Review*, where he has worked for a decade, except for two years spent as a senior writer with *Time* magazine. Earlier Callick lived and worked in Papua New Guinea. He has won several journalism prizes and is author of *Comrades and Capitalists: Hong Kong Since the Handover* (Sydney: University of New South Wales Press, 1998).

Jorge Carrasco Araizaga is a journalist in Mexico.

Gabriel Chávez-Tafur is a journalist in Peru where he is affiliated with the Instituto Prensa y Sociedad.

Florence Chong is a journalist in Australia.

Sheila Coronel is Executive Director of the Philippines Center for Investigative Journalism.

Penny Dale reports on Africa for *Africa Confidential, NewsAfrica*, the *Financial Times, International Trade Finance, Oxford Analytica* and *The Voice*. She has also contributed to the BBC, the *Economist*, and Control Risks Group reports. Dale previously worked as assistant editor at *Africa Analysis*.

Carolina De Andrea is a journalist in Peru where she is affiliated with the Instituto Prensa y Sociedad.

Dini Djalal writes regularly for *Far Eastern Economic Review, Asian Business* and the *Bangkok Post*. She has also worked for radio and television, including as a reporter/producer for CNBC Asia. Djalal is based in Indonesia.

Yves-Marie Doublet is an advisor to the French National Assembly in its European Affairs division. He is the author of *Le financement de la vie politique* (Paris: Presses Universitaires de France, 1997).

Jeremy Druker has been a staff writer at *Transitions* magazine and Transitions Online (TOL). He became Director and editor of TOL three years ago. Druker has worked as a freelance consultant and correspondent for the Freedom Forum Media Studies Centre, *International Press Institute Report* and the European Journalism Network. He has also contributed to *US News & World Report, Columbia Journalism Review* and *Media Studies Journal*.

Peter Eigen is Chairman of Transparency International. He holds teaching positions at Harvard University's John F. Kennedy School of Government and Johns Hopkins University's School of Advanced International Studies. Prior to founding TI in 1993, Eigen worked for more than two decades at the World Bank, where he held senior management positions in South America and East Africa.

Keith Ewing is Professor of Public Law at King's College, University of London. He is the author of numerous books and articles on constitutional, administrative and human rights law. Ewing has acted as advisor to the British Labour Party on party funding issues.

Rossana Fuentes Berain is a journalist in Mexico. She is the managing editor of the Spanish edition of *Foreign Affairs*.

Fredrik Galtung is a founding staff member of Transparency International, where he is now head of research. Galtung has published widely on corruption and has been affiliated with Wolfson College, Cambridge University since 1997.

Miren Gutiérrez was business editor at *La Prensa* in Panama from 1996 to 2001. She contributes to *El País* and TVE and previously worked as a correspondent in Hong Kong for Agencia EFE. Gutiérrez has also written for the *Wall Street Journal, Wall Street Journal Americas, El Mundo, El Sol de México* and *Latin Finance*.

Djillali Hadjadj is a journalist for *Le Soir d'Algérie* and author of *Corruption et démocratie en Algérie*, now in its second edition (Paris: La Dispute, 2001). He is a founding member of the Association algérienne de lutte contre la corruption.

Hakeem Jimo reports for the Deutsche Presse Agentur, ARD-Public Radio, *Der Spiegel, Neue Zürcher Zeitung, Handelsblatt* and *Die Tageszeitung*. He is based in Benin. Jimo has also previously worked as business editor for AOL Germany.

Kristjan Kaljund is a journalist in Estonia.

Juca Kfouri is a journalist in Brazil.

Alisher Khamidov is a journalist in Kyrgyzstan.

Sophia Kornienko is a journalist in Russia.

Paul Lashmar began his journalism career with the UK's *Observer* in 1978. He has contributed to the *Washington Post* and *New Statesman*, and he worked for a number of years as an investigative journalist for television. From 1998 –2001 Lashmar was an investigative journalist with *The Independent*.

Michael Levi is Professor of Criminology at Cardiff University. Levi has written several books and articles on fraud, cross-border policing and money laundering, most recently *White Collar Crime and its Victims* (Oxford: Clarendon, forthcoming 2001), which he co-edited. Levi is currently editing a special issue on organised crime for the *Howard Journal of Criminal Justice*. In 1997, he was appointed 'scientific expert' on organised crime at the Council of Europe.

Telma Luzzani has worked as a journalist since 1982. She has reported for *Tiempo Argentina*, *Le Monde* and *Clarín*. Luzzani worked as foreign correspondent and is now an editor of *Clarín's* international politics section. She is also editor of the *Clarín* yearbook.

Patrick Mawaya is a journalist in Malawi.

Rigoberta Menchú Tum won the Nobel Prize for Peace in 1992, in recognition of her work against repression, racism and poverty in Guatemala. She now heads a foundation that focuses on human rights, especially of indigenous peoples. Menchú is also a UNESCO Goodwill Ambassador.

Kumi Naidoo is Secretary General and CEO of the NGO CIVICUS, the World Alliance for Citizen Participation. A long-time activist in the anti-apartheid movement, he contributed in various capacities to South Africa's transition after 1990. Naidoo is on the board of the Association for Women's Rights in Development and the Partnership for Transparency Fund.

Gerald Ndikum works on transparency issues in Cameroon.

Erich Ogoso Opolot is a journalist in Uganda and Kampala bureau chief for the Nation Media Group.

Enery Quinones is head of the Anti-Corruption Unit within the Directorate for Financial, Fiscal and Enterprise Affairs at the OECD.

Altin Raxhimi is a journalist in Albania.

Aqil Shah is a public policy analyst and writer based in Pakistan. He has worked for several think-tanks and international organisations, including the UNDP, and specialises in the political economy of corruption, public sector reform and democratisation.

Nicholas Shaxson is the author of country reports on Angola and Gabon for the Economist Intelligence Unit and a regular contributor to the BBC, *Financial Times, Financial Times Energy* and *Business Day*. He also reports for Reuters on the oil, gas and diamond industries.

Clare Short is Secretary of State at the Department for International Development of the UK government. She has been a Member of Parliament since 1983.

Daria Sito is a journalist in Bosnia.

Tidiane Sy is a Senegal-based correspondent for Agence France Presse. He also contributes regularly to Network Radio Services, Radio France International and *West Africa* magazine. Sy worked for several years as a journalist in South Africa.

Jennifer Tracy has been a staff writer and editor for the *St Petersburg Times* and *Moscow Times*. She has written for *Industry Standard, Business Central Europe*, and was until recently managing editor at Transitions Online in Prague.

Dame Wade is a journalist in Senegal where he has written for *Le Devoir* and *Le Nouvel Horizon*.

Gitau Warigi has worked as a reporter for *The Weekly Review*, Kenya's leading current affairs periodical, and as a senior writer for *The EastAfrican*. He is currently a national political correspondent for *The Sunday Nation* in Nairobi and also works as a development consultant in the region.

Alex Znatkevich is a journalist in Belarus.

Global Corruption Report 2001 editorial team

TI editors: Robin Hodess, Jessie Banfield and Toby Wolfe

Outside editors: Sarah Burd-Sharps and Michael Griffin

Acknowledgements

We extend our sincere thanks to all those who have helped make the *Global Corruption Report 2001* possible.

Thanks are first due to our many contributors, who worked to tight deadlines to help produce this first *Global Corruption Report*. We also thank the artists from around the world – Bonil, Anna Cechová, Samuel Githui, Si-Beck Park, Polyp, Sam Sarath, Rashid Sherif and Zapiro – who shared their work with us.

We are grateful to those who devoted their time and expertise to referee our reports. In addition to many from within the TI movement, we thank Colm Allan, Daniel Bilak, Donald Bowser, Lala Camerer, Christian Dietrich, Damian Fernandez, Odd-Helge Fjeldstad, Terence Gomez, Amy Hawthorne, Kristinn Helgason, Paul Heywood, Les Holmes, Mohammad Kisubi, Neville Linton, Xiaobo Lu, Corbin Lyday, Jean-François Médard, Marta Muço, Olga Nazario, Juanita Olaya, Véronique Pujas, William Reno, Susan Rose-Ackerman, Alan Rousso, Charles Sampford, Ian Smillie, Daniel Smilov, Charles Taylor, Mahaman Tidjani Alou, Chris Toensing, Will Wechsler and Laurence Whitehead.

Special thanks to our informal steering committee: Tunku Abdul Aziz, Laurence Cockcroft, Hansjörg Elshorst, John Githongo, Rosa Ines Ospina, Jeremy Pope, Peter Rooke and Frank Vogl. We also owe a great debt to the TI national chapters, many of whose members dedicated time and energy to providing ideas and comments throughout the editorial process.

This report would not have been possible without the support and assistance of the entire staff at the TI Secretariat in Berlin.We are especially grateful to Hansjörg Elshorst and Roslyn Hees for their commitment and encouragement. We also want to thank the many interns who, for a short time, greatly enriched our work: Liam Campling, Thomas Friis, Susanne Krueger, Andrea Paar, Tara Polzer, Frauke Rolenc, Rebecca Townsend, Inken Wiese and Aled Williams.

Additional thanks to Sarah Burd-Sharps for her publications wisdom and clear way with words; Michael Griffin for his expert editing; John Whaley for his diligent research; NetScript for a seamless website design; and our book designers, Iris Farnschläder and Jörg Mahlstedt, for bringing the book to life.

Publication of the *Global Corruption Report* has been made possible with the financial support of the Utstein group, comprised of the governments of Germany, the Netherlands, Norway and the United Kingdom.

Robin Hodess, Jessie Banfield and Toby Wolfe

Editor's note

The *Global Corruption Report 2001* concentrates on events in the period July 2000 to June 2001. It uses Transparency International's definition of corruption as the misuse of entrusted power for private gain. This includes both public and private sector corruption, at petty and grand levels. The *Global Corruption Report 2001* is divided into three main sections.

The first section explores corruption across the world in 12 regional reports. These have been written by independent journalists who are, for the most part, from and based in the region on which they report. Regional reports are not works of investigative journalism, but offer summaries of prominent events relating to corruption and the fight against it in 2000–01. Due to this news-driven method, not all countries in each region are included with equal attention, or in some cases at all. Regional reports also focus on region-wide 'trends' in corruption or anti-corruption activities. A trend is defined as a recent development common to a number of countries and manifest in a series of events or initiatives.

The second section of the book focuses on a number of issues that have been of particular importance to the global fight against corruption in 2000–01. Global issues reports, authored by experts, examine the relationship of these issues to corruption, as well as the extent to which public and private sector anti-corruption efforts may have changed the global environment for politics and business. Global issues in this year's report include party financing, money laundering and the international diamond trade. We have also included an update from the OECD on the implementation of the Anti-Bribery Convention.

The final section of the *Global Corruption Report 2001* turns to the findings of research on corruption. This data and research section presents snapshots of ongoing or recently completed research projects – by international organisations, governments, the private sector, NGOs and academics. It focuses on research that is comparative or has used comparative data.

Transparency International chapters, independent journalists and NGOs from around the world present short contributions throughout the GCR about how corruption affects their countries, their concerns and their daily lives. We believe these add a sense of the challenges – and hope – that characterise the present-day fight against corruption.

List of acronyms and abbreviations

ADB Asian Development Bank

APEC Asian Pacific Economic Cooperation forum

BIS Bank for International Settlements

BPI Bribe Payers Index

CIS Commonwealth of Independent States

CPI Corruption Perceptions Index

CSO Civil society organisation

EBRD European Bank for Reconstruction and Development

ECOWAS Economic Community of West African States

EU European Union

FATF Financial Action Task Force (on Money Laundering)

FDI Foreign direct investment

G7 Group of seven major industrial democracies (Canada, France, Germany, Italy, Japan, United Kingdom and United States)

GDP Gross Domestic Product

GNP Gross National Product

GRECO Council of Europe Group of States against Corruption

HDI Human Development Index

HIPC Heavily Indebted Poor Countries

IDB Inter-American Development Bank

IMF International Monetary Fund

Interpol International Criminal Police Organisation

Mercosur Mercado Común del Sur (Southern Cone Common Market)

NGO Non-governmental organisation

OAS Organisation of American States

OAU Organisation of African Unity

OECD Organisation for Economic Cooperation and Development

OSCE Organisation for Security and Cooperation in Europe

SADC Southern African Development Community

TI Transparency International

UEMOA Economic and Monetary Union of West Africa

UN United Nations

UNCTAD	United Nations Conference on Trade and Development
UNDP	United Nations Development Programme
UNESCO	United Nations Educational, Scientific and Cultural Organisation
UNICRI	United Nations Interregional Crime and Justice Research Institute
USAID	United States Agency for International Development
WBI	World Bank Institute
WEF	World Economic Forum
WTO	World Trade Organisation

Introducing the
Global Corruption Report 2001

By Peter Eigen
Chairman, Transparency International

Corruption respects no national boundaries. It deepens poverty around the globe by distorting political, economic and social life. Transparency International (TI) was born from the experience of people who witnessed first hand the real threat to human lives posed by corruption – and from its founders' frustration that nobody wanted to talk about it.

Today, corruption at the highest levels captures headlines everywhere, and people are becoming aware of its disastrous consequences. But there is a real danger that the world's citizens will grow weary of bad news and continue to feel powerless. Those engaged in the fight against corruption must continue to expose the way it works and to promote remedies and successes that can turn the tide. Sustained vigilance is required, and much more remains to be done.

Since its foundation in 1993, TI has consistently invited people and institutions from all walks of life to join the global movement against corruption. It is in this spirit that we embarked upon this new publication. I urge you to read on and learn not only how the curse of corruption afflicts societies around the world, but also what concerned people can do, and are doing, to counter it.

What is the *Global Corruption Report*?

The *Global Corruption Report 2001* examines the current 'state of corruption' around the world, analysing recent developments, identifying ongoing challenges and pointing to possible solutions. TI commissioned outside journalists and experts to take a hard look at corruption and to provide their perspective on its impact. As a result, the report adds a new dimension to TI's efforts to raise awareness of corruption in all its guises.

The *Global Corruption Report 2001* highlights the bravery of those tackling the problem, from new political leaders elected on anti-graft platforms, to whistleblowers risking their own livelihood, to the growing number of NGOs that make up the global movement against corruption. The report helps us to understand the realities that underlie the Corruption Perceptions Index (CPI), our annual ranking of countries according to their perceived levels of corruption. It also contributes a global dimension to the concept of National Integrity Systems, as set out in the *TI Source Book*.[1]

The *Global Corruption Report 2001* is not exhaustive, but it provides a unique overview of corruption for the year 2000–01. The individual reports are assessments made by each author. They do not always reflect the views of TI national chapters, or of the TI movement as a whole. But we stand proudly behind this work, which we think offers a revealing portrait of corruption today.

Lessons from the *Global Corruption Report 2001*

Not surprisingly, the *Global Corruption Report 2001* provides a mixed evaluation of the state of corruption – though some notable patterns do emerge.

Corruption scandals dominate the news and public discussion of corruption. The good news is that corruption is attracting more public scrutiny than ever before. In the past year, we have witnessed the exposé of high-level officials and politicians in India by internet reporters who filmed alleged pay-offs on weapons contracts; the Elf Aquitaine affair, which led to the conviction of leading French officials; and, in Peru, a daily television diet of secretly made video films of political leaders taking bribes. In the Philippines, public outrage at corruption forced a national leader out of office. The secretive web that once shrouded corruption is fast unravelling.

Numerous and prominent elections have centred on the fight against graft. Mexico is one striking recent example where people demonstrated that they had had enough of many decades of pervasive corruption, by electing Vicente Fox as President. But scandals in Germany, and in several countries in Southeast Asia and South America, have intensified concerns about corruption in party and election financing. In the US, a crisis of integrity and accountability is evident in the system of political campaign finance: Senator John McCain won a national following in the 2000 presidential elections due to his critique of 'soft money'. The *Global Corruption Report 2001* looks at the possibility of international standards to tackle this problem.

A downside of the increase in attention to corruption is the way the issue is often politicised and exploited, a phenomenon that is pronounced in the politics of several countries in South Asia, Southeast Asia and West Africa. The danger of corruption-related witch-hunts is very real, the report shows. Such political manipulation threatens other efforts to expose corruption and bring perpetrators to justice.

There are signs of increasing commitment by political leaders to anti-corruption reforms, but national anti-corruption programmes have had mixed results. The increasing prominence of corruption in public debate has pushed leaders, both new and not so new, to try and address it. Russia's President Vladimir Putin, in his quest to enforce the rule of law, has had to face the reality that corruption is rampant throughout the Russian establishment: a single decade of privatisation of state assets resulted in the outflow of tens of billions of dollars into the personal overseas bank accounts of former state officials. In Japan, the new leadership seems to recognise that economic recovery requires a loosening of the stranglehold that has kept corruption a taboo in political debate. Accused of foot-dragging until recently, the Japanese government, along with the re-elected Labour government in Britain, have started bringing national legislation into line with the OECD Anti-Bribery Convention.

In China, the authorities declared war on corruption, tacitly accepting international pressure to clean up for entry into the World Trade Organisation. Huge schemes to defraud the state have been exposed and brought to court, but continued use of capital punishment against offenders is a draconian measure that must be condemned. Hong Kong's Independent Commission Against Corruption is a model anti-corruption agency, and the Chinese government may yet find a way to apply the lessons of its success. Repression of the media in China remains a key area of concern, however.

National anti-corruption efforts are undermined across the world by ongoing corruption in procurement practices. The *Global Corruption Report 2001* highlights the way military procurement in particular can fall prey to illicit deals and kickbacks, as in Southern Africa and South Asia, with dangerous ramifications for regional security, and at the expense of basic public services. Procurement the world over needs to be rid of the secrecy, conflict of interest, and systems of patronage that prevent transparency at this critical juncture of the public and private spheres.

Dedicated anti-corruption agencies stand little chance of success if they are not independent. In Kenya, the High Court declared the Kenya Anti-Corruption Authority unconstitutional in December 2000, with serious implications for Kenya's relations with its foreign donors. In South Africa, the head of the Special Investigating Unit mandated to probe corruption was excluded by a constitutional commission from taking part in a high-profile investigation.

Public institutions need to be strong, effective and the right size to ensure that opening up to the global market does not allow the state to be captured by private interests, which the report shows has had harmful effects in many of the countries of the former Soviet Union. Moreover, national anti-corruption programmes that succeed do not stop at the enactment of laws and establishment of institutions, but demonstrate serious intent through realistic and creative strategies for implementation and monitoring. In many cases, the input of civil society, as in Slovakia or Colombia, has helped to strengthen these programmes, providing greater credibility and wider public exposure.

Greater transparency in all areas of government practice is probably the most effective single instrument against corruption. New approaches to transparency are starting to become more standard in some areas. E-government, through internet bidding for procurement deals for instance, has taken hold in Chile, Estonia and the city of Seoul. Increasingly, governments are putting records, income statements and other documentation on-line. The Latvian Finance Minister went so far as to put a web camera in his office to show what he is doing to anyone who cares to look. The doors to power continue to be forced open by the strength of new technology.

Business has begun to address corruption and has made efforts to introduce new standards to identify and prevent it. The *Global Corruption Report 2001* demonstrates that the private sector cannot escape its responsibility as part of the corruption equation. This echoes TI's Bribe Payers Index, due to be updated in 2002, which points out the ongoing propensity to bribe among firms from leading exporting countries. Initiatives from business have made an enormous difference in the fight against corruption – and business is a crucial player in any anti-corruption coalition.

In recent years, the hushed tones of international private banking led to cries of public outrage, as it emerged that a number of banks kept shamefully quiet about, or negligently failed to notice, enormous deposits of dubious origin. Efforts to stamp out money laundering now focus on introducing transparency and making the rules and requirements in banking more consistent in all jurisdictions. Voluntary steps are also being taken: TI had a vital role to play in facilitating a 'know your customer' initiative of 11 leading international banks, known as the Wolfsberg Principles. The sum effect of new efforts may be that the market for depositing illicit funds is shrinking.

Similar voluntary initiatives have emerged in the international diamond trade, where leading players have responded to the demand for clean diamonds by advocating certification or chain of custody schemes. The *Global Corruption Report 2001* includes this account of an entire industry reacting to civil society and international advocacy as an example of a mutually-beneficial process and of steps taken toward more transparent business practices. The anti-corruption movement can learn from such cases.

The initiative of the business community is particularly important in areas that legislation cannot tackle alone. With increased pressure for ethical trading and corporate social responsibility, many business leaders have launched efforts to secure compliance with codes of conduct that incorporate anti-corruption provisions. Companies that want to remain clean have already indicated that they try to avoid investing in corrupt countries, as empirical contributions to the *Global Corruption Report 2001*'s data and research section show. While this is a good sign, the private sector must continually be encouraged to hold itself to the highest possible standards of transparency.

On balance, the international community's efforts to fight corruption have had a positive impact. This is one of the encouraging lessons that we can take from the *Global Corruption Report 2001*, though there are important exceptions. In Bosnia and Herzegovina, international institutions failed to cooperate effectively. In parts of Africa, as in many developing and transition countries, the impact of international involvement is contested and complex: activists have underlined for several years that privatisation and liberalisation have been advocated too uncritically as means of reducing corruption. The *Global Corruption Report 2001* demonstrates that such remedies, promoted internationally but applied locally without sufficient caution, can present opportunities for increasing corruption.

At the regional level, the Organisation of American States has been particularly active in the anti-corruption field. More recently, regional organisations as varied as the Southern African Development Community, the Economic Community of West African States and the European Union (EU) have also brought anti-corruption reform onto their agendas, indicating new sources of regional pressure to stop corruption. The EU has had a major impact on the countries of Central and Southeast Europe in the run up to their accession, and, along with the Council of Europe, has taken first steps toward tackling corruption in party funding. The Council of Europe, for its part, has developed criminal and civil law conventions on corruption and has been actively engaged in a programme of evaluation of anti-corruption strategies in its member states.

Other international efforts have also met with some success: a recent Financial Action Task Force blacklist of countries that had failed to cooperate in combating money laundering resulted in considerable reform in a number of the 'listed' countries. The implementation of the OECD Anti-Bribery Convention, which came into force in 1999 and makes bribery abroad a crime in signatory states, is a landmark measure which promises important results. Bribes can no longer be deducted from taxable income as a legitimate business expense. These are major achievements for the anti-corruption movement, but it remains necessary to look ahead, towards sealing loopholes in the Convention and pressing for its enforcement, which must be monitored closely.

Increased international cooperation is essential to turn the tide against corruption. The institutions responsible for multilateral and bilateral development cooperation are now focusing more than ever on anti-corruption measures, and should continue to do so. A forthcoming opportunity to promote anti-corruption work at the international level might be a UN convention against corruption. We expect that this UN initiative will concentrate on areas currently not adequately addressed – such as the repatriation of stolen funds and mutual legal assistance – and, therefore, that it should not delay or displace other efforts to strengthen integrity, particularly at the national or regional levels. A UN convention against corruption could pave the way for a more powerful and universal consensus about the unacceptability of the problem, and about the need to provide an enabling environment for worldwide support for the anti-corruption movement.

Civil society groups around the world have unleashed an 'anti-corruption eruption'. Citizens are mobilised as never before to demand greater transparency and to hold to account those entrusted with power. When aided by the news media and the power of the vote, civic action has played a key control function in the struggle to stop corrupt practices. Civil society showed its strength in the past year in many countries, both as watchdog and partner of those in power. In Peru, for example, civil society helped to forge a new path forward following allegations of bribery and abuse under Fujimori and Montesinos. Almost all 12 regional reports in the *Global Corruption Report 2001* pay tribute to the courage of civil society, including the news media, in the fight against corruption.

Civil society groups have demonstrated their ability to innovate and adapt. But despite their growing capacity, the perseverance of activists and journalists, and the important voice they provide to citizens, civil society is not always welcome at the table. And many governments still prohibit freedom of information and the press, as in Zimbabwe, or tolerate overwhelming media concentration in the hands of politicians, as in Honduras and Italy.

The importance of a free press cannot be over-emphasised. The media spotlight has resulted in widespread awareness that corruption is strangling societies around the globe. Despite the dangers journalists have faced, news media reported vigorously during the year, whether tracking bribery in the Argentinian senate or exposing electoral malpractice in Ghana. In relative terms, news media also managed to become more active in places not known for press freedom, such as the Middle East and North Africa.

Next steps

The *Global Corruption Report 2001* has reaffirmed that the problem of corruption is enormous and varied, affecting all societies, rich and poor. The report serves as a strong reminder of the centrality of political and public sector corruption in popular discussion of the issue. But it also shows how the private sector is part of the problem – and the solution. By demonstrating that bad governance, disaffected citizens and poverty are corruption's inevitable outcomes, the report reaffirms that the fight against corruption must not be a passing fad – but has to be sustained if it is to be successful. Planting corruption firmly on the international political agenda is but a beginning.

When assessing what has worked in the fight against corruption, time and time again the necessity of coalition building is apparent. The brave men and women in TI's national chapters who fight corruption, often at personal risk, have shown that to do so takes courage, commitment and the capacity to build broad alliances that can stand the test of time. Linkages must be made within and across societies both to reduce incentives to bribe and to enforce anti-corruption commitments. Recent efforts, such as the Wolfsberg Principles, Integrity Pacts in Colombia, and civil society monitoring of the sale of state assets in Bulgaria and Slovakia, all show the way such creative alliances can bring positive results.

At the international level, we at Transparency International are working hard to build public awareness and coalitions, and pressing for stronger anti-corruption efforts from international financial institutions, intergovernmental organisations and multinational companies. Global norms for integrity and transparency have much to recommend them, as the *Global Corruption Report 2001* demonstrates. But the battle against corruption also has to be fought country by country. As this report shows, however, we are only beginning to gather lessons and learn what works.

Like the anti-corruption movement it serves, the *Global Corruption Report 2001* is a work in progress. The contents of the report may make uncomfortable reading for some. For others, they may point to problems that urgently need to be addressed. We are keen to hear the reactions of our many partners, supporters and critics. We want to improve and refine the process of reporting on global corruption, to create a publication that serves the broad needs of the international anti-corruption coalition.

1 TI's Corruption Perceptions Index is an annual index of countries, ranked according to their perceived level of corruption, and drawn from multiple surveys. See p. 232 for the 2001 CPI. TI's *Source Book*, now translated into over 20 languages, argues the case for a holistic approach to transparency and accountability, using TI's concept of a National Integrity System. Jeremy Pope, *TI Source Book 2000 – Confronting Corruption: The Elements of a National Integrity System* (Berlin: Transparency International, 2000).

Regional reports

East Asia and the Pacific

Australia, China, Fiji, Japan, Mongolia, New Zealand, North Korea, Papua New Guinea, South Korea, Taiwan, and other Pacific island states

By Rowan Callick

Introduction

The East Asia and Pacific region contains the world's largest and smallest countries, ranging from the People's Republic of China to the island state of Nauru. Australia, Hong Kong and New Zealand have grappled with corruption for decades, devising effective strategies to contain it, while South Korea and Japan show clear signs of wanting to follow suit. But China and Papua New Guinea have an immense task ahead. Though both have recently introduced anti-corruption measures, making them work may involve confrontation with influential sectors of the body politic.

In the first decades after World War II, the focus of public attention was overwhelmingly on political development, as independence struggles, the divisions of the Cold War, and the emergence of new elites and institutions took their course. The thrust of the last 20 years has been more on economic change, with aid and foreign investment reinforcing the pursuit of ever faster growth.

After the financial crash of the late 1990s, attention is again firmly fixed on the need to address political reform, in part because of a valid popular perception that the economic crisis was spurred by failed governance and excessive cronyism, and that public and private corruption are hindering economic recovery. As the 21st century begins, a consensus is developing across much of the region that there is no serious alternative to democracy. As the Asian middle classes grow ever larger, the rule of law and meritocracy are increasingly viewed as more likely than cronyism and feudalism to bring stability in the longer term.

The Asian economic crisis also focused attention on the volatility of foreign investment. Foreign investors are frequently blamed for a fickleness that fostered corruption, which is now widely viewed within the region as having contributed to the crisis. Previously, investors looked favourably on the region's 'stable' – often undemocratic and corrupt – regimes. Afterwards, the international investment community railed against the 'moral hazard' that this fostered.

But despite the 'wake-up call' from the crisis, 'the perception is that corruption clearly remains a serious problem in most countries' in Asia, according to Hong Kong's Political and Economic Risk Consultancy.[1] The companies that suffered most from the economic downturn were those that depended most on corrupt arrangements, rather than open competition. Many of those companies have since been resurrected, in part through international support for the region's economies. The ascendancy of *guanxi* (Chinese for 'special connections') over skills and sound business plans has never been stronger, though significant changes are taking place, for instance in Japan and South Korea.

News review

China faces the region's greatest challenge in reining back corruption. While corruption is far from a new phenomenon, economic transition has presented new opportunities. Morgan Stanley Dean Witter economist Andy Xie estimated the cost of corruption to China's economy at 2–3 per cent of the country's GDP.[2] But Professor Hu Angang of Tsinghua University, Beijing, put the cost as high as 13–16 per cent of GDP, and estimated that 15–20 per cent of public project funds 'leak' into private hands.[3] Cases of corruption received more attention than ever in the Chinese media in 2000: the number of accusations investigated in the year numbered 45,000, a 15 per cent increase from 1999.[4]

China's senior officials acknowledge the extent of the challenge facing them. Annual meetings of the National People's Congress are the scene of frank admissions of the distortions caused by corruption to the economy, to the social fabric and to the credibility of the Communist Party. On 9 March 2001, Li Peng, Chairman of the Standing Committee of the National People's Congress, warned: 'Historical experience has proved that the exercise of power without restraint and supervision inevitably leads to corruption. We face the destruction of our party and of our nation if we fail to fight corruption and promote clean government.'[5]

The Chinese government's move to de-link the military and police from their considerable past business involvement gives confidence that progress can be made in such areas. The government has also begun to streamline the approval process for business activities, in part to reduce corruption, in part because of its need to raise funds. And to combat corruption in building the ambitious Qinghai-Tibet railway, China's vice minister of railways announced a process of public bidding for the contract – an example of the recent shift towards market mechanisms in project approvals and administration.[6] China's stepped-up 'strike hard' anti-crime campaign of 2000–01, which included the execution of a number of senior officials over corruption, was criticised by human rights activists for its infringement of civil liberties. Those executed included former National People's Congress vice-chairman Cheng Kejie, convicted of embezzling 41 million yuan (US $5 million), and the former deputy governor of Jiangxi province, Hu Changqing, convicted for accepting 5 million yuan (US $650,000) in bribes.[7]

Hong Kong's Independent Commission Against Corruption is widely viewed as a model of toughness and what can be achieved given sufficient resources. In 2000 it received 4,390 corruption reports, of which 3,140 were considered pursuable, up by 23 per cent on 1999. There were 602 reports against the police, up 19 per cent, and 2,402 reports against corruption in the private sector, up by 26 per cent. Commissioner Alan Lai argued that the Asian economic collapse of 1997–99 'exposed some graft-facilitated frauds that took place when the economy was going well'.[8]

In March 2000, in Taiwan, a president was elected for the first time from outside the Kuomintang (KMT) party that dominated the island's politics from 1949 to the 1990s (with martial rule continuing until 1987). President Chen Shui-bian of the Democratic Progressive Party campaigned against 'black gold' politics: the involvement of organised crime in political life. Lien Chan, the new KMT leader said: 'KMT today is quite different from KMT yesterday.'[9] Part of its US $2 billion assets have been placed in a blind trust in an attempt to make the party more

Ban-Bu-Pae (Against Corruption)
Si-Beck Park, South Korea

transparent. Vote buying persists in Taiwan, but Chen's victory demonstrated that both the practice and its effect have waned. However, the fight against 'black gold' politics is a formidable challenge to the new government.

South Korea's Ministry of Government Administration and Home Affairs revealed in early 2001 that it knew of 8,200 officials who had accepted bribes. But provincial government officials warned that an excess of zeal in the anti-corruption campaign risked charges of political persecution during the 2002 elections.[10] The intimate entanglement of *chaebols* (conglomerates) with successive governments and leading politicians in South Korea is regarded by many as dangerous and corruptly collusive. Their domination by single families in the past reinforced their control of the markets in which they operated and of government procurement business. The collapse of Daewoo, the second biggest *chaebol*, with debts of US $80 billion, sent shock waves through Korea just as many thought recovery had begun to consolidate. The bankruptcy raised questions about auditing – an auditor faced criminal charges for the first time in South Korean history – and the efficacy of the new Financial Supervisory Commission. It also brought concern about the failure of the banks and trusts that had kept the company afloat to provide any earlier warning. Attention focused on the extent of alleged bribery on the part of group founder and former chairman Kim Woo-Chong, who became a fugitive shortly before the company's final failure.[11]

North Korea has one of the least transparent government structures in the world. It nevertheless laid itself open to a degree of accountability by accepting UN aid to counter its continuing famine, and by starting to accept modest investment, chiefly from South Korea. Aid workers complained of difficulties in monitoring programmes; they simply could not tell if supplies reached their intended destination.[12] Mark Galeotti, Director of the Organised Russian and Eurasian Crime Research Unit at Keele University in the UK, warned of 'the economic links between the two Koreas broadening the opportunities for personal corruption'.[13]

Japan's ten-year economic crisis fostered a succession of allegations of corruption and of electoral campaign finance scandals. Three cabinet ministers were forced to resign from the 2000–01 Yoshiro Mori government, including Fukushiro Nukaga – State Minister of Economic and Fiscal Policy – who admitted that he received bribes to influence government decisions from insurance company KSD.[14] A Foreign Ministry report in early 2001 revealed the existence of hitherto secret 'discretionary funds' used by prime ministers and officials for overseas trips and for other activities, including espionage.[15] This behaviour was widely viewed as corrupt inside Japan, and its revelation in an official document indicated the emergence of new attitudes to transparency and accountability. Labour Minister Masakuni Murakami, one of the 'Gang of Five' who selected Yoshiro Mori as Prime

Minister, was arrested in March 2001 on charges of bribery, an indication of the growing zeal of police and prosecutors to pursue even the most powerful in Japanese politics.[16] In April 2001, Junichiro Koizumi became Japan's new Prime Minister. At first an outsider in the race within the Liberal Democratic Party to replace Mori, he defeated the party's established hierarchy, pledging to reinvigorate political and economic reform in Japan – and received unprecedented public support.

Australia's federal criminal code was amended to include a new chapter, the Proper Administration of Government, that covers theft, fraud, bribery and related offences, with new penalties of up to ten years' imprisonment for bribery. The amendment came into effect in May 2001. New Zealand still enjoys a low perception of domestic corruption though, as in Australia, attention to the issue was increased by the international cricket bribery scandal. The Indian Central Bureau of Investigation named the former captain of the New Zealand cricket team, Martin Crowe, as having contact with a bookmaker.[17]

Papua New Guinea's (PNG) Prime Minister Sir Mekere Morauta is widely perceived to be at the forefront of a tough battle against entrenched corruption. In 2001 the PNG police fraud squad began investigating four provincial governments over allegations of corruption.[18]

Developing institutions to combat corruption

Increasing numbers of countries in the Asia-Pacific region have introduced or reinforced high-profile independent anti-corruption agencies, as they have discovered that diverting existing institutions in this direction often achieves little. In the wake of the economic crises of the late 1990s, the increased exposure given to the economic and social problems caused by corruption has accelerated decisions in favour of a pro-active stance. The success of one-off inquiries has tended to be an interim route in that process. Older anti-corruption agencies, such as those in Hong Kong, Singapore and the Australian state of New South Wales, have become working models of the institutions that NGOs and the private sector want to see replicated in their own countries.[19] Such models are being increasingly considered as options in South Korea, Japan, PNG, Vanuatu, and in a number of other Australian states, but the economic and political costs are a major deterrent. The spread of anti-corruption agencies has therefore been slow. China has not followed these models, but the Communist Party's Central Discipline and Inspection Commission, though it lacks transparency and operates in an uncertain judicial environment, has become a feared anti-corruption agency.[20]

The institution of the ombudsman is not new in the region: New Zealand introduced the institution as early as 1962. In recent years, ombudsmen in PNG,

Fiji and Vanuatu have produced sensational reports and come under political fire as they have become more pro-active in investigating corruption. Ombudsmen maintain a difficult balance between their oversight role and more dramatic investigative work. Vanuatu's first Ombudsman failed to be reappointed by the President after a series of hard-hitting reports.[21]

The wide variation in the strength of institutions across the region and their different capacities in the fight against corruption are visible even between the Pacific island states, which were pulled in very different political directions in 2000–01. In PNG, Mekere Morauta, Prime Minister since 1999, initiated a range of efforts against the country's deeply entrenched corruption. Reforms included legislation to enhance the independence of the central bank; the 'revitalisation' of watchdog institutions such as the Ombudsman Commission, Auditor General and Parliamentary Public Accounts Committee; legislation on the integrity of political parties; and the establishment of a judicial inquiry into the collapse of the National Provident Fund.[22] By contrast, in the Solomon Islands institutional development has been very tentative. Morale has been depressed by the extent of the environmental, social and economic damage caused by Southeast Asian loggers, who have become enmeshed with the governing elite.[23] Following a coup in mid-2000, the country has effectively been in the hands of ethnic militias.

Ethics in the public service and beyond

There is a growing perception in East Asia and the Pacific that public services are failing to shield people from corruption, particularly in a period that has seen bureaucracies and budgets reduced in size. The quality of public service varies enormously within countries and between them. In Australia, Hong Kong and New Zealand, a high level of professionalism prevails at the national and provincial level and standards of ethics are high. But elements of China's public service are notorious for their susceptibility to petty corruption, reflecting low pay levels, although the government is seeking to redress this in the face of burgeoning wage growth in the private sector.

A number of countries have seen both public and private sector reforms. New 'whistleblower' legislation – the Protected Disclosures Act – took effect in New Zealand on 1 January 2001 and ostensibly protects employees who notify the authorities of corruption from civil, criminal or disciplinary proceedings, and retaliatory action by their employer.

In Japan, a belated shift towards a stronger sense of public service was signalled by the Cabinet's appointment of a board to administer the National Public Service Ethics Law of 1999. This law requires that fair treatment be given to all members of the public and distinguishes between public and private dealings.

New party law in Papua New Guinea

The Integrity of Political Parties and Candidates Act, passed unanimously on 7 December 2000, offers hope that elected governments in Papua New Guinea (PNG) will finally come to fulfil their national mandates. The law aims to end the criss-crossing of the parliamentary floor by MPs that has hampered PNG's political development.

The Act is intended to develop and nurture political parties that, despite 25 years of independence, have failed to supplant traditional alliances. Political parties have not yet developed to the point where they offer alternative platforms and policies to the voting public. Instead, individual candidates offer material benefits, such as food and drinks, and promises of future rewards, in return for votes from their constituencies.

Politicians in PNG often run as independents – more than half did in the last election – or join political parties as a matter of convenience only after winning their seats. The constantly shifting alliances that characterise political life in post-independence PNG have led to rampant corruption.

The majority of members of parliament, often elected with as little as ten per cent of the vote, are rarely re-elected. They tend to see their term in office as an opportunity to advance their personal fortune at the expense of the national interest.

The Integrity of Political Parties and Candidates Act is intended to change that pattern by nurturing political parties. It requires all parties to be registered and provides state funding to candidates who belong to them.

It is hoped that this will minimise the need of members of parliament to raise money from unscrupulous sources seeking political favours. The law also ensures accountability by requiring parties and candidates to declare to the public who their members are, where they get their money from and how they spend it.

The new law discourages politicians from running as independent candidates by restricting their voting rights on votes of no confidence, the budget and constitutional amendments. This clause is intended to prevent independents from threatening to join the opposition ranks and bringing down the government if they do not get what they want.

While the rights of independent candidates have been limited, the rights of women candidates have been expanded. The Act does not set aside seats specifically for women, as some women had wanted, but it does include incentives to encourage women to run for office. Registered parties that endorse a female candidate will be reimbursed for expenses incurred in her campaign if she secures at least ten per cent of the vote in her constituency.

Hopes are high that the Integrity Law will make a real difference to PNG's political evolution, but the challenge lies in its implementation. If applied in the spirit in which it was intended, the law offers the possibility of meaningful democratic change. But if it is subverted by political self-interest, democracy in PNG will continue to be undermined.

TI-Papua New Guinea

State employees now require approval before giving a speech or making a TV appearance for which payment by an 'interested party' has been promised.[24]

Such measures help to raise the standards of public service behaviour, but the real challenge requires the creation of more robust anti-corruption agencies. Endowing such agencies with powers of criminal prosecution would allow them to benefit from police-level cooperation at an international level.

International pressure for change

The widespread acceptance of globalisation as a force for progress and improved living standards has encouraged international and regional bodies to take an active role in guiding patterns of governance. This has increasingly included making funding conditional on improved standards. International pressure is encouraging countries to develop appropriate institutions for combating corruption as an indication of their determination to take the issue seriously.

International pressure for better governance gained critical leverage from the need of ailing Asian economies for increased external capital inflows. South Korea received a massive support programme initiated by the IMF, following the 1997 downturn. The conditionalities demanded by lenders led in turn to increased deregulation of domestic markets, diversified ownership of business and enhanced accountability through a higher status accorded to shareholders. Pacific Island finance largely flows through official aid channels that increasingly arrive with attached conditions of better governance. For the Australian government, the largest donor in the islands region, this is a major element in aid decisions.

Among the conditions attached to packages coordinated by international financial institutions, anti-corruption measures tend to attract most public support. Inevitably they also risk antagonising governments that resent being treated as corrupt, and the concomitant 'invasion' of their sovereignty. The PNG government, currently implementing a structural adjustment programme, asked the World Bank in February 2001 to remove its coordinator from Port Moresby, the capital. Concern was expressed in the private sector that this request was in part due to World Bank pressure for anti-corruption conditions, although the government denied this.[25]

China's accession to the World Trade Organisation, expected to be completed by the end of 2001, was viewed as a crucial opportunity to harness the country's economic dynamism to a rules-based structure. Modernising planners in China and representatives of the international investment community regard this as more likely to improve governance than any single domestic factor.

At its second annual meeting in Seoul in December 2000, the Anti-Corruption Initiative for Asia-Pacific, led by the ADB and the OECD, endorsed the concept of an 'anti-corruption compact' for regional cooperation. The compact is being formulated for submission at the next annual meeting of the Anti-Corruption Initiative in Tokyo in November 2001. The draft compact highlights the roles that governments, the private sector and civil society can play.

As members of the OECD, Australia, Japan, Korea and New Zealand have all signed the Anti-Bribery Convention. New Zealand ratified the Convention in June 2001. Japan was one of the first countries to ratify the Convention, implementing it through an amendment to its Unfair Competition Prevention Law which came into force in February 1999. However, an OECD Working Group review of Japan in October 1999 argued that a 'major loophole' remained.[26] In response, the government eventually adopted amending legislation in June 2001.

In the Pacific, the OECD put pressure on the Cook Islands, Marshall Islands, Nauru, Niue, Samoa, Tonga and Vanuatu to strengthen their anti-money laundering mechanisms and threatened sanctions if performance was not improved.[27] With around 10,500 inhabitants, the Micronesian island nation of Nauru for a few years claimed the highest per capita income in the world from phosphate mining and its 400 offshore banks. The US Department of State said the Russian mafia was laundering billions of dollars through Nauru's banks.[28]

> International pressure for better governance gained critical leverage from the need of ailing Asian economies for increased external capital inflows.

The Pacific Islands Forum is beginning to support improved governance among its 16 members, who comprise most of the island nations, along with Australia and New Zealand. In October 2000, the Forum approved rules including 'the inalienable right to participate by means of a free and democratic political process'. Members formerly refused to countenance intervention in their domestic affairs. The new declaration – driven by shock at the attempted coups in Fiji and the Solomon Islands – committed Forum nations to good governance, and established an action plan to respond to future crises.[29]

Bilateral commercial bodies play an important role in boosting mutual trade and investment. Increasingly, they have begun to raise issues that hamper this, including corruption. The Australia-PNG Business Council said in February 2001 that, in spite of its general approval of the Morauta government's reforms, 'business groups are despondent about PNG's feeble response to the endemic corruption that is clogging the wheels of the administration and the judiciary. Few if any of the perpetrators face punishment.'[30]

Growing internationalisation has also had an impact on various professions, with central bankers meeting frequently to compare notes on threats to governance, and judges increasingly sitting on courts of appeal in neighbouring countries in a bid to enhance impartiality. Most Pacific Islands courts use the services of foreign judges. A Pacific Legal Network was formed in early 2001 comprising private law firms in different island jurisdictions cooperating on cases.[31]

Civil society targets corruption

Civil society is strongest in the oldest democracies, Australia and New Zealand, but is also taking firm root in South Korea, which has a tradition of stubborn trade unions and feisty student activists, and Taiwan, whose environmental activists are among the most effective in Asia. Civil society is less robust in Japan and Hong Kong. In China the government maintains the right to control all significant institutions in the country, including 'NGOs' and the media. In the Pacific Islands, civil society is growing in strength as disillusionment grows with political elites.

Where progress towards establishing independent anti-corruption agencies is slow, it is the institutions of civil society that can do most to fill the gap. But civil society groups face constraints in responding to corruption, including a lack of the resources required to conduct investigations that can be sustained in court, and a fear of alienating politicians or political parties.

Years of lobbying by civil society groups in Japan resulted in an Information Disclosure Law that came into effect on 1 April 2001 and which could have a large impact on the ability of civil society to hold public officials to account. During the 1980s and 1990s NGOs lobbied for information disclosure ordinances at local government level, achieving them in many administrations. Under the new law, the national administration must also become more transparent. Civil society groups such as Information Clearinghouse Japan and the Freedom of Information Citizen Centre work to help citizens make use of this new law. However, limitations remain. Officials enjoy considerable discretion in deciding which documents fall into 'exempt' categories, and the law does not apply to *tokushu hojin* (public corporations), though draft legislation has been submitted to address this.[32]

The two major NGO associations in South Korea, the Korea Council of Citizens Movement, with 65 civic groups, and Reform Solidarity, with another 100 groups, agreed in early 2001 to campaign together on a range of issues of which corruption is central. And in January 2001 a group of 23 young legislators formed the Lawmakers' Council for Political Reform, which aims in part to promote more effective legislation against corruption.[33]

In response to popular anger about corruption in China, the authorities have taken tough action, resulting in arrests and convictions. However, this approach could backfire politically if corruption is perceived still to be growing.

In PNG, talkback radio has become a focus for popular discontent, especially concerning corruption and environmental abuses, and the morning shows of Roger Hau'ofa are regularly listened to in business and government offices. Further cases of corruption in public life such as the issuance of false passports and a visa racket were brought to light in the year 2000 by the PNG media.[34]

Civic groups in Fiji, most prominently the Citizens' Constitutional Forum, have emerged to play a significant watchdog role on corruption issues as part of a broader brief to defend human rights and democratic institutions. As a result of their pressure and that of the courts, elections in Fiji were brought forward to August 2001.

In Hong Kong, extensive media coverage of major ICAC cases is encouraging more people to come forward and inform about corruption. The ICAC said in its annual report for 2000, 'the private sector has demonstrated less tolerance towards corruption as evident in the rising numbers (188 in the year 2000) of management referrals'. And 70 per cent of total complaints were not anonymous, greatly enhancing follow-up capacity.[35]

> Where progress towards establishing independent anti-corruption agencies is slow, it is the institutions of civil society that can do most to fill the gap.

Members of the private sector are reluctant in many countries to take a more prominent role in anti-corruption activities, out of concern that they could attract the criticism of their peer groups for inviting regulation. However, NGOs are having some influence on the private sector. The Minerals Council of Australia, for example, introduced a framework for improvements in the governance of companies operating overseas. The code, which the Council wants its members to sign, would result in public scrutiny through a compulsory reporting process reviewed by a new independent advisory group.[36] This code results in part from NGO campaigns on the activities of mining houses overseas.

Conclusion

While corruption remains a severe problem in many countries in East Asia and the Pacific, recent reforms have led to a number of new institutions and processes to fight it. The lessons from Hong Kong and Australia's state of New South Wales are that the fight against corruption can be effective when institutions focus exclusively on corruption and have the authority to pursue criminal prosecutions. The trend towards stronger anti-corruption bodies coincides with civil society demands for change.

Greater public concern about the effects of corruption is a clear trend across the region. As non-executive parts of government grow in authority and accountability and non-governmental forces emerge, there is a new counterweight demanding an end to corruption in a number of East Asian and Pacific societies. The details differ from country to country. In some, civil society remains weakly organised and, especially in China, constrained by the state. Public attention to corruption relates to the dislocation between the high expectations of constant rising living standards and the negative impact of the economic slowdown in the wake of the Asian economic crisis of 1997–99.[37] Another reason for increased public concern is the rapid growth of new media, multiplying the spread of information – and rumours – about the state of national corruption.

International cooperation in the fight against corruption is growing, and it may bring significant change to the region. Institutions, including the World Bank, the OECD and the ADB, now tie anti-corruption efforts to their loan activities. The importance of good governance has been stressed in the new Cotonou Agreement, which underpins relations between the EU and the Pacific island states. And in response to coup attempts in the Solomon Islands and Fiji, the Pacific Islands Forum firmly committed its member states to the promotion of democracy and good governance.

As East Asian countries begin again the process of launching fresh rounds of investment and trading overseas, it is important that their businesses take with them the lessons of improved governance at home, and do not adopt, as too often in the past, the view that abroad 'anything goes'.

1 Agence France Presse, 19 March 2001.
2 Interview with author.
3 *Asian Wall Street Journal* (Singapore), 8 March 2001.
4 Figure reported by the Prosecutor General's Office to the National People's Congress (China's parliament) in March 2001. *South China Morning Post* (Hong Kong), 19 March 2001.
5 Xinhua News Agency (China), 10 March 2001.
6 Xinhua News Agency (China), 10 March 2001.
7 Associated Press, 14 September 2000; Reuters, 7 May 2000.
8 Independent Commission Against Corruption, press release on the *ICAC 2000 Annual Report*, 23 February 2001.
9 Reuters, 19 March 2001.
10 *Korea Times* (Korea), 7 February 2001.
11 Economist Intelligence Unit (UK), 8 March 2001.
12 *The Australian* (Australia), 20 November 2000.
13 *Jane's Intelligence Review* (UK), March 2001
14 Forbes.com, 23 January 2001.
15 *Kyodo News* (Japan), 18 March 2001.
16 *Asia Intelligence Wire* (UK), 6 March 2001.
17 *Pakistan Press International* (Pakistan), 2 November 2000.
18 *The National* (PNG), 15 February 2001.
19 For more on Singapore, see the regional report on Southeast Asia, p. 23.
20 Economist Intelligence Unit, Business China, 12 March 2001.
21 Economist Intelligence Unit, 'Pacific Islands: Fiji, New Caledonia, Samoa, Solomon Islands, Tonga and Vanuatu,' October 2000.
22 PNG Prime Minister Mekere Morauta, speech to the Institute of Directors, 1 March 2001.
23 *Sydney Morning Herald* (Australia), 3 March 2001. For more on logging in Southeast Asia, see p. 26.
24 *South China Morning Post* (Hong Kong), 6 September 2000.
25 *Australian Financial Review* (Australia), 19 March 2001.
26 OECD, 'Japan: Country Report on the Implementation of the Convention on Combating Bribery of Foreign Public Officials in International Business Transactions and the 1997 Revised Recommendation,' 2000.

27   Pacific Islands Forum Secretariat, press release, 28 April 2001.

28   Agence France Presse, 18 March 2001.

29   *Australian Financial Review* (Australia), 30 October 2000.

30   Australia-PNG Business Council, joint statement, February 2001.

31   *Australian Financial Review* (Australia), 9 February 2001.

32   *Nikkei Weekly* (Japan), 2 April 2001.

33   *Korea Herald* (Korea), 15 February 2001.

34   *The National* (PNG), 8 June 2001.

35   Independent Commission against Corruption, *ICAC 2000 Annual Report*
     (Hong Kong: ICAC, 2001): <http://www.icac.org.hk/eng/public/index.html>.

36   Author's interview with the Executive Director of Minerals Council of Australia.

37   Minister Byoung-Woo Ahn, Office of the Prime Minister, South Korea, in an address
     to the Seoul Conference on Combating Corruption in the Asia-Pacific Region,
     11–13 December 2000.

Southeast Asia

Brunei, Cambodia, East Timor, Indonesia, Laos, Malaysia, Myanmar,
Philippines, Singapore, Thailand, Vietnam

By Dini Djalal

Not so very long ago, most Southeast Asian countries were known as 'Asian tigers' for their double-digit economic growth rates. The Asian financial crisis of 1997–99 was varied in its impact, but the region as a whole was hit hard, with many countries experiencing a rapid withdrawal of foreign investment, high bankruptcy rates and falling currencies. The human costs of the crisis were enormous. More than 13 million people lost their jobs, real wages fell, and crime and violence rose sharply.[1] The upheaval that followed the crash brought a marked change in political rhetoric: politicians' traditional rallying cry of 'growth' changed to calls for 'reform'. Increased prominence is now given to corruption, though the rhetoric has not been matched by action.

Differing responses to the financial crisis reflect the array of political, economic and cultural systems found in the region. The shift in political rhetoric meant something very different in the democratic Philippines than it did in communist Vietnam. And the experience of the stable city-state of Singapore, which has one of the lowest levels of corruption in the world, was quite different to that of Indonesia, the most populous country in the region, which has seen economic turmoil and violent sectarian tensions in the last few years.

Dramatic political change took place after the 1997–99 financial crisis, from the overthrow of the long-time president of Indonesia to the election in Thailand of Thaksin Shinawatra of the Democratic Party – and across the region corruption has become a key political theme. Anti-corruption groups have multiplied, and their case has been strengthened by the campaigns of governments eager to prove their reformist credentials.

Good governance and structural reforms were among the conditions imposed by the IMF and other donors in exchange for the massive bailout packages required to salvage the economy in Thailand and elsewhere. Yet while donors may have stepped up the monitoring of aid, corruption remains rife in other areas, particularly in the political process. Many in the region fear that democratisation has not been accompanied by legislation or the creation of institutions strong enough to resist the influence of 'money politics'. And political instability may divert attention from the tasks of legal reform and institution building.

Southeast Asian countries share an absence of strong institutions, independent of the state, which are essential to combat pervasive corruption. Activists are supported by those reform-minded politicians and business people who are working to set a new standard of good governance. Their determination is testimony to how much stronger civil society has become in a few short years, but their struggle is far from over in much of the region.

News review

The simultaneous investigation of three heads of government for alleged corruption – Indonesia's President Abdurahman Wahid, Thailand's Prime Minister Thaksin Shinawatra and former president Joseph Estrada of the Philippines – is a unique indication that the demand for political accountability has taken root.

As the *Global Corruption Report 2001* went to print, legislators were seeking the impeachment of President Wahid after a parliamentary investigating team suspected his involvement in two corruption cases. Wahid denied any wrongdoing. His supporters said the spotlight should rather fall on the family of former president Suharto, which has evaded prosecution despite alleged thefts from the state of funds that run into billions of dollars. Suharto's youngest son Tommy has been Indonesia's most famous fugitive from justice since he was convicted of corruption in November 2000. Among Suharto's business associates, only the flamboyant timber tycoon, Mohamad 'Bob' Hassan, has been tried and imprisoned.[2]

> The simultaneous investigation of three heads of government for alleged corruption is a unique indication that the demand for political accountability has taken root.

Politicians in Thailand were in an equally difficult bind after the election of Thaksin Shinawatra as Prime Minister. The National Counter Corruption Commission alleged that Thaksin misrepresented his wealth while serving as deputy prime minister in 1997, having transferred his stake in a multi-million-dollar business empire to his family and household staff. The Prime Minister responded that the money was in the form of loans and that the incorrect disclosures arose from a 'misunderstanding'.[3] A recent scandal involving a deceased general may shed light on why Thais are sceptical of the Prime Minister's protestations: though his monthly salary was little more than US $1,000, the late General Sunthorn Kongsompong allegedly amassed a fortune worth millions of dollars. The matter is under investigation by a panel of senators.[4]

An August 2000 survey by the Civil Service Commission found that the majority of Thais believed that corruption is getting worse, especially among politicians.[5] Elections in January 2001, considered by many to be some of the most fraudulent ever, did little to dispel these fears: new polls had to be called in 62 of the country's 400 constituencies.[6]

A similar tale of problematic ballots occurred in the Philippines during the Senate elections in May 2001. Incomplete voter lists were cited in several constituencies while, in other locations, armed men burned the ballot boxes.[7] The election served to cement the administration of Gloria Macapagal Arroyo, installed as President following an uprising against Joseph Estrada, now on trial for corruption. Estrada stands accused of abusing his position to gain more than US $80 million illegally. Although the charges sparked riots by his supporters, his detention was a landmark in the Philippines' long campaign against corruption.[8]

Another anti-corruption drive picked up steam in Malaysia where there is public concern about alleged corruption in the administration of Prime Minister Mahathir Mohamad, particularly in relation to a number of government-financed rescues of businesses.[9] So strong was concern that the American-Malaysian Chamber of Commerce publicly warned about the 'high level of corruption in the Malaysian economy'.[10] By way of response, the government suspended six members of the ruling United Malays National Organisation on corruption charges in May 2001.[11] One month later Finance Minister Daim Zainuddin, who was closely linked to the bailouts, resigned.[12]

The anti-corruption campaign in Vietnam began on a high note in November 1999 with the dismissal of then deputy prime minister Ngo Xuan Loc. His return to a key government post six months later was a blow to public enthusiasm, however, and rural villagers, angry at Ngo's apparent impunity, came out in force. The new leaders of the Communist Party promised more action, but political instability and the bottlenecks created by a corrupt bureaucracy in Vietnam continue to deter foreign investors.[13]

Corruption takes a heavy toll on the environment, particularly in communist Laos, where residents said it has increased in tandem with the growth in illegal logging.[14] Most of the logging in Cambodia is also illegal,[15] and military factions and other groups continue to plunder the forests at a rate five times the annual sustainable yield. The government has made efforts to shut down illegal logging operations, but growing encroachment on remote areas indicated that concession holders, and the illegal loggers who follow, may prevail.[16]

Laws and lawlessness: the battle for legal reform

A functioning legal system and vigorous enforcement are vital to cleaning up corruption. No country in Southeast Asia can make this claim better than Singa-

Illegal logging in Cambodia

A daily drama is played out in remote areas of Cambodia where villagers are struggling to protect their rights. Illegal deals between government officials and logging companies have led to companies using armed soldiers to terrorise local villagers into selling their trees.

Under the 1988 Forest Practice Rule, and subsidiary laws passed since, the government grants concessions for companies to log in specified areas. The law is supposed to protect so-called 'old' logs by requiring concessionaires to maintain sustainable forestry, and to defend the interests of villagers who depend on the forest for their livelihood.

But companies circumvent the law by bribing government officials, including the military. Illegal activities, such as felling protected species, avoiding royalty payments and the abuse of local villagers, are widespread.

A typical example is the plight of 270 villagers in Tbeng Meanchey District, some 200 km from the capital, Phnom Penh. For generations, they have eked out a livelihood from resin-tapping. Each family has customary tenure parcels of between 500 and 2,000 trees. The resin provides them with 500,000 to 1.5 million riels (US $130 to $390) in monthly income. Traditionally, villagers in forest areas farm rice for food and tap resin for cash.

In February 2001, the desperate villagers turned to a Cambodian NGO for help. They said that a Taiwanese-owned company was attempting to 'steal' their resin trees. It had hired soldiers to stop them collecting the resin in the forest and tried to force the villagers to sell their trees. Any resistance to selling, the villagers said, was met with retaliation, such as the imposition of roadblocks that prevented them accessing the market. Fourteen families had apparently lost their livelihood in this way.

In a village in north Kampong Thom, 70 families are under similar pressure to sell their trees for between 2,000 and 5,000 riels (US $0.50 to $1.30) each to a logging company.

The threat is likely to continue as long as the law is not enforced, according to an NGO source.

For Cambodia, the problem goes beyond those who make their living from forest products. The adverse ecological and socio-economic effects of excessive logging on the country's waterway system are well documented.[1]

Collusion between officials in the Department of Forestry and Wildlife (DFW), the Ministry of Agriculture, Forestry and Fisheries and the legal concessionaires is the cause of the illegal activity, according to the NGO Global Witness. The military controls much of the illegal logging, either privately or on behalf of the concessionaires.

Illegal logging comes at a high cost to the government. Forest income is currently estimated at about US $13.5 million annually.[2] Without the illegal logging, the figure could be up to US $100 million higher.[3]

The only mechanism available for tracking the concessionaires' activities is the Forest Crime Monitoring Unit (FCMU). The FCMU is an independent enforcement unit, jointly run by Global Witness, DFW and the Ministry of Environment. While short on dramatic outcomes, the FCMU has made some inroads, with its findings leading to corrupt government officials being sacked and illegal loggers arrested. But its work was interrupted when the unit was temporarily suspended in February 2001.

Meanwhile villagers, such as those from Tbeng Meanchey District who eke a living from Cambodia's forests, continue to suffer.

Florence Chong

1 Kirk Talbot, *Logging in Cambodia: Politics and Plunder* (New York: Asia Society, 2000).
2 Fraser Thomas, 'Cambodian Forest Concession,' Asian Development Bank Review Report, 28 April 2000. The income comes from 'stumpage' – a fee for each log felled.
3 Keat Chhon, Minister of Economy and Finance, speaking at a conference of the Asian Free Trade Association, in Phnom Penh, 2000.

pore, whose 40-year-old anti-corruption campaign is often hailed as a model for the region. Once burdened with a corrupt police force and customs office, Singapore is now an efficient commercial hub envied by its neighbours.

Its secret? High civil servant salaries, often exceeding parallel wages in the private sector, according to some observers. But Singaporean officials argue that the introduction of tough anti-corruption legislation and its enforcement by a strong anti-corruption commission and an independent judiciary were more effective than high wages, which were introduced only gradually in the 1970s and 1980s. The new laws stated that suspects could be found guilty of corruption even if no payment had actually been received – intent was sufficient to secure conviction – and the penalty for corruption was five years' imprisonment or a substantial fine. Political will has also been a key factor. Singapore's anti-corruption commission is located in the office of the Prime Minister. Such an arrangement often runs the risk of limiting such a commission's independence and even facilitating corruption, but Singapore has avoided this in part through the personal commitment of its Prime Minister.[17]

A number of other Southeast Asian nations have introduced anti-corruption measures and watchdog institutions. Malaysia's 800-member Anti-Corruption Agency, for example, has arrested more than 5,000 people over the past two decades, and the Anti-Corruption Act of 1997 further strengthened its investigative powers.[18] Unlike Singapore, the impact of such institutions is often limited by such factors as a lack of political will, imperfect legislation or low prosecution rates due to the judiciary's lack of independence.

In the Philippines, the Ombudsman has filed cases against dozens of high-ranking officials, but only 2 per cent result in conviction.[19] The proportion of officials prosecuted for corruption is as low as 0.5 out of 10,000, compared to eight out of 10,000 in Hong Kong.[20] President Arroyo has revived a Presidential Commission Against Corruption, and proposed an independent body to investigate the wealth of senior government officials.[21] But it remains to be seen whether these watchdog agencies, hampered by lack of resources and resentment from certain quarters, can claim successful prosecutions.

Concern over the extent of political will in Thailand is reflected in the difficulties faced by watchdog agencies there. The National Counter Corruption Commission (NCCC) is an offspring of Thailand's widely praised 1997 constitution, which was drafted with the participation of various sectors of society. The NCCC complains that its 300-member staff struggles to investigate the country's more than 6,000 municipalities.[22] In the area of electoral fraud, Thailand's watchdog is the Election Commission but many saw this year's elections as an indication of its limitations. There were over 1,000 allegations of fraud, but only eight candidates were disqualified. And old-guard officials seemed intent on weakening the body. In October 2000, the Council of State, a conservative government arm, was given the right to review the Commission's findings of electoral fraud, a move that threatened to erode its independence.[23] Some also claim that weaknesses in both the NCCC and the Election Commission are internal, with allegations of kickbacks and other forms of corruption.[24] While some of the allegations may have been deliberately intended to weaken the institutions, they have taken their toll – the integrity of the Election Commission and the NCCC are now doubted by some.[25]

Gaps in legislation or procedural requirements can be key constraints on conviction rates. Campaigners in the Philippines point out that current legislation places the burden of proof on the prosecutor, making convictions difficult when the required documents – details of bank transfers, for example – are impossible to obtain. The amendment of bank secrecy laws would ease this obstacle.[26] The same legal hurdle exists in Indonesia, where the government is currently preparing legislation to transfer the burden of proof to the accused. The suspect will then have to prove that he or she obtained wealth without breaching the law. There have also been moves to strengthen protection of witnesses in corruption trials.

But the key to effective implementation of anti-corruption laws is often the strength, independence and integrity of judiciaries. In Malaysia, the independence of legal institutions is a cause for concern to many: a recent survey found that eight out of ten people were unhappy with the courts.[27] In the Philippines, 57 per cent of respondents to a 1999 World Bank survey said that most judges could be bribed.[28] Only 4 per cent bothered to report incidents of bribery, saying that reporting them would be futile. Activists lament that some cases are given attention, particularly where politicians have axes to grind against their opponents, while others are neglected. However, attempts are being made in both countries to address these concerns: in Malaysia the newly-appointed Chief Justice has been attempting to restore the image of the judiciary, and the Supreme Court of the Philippines has formulated an Action Programme on Judicial Reforms for the period 2001–06. The law's seeming discrimination must be addressed if public trust in the judiciary is to be restored.

The reputation of the courts in Thailand is no better. Few Thais know how the legal system works, avoiding it whenever possible.[29] According to a recent survey, one third of those who went to court said they were asked for bribes while there.[30] Laotians also have little knowledge of their legal system, and their one-party state is less than transparent about the workings of government.[31]

Indonesians complain about their weak judiciary, but there is some hope. In the last year, more than 150 cases of corruption were reported by state oil firm Pertamina and a dozen by the Forestry Ministry: few prosecutions ensued, however, due to 'insufficient evidence'.[32] Exasperated, the government now plans to transfer anti-corruption duties to an Anti-Corruption Commission armed with powers both to investigate and prosecute, and it will create a special court for corruption cases.[33] Unfortunately, the death in July 2001 of the newly-appointed Attorney General, who had won a tough reputation as justice minister, raised concerns that the pace of prosecutions may slow down once again.[34]

Difficulties in the implementation of legislation must be put in context: in some countries in the region, there is almost no law at all. When Myanmar's ruling junta suspended the constitution in 1988, the law automatically ceded to the whims of the military. The establishment in 1991 of the Law Scrutiny Central Board, which can amend laws deemed 'non-beneficial to the state and the people', further emasculated the legal system. By 1996, when this agency repealed 115 laws, few people in or outside the country had any idea what laws, if any, still functioned in Myanmar.[35]

In Vietnam, the courts are subservient to the Communist Party. Until recently, dismissal of senior party officials required the approval of the Politburo's standing board. The lawlessness and lack of transparency is driving away investors. According to the police, only 79 out of the 14,200 cases of smuggling, trading in illegal goods and tax avoidance reported in 1999 were brought before the courts.[36] A 1998 decree that required officials to declare their assets produced few public results.[37] There have been some well-publicised executions, yet unless there are more convictions the public will remain unconvinced by the anti-corruption campaign.

In Cambodia, scores of judges and lawyers were killed during the Khmer Rouge regime, and as a result many of the current judiciary have little more legal education than the general public.[38] The institution of the Investigating Judge is also a hindrance to justice, since the office can obstruct police investigations even though its mandate is not endowed by the constitution. The NGO Centre for Social Development, is currently helping the government draft an anti-corruption law, but the legislation has awaited completion for several years now.

If Southeast Asian nations want to eradicate corruption, they must not only tighten legislation, but also ensure that both watchdog agencies and judiciaries have the capacity and independence to investigate comprehensively and, in turn, prosecute wherever appropriate. In particular, political will is required to install independent judges of high integrity. Without judicial support, watchdogs can bark, but not bite.

Sam Sarath, Cambodia

Politics and patronage: democratic ideals compromised

In its annual report this year, the anti-corruption NGO Indonesia Corruption Watch (ICW) claimed that political parties are now the vanguard of corruption, which has a hand in every public decision from the appointment of Supreme Court justices and provincial governors to the abrupt termination of investigations into a tycoon's suspect business dealings.[39]

Vote buying and campaign financing

Vote buying, whether at the polls or in the legislature, is widespread across the region. With the possible exception of Thailand, officials in Southeast Asia still face weak sanctions for questionable campaigning methods or affiliations. There is little deterrence to offering and taking what are referred to as 'gifts'. This entrenched system of political patronage has an adverse impact on the quality of leadership and the democratisation process.

In Thailand, the lack of grassroots support for business people who run for office compels them to buy votes. While democracy in Thailand took a step forward in 2000 with the first democratic elections to the Senate, it required five rounds of voting over a period of five months before the Election Commission approved the results.[40] Changing methods of vote buying are a particular problem. While the Election Commission has achieved a considerable amount, allegations have surfaced that politicians are now attempting to pay off rural and local representatives of the Commission so that discrepancies go unnoticed.[41]

A 1999 World Bank report documented the high cost of elections in the Philippines: a presidential campaign can cost up to US $8.5 million in a country where GNP per capita is US $1,020.[42] Corruption begins when politicians attempt to recoup the cost of standing for office. At work is a complicated web of patronage politics. The Philippines has a tradition of awarding governors with appointments in return for votes, and business people with contracts in return for funds.

Only in February, when President Arroyo transferred the authority of reviewing large government contracts from the Presidential Office to the National Economic Development Authority, did Filipinos begin to see some hope of a reduction in the buying of favours.[43] But observers say President Arroyo's promises of reform are compromised by the appointment of officials from the former administration. Filipinos are concerned that she is paying back these old-regime politicians for their support during her campaign against Joseph Estrada. In February, President Arroyo chose as her official 'gambling consultant' Governor Luis Singson, the whistle-blower who broke the Estrada corruption scandal, but a self-confessed corrupter. Arroyo picked for her Tourism Secretary an official with past allegations of corruption against him, though the Senate quickly moved to block the appointment.[44]

Elsewhere fickle allegiances are not out of the ordinary. Thai pundits say: 'Old politicians never die, they just switch parties.' Thaksin Shinawatra became Thailand's Prime Minister with the help of old-regime politicians, including discredited former prime minister Chavalit Yongchaiyudh. Key figures in Thaksin's Thai Rak Thai party were the interior minister in a previous regime and a former finance minister, forced to resign in 1996 for mishandling a banking scandal.[45]

Such ironies could be avoided if political parties had access to independent sources of funding, if politicians were paid sufficient salaries, and if exemplary punishment awaited those violating election laws. But in the absence of transparent or viable fundraising alternatives, new political parties often have to join hands with politicians from old regimes, or their business affiliates, in order to survive. There is often no legal deterrence to this taking place.

The use of corruption accusations as a political tool

Corruption charges are increasingly used as a means to discredit rivals, rather than as an effort to clean up politics. Because of public reaction, corruption accusations are a sure means of shoring up political support and, for veteran politicians, retaining power.

Some Indonesians judged the campaign to impeach President Wahid as driven by short-term goals: a cabinet position or a directorship at a lucrative state-owned enterprise. But two can play this game and, to counter the allegations, Wahid's allies launched a corruption probe into the opposition legislators targeting the President. Opposition politicians then accused Wahid of seeking to deflect the spotlight from his impending impeachment and attempted to accelerate the impeachment process.[46]

The tendency to use corruption charges to settle political scores is widespread. In Vietnam, observers dismissed the Communist Party's three-year-old 'self-criticism' campaign as an opportunity to 'lick official boots and kick their colleagues' – and a chance for conservatives to weed out reformers. The former deputy prime minister was sacked but eventually reinstated into government, yet a general widely regarded as a reformer was expelled from the party for criticising it too openly.[47]

In Cambodia, Prime Minister Hun Sen seized on a campaign against illegal logging as an opportunity to discharge military officers he regarded as threatening his power.[48] Hun Sen was also accused of buying off members of the opposition to weaken it, particularly during the period leading up to the 1997 coup.

Former Malaysian deputy prime minister Anwar Ibrahim was charged with corruption, among other things, but he and his allies refuted the charges.[49] Ibrahim, regarded as the popular successor to long-serving prime minister Mahathir Mohamad, was seen by observers as a scapegoat for politicians trying to protect their business interests.[50] Corruption charges yet again served as an effective way of silencing the opposition.

Democratisation processes and anti-corruption campaigns in Southeast Asia remained fragile during 2000–01. Their sustainability hinges on the ability of politicians to maintain independence. In the absence of strong legislation to regulate campaign financing and sources of funding that will not compromise a political party's subsequent decision-making power, 'money politics' will remain a reality for years to come. So too will accusations of corruption by politicians against their rivals, accusations that often serve political ends rather than the desire to eradicate corruption.

Public patience wanes

In a number of countries in the region, public exasperation with corruption is widespread. Protests demanding President Wahid's resignation echoed Indonesians' desire to seek greater accountability in their leaders. Similarly, the 'People Power II' movement on the streets of Manila may not be representative of the majority, but many Filipinos would welcome an end to the opaque deals and kick-backs that define the country's patronage politics.

Attitudes to corruption are complicated by the desire for economic progress. Millions of Filipinos voted for former president Joseph Estrada, who campaigned on a pro-poor platform.[51] Indeed, it is argued that President Arroyo's popularity is less due to her attacks on corrupt practices than her pledge to deliver economic growth. Many are sceptical that Arroyo can break the habit of political patronage, but they do not doubt her credentials as an econo-

> A successful anti-corruption campaign requires not only a free press and strong civil society organisations, but also wide public support.

mist. Similarly, many Thais voted for Thaksin not because they considered him clean, but because they admired his wealth and hoped he would run Thailand as a successful business concern. An increasing number of Thais say that their main worry is not corruption, but poverty.[52]

In villages across Indonesia there is nostalgia for the so-called 'good old days' when putting food on the table was cheaper than today, whatever the brutalities of Suharto's dictatorship. A May 2001 newspaper poll showed that respondents viewed Suharto's 32-year rule more favourably than the administration of

A citizens' revolt in the Philippines

Nowhere was corruption more central an issue this year than in the Philippines, where it determined the fate of Joseph Estrada's government.

At about 10 pm on 16 January 2001, a majority of senators presiding at the impeachment hearing of President Joseph Estrada voted against accepting evidence that would incriminate him on charges of receiving millions in pay-offs from businessmen. The Senate vote indicated that the establishment was inclined to acquit Estrada, confirming Filipinos' worst suspicions that the trial was merely a charade.

Within an hour after the court adjourned, hundreds of citizens went out on the streets demanding Estrada's resignation. By midnight, thousands had gathered on Edsa, the same highway where the 'People Power' revolt against dictator Ferdinand Marcos took place in 1986. Over the next four days, citizens massed on Edsa, refusing to budge until the President left his post. When Estrada was finally escorted out of the presidential palace on 20 January, it was apparent that he no longer had the support of the people, the armed forces or Congress.

The revolt against Estrada showed the effectiveness of direct citizen action in holding officials accountable, when democratic institutions are unable, or unwilling, to do so.

The uprising happened because it was clear to those following the trial that the senators would not deliver justice. But it would not have succeeded without the combined efforts of citizens' groups from a broad political spectrum, including the Catholic Church and the opposition. These groups temporarily set aside their differences to coordinate rallies, forums and other events to raise popular awareness about Estrada's excesses. They mobilised their constituencies for a series of protests that began in October 2000 and culminated in Estrada's arrest 12 weeks later.

The emergence of a broad anti-corruption coalition during the Estrada administration indicated the depth of popular outrage against malfeasance in high office. Corruption is a long-running theme in Philippine politics but, for the most part, the complacent citizenry tolerated corrupt and unaccountable leaders, voting them into office despite their crooked deals. The revolt showed the limits of that tolerance.

That limit was reached because of Estrada's sheer effrontery. The picture that emerged from the impeachment testimony was of a president who accumulated millions in deals that ranged from the most sophisticated sectors of the economy – the stock market and the formal banking system – to the most primitive and illicit, such as gambling and smuggling. Estrada combined the vintage methods of plunder perfected by Marcos, like preferential loans to cronies, commissions from contracts, and the use of foundations as fronts, with newer machinations: the use of state pension funds for stock market speculation and corporate takeovers. Estrada is estimated to have stolen as much as P20 billion (US $400 million) during his two-and-a-half year presidency.

Such thievery infuriated the middle class and the business community, which mobilised their resources in support of the protests. These sectors were most affected by an economic decline triggered by the loss of investor confidence. The Catholic Church attacked Estrada on moral grounds: the presidential lifestyle, which included keeping five households in grand style, was particularly scandalous. Trade unions, grassroots groups and leftist organisations formed the core of the protests. Most of those who took part in the revolt did so out of a sense of righteous anger.

The media played a key role by providing information on presidential malfeasance and encouraging participation in protests by reporting them. The impeachment trial was covered live on television and radio, allowing Filipinos to make an independent assessment of the evidence and the conduct of the hearing. And, for the first time, demonstrators were able to text-message one another to mobilise for rallies, spread the news and raise awareness.

While the fall of Estrada renewed faith in 'people power', it also showed the fallibility of Filipino institutions and the urgent need to strengthen them. Even as a new government assumed power, the old structures remained. The judiciary is weak and pliable and high-level corruption is endemic in a system where 'money politics' reigns. Electoral campaigns are among the most expensive in the world and candidates are beholden to personal and corporate contributors.

These problems will not be resolved quickly. The danger is that citizens will lapse into apathy once they see that corruption persists. While the organisations that took part in the revolt remain energised, it requires a great deal of resources and effort to keep vigilance alive. Electoral politics must be reformed and the judiciary strengthened if the battle against corruption is to be truly won.

Sheila Coronel

Wahid, Indonesia's first freely-elected president.[53] Analysts say that the reactionary gloom is caused partly by the pervasive corruption of recent years. Economic despair brought on by the financial crisis has led to a higher incidence of corruption among the bureaucracy, many of whom were underpaid even before the currency depreciation.[54]

These developments are cause for concern since a successful anti-corruption campaign requires not only a free press and strong civil society organisations, but also wide public support. The struggle within civil society against corruption may be weakened by scepticism about the effectiveness of anti-corruption institutions, and by corruption allegations against anti-corruption bodies. The press too faces increasing scepticism. In both Indonesia and the Philippines, there are allegations that sections of the media are politically partisan and subjective about which corruption scandals they report, though journalists dismiss such accusations.

However, tendencies to prioritise economic stability and to be sceptical of anti-corruption efforts should not be exaggerated. Perhaps concerned by the public's increasing disillusionment and by the spectre of the old-guard returning to power, anti-corruption activists have stepped up their campaigns.

In Thailand, the October Network watchdog group can call on a team of whistle-blowers, including bureaucrats and company managers. And reform-minded senators, armed with oversight powers, have set up committees to monitor government ministries and the implementation of economic policy.[55] In the Philippines, where citizens are responding energetically to the Estrada trial, anti-corruption groups are volunteering to guard ballot boxes and to monitor the procurement of government projects.[56]

In many places the anti-corruption movement can boast victories, and these are important reminders to the public that the battle against corruption is not in vain. In the Philippines, the testimony of the vice-president of a bank during the

Estrada trial was a watershed for the business community, many of whom now prefer professionalism over cronyism. In Malaysia, the state of Terengganu created a local Ombudsman office and adopted an Integrity Pact.[57] In Cambodia, a Transparency Task Force has been established by the NGO Centre for Social Development in conjunction with the Ministry of Education, and is developing a curriculum of ethics, transparency, accountability and good governance studies for the public school system.[58]

Signs of change are even evident in Vietnam. Though press freedom is curtailed, reporting by journalists of irregularities in a government body led recently to an official investigation. Analysts hope that the election of Nong Duc Manh as Secretary General will lead to greater openness; Manh has already allowed meetings between legislators and ministers to be televised.[59]

Efforts such as these are indicative of the perseverance of those fighting corruption. But in a region-wide climate of political instability and economic difficulties, activists face an uphill struggle, not least in rallying public opinion behind them. As the window of opportunity narrows, activists are realising that they must work fast to prove to the public that corruption can be challenged.

Conclusion

The most prominent development in Southeast Asia over the last two years has been the prosecution of many of its heads of government and other high-ranking officials for alleged corruption. Yet upon closer inspection of events in Cambodia, Indonesia, Malaysia, the Philippines, Thailand and Vietnam, it becomes clear that corruption has survived the various impeachment proceedings and sackings. This begs the question: were the politicians who called for justice truly trying to fight corruption, or were the accusations simply a political tool?

Democratisation in Southeast Asia has not been accompanied by strong institution building, even within political parties. Politicians' desire for short-term political gains over their rivals has limited longer-term efforts to reduce opportunities for corruption. Parties and politicians continue to rely on patronage, and this leads to alliances between old and new regimes that may compromise the drive for good governance.

Democracy requires strong legislation if it is to ensure that no one is above the law. Legal reform in Indonesia has fallen far short of weeding out impunity for the corrupt, and the public has reacted by taking the law into its own hands: vigilantism is on the rise. In the Philippines and Thailand, the low credibility of the judiciary and police hinders the reporting of corruption. If this trend continues, it will be doubly difficult to pursue prosecutions. Intervention by the government in the legal battles of many Southeast Asian countries has not helped. As Singapore has shown, the fight against corruption requires a strong judiciary that serves justice no matter who the perpetrators of crime may be.

The urgent need to tackle these issues cannot be sufficiently stressed. In many countries in the region, patience with promises of reform is running out. In spite of the pressure being applied by the IMF and the World Bank, and the revelation of high-profile corruption scandals, corruption remains. Many increasingly want to prioritise economic stability at the expense of political and institutional reform.

Civil society today is stronger and better equipped to carry out the daunting task of empowering communities. Whether as election monitoring crews or microcredit teams, grassroots groups can provide the social, economic and political education the population needs to demand change. Because of the increasing assertiveness of civil society groups in most countries in Southeast Asia, the challenges outlined may be surmountable.

1   UNDP, *Human Development Report 1999* (New York: Oxford University Press, 1999).
2   *South China Morning Post* (Hong Kong), 25 April 2001.
3   *Far Eastern Economic Review* (Thailand), 26 April 2001; Associated Press, 13 April 2001; *Financial Times* (UK), 14 June 2001.
4   *Asiaweek* (Hong Kong), 20 April 2001; *Time Asia* (Hong Kong), 24 May 2001; *Bangkok Post* (Thailand), 16 May 2001. As a result of the investigation, a graft monitoring panel called for mistresses of senior officials to be forced to declare their assets.
    Bangkok Post (Thailand), 20 June 2001.
5   *Far Eastern Economic Review* (Thailand), 7 September 2000.
6   *Far Eastern Economic Review* (Thailand), 8 February 2001.
7   Associated Press, 15 May 2001.
8   Australian Broadcasting Corporation, 17 April 2001.
9   Reuters, 21 February 2001; *Far Eastern Economic Review* (Thailand), 5 April 2001.
10 Agence France Presse, 30 January 2001.
11 *Sunday Star* (Malaysia), 6 May 2001.
12 *Far Eastern Economic Review* (Thailand), 14 June 2001.
13 *South China Morning Post* (Hong Kong), 8 June 2000; Reuters, 8 September 2000.
14 Associated Press, 27 March 2001.
15 *Time Asia* (Hong Kong), 19 April 1999.
16 Global Witness, 'Corruption, War, and Forest Policy,' April 2000; *Time Asia* (Hong Kong), 11 September 2000.
17 Jon Quah, 'Corruption in Asian Countries: Can it be Minimised?', *Public Administration Review*, November-December 1999.
18 R.S. Milne and Diane Mauzy, *Malaysian Politics under Mahathir* (London: Routledge, 1999).
19 World Bank, *Combating Corruption in the Philippines* (Washington DC: World Bank, 1999).
20 Segundo Romero, 'Civil Society-Oriented Measures for Enhancing Transparency and Accountability in Governance and the Civil Service,' Friedrich Ebert Stiftung, November 2000.
21 *Philippine Star* (Philippines), 22 February 2001.
22 *Bangkok Post* (Thailand), 8 October 2000.
23 *Far Eastern Economic Review* (Thailand), 8 February 2001.
24 Associated Press, 22 March 2001; *Far Eastern Economic Review* (Thailand), 8 February 2001.
25 *Far Eastern Economic Review* (Thailand), 26 April 2001.
26 *Far Eastern Economic Review* (Thailand), 18 January 2001.
27 Reuters, 21 February 2001.
28 World Bank (1999).

29 Author's interview with Election Commissioner Gothom Arya.
30 P. Pongpaichit, 'Household Survey on Corruption,' 2000.
31 Associated Press, 27 March 2001.
32 *Petromindo* (Indonesia), 25 January 2001; *Jakarta Post* (Indonesia), 15 March 2001.
33 Author's interview with Frans Winarta, member of the team drafting the anti-corruption law.
34 Reuters, 4 July 2001.
35 Burma Centre Netherlands & Transnational Institute, *Strengthening Civil Society in Burma* (Thailand: Silkworm Books, 1999).
36 *South China Morning Post* (Hong Kong), 8 June 2000.
37 Reuters, 17 May 2000.
38 *The Washington Post* (US), 14 January 2001.
39 Interview with author.
40 M. Backman, *Asian Eclipse: Exposing the Dark Side of Business in Asia* (London: John Wiley & Sons, 2000).
41 *Far Eastern Economic Review* (Thailand), 8 February 2001.
42 World Bank (1999); World Bank, *World Development Report 2000* (New York: Oxford University Press, 2000).
43 *The Philippine Star* (Philippines), 16 February 2001.
44 *Far Eastern Economic Review* (Thailand), 1 March 2001.
45 *Far Eastern Economic Review* (Thailand), 18 January 2001.
46 *Jakarta Post* (Indonesia), 15 June 2001.
47 Reuters, 8 September 2000; A. Pierre, 'Not a Syndrome, But a Country,' *Foreign Affairs*, November–December 2000.
48 Global Witness (2000).
49 *Asian Wall Street Journal* (Hong Kong), 21 June 2000; Reuters, 21 February 2000.
50 Milne and Mauzy (1999).
51 *Far Eastern Economic Review* (Thailand), 14 December 2000.
52 Pongpaichit (2000).
53 Agence France Presse, 21 May 2001.
54 Author's interviews with UNDP consultants and the government's Joint Investigation Team to Eradicate Corruption.
55 *Far Eastern Economic Review* (Thailand), 1 April 2001.
56 *Philippine Inquirer* (Philippines), 21 March 2001.
57 An Integrity Pact is a contract in which bidders in a given public procurement process explicitly promise each other and the respective government not to offer or pay bribes, and to subject themselves to specific fines if they fail to live up to this promise.
58 The Centre for Social Development: <http://www.bigpond.com.kh/users/csd/>.
59 *Far Eastern Economic Review* (Thailand), 25 January 2001 and 3 May 2001.

South Asia

Bangladesh, Bhutan, India, Maldives, Nepal, Pakistan, Sri Lanka

By Aqil Shah[1]

Introduction

Corruption afflicts South Asia at all levels of state and society. Scarce government resources that ought to be financing basic health, nutrition and education programmes are often allocated to huge arms deals and infrastructure projects that offer officials and politicians prospects of lucrative kickbacks. At the individual level, high levels of corruption impose disproportionate costs on the majority of South Asians, as they are forced to pay bribes in order to gain access to basic social services. Democratic and authoritarian governments alike wax lyrical about the need to combat corruption, but the region's political, bureaucratic and military elites are rarely held accountable.

The largest country, India, has the strongest democratic institutions in the region, but it is as plagued as Bangladesh, Nepal and Pakistan by systemic public and private sector corruption. Sri Lanka, which has the highest Human Development Index ranking, also suffers from this menace.[2]

Foreign donors have played a significant role in influencing the region's development as a whole over the past decades, pushing in recent years for good governance. But their role in the fight against corruption generates much controversy. Some argue that the direction of foreign aid in the region is still dictated by political and strategic considerations, rather than the economic needs and policy performance of recipients. There is no evidence that less corrupt governments receive more aid.[3]

Recent opinion polls indicated mounting public awareness that corruption has increased in politics, administration and the judiciary.[4] Growing democratisation, coupled with the liberalisation of media ownership, has stimulated the emergence of a vocal civil society. People understand that corruption cripples their institutions, undermines the rule of law, hurts the environment and distorts social and economic development. For government officials, corruption has emerged as a key issue around which political battles are fought. Increasingly, South Asian governments stake their own legitimacy on the lack of accountability of political opponents, as events during 2000–01 clearly showed.

The state's standard response to the demand for corruption control is to implement new strategies, laws, regulations and institutional mechanisms. These provide governments with a measure of legitimacy and serve to deflect public pressure, but it is questionable whether fundamental change is thereby achieved.

News review

In India, convictions of high-level politicians in the year 2000 restored a small measure of hope in the rule of law. In October 2000, P. V. Narsimha Rao became the first Indian prime minister to be convicted on charges of corruption. Along with a former home minister, he was sentenced under the Prevention of Corruption Act of 1988 to three years' imprisonment for bribing four minority MPs to alter their vote. In the same month, the leader of the All India Anna Dravida Munnetra Kazhagam (AIADMK) party, Jayaram Jayalalitha, was sentenced to five years' imprisonment in two cases relating to the purchase of state-owned land at undervalued prices while she was chief minister of Tamil Nadu. Despite electoral disqualification, Jayalalitha was again sworn in as chief minister when her party swept the state elections the following May.[5]

At an All India Conference of State Vigilance Commissioners in January 2001, Prime Minister Atal Behari Vajpayee vowed to 'provide a clean, efficient and transparent administration' and to 'adopt a policy of zero tolerance while dealing with corruption'.[6] His words boomeranged as an arms bribery scandal exposed by the news website Tehelka.com rocked the ruling coalition government of the National Democratic Alliance (NDA). A video-taped sting operation conducted by two journalists posing as arms dealers appeared to show politicians, senior military personnel and Defence Ministry bureaucrats receiving bribes.[7] Minister for Defence George Fernandes subsequently resigned, although he had not been filmed. Bangaru Laxman, President of the Bharatiya Janata Party (BJP), and Jaya Jaitley, President of the Samata Party and close aide of Fernandes, also stepped down.[8]

The Central Bureau of Investigation (CBI) – the primary law enforcement agency entrusted with investigating corruption – arrested the chief of India's Central Board of Customs and Excise in April 2001 for possessing assets disproportionate to his known sources of income. The CBI later raided other senior officials for alleged involvement in a smuggling racket. Earlier, in October 2000, the CBI charged the three Hinduja brothers for their role in the Bofors scandal that had led to Rajiv Gandhi's defeat in the 1989 elections. Allegedly Bofors paid them millions of dollars in illegal commissions. The Hindujas admitted receiving the payments from the Swedish firm, but denied they were linked to a controversial howitzer deal. In January 2001, the Hindujas appeared in a CBI court charged with 'conspiracy to bribe and cheat'.[9]

In December 2000, the Board of Control for Cricket in India imposed a life ban on former captain Mohammad Azharuddin and test-player Ajay Sharma, and suspended two other team members for five years, for fixing matches in exchange for bribes. The decision came in the wake of a CBI report on match fixing which blew the whistle on a global cricket-betting racket.

In Pakistan, the military regime of General Pervez Musharraf that ousted a democratically elected government in 1999 pursued a vigorous 'accountability' campaign, ostensibly aimed at recovering defaulted loans worth Rs211 billion (US $4 billion) from the country's politicians and industrialists. The military's anti-corruption arm, the National Accountability Bureau (NAB), secured its first major conviction in July 2000 when a court sentenced ousted prime minister Nawaz Sharif to 14 years' imprisonment. Though several other corruption charges were pending against Sharif and his close family members, he was pardoned and exiled to Saudi Arabia in December 2000. In June 2001, General Musharraf consolidated his authority further when he declared himself President.

In August 2000, allegations of kickbacks in arms deals, which implicated two army chiefs, one naval chief and two air force chiefs, hit the Pakistani headlines.[10] The arms deals reportedly amounted to US $2.7 billion worth of submarines, jets and tanks from French and Ukrainian companies. In April 2001, at the request of the Pakistani government, the US authorities arrested former naval chief Admiral Mansur ul-Haq, who opted for voluntary extradition. A corruption charge against him is pending before a Pakistani accountability court.

In 2000, the Auditor General of Pakistan reported misappropriation of Rs12 billion (US $240 million) in the World Bank Social Action Programme, prompting the Bank to dispatch a team to investigate the embezzlement.[11]

In March 2001, the Supreme Court set aside the conviction of former prime minister Benazir Bhutto and her husband on corruption charges and ordered a retrial in the wake of an exposé of intelligence tapes revealing the manipulation of her trial by the Sharif government.[12] Meanwhile, the Court also instructed the government to amend the NAB ordinance and reduce the remand period of suspects in corruption cases from 90 days to 15 days, and the disqualification period for public office from 21 years to 10 years.[13] The Court ruled that from 2002, accountability courts should be under the discipline of high courts, and not the government.[14]

In Sri Lanka, allegations of major irregularities in defence deals surfaced in June 2000 as bidding procedures were reportedly set aside to put the government's US $800 million arms procurement drive on a fast track.[15] In March 2001, the chief of the navy cancelled a US $20 million gunboat deal with a state-owned Chinese firm amid allegations of kickbacks pocketed by defence officials and middlemen.[16]

Allegations of corruption led to resignations of the President of the Ceylon Electricity Board and the Chairman of the Board of Investment in 2001. Meanwhile, a multi-billion rupee expressway project was in disarray as President Chandrika Kumaratunga, in her capacity as Finance Minister, sought cabinet approval to award the tender to a South Korean joint venture, Daewoo-Keangnam, despite its disqualification in the initial bidding process.[17]

Mass rigging, electoral malpractice and violence in many districts that, according to the Centre for Monitoring Election Violence, had a major distorting impact on the outcome of the polls, marred parliamentary elections held in Sri Lanka in October 2000.[18] Mylvaganam Nimalrajan, a Jaffna-based journalist investigating the electoral malpractice, was shot dead at his residence by unidentified attackers during a curfew.

The Swiss newspaper *Le Courrier* made startling disclosures of the heroin smuggling, money laundering, extortion and human trafficking networks that greased the war machine of the Liberation Tigers of the Tamil Ealam (LTTE), who are fighting the Sri Lankan government in the north of the country.[19]

The Central Bureau of Investigation report on match fixing also accused two star Sri Lankan cricketers, Arjuna Ranatunga and Aravinda De Silva. In November 2000, the Board of Cricket Control in Sri Lanka (BCCSL) appointed an inquiry committee to look into the allegations. A few months later, the BCCSL was itself dissolved amidst allegations of financial irregularities.

In Nepal, the government of Prime Minister Girija Prasad Koirala, which came to power on an anti-corruption platform in 1999, announced plans to combat corruption through three proposed anti-corruption measures: a Prevention of Corruption Bill, an amendment to the Commission for Investigation of Abuse of Authority (CIAA) Act, and provisions for a special Anti-Corruption Court. Ironically, parliament remained deadlocked in early 2001, with opposition parties calling for Koirala's resignation for his alleged involvement in a controversial Boeing lease fraud.[20] After months of investigation, the CIAA filed corruption charges against officials accused in the case, including the civil aviation minister at the time. Stopping short of prosecuting the Prime Minister, the CIAA strongly rebuked him for his role in approving foreign exchange for the deal.

In March 2001, the CIAA sought the Prime Minister's permission to proceed against Govindaraj Joshi, the Minister for Local Development, for his allegedly dubious intentions in amending selection guidelines for teachers when he was education minister in 1997. Joshi filed a petition in the Supreme Court challenging the CIAA's action. The CIAA is also fighting another battle in the Supreme

Court against the Attorney General, who filed a writ petition challenging the CIAA's authority to question his decision to drop proceedings in a currency smuggling case.[21]

In Bangladesh, official anti-corruption efforts continued to target political opponents of the ruling Awami League government. In August 2000, Hussein Mohammed Ershad, head of his own faction of the opposition Jatiya Party, was sentenced to five years' imprisonment, banned from contesting elections for five years and fined Tk50 million (US $1 million) for misuse of office and corruption during his presidency. A month later, Khalida Zia, a former prime minister and now leader of the main opposition Bangladesh National Party, along with two former ministers and seven officials, was charged with receiving kickbacks of Tk1.7 billion (US $32 million), allegedly paid during the purchase of two French airbus passenger jets for state-run Biman Airlines during the party's 1991–95 rule. Ershad was released on bail in April 2001.

The year 2000–01 was one of the worst for freedom of the press in Bangladesh as several journalists were killed, harassed, assaulted or received death threats for reporting on corruption and other criminal activities.[22]

Partisan anti-corruption drives

The thin line between accountability for corruption and political victimisation often appears blurred in South Asia. In India, the decline of the opposition Congress Party and the rise of new regional and sectarian parties has intensified political competition. Indian politicians now find it expedient to use anti-corruption accusations as a strategy against political opponents.[23] Similarly, increased political instability and electoral competition in Pakistan and Bangladesh have spurred insecure governments to settle political scores using official anti-corruption drives. 'For maximum political mileage,' argued Pakistani political analyst Mohammad Waseem, 'special emphasis is placed on high-profile convictions of opposition leaders.'[24]

In India, the government in power often uses the Central Bureau of Investigation (CBI) to promote its partisan objectives. The filing of the charge sheet in the Bofors arms case in October 2000 was seen in political and media circles as an attempt to malign Sonia Gandhi, President of the Congress Party. This

> The thin line between accountability for corruption and political victimisation often appears blurred.

was also the case with the disproportionate assets case filed against her personal secretary. The misfortune of the former Tamil Nadu chief minister Jayalalitha after falling out with the BJP was captured by *The Hindu* newspaper: 'As long as the AIADMK leader Ms Jayalalitha was part of the Vajpayee political entourage, questions about her corruption were conveniently put on the back burner. The moment she parted company with the BJP, she was again discovered to be corrupt.'[25] When it was the government's turn to clean up its act in the wake of the Tehelka allegations, the focus of its inquiry was superficial to the point of cynicism: corruption was not the issue, but rather the fact that allegations of corruption had been made and published at all.

In Pakistan, five successive elected governments have been dismissed on charges of corruption and mismanagement since 1988. Most recently, the Sharif government's alleged manipulation of the trial judge in the Bhutto case, and Sharif's exile to Saudi Arabia in the 'national interest', left little doubt as to the political motives of official anti-corruption drives.

Political observers and human rights activists in Pakistan questioned the legality of the National Accountability Bureau (NAB) ordinance that until recently allowed detention of suspects for 90 days without a trial, but which explicitly excluded from its purview serving military personnel and judges. While politicians useful to the military's political machinations were also excluded from investigation, those belonging to Sharif's faction of the Pakistan Muslim League (PML) were prime targets as the regime tried to use the stick of accountability to effect defections to the pro-military faction of the PML. 'The cases brought by the NAB look politically motivated, and none has seriously touched the army, source of much of the graft,' said *The Economist*.[26] The only high-level case, brought against former navy chief Admiral Mansur ul-Haq, also seemed to be driven by political motives.[27]

In Bangladesh, the anti-corruption drive of the Awami League (AL) government fares no better. In 1999, as many as 70 cases were pending against opposition MPs and activists, ranging from corruption to murder.[28] Political observers claim that the Bureau of Anti-Corruption (BAC), which investigates cases after approval from the Prime Minister's office, is engaged in political witch-hunts. This behaviour is not limited to the current government. The opposition Bangladesh National Party (BNP) also used the Bureau to settle its political scores when it was in power. The case against former president Ershad is an example of these pendulum politics. Jailed for corruption in 1990 by the BNP, Ershad was released on bail in 1997 after he decided to support the AL's 'government by consensus'. Soon after he parted ways with the AL and joined the opposition BNP in August 2000, Ershad was again convicted of corruption.[29] After he was released on bail in April 2001, Ershad bade farewell to the four-party opposition alliance, lending credence to allegations that he had struck a deal with the AL government. The *Daily Star* said in an editorial: 'Such alternating political expediency on the part of major

The costs of corruption in Bangladesh

Bangladesh laid the foundations of its democracy in 1991 when its long-standing military regime was ousted through mass protest, but good governance, transparency and accountability have yet to be fully established. Corruption in public agencies and authorities remains extensive, imposing a considerable burden on the economy.

It is estimated that Bangladesh received 50 per cent less foreign direct investment during 1999 because of corruption.[1] Corruption at the country's port, according to the American Chamber of Commerce, costs the economy US $1.1 billion every year.[2] The electricity system suffers significant losses because of unauthorised power supply – approximately US $1 billion worth of industrial output is lost as a result.[3] Telephone lines cannot be installed without payment of bribes. Citizens trust neither the law enforcement agencies nor the judiciary. The public health and education sectors fail to meet demands. Most painfully, in a country with extreme levels of poverty, petty corruption imposes high costs at the grassroots level.

The absence of transparency and accountability in public life can in large part be attributed to a lack of political will, a result in turn of the confrontational nature of politics in Bangladesh. Since its resurrection in 1991, parliament has not functioned to its full potential. Sessions are often abandoned because of opposition boycotts. *Mastaans* (thugs) are commonly deployed by politicians to realise their goals. Meanwhile, political party funding procedures are far from scrupulous, and corrupt networks between politics and local businesses are entrenched.

Concerned members of civil society are actively engaged in tackling these problems. NGOs strongly advocate a change in political priorities to curb corruption. At present, civil society groups are preparing to monitor transparency in the elections due in October 2001. Politicians, meanwhile, are beginning to show concern for the fight against corruption, with parties accepting the creation of a 'caretaker government' system to monitor elections.[4]

Curbing corruption demands administrative reform. To this end, a Public Administration Reform Commission was set up in 1997. A report by the Commission advocated breaking the state monopoly in the telecom and power generation sectors, among other measures. These processes have subsequently begun, though at a slow pace.

The media plays an important role in pushing for change in Bangladesh's political life. All print media are privately owned and, in addition to the one state-controlled television channel, two private stations were recently launched following liberalisation of the sector. Provision for establishing an independent broadcasting commission to govern the state-owned TV channel has also been sanctioned. It is hoped that as a result of these developments, government influence over programming may soon be curbed.

Though several journalists have been killed, harassed and assaulted during the year for reporting on corruption and criminal activities, the independent media continues to encourage investigative journalism. An active civil society combined with a free media represents a slow but sure means of challenging corruption in Bangladesh.

TI-Bangladesh

1 UNCTAD, *World Investment Report 2001* (New York: UN Publications, 2000).
2 AmCham, 'Chittagong Port: Concerns and Solutions,' press release, 31 January 2001.
3 *The Independent* (Bangladesh), 2 October 2000.
4 Bangladesh's caretaker government system was created by constitutional amendment in 1996, in order to ensure that the 1996 and subsequent general elections were conducted fairly. Caretaker governments – unique to Bangladesh – rule for the three months leading up to an election, and are made up of a former chief justice and members of civil society.

political parties in the country, centring around a single person with a reputation for changing loyalties, hurts people's political sensibilities and diminishes their faith in democracy.'[30]

However, the independent Commission for Investigation of Abuse of Authority (CIAA) in Nepal may be making more progress. The anti-corruption agency filed corruption cases against high-profile officials and an ex-minister and rebuked the Prime Minister for approving the Lauda Air deal. It is too early to assess the long-term impact of these developments on official corruption levels, and they clearly represent only a beginning. Nevertheless, in 2000–01, CIAA initiatives demonstrated to South Asia that autonomous public anti-corruption agencies backed by constitutional provisions can make a difference, and avoid falling under the sway of partisan objectives.

Even so, the prevailing climate of political competition mobilised around corruption issues remains a threat to the fight against corruption, in Nepal as elsewhere. A further problem is the absence in the region of functioning judicial systems. While all South Asian countries have rigorous anti-corruption laws, conviction rates are low and sentences rarely carried out. The judicial process is open to manipulation and cases drag on for years.[31]

In the name of national security: corruption in defence procurement

The intensification of the India-Pakistan conflict in the aftermath of the May 1998 nuclear tests, the Kargil conflict in 1999, and the raging civil war in Sri Lanka, continue to fuel strategic priorities and the demand for military hardware in the region.

The heavy secrecy that shrouds arms deals in South Asia makes it difficult to corroborate the allegations of widespread corruption relating to them. Many defence analysts and former officials agree that defence purchases offer the widest scope for corruption as governments invoke national security considerations to avoid scrutiny. 'If corruption is pervasive in civilian procurement despite extensive checks and balances,' argued a defence analyst, 'one can imagine the extent of corruption in secret arms deals involving billions of dollars.'[32]

Military spending in South Asia is higher than in any region other than the Middle East.[33] In 1999 alone, the region spent a whopping US $20 billion on military expenditures, with Pakistan, India and Sri Lanka allocating 5.7 per cent, 3.4 per cent and 5.1 per cent of their respective GDPs to defence.[34] This contrasts sharply with the GDP allocated for health, which hovers around 1 per cent across the region.

In India, the evidence of high-level arms bribery revealed by the Tehelka tapes was a crude reminder of the rot that plagues defence procurement. The editor-in-chief of Tehelka.com wrote that: 'Of course all Delhi knows that an entire sub-culture of staggering influence … survives on defence kickbacks.'[35] While an interim report by the Central Vigilance Commissioner (CVC) on irregularities in defence deals gathers dust in the Defence Ministry, the Tehelka tapes provided stunning disclosures of the nexus of middlemen, politicians, military officers and their civilian counterparts 'who make hundreds of *crores* cranking the machinery of Indian defence'.[36]

In Pakistan too, defence procurement deals are notoriously corrupt. 'The military in Pakistan, which takes away most of the budget, is accountable to no one,' according to a Pakistani defence analyst.[37] 'There is no procurement system, little accountability and the interaction of buyers and sellers is dangerously close,' argued another.[38] The former chief of the defunct Accountability Bureau claimed in an interview in September 2000 that US $1 billion was paid to senior military officers in kickbacks in eight defence deals. The amount, he alleged, was more than the combined misappropriations in all the civilian projects his team had investigated.[39]

> Defence purchases offer the widest scope for corruption as governments invoke national security considerations to avoid scrutiny.

In Sri Lanka, arms deals 'spawn billionaires' overnight.[40] According to independent observers, politicians and officials don't want the civil war to end, since defence deals promise the most lucrative payoffs. 'There is no transparency or oversight,' according to defence journalist Iqbal Athas. 'Deals are shrouded in secrecy and bidding procedures are usually set aside for crisis purchases.'[41] Basic consumer items are subject to a 6.5 per cent defence tax and prices are frequently increased to raise extra money for arms procurement. 'Sri Lankans are compelled to pay for the sins of those who make millions and get away with it,' Athas pointed out.

In Bangladesh too, corruption in arms deals is endemic. Opposition leader Khaleda Zia claimed in April 2000 that the Awami League government had misappropriated Tk4 billion (US $75 million) during the purchase of MIG 29 fighter jets from Russia.[42] The Parliamentary Standing Committee on Defence is investigating allegations of kickbacks in another deal involving the purchase of frigates worth Tk5 billion (US $90 million) from South Korea.

No discussion of corrupt arms deals in South Asia would be complete without mentioning the ubiquitous role of the foreign arms manufacturers, who factor in commissions to deals. Journalists and officials often accuse armament firms of handing out millions to win contracts. In the late 1980s, the Swedish firm

Bofors paid vast kickbacks to President Rajiv Gandhi and middlemen in what became the worst corruption scandal in Indian history.[43] The government of Pakistan collected evidence against three French firms who allegedly paid US $8.3 million in kickbacks to former navy chief Admiral Mansur ul-Haq, in connection with the purchase of submarines and related equipment.[44] Defence and political observers in the region welcome the OECD Anti-Bribery Convention, but say that it remains to be seen whether OECD governments will enforce its standards, at the risk of alienating a powerful industry that provides extensive revenue and employment to their domestic economies.

News media and civil society target corruption

Investigative capacities are low, employment conditions poor and ownership-related political influence and other forms of censorship constrain reporting. However, with the onset of democratisation and overall liberalisation of information media, a vibrant press, with a healthy tradition of exposing corruption in high places, is emerging. Corruption exposés are turning the heat on governments and providing an impetus for reform.

The Tehelka revelations, which spurred the Indian government to speed up defence procurement reforms, are a spectacular instance of this dynamic. In the aftermath of the devastating Gujarat earthquake, media exposure of collusion between cabinet ministers, senior officials and construction firms to allow lax building codes provided further evidence of the investigative tradition in the Indian media coming into its own. In a region where the electronic media is still largely state-controlled, satellite news channels are now breaking news 'as it happens', making it doubly difficult for governments to hide their misdeeds (as Zee TV's airing of the Tehelka.com tapes as the scandal erupted showed).

In Pakistan, the media has clawed back some of the ground lost during decades of authoritarian censorship. The power of the press was evident in the way the Sharif administration was pressured to abandon its intimidation campaign against the Jang Group, the country's largest newspaper company. The regular exposure of corruption reinforces a strong public appetite for 'frying the big fish' – and for pushing governments to institutionalise accountability. Exposure of corruption in the military has tainted the army's 'sacred cow' status in popular perceptions, spurring a lively debate in the media on the need to regulate arms procurement in particular, and military budgets in general.

In Nepal, the media adopted corruption as its main theme in 2000–01. 'Brazen corruption prevalent five years ago,' said the editor of *Himal* magazine, 'is impossible now as the media will take anyone to town.'[45] While news programmes on the radio can only be broadcast on government stations, private FM stations sidestep regulations by hosting lively discussions with intellectuals and officials on corruption and other issues of popular concern.

In Sri Lanka, the tradition of investigative journalism is kept alive by the private media which regularly exposes official corruption despite draconian censorship regulations. The press is lobbying parliament for comprehensive media reform, including the enactment of a freedom of information act and an independent press complaints commission.

Democratisation, though incomplete and reversible in some cases, has created an opportunity in South Asia for public debate on corruption, including the hitherto taboo subject of corrupt practice in defence procurement. In the last five years, the perception that corruption hurts the economy, undermines institutions and impedes human development has led to vigorous debate among the informed public on the need for reform. It is clear that without adequate public pressure, governments are unlikely to enforce probity in public office. But groups such as the Centre for Media Studies in India, Transparency International in Bangladesh, and Media Services International in Nepal are articulating public perceptions through opinion surveys, making it harder for governments simply to dismiss corruption allegations out of hand. The Public Interest Litigation Centre, Common Cause in India and other NGOs and individuals are effectively employing public interest litigation to redress public grievances.

> Corruption exposés are turning the heat on governments and providing an impetus for reform.

At the local level, grassroots movements have demonstrated the crucial role collective citizen action has to play. The Mazdoor Kisan Shakti Sangathan (MKSS), or Association for the Empowerment of Farmers and Workers, in Rajasthan, India, is campaigning for the right of ordinary citizens to access official information and organising public hearings where government records are cross-checked against the evidence provided by service users. While authorities are reluctant to supply information and few officials have been punished for corruption, the movement has been instrumental in 'mobilising rural people to prioritise the seemingly abstract right to information as a key element in their struggle to achieve accountability from local authorities and enhance their livelihood prospects'.[46]

The Nepalese government introduced its key anti-corruption measures under sustained pressure from the media, the public and NGOs. In Sri Lanka, the government moved to institute a parliamentary select committee to investigate allegations of corruption in arms deals amid demands for accountability from the opposition and media. Freedom of information bills, the distinguishing mark of democracy around the world, are on the legislative table in India, Nepal and Pakistan. The region's judiciaries, parliamentary committees, auditor generals and independent election commissions are also turning the screw on corruption.

Growing anti-corruption sentiment is reflected in the aggressive postures of influential public figures. The Central Vigilance Commission in India posted lists of corrupt officials on its website. Sri Lankan Justice Minister Batty Weerakoon openly attacked politicians and bureaucrats for their collusion with arms dealers and plans to bring amendments to the Bribery Act, including provision for forfeiture of assets acquired through illegal means. In Nepal, the Speaker of the House of Representatives Tara Nath Ranbhat castigated the Prime Minister and the cabinet for corruption; and the Public Accounts Committee chairman earned the public's respect for his committee's active role in probing corruption in ministries.

Conclusion

Official accountability drives in South Asia have capitalised on the need to weaken and undermine political opposition as insecure leaders seek to legitimise their hold on power. Governments claim the moral high ground by pursuing one-sided accountability investigations in the belief that, as long as the public's attention is focused on the corrupt deeds of previous regimes, their own will be overlooked. The seesaw politics of official anti-corruption drives has served to politicise administrations and the judiciary, increasingly calling on them to take sides in political battles.

Grand corruption in arms deals imposes huge economic costs on one of the world's poorest regions, as its resources are diverted from social development priority areas. Corrupt arms deals also undermine genuine national security needs, as procedure is bypassed in favour of pay-offs. The need for greater transparency in military expenditures and arms deals calls for urgent attention. Regulating the role of middlemen, reducing discretion and secrecy, ensuring the participation of all civilian and military actors in the decision-making process, and parliamentary oversight are some options for making arms deals more transparent. There is a belief in the region that the OECD Anti-Bribery Convention fails to make parent companies act with sufficient responsibility for the corruption of their subsidiaries or local agents. Defence analysts recommend that firms involved in bribery in South Asia should be blacklisted. Analysts also draw attention to the menacing role of the global arms trade in fuelling a nuclear arms race in the region that has grave consequences for international security.

While the anti-corruption movement still has a long way to go, the proactive stance of the news media, civil society groups and key public figures pushed corruption to the top of the public policy reform agenda in 2000–01. Growing public anger against petty and grand corruption is due in no small measure to the media, which routinely points out corruption at the highest levels of state. The deterrent effects of the threat of public exposure remain a potent check on malfeasance in public office. However there is a danger that frequent allegations of corruption may create widespread public disillusionment with leaderships of all persuasions. Ironically, the electoral fortunes of politicians so far remain largely unaffected by corruption investigations, as shown by the continued popularity of many leaders accused of corruption.[47]

As South Asian countries grapple with critical social, political and economic transformation, corruption is unlikely to decrease in the short run. Political instability, underpaid civil servants and unresponsive state institutions are compounded by rising poverty and unemployment. Political violence, increasing military expenditures spawned by intra-state and inter-state conflict, and massive debt burdens are also major problems. All these factors limit the capacity of states to institute the meaningful institutional reforms necessary for economic development and reducing corruption. Media and public pressure, collective citizen action and the consolidation of democratic institutions could, however, turn the tide in the medium term.

1 The author would like to thank Paul Oquist, Mohammad Waseem, Hannah Bloch and Gurharpal Singh for their assistance. Thanks are also due to Manzoor Hassan of TI-Bangladesh and Ashish Thapa of TI-Nepal.
2 The Human Development Index (HDI) is a composite index of GDP per capita, life expectancy and education. Sri Lanka's HDI ranking at 81 is the highest in the region, followed by India at 115, Pakistan at 127, Nepal at 129 and Bangladesh at 132. See UNDP, *Human Development Report 2001* (New York: Oxford University Press, 2001).
3 Alberto Alesina and Beatrice Weder, 'Do Corrupt Governments Receive Less Foreign Aid?' National Bureau of Economic Research, Working Paper No. W7108, May 1999.
4 Media Services International, 'Survey on Corruption,' 2001; Citizen's Survey, *Human Development in South Asia 1999: Crisis of Governance* (Karachi: Oxford University Press, 1999).
5 India Abroad News Service, 14 May 2001.
6 *The Hindu* (India), 23 January 2001.
7 Aniruddha Bahal and Mathew Samuel, 'Operation Westend: How the Suitcase People are Compromising Indian Defence,' 2 April 2001: <http://www.tehelka.com/operation1.htm>.
8 The army was quick to form a court of inquiry which found *prima facie* evidence of corruption against the six officials implicated in the tapes. *Indian Express* (India), 17 May 2001.
9 *Asian Age* (India), 13 December 2000.
10 *The News* (Pakistan), 29 August 2000; *Newsline* (Pakistan), July 2000; *The Guardian* (UK), 2 September 2000.
11 *The News* (Pakistan), 30 April 2000.
12 *The Sunday Times* (UK), 4 February 2001.
13 The Supreme Court issued these instructions while disposing of several constitutional petitions challenging the validity of the National Accountability Bureau (NAB) ordinance. Under the ordinance, the NAB enjoys sweeping powers of detection, investigation and prosecution in corruption cases.
14 *Dawn* (Pakistan), 25 April 2001.
15 *The Sunday Times* (Sri Lanka), 25 June 2000.

16   *The Sunday Times* (Sri Lanka), 4 March 2001.
17   *The Sunday Times* (Sri Lanka), 23 July 2000.
18   *The Sunday Times* (Sri Lanka), 15 October 2000.
19   *Le Courrier* (Switzerland), 17 August 2000.
20   *The Telegaph* (Nepal), 14 March 2001.
21   Article 110 (2) of the Constitution of Nepal gives the Attorney General final authority for initiating proceedings on behalf of the government. Under Article 98 (1) of the Constitution, the CIAA has the authority to investigate public office-holders.
22   *Daily Star* (Bangladesh), 17 March 2001.
23   Gurharpal Singh, 'Understanding Political Corruption in Contemporary Indian Politics,' in Paul Heywood (ed.), *Political Corruption* (Oxford: Blackwell, 1997).
24   *Dawn* (Pakistan), 1 October 2000.
25   *The Hindu* (India), 5 March 2000.
26   *The Economist* (UK), 14–20 October 2000.
27   *The Friday Times* (Pakistan), 27 April–3 May 2001.
28   US Department of State, 'Country Reports on Human Rights Practices 2000,' <http://www.state.gov/g/drl/rls/hrrpt/2000/>.
29   In February 2001, the Supreme Court ruled that Ershad could be released on bail after payment of a fine. Before the decision could take effect, however, the government moved to detain him under the Special Powers Act.
30   *Daily Star* (Bangladesh), 27 August 2000.
31   It took five years to convict Ershad; Rao's case took seven. Commenting on the tortuous course of court cases in India, a former CBI official wrote in his memoirs: 'The accused have succeeded in stalling the JMM bribery case by forcing adjournments on grounds of interpretation. Like many similar cases, this trial too will drag on: witnesses will forget, some turn hostile, some may expire and eventually nothing may come of the case.' N. K. Singh, quoted in *The Statesman* (India), 11 February 1999.
32   Interview with author.
33   After the end of the Cold War, military expenditures steadily rose in South Asia though they declined in most other regions. According to the Stockholm International Peace Research Institute (SIPRI), military expenditures in the region rose by 27 per cent between 1988–98. SIPRI, *SIPRI Yearbook 1999* (London: Oxford University Press, 1999).
34   International Institute of Strategic Studies, *The Military Balance 2000–01* (Oxford: Oxford University Press, 2000).
35   Tehelka.com, March 2000.
36   Ibid. A *crore* is ten million rupees (US $215,000).
37   Interview with author.
38   Ayesha S. Agha, *Pakistan's Arms Procurement and Military Build-up, 1979–99: In Search of a Policy* (London: St Martin's Press, 2001); interview with author.
39   *The Nation* (Pakistan), 26 September 2000.
40   A senior defence official quoted in *The Sunday Times* (Sri Lanka), 4 March 2001.
41   Interview with author.
42   *Daily Star* (Bangladesh), 24 April 2000.
43   Swedish radio alleged in April 1987 that Bofors planned to pay a total of US $16 million in kickbacks to Indian politicians and key defence figures, of which US $5 million was paid in the last two months of 1986. *Indian Express* (India), 17 April 1987.
44   *The Herald* (Pakistan), October 2000.
45   Interview with author.
46   Rob Jenkins and Anne Marie Goetz, 'Accounts and Accountability: Theoretical Implications of the Right to Information Movement in India,' *Third World Quarterly*, Vol. 20, No. 3, June 1999.
47   The resilient comebacks of Jayaram Jayalalitha in India, and Benazir Bhutto and Nawaz Sharif in Pakistan are cases in point.

Southern Africa

Angola, Botswana, Lesotho, Madagascar, Malawi, Mauritius,
Mozambique, Namibia, South Africa, Swaziland, Zambia, Zimbabwe

By Penny Dale

Introduction

Far-reaching political and economic reform has been undertaken across
Southern Africa in the past decade: multi-party politics has taken root in most
countries, though economic growth has been elusive. In Zambia, up to 80 per cent
of people live on less than US $1 a day,[1] while average incomes in Lesotho are less
than US $500 a year.[2] Botswana, Mauritius and South Africa are classified as
upper middle-income countries, comparing well to other emerging market
economies, but this disguises widely divergent living standards, particularly in
South Africa.[3] The marginalisation of the region's struggling economies, vis à vis
the global economy, is an ongoing obstacle in the fight against corruption, as is
the context of increasing poverty and the HIV/AIDS epidemic that is sweeping
Southern Africa.[4]

Donor agencies have played an extensive role in assisting development in the
region since the 1980s, most recently by building into their recommendations a
focus on fighting corruption. But Southern Africa has a history of suspicions of
Western agendas. Some welcome the increased attention paid by donors to
poverty reduction and the strengthening of governance, but others argue that
tying aid packages to new conditionalities in the shape of anti-corruption strategies further undermines national sovereignty.

A recent survey of civil society, media and private sector players revealed
that corruption, and the perception of corruption, are endemic in the region.[5]
Another study showed that almost 90 per cent of Zambians believe that politicians, including government ministers, are the most corrupt in society.[6] However,
perceptions of corruption are sharply skewed along race lines, particularly in
South Africa. A Human Sciences Research Council survey found that 72 per cent
of whites gave the African National Congress (ANC) government low marks on
combating corruption. Black respondents were the only group among whom a
substantial number of respondents (40 per cent) felt sufficient attention was paid
to prioritising clean government.[7] Interestingly, across the region actual experience of corruption does not match perception.[8]

But the political will of leaders to combat corruption actively is a major issue in Southern Africa, and events in 2000–01 did little to settle public doubts. Though numerous anti-corruption institutions have been established in recent years, their autonomy is weak, and prosecution of senior officials on corruption charges is the exception, not the rule. The role of foreign companies paying kickbacks to officials in order to win contracts has also been thrown into the spotlight.

Political stability – in a region notable for its democratic aspirations – is under threat from a growing trend of autocracy, most vividly in Zimbabwe where the regime of President Robert Mugabe unleashed a cycle of violence and intimidation in a bid to cling to power beyond its constitutional term of office. Malawi, Namibia and Zambia also face challenges in the near future, though hopefully of a different order, as established heads of state near the end of their electoral mandates. Two major conflicts, in Angola and in the Democratic Republic of Congo (DRC), continued to embroil states in the Southern Africa region during 2000–01. Both wars have been fuelled by a scramble for natural resources by governing elites, generals, rebels and foreign companies.

News review

In South Africa, the region's most economically influential state, a long-running controversy over a US $5.5 billion arms deal with contractors in Germany, Italy, Sweden and the UK dominated the headlines this year. Close links between subcontractors and high-ranking government officials were exposed. Though the ANC government denied impropriety, the scandal cast a long shadow. A team composed of the Public Protector, the Auditor General and the National Directorate of Public Prosecutions launched a probe. But the exclusion from the inquiry of the Special Investigating Unit, headed by Judge Willem Heath until his recent resignation, raised suspicions of a half-hearted investigation.

Numerous allegations of corruption by local level officials and members of the police force appeared in the media throughout the year. South Africa has a wide range of institutions and initiatives designed to tackle the corruption issue, however. The Public Service Commission is currently preparing a national strategy against public sector corruption and, in June 2001, a National Anti-Corruption Forum was established, made up of representatives from government, business and civil society.

In Lesotho, court proceedings in the long-running US $8 billion Lesotho Highlands Water Project case began in June 2001. The former head of the Lesotho Highlands Development Authority, responsible for awarding construction contracts since 1986, faces multiple charges of bribery and fraud. Charges are also being brought against the beneficiary contractors – including some of the world's leading construction companies from Canada, France, Germany, Italy, South Africa, Switzerland and the UK – who allegedly offered the bribes.[9]

In December 2000, an arms-for-oil scandal erupted with the arrest of Jean-Christophe Mitterand, son of the late French president, and international trader Pierre Falcone. Both were accused of involvement in US $500 million worth of arms sales to Angola in contravention of a UN embargo.[10] There were also allegations that large-scale kickbacks had been paid. The probe, called 'Angolagate' by the French press, brought attention to the financial affairs of Angolan President Eduardo José Dos Santos, the procurement methods of Angola's army general staff, and the transparency of international oil company accounting methods.[11]

The murder in Mozambique of Carlos Cardoso, one of the country's most respected journalists, was a sharp reminder of the risk to reporters who attempt to secure evidence of corruption by senior officials. Cardoso's investigation into a US $14 million bank fraud, linked to the privatisation of Banco Commercial de Moçambique under an IMF structural adjustment programme, is widely thought to have led to his assassination in November 2000. After considerable delays, Maputo police arrested and charged two wealthy businessmen and the former Maputo branch manager of the bank, along with five local contract killers.[12] The dismissal in April 2001 of 39 police officers, now facing legal action for their links with organised crime, indicated the considerable corruption in Mozambique's law enforcement services.[13]

> The autonomy of anti-corruption institutions is weak in parts of Southern Africa, and prosecution of senior officials is the exception, not the rule.

In Malawi, one of the poorest countries in the region, revelations in October that the government spent US $2.5 million on limousines for ministers soured relations with donors. President Bakili Muluzi was pushed to investigate after awkward questions were posed in the UK parliament about whether British aid money was used for the purchase of the vehicles.[14] A report by a parliamentary committee in Malawi meanwhile revealed that senior officials, including five ministers, were implicated in the embezzlement of millions of dollars of government money. Some US $2.3 million went missing from the Education Ministry alone.[15]

In Zambia, which once promised to be one of the more stable democracies in the region, President Frederick Chiluba's quest to hang on to power beyond his second term created instability and split the ruling party. Meanwhile, both the Speaker of the National Assembly and the Anti-Corruption Commission launched inquiries into allegations that state money was illegally diverted to fund a recent

Learning the wrong lesson in Malawi's schools

Serious fraud relating to the issuing of contracts to build schools, involving K187 million (US $2.3 million), was reported at Malawi's Ministry of Education in 2000 by the Public Accounts Committee of the National Assembly. Two cabinet ministers were charged, taken to court – and then acquitted. In fact, no one has been convicted in connection with the case. The Anti-Corruption Bureau (ACB) is following up, but with no results as yet.

While those responsible for the theft appear to have escaped unscathed, teachers and pupils continue to pay the penalty of having to work within a corrupt and under-resourced system.

Large classes, scarcity of teaching materials and limited teacher training are the norm. Only 53 per cent of children are in school; there is one teacher for every 70 pupils; and 58 per cent of the population cannot read.[1]

Major problems, most notably the country's HIV/AIDS epidemic, face education and other public sectors in Malawi. In this context, the government's commitment to facilitating the transparent and accountable management of education is all the more critical. The recent mushrooming of poor-quality private schools in Malawi allows more children access to education, though not necessarily of a very high standard. The challenge of monitoring the quality of these new schools is not being addressed. Individuals who have never seen the inside of a classroom are opening schools with the government's blessing. Foul play is suspected in the way licences are granted.[2]

In 2000, the yearly exams were cancelled when students were found in possession of the test papers beforehand. The Director of Malawi's examination board ordered new papers to be prepared and postponed the sittings for a month. President Muluzi ordered an inquiry and the Director was fired. Candidates in December 2000 found themselves in the unusual position of sitting exams supervised by a heavy police presence.

Anthony Ndau, an eighth-grade pupil at Chilinde primary school in Lilongwe, complained about corruption. 'What happens is that pupils who don't even work hard in class pass examinations through dubious means. It's a drawback.' Anthony was quick to add that he believes the trend of bribing teachers has a negative impact in the long run. 'A person cannot measure his or her ability,' he said.

Maenad Nyirenda, who operates a mini-bus in Lilongwe, said his two sons fell victim to the practice of bribing teachers. 'My two boys dropped out of school because they were not able to continue with education at the higher level. Surprisingly though, they had good grades at primary level. I later realised they used to give money to teachers so that they would give them a good report, just to convince me they were working hard.' Nyirenda added: 'The impact of the practice on my sons is grave. I cannot trust them to run my business.'

The education system in Malawi is a clear tale of how rot at the top seeps down through all levels. If senior officials go free, how can teaching staff be expected to act with integrity, above all on so little pay? If licences for schools are issued with no care as to their merit, how can pupils be expected to work hard and perform?

At stake is the next generation, who are burdened by this system, in terms of both their own personal development and the socio-economic future of their country.

Patrick Mawaya

1 Panos, 27 April 2001.
2 *The Nation* (Malawi), 7 June 2001.

convention of the ruling party.[16] The Chief Justice was asked to probe three ministers for their alleged involvement in political funding irregularities.[17]

The new government in Mauritius promised to make anti-corruption a key plank in economic recovery plans after the old regime foundered amid a series of scandals. Prime Minister Anerood Jugnauth, elected in September 2000, said he would establish a code of ethics for public officers, revise the Declaration of Assets Act and reinforce legislation to combat fraud and corruption in the private sector.[18] A high-powered committee composed of members of the National Assembly was created to study all aspects of corruption in the country. Its report, due in 2001, is expected to lead to new anti-corruption legislation.

In March 2000, four years after it was proposed, the Namibian cabinet finally approved an independent anti-corruption body, to be set up within 12 months. In January 2001, the government announced that it would also pass a long-awaited anti-corruption law.[19] Business and civil society welcomed the moves, as corruption is seen to be once again on the rise after determined efforts to stamp it out in the first years after independence in 1990. The law was still awaited as the *Global Corruption Report 2001* went to print.

Although not devoid of corruption, Botswana nevertheless stands out in the region. Major scandals are rare and the public and business community tend to view the government as accountable and transparent. In April 2001, the government promised to investigate allegations of corruption in the tender process for the management of the Public Officers Pension Fund.[20]

Regionwide, the ministers of justice and home affairs of the Southern African Development Community (SADC) adopted a draft anti-corruption instrument in November 2000 after two years of patchy dialogue. The draft protocol defines corruption in both the public and private sectors and provides for the confiscation or seizure of properties and proceeds acquired in a corrupt manner.[21] All SADC member states will have to develop their domestic anti-corruption laws or strengthen existing laws within the protocol's framework once it is ratified. In June 2001, anti-corruption institutions from eight SADC countries founded an informal coalition, the Southern African Forum Against Corruption (SAFAC), to facilitate networking and information exchanges.

Limits to political will

Official anti-corruption policies became common during the 1990s when corruption emerged as the latest donor buzzword. But local experts say the region's many anti-corruption mechanisms are hampered by lack of independence, funding constraints and capacity limitations.[22]

Most anti-corruption agencies report to the head of state, making them dependent on the will of a single political leader. Some are limited to reactive rather than proactive roles. Even in South Africa, which has a comparatively sophisticated anti-corruption infrastructure, the independence of official anti-corruption bodies is limited by their politicisation: all of the agencies authorised to participate in the arms procurement investigation, with the exception of the Auditor General, are headed by former senior ANC politicians.[23]

Noria Mashumba of the Human Rights Trust of Southern Africa distinguished between 'quantitative' and 'qualitative' political will to fight corruption in public service provision. With regard to the first, which includes efforts to establish anti-corruption institutions, legislation and processes, 'tremendous progress has been made within the region'.[24] But beyond this, 'qualitative' political will is also essential, she said. This means concrete action by those who make commitments to ensure the effectiveness of their policies.

A damaging blow was dealt to one of the region's more outspoken anti-corruption activists when South Africa's President Thabo Mbeki publicly denounced Judge Willem Heath, head of the Special Investigating Unit, which is mandated to investigate corruption cases and recover plundered public funds. Mbeki excluded the Heath Unit, as it was known, from the arms scandal inquiry following a ruling by the Constitutional Court that a judge could not head such a unit since this blurred the line between the executive and the judiciary. Heath subsequently resigned.

The suspicion of political interference was also raised in Malawi when the head of the country's Anti-Corruption Bureau (ACB) was summoned by President Miluzi to report on the ACB investigation into the embezzlement of millions of dollars of government money. The integrity of the ACB head, who has publicly accused top officials of allowing Malawi's financial management system to break down in order to be able to abuse it, is not in doubt. Critics are less generous about the President's motives.[25]

Political will to fight corruption showed its limits most starkly in Zimbabwe. President Mugabe's violent 'land reform' process was used as a means of transferring white-owned farms into the hands of political cronies. The majority of commercial farms invaded last year by war veterans groups, avowedly to resettle landless citizens, were reallocated at giveaway prices to party officials or the employees of private and state-owned corporations.[26] The involvement of the governing elite in profiteering from the DRC conflict similarly gives little cause for optimism.[27] The judiciary has also been under sustained attack.

Of the region's governments, Lesotho gave the firmest possible indication of its determination to fight corruption when it announced that it was pursuing legal

Transparency and participation in South Africa's budgetary process

The last few years have seen a rapid growth in the number of NGOs, researchers and activists scrutinising their countries' budgets. Their efforts are motivated by a growing belief that an open budgetary process serves both to detect and prevent corruption, and to ensure that spending policies respond to public needs.

As part of this trend, the Institute for Democracy in South Africa (IDASA) and the US-based NGO International Budget Project (IBP) shed some welcome light on South Africa's budgetary process in a recent report. The IDASA/IBP report was based on interviews, information audits, budget and systems analysis, and other published research.[1]

At the start, the effort relied heavily on the IMF Code of Good Practices for Fiscal Transparency, first issued in 1998. As the study progressed, it modified the IMF standards to suit the South Africa context and the concerns of civil society by adding a new focus on participation.

With regard to the first area of investigation, the legal framework for transparency, South Africa achieved a medium score. It has a legal framework to assign fiscal management responsibility to the executive and there is a strong legal basis for the taxation system. However, it has failed to adopt legislation on the role of parliament in the budget process.

The second area addressed the roles and responsibilities of different tiers of government. These were found to be weakly defined. Though the constitution assigns clear expenditure responsibilities, the assumption of roles in practice has been murky, enabling different tiers to point fingers at each other over accountability. But a robust disbursement and reporting system that relates actual expenditure to budgets has tightened inter-governmental financial management, decreasing the scope for corruption.

For the third area, public availability of budget information, South Africa was rated as 'medium'. On the positive side, more comprehensive budget information is now available than five years ago. But the report concluded that it is too soon to say whether this progress will stick. Recent legislation further tightened financial management, placing stringent reporting obligations on public officials. If enforced, it could oblige departments to improve information systems, thereby lessening the scope for misappropriation.

The fourth area examined was the independent checks and balances on budget execution and government data. These were found to be strong. The Auditor General is guaranteed independence in the constitution, and Statistics South Africa (SSA) has been set up as an independent institution. An early-warning system exists and is now backed by reporting requirements. Both emergency expenditure and procurement are governed by regulations. Procurement regulations, however, are not observed in practice, so the procurement process remains an area of concern.

The final area reviewed by IDASA/IBP was the country's budget decision-making process, which was weak. Budget preparation still happens behind closed doors, with the exception of a medium-term statement that makes the budget framework available two to three months in advance. The legislature has no formal power to amend the budget.

Publication of this research prompted comparable studies in Argentina, Brazil, Chile, Ghana, Kenya, Mexico, Nigeria, Peru, South Africa and Zambia, as well as work in Croatia, Poland and Russia.

Institute for Democracy in South Africa

1 IDASA/IBP 'Transparency and Participation in the Budget Process: South Africa, A Country Report,' 2001. Contact Alta Folscher (alta@idasact.org.za), lead author of the report, or co-authors Isaac Shapiro (shapiro@cbpp.org) and Warren Krafchik (krafchik@cbpp.org) of the IBP.

action against 14 foreign companies involved in the Lesotho Highland Water Project case. Elsewhere in the region however, governments have displayed a more limited determination to curb corruption, especially when it affects their own ministers or senior officials.

Civil society and the press

While political will to tackle corruption in Southern Africa is variable, civil society organisations are developing rapidly, with strong links to the emergent independent media in many formerly one-party state systems. Anti-corruption NGOs are now visible in most countries in the region.

In Mozambique and Angola, where socialism and war largely suppressed civil action for a generation, NGO impact is still weak, as indeed it remains in Malawi.[28] Anti-corruption campaigns are more effective in Zambia and Zimbabwe, where civil society groups play a key role in pushing for political change and greater transparency. For decades, citizens' organisations in apartheid South Africa provided the majority of the population with a well-developed network of alternative services in the fields of law, education and social organisation, and civil society is therefore strong.

Regional civil society initiatives are now also emerging. In March 2001, representatives of Transparency International from 11 African countries, including Botswana, Malawi, South Africa, Zambia and Zimbabwe, signed the Nyanga Declaration. Its aim is 'to spearhead an international campaign for the tracing, recovery and repatriation of Africa's stolen wealth and the formation of a global coalition ... to pursue this end'.[29]

The independent print media in the region plays a vital role in investigating allegations of corruption and disseminating information to their largely urban readerships, a function that led to retaliation from some governments during the year. In its latest annual report, the Media Institute of Southern Africa (MISA) warned of a 'clear trend of growing antagonism toward the media', with attacks on journalists in SADC countries rising from 84 in 1994 to 182 in 2000.[30] Figures for 2001 are expected to demonstrate a further rise. Namibia's early image as a shining example of press freedom has been severely tarnished. In the last year, MISA recorded 22 violations of media freedom and freedom of expression by government departments or officials. In Zimbabwe, government-condoned violence toward journalists and their newspapers soared, culminating in a bomb attack on the printing presses of the independent *Daily News* in January 2001 that caused damage estimated at US $2 million.[31] The bombing followed a series of articles alleging massive kickbacks in the tendering for Harare's new international airport, involving President Mugabe's nephew and others. In addition to the use of

Governance
in Zimbabwe

Discussions about corruption – its nature and manifestations – most commonly relate to financial transactions or other material gain. In Zimbabwe at the present time, corruption is very much a governance issue – hence talk of the corruption of governance.

Zimbabwe has seen dramatic and traumatic developments over the past year. General elections held at the end of June 2000 proved to be the most violent in the history of the country. The results reflected the mood of the electorate for change, with the opposition Movement for Democratic Change winning 57 of the 120 contested seats in parliament despite the open intimidation of voters. This was the first time in Zimbabwe's 20-year history that a substantially large and viable opposition had emerged to challenge the dominance of the ruling Zanu-PF party.

This situation brought about a crisis of governance in Zimbabwe. In order to restore its fortunes and maintain its grip on power, the ruling party resorted to extraordinary measures. These included: attacks and intimidation of the judiciary, ultimately leading to the forced resignation of the Chief Justice; invasion of commercial farms; selective application of the law in favour of ruling party elements/sympathisers; violation of the rule of law by state agents; harassment and tightening of government control over the media; the fast-tracking of retrogressive and in some cases unconstitutional legislation, including measures to prevent political parties from receiving financial support; and a bill to ban any external funding for local civil society organisations, which is now anticipated.

All these actions and measures have the sole intention of ensuring that the ruling party wins the forthcoming presidential election due to be held no later than April 2002. They also reflect a specific brand of corruption, which manifests itself through abuse of power for political gain. In the case of Zimbabwe, it is possible for the government to abuse power constitutionally. Its absolute majority in parliament for the last 20 years and its current working majority have allowed a situation where the head of state can act in direct contravention to the wishes of the people.

The government has steadfastly refused to overhaul the current, hugely unpopular constitution. Its refusal is based on the fact that the last attempt to introduce a new constitution was rejected by the people because it sought to entrench provisions that had been expressly rejected as undemocratic.

In this scenario, where the very principles of governance are corrupted, the task of tackling corruption in civil society, business and in government becomes academic. Currently the government is involved in a massive vote buying exercise. Huge amounts of money are given to mostly unemployed youths and rural folk to persuade them to support Zanu-PF. This strategy has been carried out openly, as widely reported in the country's independent media (the *Daily News*, the *Financial Gazette* and *The Independent*). It worked for the ruling party in the general election and in the by-elections – and no doubt in their view, it will also work in the presidential election.

How does one address corruption issues in such a situation? The call to fight corruption in this context amounts to a call for the removal of the ruling party from government, a dangerous position to be in, and a situation that places activists in the same camp as opposition politicians.

However, any other method is akin to pruning a tree whose roots are totally rotten. The basic tenets and principles that govern the legal and social relations of citizens are encapsulated in the constitution of a country. If these are being undermined, any attempt at addressing corruption within that country must begin with restoring the respect for those tenets and principles, since they form the parameters of accountable governance.

TI-Zimbabwe

criminal defamation to silence critics, the authorities in Zimbabwe make frequent recourse to old colonial legislation that makes it an offence to 'spread fear or despondency'.

In Botswana, the head of television news and current affairs resigned in April claiming government interference prevented him from carrying out his task properly. Two of Botswana's leading newspapers, *The Guardian* and *The Midweek Sun*, were in danger of closing, following instructions to all ministries, state departments, parastatals and private businesses associated with the government to freeze their advertising in the papers.

Government pressure on the media indicated the weakness of political commitment to anti-corruption measures and increased transparency. However, observers are optimistic that the growth in civil awareness that has occurred during a decade of democracy is irreversible: 'However much they wriggle, governments are becoming more accountable,' said a leading source of news and commentary.[32]

Corruption in privatisation and public procurement

The ambitious economic reform programmes of the last two decades were intended to dismantle heavily nationalised economies, spur growth and development through private sector participation, and reduce corruption. But privatisation has not proven to be the panacea that the international financial institutions envisaged. Many of the debilitating features of the one-party state persist, including cumbersome bureaucracies and entrenched patronage networks. Some analysts say this is because 'speed rather than transparency in the privatisation process has been the top priority'.[33] By overlooking the parallel existence of corrupt practices in commercial business, critics say, donors who pushed for speedy divestment and companies that invested in former parastatals have been complicit in the creation of greater opportunities for private corruption.[34]

The experience of Zambia – widely seen as a classic example of how not to privatise – is a case in point. 'Corrupt politicians are using the [Zambian] state with impunity as a resource for private accumulation at the expense of the public,' said a recent study.[35] The most prominent case relates to sale of the country's key assets, the copper mines, formerly run by the parastatal Zambia Consolidated Copper Mines. The saga has dragged on for years, but it came to a head in November 2000 when the Luanshya Mine, sold in 1997 to the Binani Group amid allegations of corruption, was placed in receivership. A critical parliamentary report identified asset-stripping, gross negligence, abuse of the Privatisation Act and other malpractices.[36]

In a case that had tragic consequences, journalist Carlos Cardoso's investigation of the plundering of the assets of Banco Commercial de Moçambique (BCM) during its privatisation in 1996 led to his assassination in 2000.[37] The BCM case took years to come to court, due to alleged corruption in the Attorney General's office, and it provided further evidence of the difficulty in ensuring transparency during privatisation programmes. A warrant has now been issued for the arrest of the former attorney general.[38]

Procedures for public procurement also offer extensive opportunities for corruption, because of the scale and volume of such transactions, as well as poor regulation. The provision of goods and services to the public sector was historically at the core of African patronage networks, which revolve around familial and social ties, and it continues to be an important means of political settlement.[39] Allegations of abuse in the tender for Harare's new international airport, which led to its opening being stalled by order of Zimbabwe's High Court, provided a recent example.[40]

OECD countries have agreed measures to criminalise bribe paying abroad by their companies. The Lesotho government, currently prosecuting foreign contractors involved in the Lesotho Highlands Water Project, is also taking a vigilant stand. The World Bank is paying for the prosecution of this case, a move welcomed by critics who had accused the Bank of trying to sweep revelations of corruption under the carpet so as not to delay completion of the project.[41] The Bank also recently proposed blacklisting companies found guilty of corruption in the trial.[42]

Meanwhile, the multi-billion dollar arms scandal in South Africa exposed links between foreign contractors and senior ANC government officials, non-compliance with tender regulations, nepotism, conflict of interest, internal manipulation and lack of transparency.[43] The Auditor General's report on the arms purchase, released in September 2000, identified 'material deviations from generally accepted procurement practices' and called for a forensic audit of the process and of subcontractors.[44]

Also under investigation in Pretoria was a secret oil trading deal that allegedly cost the Treasury millions of dollars. London-based Trafigura's joint venture in South Africa, High Beam Trading International (HBTI), was accused of bribing officials of the holding company responsible for the state's energy assets in order to secure a R1.5 billion (US $191 million) oil trading contract.[45] The government acted more decisively in this case than it had with the arms inquiry. According to an independent investigation by Kroll Associates, the deal was found to have been 'unduly advantageous' to HBTI and 'potentially prejudicial' to the state.[46] Trafigura denied the allegations. In December 2000, the government fired Keith Kunene who, in addition to chairing the holding company concerned,

Zapiro, South Africa

is a leading South African businessman and outspoken advocate of black empowerment.[47] The speed of the official reaction was interpreted as an attempt to head off criticism in the largely white-owned media of the government's support for black empowerment schemes and again pointed to the racial tensions that permeate many corruption cases in the country.

The spoils of war

The spoils of war are particularly lucrative in Southern Africa, which is rich in diamonds, gold, copper and oil. Angola, ravaged by civil war since independence 30 years ago, offers a prime example of how the struggle to control these commodities can feed conflict and lead to the collapse of governance. The importance of diamonds in arming UNITA rebels has long been common knowledge, though this was given a sharper focus recently.[48] Less well known is the MPLA government's plunder of Angola's oil wealth, a side of Angola's story which an increasingly activist diaspora is now lobbying to publicise.

According to Simon Taylor of Global Witness, legal proceedings against oil giant Elf Aquitaine in France revealed 'a gruesome tale of money laundering and state robbery at the expense of the long-suffering Angolan people'.[49] At the centre of the scandal was the lack of accountability over how loans were guaranteed by future oil production and then used to purchase weapons in the global market at inflated prices. Global Witness argued that there is no serious political commitment to peace because, under the cover of conflict, the proceeds of oil exports are easily siphoned off for personal gain, while the war generates additional profits for senior generals and politicians.

In April 2000 the IMF, the World Bank and the Angolan government agreed to monitor oil funds, contracting an international consultancy firm to implement a 'diagnostic' of oil industry accounts. At present no official records of the oil audit are publicly available, and international oil companies in Angola are not required to file annual accounts that would detail tax and royalty data. No record exists of where the controversial 'signature bonuses', paid by multilateral oil companies to secure oil blocks, actually go.

The war in the DRC, meanwhile, enmeshed at least six nations. Angola, Namibia and Zimbabwe entered on the side of the late president Laurent Kabila.[50] In return for Zimbabwe's help, crucial to Kabila's defence against Congolese rebels, mining concessions were given to senior officers in the Zimbabwe Defence Force. One of the Zimbabwean companies known to have enjoyed preferential access to the DRC's diamond wealth is Osleg. Among its directors were a Lieutenant-General in the army, the head of the Minerals Marketing Corporation, and the Permanent Secretary in the Ministry of Defence.[51] Zimbabwe's Congolese involvement directly contributed to the collapse of its own economy. While individuals found lucrative pickings across the border, national GDP fell by 6 per cent in 2000, and the war cost the economy up to US $1 million a day at its peak.[52]

Observers are hopeful that the advent of Joseph Kabila to power in the DRC may signal the beginnings of the end of a conflict that has drawn in so many countries from such a vast geographical region. However, the militarisation, fragmentation and destitution that are the legacies of conflict there and in Angola indicate that recovery will be difficult. Against this backdrop, the predatory ambitions of elites and their foreign trading partners remain a menace to peace.

Conclusion

The donor push for rapid economic liberalisation during the 1990s, which included a belief that freeing markets from state control would automatically result in less corruption, proved too simplistic. The overhaul of state-dominated, overly bureaucratic economies did not lead to increased transparency as soon as was expected. In fact, in the short term these measures created new opportunities for abuse, especially in the privatisation of state-owned companies and assets. Public procurement also represents a lucrative arena for opportunists, drawing in civil servants, politicians and international companies.

Wavering of political commitment to tackling both old and new forms of corruption was notable during 2000–01. Lesotho showed rare determination, but other governments took the opposite path, using cronyism to maintain a grip on political power or a share of national resources. Across the region the efficacy of current anti-corruption institutions and legislation is questionable, whether due to their lack of independence and funding or because of the absence of a strong, independent judiciary. It is vital that anti-corruption activists continue to pressure governments to reinforce these institutions.

On the whole, civil society is still too weak to lead an effective drive against corruption, but independent media and NGOs do play an increasing role exposing wrongdoing and raising awareness of corruption issues. The autocratic tendencies of governments in Southern Africa persist despite democratic transition, resulting in ongoing intimidation of independent media and journalists. And deep-seated racial tensions are a further problem that undermines concerted civic action against corruption, particularly in South Africa and Zimbabwe.

Events during the year underlined the role of foreign companies in sustaining corruption. Foreign companies, international banks and other financiers must confront their own complicity in perpetuating corruption in the region: several high-profile cases may soon force them to do so. Bribery conceals hidden social costs that are ultimately paid for by ordinary people. In the impoverished Southern Africa region, such costs are unsupportable.

1 Zambia Central Statistical Office, 'Living Conditions Monitoring Survey,' 1998.
2 UNCTAD, *The Least Developed Countries 2000 Report* (New York: UNCTAD, 2001).
3 In 1999, 95 per cent of South Africa's poor were black, according to a survey published in *New People* (Kenya), 1 January 1999.
4 Launching Transparency International's Corruption Perceptions Index 2001, TI Chairman Peter Eigen highlighted the health impact of corruption in Africa. The rapid spread of HIV/AIDS in recent years has exacerbated the region's poverty, claiming 2.4 million African lives in 2000 and placing a heavy strain on social infrastructures.
5 Philliat Matsheza and Constance Kunakas, *Anti-Corruption Mechanisms and Strategies in Southern Africa* (Harare: Human Rights Research and Documentation Trust of Southern Africa, 1999).
6 Zambia's Foundation for Corruption Awareness, December 2000.
7 Panafrican News Agency, January 2000.
8 Robert Mattes, Derek Davids, Cherrel Africa, 'Views of Democracy in South Africa and the Region: Trends and Comparisons,' IDASA Afrobarometer Series, No. 2, October 2000. See p. 307.
9 Companies allegedly involved include ABB of Switzerland; Alstom, Dumez and Spie-Batignolles of France; Lahmeyer International of Germany; Acres International of Canada; Impreglio of Italy; Group Five of South Africa; and Balfour Beatty, Sir Alexander Gibb and Co., Stirling International and Kier International of the UK. The companies deny the allegations. *Business Report* (South Africa), 10 June 2001; *The Guardian*, 19 June 2001.

10 At the time of going to print, charges had been dropped on a legal technicality.
    The Scotsman (UK), 28 June 2001.
11 *Africa Confidential* (UK), 8 December 2000; *Le Monde* (France), 23 January 2001.
    For more on the Elf case see p. 145.
12 Mozambique News Agency, 13 March 2001.
13 BBC News, 18 April 2001.
14 *Africa Confidential* (UK), 10 November 2000.
15 BBC News, 19 December 2000.
16 *The Post* (Zambia), 11 May 2001.
17 Panafrican News Agency, 18 May 2001; CNN.com, 6 July 2001.
18 African News Network, 15 September 2000.
19 *Business Day* (South Africa), 26 January 2001.
20 Botswana Press Agency, 2 April 2001.
21 *Business Day* (South Africa), 26 January 2001.
22 Matsheza and Kunakas (1999).
23 *Sunday Independent* (South Africa), 21 January 2001.
24 Noria Mashumba in a recent e-discussion group.
25 *Mail & Guardian* (South Africa), 20 September 2000.
26 *The Guardian* (UK), 28 April 2000.
27 *Africa Confidential* (UK), 26 May 2000.
28 In January 2001 the Luanda-based Party for Democratic Assistance and Progress of Angola
    (PADPA) went on a hunger strike, demanding an official statement over the 'Angolagate' case.
29 Nyanga Declaration, <http://www.transparency.org/pressreleases_archive/2001/
    2001.03.13.nyanga-declaration.html>.
30 MISA, 'So This Is Democracy – State of the Media in Southern Africa 2000,' 2000.
31 *Daily News* (Zimbabwe), 20 February 2001.
32 *Africa Confidential* (UK), 7 January 2000.
33 Oumar Baron Makalou, *Privatisation in Africa: A Critical Analysis*
    (Washington DC: World Bank, 1999).
34 Susan Hawley, 'Exporting Corruption: Privatisation, Multinationals and Bribery,'
    The Corner House Briefing Paper No. 19, 2000.
35 Kempe Ronald Hope and Bornwell Chikulo, *Corruption and Development in Africa*
    (London: Macmillan Press, 2000).
36 Under pressure from the government, parliament ultimately rejected the report. Its findings are
    corroborated by media and other research, notably that of the Rights and Accountability in
    Development (RAID) project at Oxford University. A RAID report points to a 'clear conflict of
    interests' characterising sale of the mines. Patricia Feeney and Tom Kenny, 'Deregulation and
    the Denial of Rights in Zambia,' April 2000.
37 *Mail & Guardian* (South Africa), 27 November 2000; Mozambique News Agency,
    13 March 2001.
38 Informationsstelle Südliches Afrika, 22 May 2001.
39 John Mukum Mbaku, *Bureaucratic and Political Corruption in Africa*
    (London: Macmillan, 2000).
40 *Daily News* (Zimbabwe), 20 February 2001.
41 Nicholas Hildyard, 'The Lesotho Highland Water Development Project – What Went Wrong?
    Or, Rather: What Went Right? For Whom?' The Corner House Briefing Paper, 2000.
42 *Business Day* (South Africa), 28 June 2001.
43 *Mail & Guardian* (South Africa), 19 January 2001.
44 *Financial Mail* (South Africa), 4 February 2001.
45 *Financial Times* (UK), 16 February 2001.
46 *Africa Confidential* (UK), 23 February 2001.
47 *Mail & Guardian* (South Africa), 16 February 2001.
48 For more on the linkages between war, corruption, and the diamond trade, see p. 214.
49 UN Integrated Regional Information Network (IRIN), 29 January 2001.
50 For discussion of the involvement of the Great Lakes countries in this conflict, see p. 68.
51 *Africa Confidential* (UK), 26 May 2000.
52 *Africa Analysis* (UK), 16 October 1998.

East and East-Central Africa

Burundi, Democratic Republic of Congo, Djibouti, Ethiopia, Eritrea, Gabon, Kenya, Republic of the Congo, Rwanda, Seychelles, Somalia, Sudan, Tanzania, Uganda

By Gitau Warigi

Introduction

War, civil strife and instability mar much of East and East-Central Africa's landscape, with Africa's 'first world war' in the Democratic Republic of the Congo (DRC), state collapse in Somalia, ethnic conflict in Burundi and civil war in Sudan. Ethiopia and Eritrea have just concluded a brief but bloody war. These conflicts each present opportunities for personal profiteering by military factions and elites, and threaten prospects for accountable and stable governance.

Levels of development are uneven and poverty high, with around 30 per cent of people living on less than US $1 per day.[1] Corruption is a prominent feature of daily public life even in the region's more peaceful countries, and imposes high costs both at the local and national levels. While data is limited, the Kenyan government is thought to have lost more than Ksh475 billion (US $6 billion) through corruption between 1991–97.[2] The country is now facing a credit squeeze from its foreign lenders, directly related to perceptions of institutionalised corruption. The NGO Uganda Debt Network estimated that Uganda lost the equivalent of US $500 million to corruption over the last five years.[3]

Economies are dependent on foreign aid, much of which is paid out again to service crippling foreign debt.[4] Donors have largely shaped blueprints for privatisation and economic reform. But the trend of liberalisation that swept the region in the post-Cold War era, though designed to accelerate development and enhance governance, has presented its own opportunities for corruption.

Anti-corruption initiatives have largely been driven by donor conditionalities. Though national institutions and laws to tackle corruption are now in place in many countries, their achievements remain limited. A relatively free press and growing civil society activism over corruption have helped to expose graft in some countries, but there is an urgent need for careful reforms that are appropriate to the economic capacity and needs of the region. Governments and foreign actors alike must show themselves determined to execute reform and stamp out corruption, if its burden on development is to be reduced.

News review

In December 2000 in Kenya, the High Court ruled that the Kenya Anti-Corruption Authority (KACA), a body created primarily at the behest of IMF and World Bank pressure, was unconstitutional. Donors promptly froze all lending, sending the economy reeling. A draft bill to create a new anti-corruption authority was published in May 2001 and is widely expected to win parliamentary support, though donors made it clear that they will issue funds only if the body is truly given teeth. The financial institutions also insist on greater transparency in the country's privatisation programme. In March 2001 a team of technocrats with an express mandate to curb official graft in the civil service was dismissed by President Daniel arap Moi with the explanation that 'the reform programme now needs to be supervised by others'.[5]

In the course of 2000, several top Tanzanian officials, among them the Minister for Tourism, were removed from office as a result of investigations under Tanzania's National Anti-Corruption Strategy. However, it seems that the strategy is faltering at a time when ongoing privatisation schemes present increasing opportunities for illegal self-enrichment. President Benjamin Mkapa gave his full support to the campaign on its launch in 1999, but observers are concerned that, faced with the choice of cracking down hard or alienating key supporters, his efforts are relenting. Corruption was recently identified by the head of the EU delegation to Tanzania as 'by far the biggest challenge for the government'.[6] The government's reticence over a controversial US $150 million Malaysian-backed power investment in Tanzania, widely criticised as wasteful and corrupt, is a key area of concern. In 2000–01, senior officials of the ruling Chama cha Mapinduzi Party, as well as government officers, were implicated in the case.[7]

Until recently Uganda enjoyed an almost stellar reputation as one of Africa's most committed economic reformers. But the way in which the government carried out its privatisation programme sullied this image, and revelations of corruption and cronyism multiplied during the year.[8] A controversial UN report in April 2001 on the looting of natural resources in the DRC conflict incriminated members of President Yoweri Museveni's immediate family.[9] Petty corruption remains high, as elsewhere in the region. The general elections in March 2001 saw anti-corruption play a more prominent role in candidates' campaign rhetoric, though activists and the independent press highlighted examples of excessive party expenditure and questionable campaign methods.[10]

In Ethiopia, draft legislation for an Ethics and Anti-Corruption Commission was completed in 2000 and subsequently approved by the House of People's Representatives. It forms part of a wider strategy that calls for a multi-pronged assault against corruption, involving not just the government but the private sec-

Corruption in Uganda's judiciary and police

Each morning they wake at six and walk 16 miles handcuffed together to the district magistrate's court. In the evening, they walk back past fields of crops and homesteads to prison, tired out after a day without food. They return to their common cell in time to eat the single meal of the day – maize porridge, boiled beans and water.

Police investigations into these men's cases are still incomplete several months after they were first remanded. These are the prisoners of Kamuge prison in rural Pallisa, eastern Uganda. Designed to accommodate remand prisoners, it has no facilities for long-term imprisonment, no transport, no basic sanitation and is in dire need of repairs.

John Oulo is suspected of stealing a bicycle; Issa Wabwire, a taxi-driver, is suspected of knocking someone over; Moses Kirya was involved in a land dispute; Sam Mugote defaulted on tax payments; and another inmate is accused of using a fake card to vote.

The longest serving is Hassan Dankaine, a sickly 70-year-old, suspected of cheating a local cotton trader. He recently fell ill and was unable to walk the distance to court, thus incurring a further penalty.

'They ask us for some money if we want our freedom. We do not have money. That is why they keep us here. Even then, our families have to come regularly to give them money. Or else they torture us and make us dig each morning before walking to court,' claim the inmates.[1]

Local police and the District Magistrate Henry Haduli deny the allegations. 'We are trying our best to deliver justice,' Haduli said. The authorities say they donated a car to transport inmates to and from prison, though both wardens and inmates deny it.

The police and judiciary are the institutions considered most corrupt by ordinary Ugandans. In a survey by the country's Ombudsman, 63 per cent of respondents claimed to have bribed a police officer, while 50 per cent had bribed a court official. Fifty-seven per cent of people interviewed thought corruption was getting worse, not better.[2]

Speaking at a recent anti-corruption workshop, the country's principal judge, Justice J.H. Ntabgoba, spoke of the difficult working conditions facing the judiciary, particularly in its lower ranks: 'No decent accommodation is provided and officials have families to feed, clothe and educate. They have limited support staff. Responsibility for collecting court fees and fines without proper accounting systems invariably results in a temptation to pocket the money, mainly as a means of survival.'[3]

The Auditor General found in 1999–2000 that over US $147,428 had been spent without authority from revenue collections by nine courts. In three courts, bail deposits of US $4,914 had been diverted, lent out or utilised in office, contrary to the law.[4]

In the last two years, the judiciary has launched efforts to clean up its image. 'The public must be encouraged to report anyone who solicits a bribe,' says Justice Ntabgoba. 'At present people don't believe such cases would ever be heard.'

A recent government inquiry into the police recommended dismissals and forced resignations of top officers. But it will take time before the police win any respect from the public. Kampala taxi driver Mohammed Mugisha said: 'All I need to know for my work is the name of the traffic officers on duty. Each time they stop me, I just give them something and they let me go.'

Uganda's police earn on average Ush120,000 per month (US $68). According to Mugisha, police officers will continue to take bribes until the government improves their wages.

Erich Ogoso Opolot

1 Interviews with author.
2 Ugandan Inspectorate of Government, 'National Integrity Survey,' 1998.
3 J.H. Ntagoba, 'The Challenges of Fighting Corruption in the Judiciary and the Way Forward,' presentation to Anti-Corruption Coalition Building Workshop, Entebbe, 2000.
4 Auditor General of Uganda, 'Report to Parliament on Public Accounts,' 30 June 2000.

tor and civil society.[11] In March 2001, corruption was at the centre of a major split in the Tigray People's Liberation Front (TPLF), the dominant party in the ruling coalition. Ato Tamirat Layne, a former prime minister and close associate of Prime Minister Meles Zenawi, was jailed for 18 years for corruption and embezzlement.[12] A former defence minister and one of Zenawi's rivals, Siye Abraha, was also accused of pocketing commissions from weapons procurement linked to the war with Eritrea and was subsequently arrested.[13] His allies in the TPLF's central committee responded by challenging the integrity of close family members of government leaders.[14] Around 20 government officials, bankers and businessmen have also been arrested on corruption charges since the government's anti-corruption campaign began.[15]

In Rwanda, Pasteur Bizimungu resigned as president in March 2000, officially for 'personal reasons'. In reality, his exit came amid a purge of top officials accused of personal corruption, profiteering and abuse of office that provided political cover for a consolidation of Tutsi elite power around post-genocide strongman Paul Kagame.[16] Patrick Mazimpaka, a powerful cabinet minister and ally of Bizimungu, was earlier pushed out of office when he was the target of an embarrassing parliamentary anti-corruption probe. And Prime Minister Pierre-Célestin Rwigema was fired in February 2000 following the 'Schoolgate' scandal, which involved the misappropriation of millions of dollars earmarked for education by the World Bank's International Development Association.[17]

In Burundi, a parliamentary commission of inquiry reported in January 2001 that 'theft, fraudulent management, corruption and embezzlement are rampant in the public sector'.[18] Among those named was President Pierre Buyoya's wife, who was mentioned in connection with sugar import fraud. According to information provided by the Inspector General's office, over BFr12 billion (US $16.5 million) have been embezzled since the civil war erupted in 1993.

In oil-rich Gabon and Congo-Brazzaville, oil and political pay-offs define the landscape of corruption. An ongoing investigation in France has focused on the secret slush funds allegedly run by state-owned oil giant Elf Aquitaine in order to pay top officials in both countries, as well as in France.[19] Elf continues to be the largest oil producer in Gabon and Congo-Brazzaville.

Conflict and opportunities for corrupt profit

Uganda and Rwanda reacted with outrage when a UN special committee released a report on their role in exploiting resources during the DRC conflict.[20] The report documented the activities of their respective forces in eastern DRC, and showed in stark detail how senior military officers and their business associates took advantage of the war to enrich themselves. It was candid about the personalities involved. Heading the list was Caleb Akandwanaho, otherwise known as Salim Saleh, who is President Museveni's younger brother, and his wife Jovia. Also mentioned was General James Kazini, commander of Ugandan forces in the DRC until last year. On the Rwandan side, the report named Colonel James Kabarebe, the army's Chief of Staff. Other officials of the ruling Rwandan Patriotic Front were also incriminated.

Despite official denial of the allegations by Uganda and Rwanda, information gathered by the UN committee indicated that the two countries recently became exporters of gold, diamonds and coltan – commodities that they do not actually produce. Opposition MPs in Uganda corroborated this information.[21] The UN report estimated that Rwanda earned some US $20 million from looted coltan every month. 'Let's make one thing clear,' said businessman Mokeni Ekopi Kane, head of the Federation of Congolese Enterprises in Kisangani, 'this is a war of plunder, looting and exploitation.'[22] Though the report recommended that sanctions be imposed on Rwanda and Burundi, political analysts are not placing much store by this, as the report was dismissed by the US, a close ally of both countries.

A web of conflict and corruption is evident throughout the war-ravaged region. In Burundi, disfigured by a slow-motion civil war since 1993, the temptations to take advantage of conflict for purposes of self-enrichment have increased since 1995 when Kenya, Tanzania and Uganda imposed an economic blockade on the country. To circumvent it, officials in Burundi, with their government's tacit support and the connivance of foreign businessmen, resorted to smuggling oil and consumables across the region.

> The corruption instigated by conflicts is bound to persist as long as states remain in violent flux.

A parliamentary report released in January 2001 accused top officials of continuing the illegal smuggling long after the blockade was lifted in 1997.[23]

Conditions created by the conflict between Ethiopia and Eritrea have meanwhile allegedly allowed officials on both sides, particularly those involved in arms procurement, to line their pockets.[24] Somalia, with no formal government (apart from the secessionist Republic of Somaliland, whose self-declared independence has yet to be recognised), has become a bandit's paradise. Warlords and their militias prosper in the anarchy, leading many analysts to conclude that they have a vested interest in ensuring that the status quo continues.[25] Outside the network of clans and militias, humanitarian organisations such as the Red Cross and the World Food Programme are the most visible players. The resources they introduce to the local economy are often the object of intense fighting among the competing groups. A similar situation prevails in southern Sudan, a region devastated by civil war that is in part sustained by the UN-backed Operation Lifeline Sudan humanitarian programme. Some analysts fear that the absence of solutions to the political disputes in Sudan and Somalia problematises relief work there, with the relationship between aid givers and recipients becoming a possible dynamic in perpetuating the conflict.[26] The corruption instigated by these conflicts is bound to persist as long as states remain in violent flux.

Developing anti-corruption institutions: donors, governments and civil society

The creation of anti-corruption bodies has become a trend in the region over the past few years, as a key feature of post-Cold War donor conditionalities. Without such institutional anti-corruption measures in place, advocates say, economic restructuring programmes will come unstuck. But the external pressure for anti-corruption institutions has been more intense in some countries than others, usually in proportion to donors' financial exposure. Anti-corruption efforts in Kenya, Uganda and Tanzania, for example, have come under far sharper scrutiny than efforts in Burundi, Eritrea or the DRC. The former now have a body of laws, institutions and procedures in place for tackling corruption, although effective implementation is missing.

The Prevention of Corruption Bureau in Tanzania and the Inspectorate of Government in Uganda are carefully designed anti-corruption institutions with mandates to investigate public sector corruption, though their work is hampered by a lack of resources and skilled personnel. Ethiopia is currently seeking to develop an Ethics and Anti-Corruption Commission in collaboration with the World Bank, the UNDP, the EU and bilateral donors, all of which have funds available to boost capacity-building initiatives.

Foreign pressure has been particularly intense in Kenya, though developements there sound a warning note as to the limits of externally-driven institutional change.[27] The international financial institutions successfully pushed for the establishment of the Kenya Anti-Corruption Authority (KACA), an independent body that would bypass the notorious corruption that hinders the investigative machinery of the Kenyan police, in an attempt to bring corrupt politicians to book. KACA's independence was an absolute condition of the disbursement of a US $220 million loan.[28]

KACA's prosecution of high-profile cases, including that of a cabinet minister and a permanent secretary, generated acute controversy and opposition among the political elite. From the first the authorities were opposed to the body's sweeping mandate. Kenyan parliamentarians were also ambivalent, as the body was

Ufisadi ni mzigo mzito kwa maskini (Corruption is a burden to the poor)
Samuel K. Githui, Kenya

also not answerable to them. KACA ran in to its most serious difficulties following claims that its mandate undermined the Kenyan constitution, according to
which only the Attorney General may authorise criminal and civil prosecutions.
International pressure to enshrine KACA's autonomy not just in statute but in the
country's constitution was seen to circumvent this exclusive authority. Opponents
to KACA used this logic to block it. The High Court declared KACA unconstitutional in December 2000.

World Bank President James Wolfensohn had also pressured President Moi
at a meeting in London in July 1999 to appoint a team of private sector technocrats to oversee reform of the corruption-ridden civil service.[29] Headed by
prominent palaeontologist and wildlife activist Richard Leakey, the unit was

quickly dubbed the 'Dream Team' by the Kenyan press. The unit motivated KACA to bring controversial and high-profile corruption cases to the fore. It also tried to speed up the stalled privatisation of Telkom, the country's national telecommunications operator – another of the donors' conditionalities for a restoration of aid. But in March 2001, the team was disbanded amid the strongest possible indications that it had fallen out with Moi. Further accusations of infringement of sovereignty were made. Installing such a prominent figure as Leakey in the post of chief inquisitor of the entire state bureaucracy was seen as a challenge to the President himself.

Complaints about sovereignty reflect genuine sensitivities, although they can also be used as a pretext for resisting efforts to investigate corruption. Whatever the motivation, murmurs of discontent have been growing among the region's aid-dependent countries. A frequent objection is that the vigour with which donors pursue the fight against corruption tends to divert attention from the failures of earlier donor-driven adjustment programmes.[30] Donor conditionalities are often unrealistic, difficult to implement and, according to one expert, can lead to new opportunities for corruption, as has happened with decentralisation reforms in Uganda and Tanzania.[31]

Those involved in shaping anti-corruption initiatives increasingly realise that another set of issues needs to be addressed. Anti-corruption strategies will only work when civil society and the media are directly involved in their creation and monitoring. This is not a model easily accommodated by the top-down approach in which a deal is struck between a donor body and a government minister. Where civil society is strong, as in Kenya, Tanzania and Uganda, it is now recognised that the anti-corruption struggle is most effectively waged when its activists are involved.

The NGO Uganda Debt Network has been especially active, publishing a periodic roll call of corrupt public figures. In May 2001 it released a lengthy report on corruption that singled out Vice-President Specioza Wandira for allegedly misusing Ush3 billion (US $2 million) in funds earmarked for dams. The group is also monitoring the proceeds of debt relief and other aid. Both the Forum Against Corrupt Elements in Tanzania (FACE-IT) and TI-Kenya play similar grassroots watchdog functions in their respective countries. Private sector groups like the Kenyan Association of Manufacturers are also beginning to take an interest. A vocal press in these three countries imposes a fierce scrutiny on the corrupt actions of public officials.

Civil society groups continue to grow in their determination to fight corruption in the more stable countries of the region, and donors are also beginning to adopt a more holistic approach. As World Bank President James Wolfensohn

Kenyan football: time for a sporting chance

The outside world associates Kenyan sporting prowess with the rigours of medium and long-distance running, but football (soccer) is the country's favourite domestic sport, with a fan base of at least ten million. But Kenyan football has been plagued for decades by ethnic antagonism and political intrigue. Now, it has become clear that the game is also a hotbed of fraud and corruption. An initiative by concerned football clubs, in partnership with TI-Kenya, is seeking to give the game a new sort of 'fix' by tackling these problems.

Widespread mismanagement of the game in the office of its organising body, the Kenya Football Federation (KFF), has long been apparent. Gross incompetence and likely bribery of referees is all too common, and the embezzlement of KFF funds has also come to light. The KFF has not sent audited accounts to its member clubs for decades. In some KFF clubs and national teams, players and coaches go unpaid for months on end. Overloaded match schedules, arbitrary changes in the appointment of match officials, the abuse of rules and manipulation in the promotion and relegation of teams regularly disappoint fans.

Eight Premier League Clubs came together in December 2000 to create the Inter-Club Consultative Group (ICCG) to petition the KFF over these trends. The ICCG protest subsequently unravelled a complex web of financial intrigue in spite of KFF resistance.

A copy of the KFF audit for 2000 was leaked, revealing major irregularities in the Federation's bookkeeping. Only Ksh2.1 million (US $26,923) was recorded for gate collections during 2000, although the year witnessed over 300 league, cup and international matches. Meanwhile, stadium expenses tripled from Ksh785,225 (US $10,066) in 1999 to over Ksh2.3 million (US $29,487) in 2000, although 150 fewer matches were played that year.

Official allowances and 'youth expenses' similarly rose massively, but inexplicably, during the same period.

In response to these alarming findings, the ICCG sent a letter to the KFF Secretary General in May 2001, asking the KFF to call a meeting of all clubs to discuss the audit issue and general levels of accountability. The letter was returned unopened with an annotation stating: 'Mail back. We do not know this group since they are not our members.' Direct appeals to the Confederation of African Football (CAF) and the International Federation of Football Associations (FIFA) also fell on deaf ears.

This lack of accountability and transparency left some ICCG clubs contemplating withdrawal from the KFF league. That would be a solemn day for Kenyan football, but it could also lead to the teams being banned by FIFA from foreign competition. The possibility of taking legal action against KFF might have a similar result if precedents are anything to go by, since FIFA actively discourages clubs from instituting legal proceedings.

The KFF and many Kenyan football clubs run a real risk of going bankrupt if efforts to improve transparency do not take place quickly. The obvious victims of this organisational and financial crisis are the players and coaches – who are often the main wage earner in their families – and, of course, the fans.

The recent emergence of corporate sponsorship and more ethnically diverse clubs in Kenyan football might give the game a fresh start. Tusker FC, sponsored by Kenya Breweries, together with 2000 Moi Golden Cup champions, the independent Mathare United FC (which gathers its players from one of Nairobi's poorest slums), are illustrative of a new direction. Together with efforts by the ICCG and TI-Kenya, these dynamics may yet save the day for Kenyan football.

TI-Kenya

acknowledged: 'A corrupt-free society cannot be legislated upon. Only a multi-pronged approach will do.'[32] The increased input of civil society should enable anti-corruption institutions to grow in scope and capacity.

Corruption in privatisation and foreign investment

The process of privatisation has been problematic in the region. Where it has occured, it has been complicated by limits both to local resources and political commitment to ensuring its transparency. By and large, privatisation is being administered with technical advice and financial support from donor institutions. But given the role of governments as the sole valuer of assets, divestiture can be easily manipulated.[33]

The Ugandan parliament and World Bank have criticised the country's privatisation programme for non-transparency, insider dealing, conflicts of interest and corruption.[34] The largest assets become concentrated in very few hands, usually those with ties to political power, as in the case of Major General Salim Saleh. Saleh has been the target of a parliamentary probe since the late 1990s, as well as regular denunciations in the media. Analysts alleged his purchase of the formerly state-owned Uganda Grain Milling Corporation was illegal and corrupt.[35]

One factor that undermines efforts to privatise is the dearth of sufficient local capital to absorb large acquisitions.[36] Capital in many countries is concentrated either within the circles of political power, or among a select group of traditionally wealthy citizens. A related impediment is the lack of capital markets. Only Kenya has a fairly well established stock exchange, though even there the trend of privatisation has been to sell to a single high bidder. Uganda and Tanzania are trying to develop their own bourses, but so far these remain rudimentary.

Without the necessary capital, many of the larger enterprises being divested are affordable only to elites or to foreign investors. Governments understandably want control to remain local, at least for what they consider strategic entities.[37] In Ethiopia, the state-controlled financial system remains off-limits to private investors, although other sectors are for sale. Kenya tentatively allowed private interests to venture into power generation, but has been reluctant to allow competition in electricity distribution. It is also considering partial privatisation of its ports, but to national investors only.[38] Gabon and Congo-Brazzaville intend to retain control over their vital oil sectors.

Retention of control based on strategic concerns may also mask baser reasoning: governments fear the loss of easy sources of political patronage. This rationale may have stalled the divestiture of Telkom Kenya. The pretext the government gave was that the price offered last year by a consortium led by South

African firm Econet Wireless was not high enough. Econet, the third largest pan-African telecom operator, made the highest bid of US $305 million for the 49 per cent stake being divested from Telkom.

Analysts familiar with the dilapidated state of Telkom's assets are convinced a better offer could not be found. Nevertheless, the government said it intended to renegotiate with bidders for a higher price, before announcing in February 2001 its intention to turn to an Egyptian company that had made a lower bid.[39] In a further turnaround, it re-opened bidding but insisted that the minimum offer must be US $350 million. Salomon Smith Barney, the merchant bankers advising on the privatisation, promptly withdrew in frustration, though they have since re-entered negotiations.[40] Analysts voiced suspicions that the government's bias against Econet had less to do with price than with the fact that the consortium refused to pay kickbacks.[41] Moreover, its local representatives are businessmen from the Kikuyu tribe, which is largely identified with the political opposition.[42]

> Governments may fear the loss of easy sources of political patronage as a result of privatisation.

Foreign investment is desperately needed in the region. Due to perceptions of instability, however, there are difficulties attracting it to most sectors, with the exception of oil and minerals. But foreign investment frequently comes at a price. French oil giant Elf Aquitaine, the dominant foreign investor in Gabon and Congo-Brazzaville, has come under investigation for allegedly offering political payoffs to top politicians[43] – though it is now moving to clean up its practices. Together with growing efforts at the international level to curtail bribery of public officials by foreign investors, the relative impunity of foreign bribery may largely be in the past. But kickbacks and corruption still continue to occur.

In the absence of local capital, and the reluctance of many foreign investors to commit to the region, 'South-South' investment is a favoured alternative. One of the most aggressive private sector players to take advantage of the liberalisation of energy in East Africa is the Westmont Group of Malaysia. In Tanzania, Westmont brokered a crucial stake in power generation, an area hitherto monopolised by Tanesco, the state-owned electricity supply utility. Westmont also has an electricity supply contract with Kenya.

The Westmont investment in Tanzania proceeded in spite of warnings by the anti-corruption agency that officials had been bribed. Press reports alleged vast kickbacks at very high levels.[44] The risk analysis of its large power project was poorly done, according to critics, and it imposed unnecessary costs by stalling development of a much cheaper power project, which would have exploited the country's abundant natural gas reserves.[45] Instead, Tanzania has been forced to use scarce foreign exchange to import the diesel for the Westmont project. In Uganda, Westmont's name cropped up in the banking sector, where allegations emerged of wrongdoing in the privatisation of the Uganda Commercial Bank in 1999.[46]

Not all privatisations are characterised by such problems, but issues of equity and fairness in the way the process is implemented remain prominent. Not only do more transparent mechanisms need to be put in place, but without them, the whole process of privatisation risks unravelling, undermining the benefits of investment in the region.

Conclusion

Discussing corruption publicly was once taboo across much of the East and East-Central Africa region. This has changed as the region opens hesitantly to globalisation and as citizens and donors enabled by democratisation and a freer press apply pressure for cleaner government. How much of the increased attention to corruption represents governments turning a new leaf is open to question. Ethiopia, Tanzania and to a lesser extent Uganda appear determined, despite setbacks, to move toward more open government. Other countries, notably Kenya and Gabon, whose leaders have each held uninterrupted power for over 20 years, are less sure. Somalia, meanwhile, is in too much turmoil to prioritise the issue of fighting corruption at all. There, as elsewhere in the Horn of Africa and the Great Lakes region, the most far-reaching networks of corruption appear to be related to conflict and aid.

Donor-inspired pressure to establish anti-corruption agencies with wide-reaching powers has perhaps inevitably led to cries of 'foreign interference', especially from governments that have much to hide. But every country in the region depends on foreign aid, and, as long as that situation prevails, donors will continue to exercise considerable influence.

Civil society groups, though still nascent, play an increasingly important role, while the media is ever more vocal. Large-scale, corruption-driven projects such as Kenya's Turkwell Gorge Project, completed in 1987 in defiance of popular and expert protests, would be unlikely to happen in today's climate, precisely because of the influence of civil society and the independent press.

The prospects for tackling corruption in the region are changing fast, as anti-corruption institutions continue to develop, civil society grows, and privatisation and investment procedures come under scrutiny. While peace is the priority for many East and East-Central African states, for others the war against corruption is now prominently on the agenda.

1 UNDP, *Human Development Report 2000* (New York: Oxford University Press, 2000).
2 Centre for Governance and Development, policy brief, February 2001.
3 *New People* (Kenya), 1 April 2001.
4 Kenya is currently paying US $4 in debt servicing for every US $1 it receives in aid grants: <http://www.jubilee2000uk.org>.
5 *The Daily Nation* (Kenya), 22 March 2001.
6 Peter Beck Christiansen, quoted in *Mail & Guardian* (South Africa), 23 June 2000.
7 *The EastAfrican* (Kenya), 5 March 2001.
8 *The Monitor* (Uganda), 12 September 2000.
9 United Nations Security Council, 'The Report of the Panel of Experts on the Illegal Exploitation of Natural Resources and Other Forms of Wealth of the Democratic Republic of Congo': <http://www.un.org/Depts/dh1/docs/s2001357.pdf>.
10 TI-Uganda, interview with author.
11 Office of the Prime Minister of Ethiopia, 'Enhancing Ethics and Anti-Corruption Effort in Ethiopia,' August 2000.
12 BBC News, 14 March 2000.
13 *Dehai News* (Eritrea), 4 March 2001; UN Integrated Regional Information Network (IRIN), 27 March 2001.
14 *Indian Ocean Newsletter* (France), 31 March 2001.
15 IRIN, 26 July 2001
16 *Mail & Guardian* (South Africa), 24 March 2000.
17 *Africa Confidential* (UK), 31 March 2000.
18 IRIN, 26 January 2001.
19 Agence France Presse, 17 January 2001.
20 UN (2001). For more on the linkages between war and corruption, see report on p. 214.
21 *The EastAfrican* (Kenya), 23 April, 2001. Ugandan and Rwandan officials have complained that the UN committee that prepared the report was 'biased', because of its francophone majority. France occupies a dominant place in Rwanda and Uganda's diplomatic demonology.
22 *Christian Science Monitor* (US), 13 April 2001.
23 IRIN, 26 January 2001.
24 *Dehai News* (Eritrea), 4 March 2001; IRIN, 27 March 2001.
25 IRIN, 20 December 2000.
26 Mark Duffield, *Global Governance and the New Wars* (London: Zed, 2001).
27 Shantayanan Devarajan, David Dollar and Torgny Holmgren, *Aid and Reform in Africa: Lessons from Ten Case Studies* (Washington DC: World Bank, 2001).
28 IRIN, 15 January 2001.
29 *The EastAfrican* (Kenya), 28 July 1999.
30 Among those who frequently made this complaint was Kenya's Finance Minister, Chris Okemo, who has sounded increasingly exasperated with donor agencies since aid to Kenya was cut off last year. 'Kenya Hansard Parliamentary Reports', February–March, 2001.
31 A researcher at Chr. Michelsen Institute, Norway, interview with author.
32 James D. Wolfensohn, 'A Proposal for a Comprehensive Development Framework,' World Bank, 1999.
33 Roger Tangri and Andrew Mwenda, 'Corruption and Cronyism in Uganda's Privatisation in the 1990s', *African Affairs,* 100, 2001.
34 *The EastAfrican* (Kenya), 18 June 2001.
35 Tangri and Mwenda (2001).
36 Roger Tangri, *The Politics of Patronage in Africa: Parastatals, Privatization and Private Enterprise* (Trenton: Africa World Press, 1999).
37 World Bank, *Anti-Corruption in Transition: A Contribution to the Policy Debate* (Washington DC: World Bank, 2000).
38 *The Daily Nation* (Kenya), 23 April 2001.
39 *The Daily Nation* (Kenya), 13 February 2001.
40 *The Daily Nation* (Kenya), 1 May 2001.
41 Wired News, 15 March 2001.
42 *The Daily Nation* (Kenya), 13 February 2001.
43 Agence France Presse, 17 January 2001.
44 *The EastAfrican* (Kenya), 4 August 2000.
45 *Mail & Guardian* (South Africa), 28 April 2000.
46 Tangri (1999).

West and West-Central Africa

Benin, Burkina Faso, Cameroon, Cape Verde, Central African Republic, Chad, Côte d'Ivoire, Equatorial Guinea, Gambia, Ghana, Guinea, Guinea-Bissau, Liberia, Mali, Mauritania, Niger, Nigeria, Sao Tome and Principe, Senegal, Sierra Leone, Togo

By Hakeem Jimo, Tidiane Sy and Dame Wade

Introduction

West and West-Central Africa includes some of the poorest countries in the world: of the 15 lowest ranking countries in the UN's Human Development Index, ten are in the region.[1] Several factors contribute to the persistence of regional poverty, and corruption is definitely one of them. Oil and gas have brought wealth to some in Nigeria, and both Equatorial Guinea and Chad are on the threshold of similar bonanzas. But the oil industry has historically provided opportunities for corruption on a massive scale, and the diamond wealth of Sierra Leone has nurtured conflict and corruption both there and in bordering countries.

Since independence from colonial rule in the 1960s, periods of dictatorship have alternated with military rule and one-party regimes, all of which have embedded corruption deep in political systems. Most countries have also seen periods of democracy, and recent years have witnessed a number of transitions to multi-party politics, frequently at the behest of international donors. Such transitions have exposed governments to greater public scrutiny. Democracy was restored in the regional 'superpower' Nigeria with the election of Olusegun Obasanjo as President in 1999. Recent elections in Ghana and Senegal offer further hope of a sustainable democratic future for the region.

A military coup and civil unrest in Côte d'Ivoire, previously an island of political stability and comparative wealth, shows how quickly change can come. In the volatile countries of Guinea, Liberia and Sierra Leone, a developing regional conflict has resulted in the displacement of hundreds of thousands of refugees. Many countries in the region are currently suffering from some form of military conflict, either with other countries or with rebel groups within their own borders – further reducing the funds available for spending on much-needed public services.

As democracy develops in some countries, civil society is beginning to establish itself. But the balance of power remains heavily weighted in favour of governments. With limited independence for judiciaries, the strength of the fight against corruption is largely determined by political will.

News review

President Obasanjo has not had an easy ride since he made anti-corruption measures the centrepiece of his administration on coming to power. While he has pushed his reform programme forward, the pace of change has been slow, which was perhaps inevitable in a country where corruption is so deeply embedded. It took over a year for the legislature to pass Nigeria's Anti-Corruption Act, and the Anti-Corruption Commission it was intended to establish was only sworn in at the end of September 2000. Observers suspected that the delay was linked to a series of corruption scandals that broke out in the legislature. The most prominent was the impeachment in August 2000 of Senate President Chuba Okadigbo, who was alleged to have misused public funds.[2]

Much of the Nigerian government's initial work in fighting corruption has addressed the legacy of former dictator General Sani Abacha. The Obasanjo administration views one of its major tasks as retrieving the billions of dollars embezzled by Abacha and deposited in overseas banks in his five-year reign.[3] The government has tried to enlist the support of financial institutions, but has so far had only partial success in reclaiming the funds.[4] Repatriation of the wealth is a subject of keen interest to the Nigerian public.

In Senegal, the victory of Abdoulaye Wade in the presidential election of March 2000, and the subsequent success of his *Sopi* ('Change') coalition in the legislative elections in April 2001, brought an end to 40 years of rule by the Socialist Party of Senegal. Evidence is now being revealed of corruption links between major state-owned enterprises and the long-running administration of former president Abdou Diouf. In March 2001, the former manager of the National Railway Company of Senegal – who is also a prominent opposition politician – was arrested, accused of the mismanagement of public funds.[5]

Former president of Mali Moussa Traoré and several of his associates recently stood trial for 'economic crimes'. Traoré was accused of misappropriating 2 billion CFA francs (US $2.6 million).[6] Investigations are also continuing into the misuse of funds belonging to pension fund Caisse des Retraites du Mali (CRM). Those under investigation include Blaise Sangharé, CRM's former director and now head of a political party.[7]

The Chief Justice of Niger's Supreme Court denounced political parties for non-compliance with financial disclosure laws. According to the judge, only eight of Niger's 30 political parties submitted the required financial statements to the

Court's accounting office, and the statements that were submitted did not fulfil all the financial disclosure obligations the law demands.[8]

Burkina Faso suffered critical damage to its international standing following UN accusations in December 2000 that it was involved in smuggling weapons to rebels in Sierra Leone and Angola and exporting conflict diamonds, collected by the Revolutionary United Front (RUF).[9]

Sierra Leone is still suffering from a civil war between government forces and RUF rebels, backed by Liberia's President Charles Taylor. Although the elected government enjoys widespread support at home and abroad, it also faces criticism because of corruption. Permanent Secretary Soloku Bockarie in the Ministry of Education was sentenced to seven years' imprisonment after he was found guilty of larceny and corruption.[10] In response, the Minister of Justice and Attorney General Solomon Berewa formed a Corruption Prevention Unit, attached to the President's Office.[11]

'If you want to do business in Liberia,' reported a US newspaper, quoting a local entrepreneur, 'you do business with Taylor.'[12] In January 2001, President Taylor invited the legislature to approve the Strategic Commodities Act, effectively giving him exclusive rights over all of Liberia's natural resources. The opposition described the Act as 'theft by legislation'.[13] In May 2001 the UN imposed sanctions on Liberia because of its role in the Sierra Leone conflict and illegal diamond trading, adding to an existing embargo on arms sales to the country.[14]

When the then military leader of Côte d'Ivoire, General Robert Guei, faced defeat in the presidential election in October 2000, he attempted to halt it by stopping the count. But he was forced from power when hundreds of thousands of Ivorians took to the streets. Guei had justified his coup in December 1999 in part because of rampant corruption in the administration of former president Henri Konan Bedie. Ivorians made it clear that Guei was not providing any solutions.[15] Côte d'Ivoire's current president, Laurent Gbagbo, faces the immediate challenge of reconciling his government with voters in the north, whose preferred candidate, Alassane Ouatarra, was prevented from standing by trumped-up allegations about his citizenship. The media have already accused ministers in the new government of corruption.[16]

In Ghana, intervention by the media played an important role in ensuring that the presidential election in December 2000 was relatively free and fair. President John Kufuor's inaugural address, which marked an end to 19 years of rule by Jerry Rawlings, announced a policy of 'zero tolerance' of corruption. Though the new government acted quickly to prevent outgoing ministers and officials from stealing public assets, including official cars, it has yet to articulate a firm anti-corruption strategy.[17]

The democratic system in Benin has been regarded as one of the better established in West Africa, but this reputation was shaken in the presidential election of March 2001. The leading opposition candidate pulled out of a second round of voting, accusing the government of electoral fraud. The second round concluded with a choice between President Mathieu Kerekou and a senior minister in his own government.

President Paul Biya of Cameroon, increasingly under pressure over alleged human rights abuses,[18] announced that he would prioritise the fight against corruption. A national Anti-Corruption Observatory was established in January 2000, and the government went on to establish Observatories within specific ministries. Cases have been uncovered – including fraud within the Education Ministry – but some questioned how far-reaching the Observatories will actually be.[19]

Equatorial Guinea has enjoyed dramatic financial advantages since oil production commenced in 1996, but the extent of corruption was such that President Teodoro Obiang Ngema forced the Prime Minister and his cabinet to resign in February 2001.[20] The President of the Supreme Court and the President of the Constitutional Court were also dismissed after a special anti-corruption commission exposed the embezzlement of funds in the judiciary.[21] The new prime minister, Candido Muatetema Rivas, claimed that his priority was fighting corruption.[22]

Inter-governmental groupings in the region have taken steps during 2000–01 to strengthen the campaign against corruption. In June 2000, the eight member Economic and Monetary Union of West Africa (UEMOA) signed a Transparency Code for the Management of Public Finances, calling for a 'qualitative change' in the conduct of public finances.[23] In November 2000, the Economic Community of West African States (ECOWAS) held the first meeting of a new Inter-Governmental Action Group against Money Laundering in Dakar.[24] As part of the growing regional concern with corruption, attorney generals and ministers of justice of ECOWAS countries issued the Accra Declaration on Collaborating against Corruption in May 2001. Member states began to develop a Community Protocol on Corruption and called for international assistance in the recovery of national wealth that had been stolen and deposited abroad.[25]

Anti-corruption campaigns: rhetoric and reality

Anti-corruption campaigns have been launched both by newly elected governments – as in Ghana, Nigeria and Senegal – and by governments trying to improve their images in advance of elections, as in Togo. Pressured in some instances by the international community and popular protest, governments in the region have established anti-corruption institutions as part of this.

Cameroon's anti-corruption campaign: a paper tiger?

Cameroon's appearance at the bottom of a ranking of 99 countries in Transparency International's 1999 Corruption Perceptions Index dealt a severe blow to domestic and international confidence in the nation's political process. But it still took two years for the government to realise that its posture of indifference to rampant corruption in the country was doing no favours for Cameroon's reputation.

Goaded by threats from the World Bank and the IMF that they would withdraw support for the economic recovery programme if nothing was done, the government reluctantly joined the anti-corruption bandwagon. The measures Cameroon took in 2000–01 marked a definite step forward, although they are still far from sufficient.

The creation of a national Anti-Corruption Observatory seemed to offer the most potential. The Observatory is responsible for monitoring the measures taken in the government's anti-corruption programme.

While the 15-member body served to raise awareness about corruption issues among government officials, its work seems far from convincing one year down the line. Despite meeting several times at Prime Minister Peter Mafany Musonge's office, little concrete action has been taken.

The Finance, Education and Transport Ministries set up their own anti-corruption observatories to complement the national body. Several months after their creation, they too are short on achievement, although the Finance and Education Ministries took punitive measures against certain officials.

Meanwhile, Cameroon's recent qualification for debt relief under the HIPC Initiative is expected to help it secure CFA Fr 218 billion (about US $300 million) from the Bretton Woods institutions over the next three years. This sum is earmarked for construction of schools, hospitals, roads and other public amenities. The funds will be deposited in an account at the Bank of Central African States. In a bid to ensure transparency in the management of the money, a 19-member consultative committee was appointed to examine all expenditure from the account. At the head of the committee is Minister of Finance Michel Meva'a Meboutou, assisted by a representative from civil society.

In spite of the new Observatories and this attempt to prevent a windfall in donor money from going astray, the fight against corruption is far from over in Cameroon. The campaign has inevitably been criticised by some as a paper tiger. The critical steps of forcing officials to declare their assets and prosecuting those guilty of corruption have still to be taken. Some fear that the government lacks the political will to commit itself this far.

Gerald Ndikum

Creating an institution, however, does not ensure its effectiveness. According to Mike Stevens, a World Bank specialist in public sector reform, far from lacking institutions to fight corruption, many countries in the region actually have too many.[26] The greatest challenge for new governments is to transform existing institutions with inherited weaknesses before vested interests 'dig in'. A key issue in several countries, therefore, is whether new governments should declare an amnesty for those who acted corruptly under previous regimes.

With the political and donor benefits that accrue to governments that are perceived to be fighting corruption, many anti-corruption crackdowns in the region are unfortunately little more than public relations exercises. Anti-corruption efforts must be backed by political will if they are to stand any chance of proving effective. In assessing their merit, the challenge is to distinguish between substantive reform and rhetoric.

In Mali, the commitment of President Alpha Oumar Konaré is seen to be behind early successes in an anti-corruption campaign launched in 1999.[27] The President, who is in his last term and therefore not responding to the pressure of re-election, is personally involved. The anti-corruption commission has issued a series of reports that reveal embezzlement within state-owned enterprises and other public bodies, and a number of senior officials have been arrested.

> The challenge in assessing anti-corruption efforts is to distinguish between substantive reform and rhetoric.

Political will is not in doubt in Nigeria, where President Obasanjo has made fighting corruption a priority, but it is too early to judge the effectiveness of his efforts. Critics complain that Obasanjo has made too little headway. After a year's delay, the Independent Corrupt Practices and Other Related Offences Commission came into being in late 2000. Its Secretary P. E. Odili called for patience. The Commission will end its training programme, which includes legal courses for selected judges in every high court in the country, by the end of 2001.[28]

In Benin, President Kerekou made the 'moralisation' of public life a key element in his political programme, though there is little evidence that action has been taken in prominent corruption cases. However following his re-election in March 2001, the President retained Minister of Finance Abdoulaye Bio-Tchané, who has a strong record on fighting corruption in public finance.[29]

Observers still need to be convinced that President Gnassingbé Eyadéma has turned over a new leaf in Togo. Eyadéma's 34-year rule, strongly criticised by human rights activists, saw aid disbursement blocked by donors because of lack of progress with democratisation. In January 2001, President Eyadéma acknowledged the negative impact of corruption. Stressing that corruption had become a real 'flaw for the country's economy', he made a strong statement against graft and embezzlement and pledged to fight them. The year 2001, he said in January, 'will be the year of an overall action against corruption, economic sabotage, mismanagement and permissiveness'.[30] But few concrete steps have been taken.[31]

After taking office in Senegal in April 2000, President Abdoulaye Wade also declared his determination to combat corruption on a number of occasions. In particular he announced an audit of all state-owned companies and other institutions involved in managing public funds.[32] Subsequently, at a meeting in January 2001 organised by Forum Civil, the Senegalese chapter of Transparency International, President Wade discussed with NGOs the building of a 'national coalition' against corruption.

Despite these and other gestures, some of his initiatives have been queried by critics, who note the absence of action in cases of corruption or mismanagement where there is no political benefit to the government. In March 2001, Mbaye Diouf, former manager of the National Railway Company of Senegal and a prominent politician in the opposition Socialist Party, was arrested for alleged mismanagement of public funds – one month before legislative elections were due.[33] In a number of cases in which members of the former ruling party, accused in auditors' reports of misappropriation or embezzlement, joined Wade's Senegalese Democratic Party, legal proceedings were not pursued. Most notably former president of the Senate Abdoulaye Diack, now an active supporter of President Wade, confessed in April 2001 to the misappropriation of public funds while the Socialist Party to which he belonged was in power. No action was taken against him.[34] Observers, including Forum Civil, called on the government to avoid any political discrimination in acting on the results of the audits.

Across the region, it is clear that the rhetoric of fighting corruption has to a greater or lesser extent been adopted by political leaders. However, many countries have yet to see firm action in rooting out corrupt officials or the establishment of strong anti-corruption institutions.

Transforming the public sector

'To many Africans, public institutions … are synonymous with poor quality services, corruption and inefficiency,' reported a World Bank study in June 2000.[35] Numerous factors have been identified as encouraging corruption within the region's public administrations: over-centralisation of power, lack of media freedom to expose scandals, the impunity of well-connected officials, absence of transparency in public fund management, clientilism and low salaries. In authoritarian regimes, 'control systems and counter-powers are precarious because there is no culture allowing the use of expertise or freedom of expression', according to Jean Cartier-Bresson, who argued that 'bad governance is at the root of the development of corruption'.[36]

Reform programmes supported by the World Bank, the UNDP and other donors focus on improving the efficiency, accountability and transparency of public services, while reducing the scale of public sector activity through privatisation. Such efforts are nothing new: they have been the focus of structural adjustment programmes since the 1980s. But donors continue to prioritise actions in these sectors with growing attention to corruption. While the need for reform is clear, often the programmes themselves have been as controversial as their effectiveness has been questionable.[37]

As one step in the process of rationalising public services, a number of governments have carried out manpower audits with striking findings. In Nigeria, the Accountant General reported in April 2001, following a manpower verification exercise, that the government had discovered 40,000 staff on the payroll who were no longer employed.[38] The same fraud is replicated elsewhere in West and West-Central Africa. In February 2001, Cameroon's Civil Service Ministry revealed that monthly salaries were paid to 7,000 personnel who had no official function, or who had left their posts years before.[39] In Equatorial Guinea, the anti-corruption commission revealed in December 2000 that more than 2,100 civil servants on the payroll did not exist, mostly within the Defence and Education Ministries.[40] The continuing need for cleaning up the civil service is clear.

The drive to improve transparency in public administration has been adopted as a policy by the African Development Bank, which is working to promote good governance in borrowing countries. In June 2000, the Economic and Monetary Union of West Africa (UEMOA) adopted a Transparency Code for the Management of Public Finances at a meeting in Dakar.[41] The finance ministers who signed the document acknowledged the weakness of their financial management systems and called for 'qualitative change' to achieve 'transparency and better management of public funds'. The code includes guidelines for greater transparency in budget procedures, more clearly defined responsibilities within administrations, the implementation of adequate judicial frameworks and other mechanisms for the monitoring of public funds. In addition, UEMOA recommended measures such as enhancing the training of public service personnel and wider dissemination of reliable information about how state monies are allocated.[42]

Privatisation

A key aspect of the dynamic to transform public services is privatisation. The push to privatise has received fresh momentum from a growing awareness that the inflow of foreign capital and improvements to services may depend on the elimination of public sector monopolies. The problems caused by these monopolies are evident throughout the region. Investigations by Mali's anti-corruption commission last year revealed corruption across a swathe of state-owned enterprises. One of the most prominent led to the conviction in May 2001 of the former CEO of the Société des Télécommunications du Mali, one of the country's largest corporations. He was sentenced to two and a half years' imprisonment and a large fine.[43]

Privatisation featured strongly in the programme outlined by President Obasanjo of Nigeria after coming to office in 1999. A National Council of Privatisation (NCP) was established and a series of sectoral steering committees were formed in September 2000.[44] The NCP, whose board includes senior ministers and the Governor of the Central Bank, is slated to see through the divestiture of a large number of state-owned enterprises – from oil marketing and cement production, to banking and insurance.

However, privatisation processes – not just in Nigeria – are fraught with opportunities for cronyism. In Benin, the privatisation of the petrol-marketing monopoly SONACOP, one of the largest enterprises in the country, was the focus of attention for the domestic media and the political opposition.[45] On completion, control of the company was handed to Séfou Fagbohoun, a close associate of the President. In July 2000, the Minister of Finance took the newly privatised entity to court over financial improprieties during the bidding process.[46]

International pressure for change

Multilateral and bilateral donors play a central role in pressing for governance reform in West and West-Central Africa. While grants and loans have for years been conditional on the adoption of structural adjustment programmes and the downsizing of civil services, donor concerns at how their funds are disbursed have led to a new interest in methods of curbing corruption.

In June 2000, the EU signed a new agreement in Cotonou governing its trade and aid relations with the African, Caribbean and Pacific (ACP) group of states. This agreement goes further than its predecessor, the Lomé Convention, in targeting inadequate governance and serious corruption as grounds for blocking aid. The EU invoked the anti-corruption clause in the new agreement for the first time in June 2001 when it declared its wish to open consultations with the government of Liberia.[47] Even under the Lomé Convention, however, proven corruption could trigger a suspension: in 1999 the EU halted aid to Côte d'Ivoire following the embezzlement of US $25 million, and funds remained frozen after the new government was formed in October 2000.[48]

An influential new instrument, particularly in Western Africa, is the HIPC initiative, which provides debt relief to the world's most 'heavily indebted poor countries'. The criteria that a country needs to meet before becoming eligible under the initiative can include good governance, accountability for public funds and the adoption of a national anti-corruption strategy. Of 23 countries worldwide that have already reached 'decision point' under the HIPC initiative, 12 are in West and West-Central Africa – the most recent being Chad.[49] But there is considerable controversy as to whether the terms on which debt relief is granted are sufficient to prevent the corrupt use of the proceeds.

Some observers question the extent to which good governance is truly prioritised in World Bank programmes. One of the World Bank's most controversial decisions in the region was to provide a loan to help finance the construction of a US $3.7 billion oil pipeline from Chad to the Cameroon coast. The project roused strong opposition from environmental activists. But the project also has a potential corruption dimension. The pipeline will bring Chad an estimated US $100 million a year in revenue – a significant proportion of the government's current budget – as well as important transit fees to Cameroon.[50]

> Donor concerns at how their funds are disbursed have led to a new interest in methods of curbing corruption.

Critics have questioned just how much of that revenue will result in improved public services in two of the poorest countries in the world.

The World Bank defended its decision in June 2000 when it said it had devised a unique programme of controls in Chad and Cameroon to prevent the misappropriation of both loan finance and proceeds from future oil exports. Its Africa spokesman Robert Calderisi said: 'There is no doubt there is a high risk of misuse of funds and we have constructed the arrangements, particularly in Chad, to insure as much as possible against that. Approval is only the first step in a long journey where all kinds of oversight are going to be exercised.'[51] The Chad government is committed to using 80 per cent of oil revenues on health, education and other social projects. However, the World Bank may find it difficult to enforce commitments. Out of an initial US $25 million to the Chad government, US $4 million was reportedly diverted for the purchase of improved weaponry.[52]

Critics of international pressure for good governance point to the role played by Western corporations and banks in fuelling corruption in the region. Speaking at the UN Millenium Summit in September 2000, Jerry Rawlings, then president of Ghana, attacked companies that pay bribes to win contracts and the banks that launder the proceeds of corruption. 'There will be less corruption in Africa if there is no place to hide the proceeds of corruption,' he said, 'or if the proceeds of corruption, once uncovered, are returned to their real owners, the people of Africa.'[53]

Strengthening civil society

Power in West and West-Central Africa remains concentrated in the inner circles of governments, but some countries have seen a growth in civil society organisations and independent media since the spread of democracy in the 1990s. More voices have begun to emerge. Most are professionals or intellectuals in urban areas, while some operate from abroad. Their constituencies are found in the independent broadcast and print media, universities, churches and mosques.

Ghana's media: winning the day for the 2000 elections

After a dozen years of authoritarian control, Ghana's media was given a fresh start by the 1992 constitution. An entire chapter of this landmark document was devoted to guarantees of free speech and encouraging an independent media to act as a watchdog on government. That vision may finally have been realised in the elections of 2000.

Convincing allegations of unfairness tarnished the first election under the 1992 constitution. Opposition parties had less than four months in which to organise campaigns against a decade-old military regime, converted into a political party that appropriated state resources to pay for re-election. Representation in the state-owned media was heavily weighted in favour of the government.

In the years that followed, the private press began to flourish. A major step forward was the arrival of private radio in 1994 with the launch of the pirate station *Radio Eye*. Previously, the government insisted that the national technical broadcast capacity was limited and that use was restricted to the state media. Following the popularity of *Radio Eye*, the government was compelled to open radio and television to the private sector.

Though the governing party was returned to power in 1996, the elections were hotly contested with near-equal exposure provided for all presidential candidates by the increasingly assertive private media. Coverage of the campaigns, voter registration process and traditional party broadcasts, heightened interest and confidence in the electoral process as a legitimate means of political expression.

By the time of the 2000 elections, the stakes were high. President Jerry Rawlings had dominated politics for nearly 20 years. Completing two consecutive terms under the 1992 constitution made him ineligible to stand again. The leading candidates for both the governing party and the opposition were largely untried personalities, fighting for the first time on a level field. The public perception was that the governing party would stop at nothing to retain power.

The media took centre stage. When the electoral roll was updated, showing more than ten million registered voters in a country of 18 million – of which 54 per cent is under 18 – the media led the nationwide protest. Forced to admit the existence of fraudulent names, the Electoral Commission cleaned up the register. The media continued to expose vote buying, the forgery of voter identification cards and the secret registration of voters.

They also provided a platform for informed debate throughout the electoral process in an environment where spin had always been king. News reports, analyses and interactive programmes in local languages and English brought politicians and the electorate together in a way never experienced before in Ghana's political history.

Voting took place on 7 and 28 December 2000. Radio stations monitored events, reported irregularities from polling stations and focused the attention of election officials on areas where there were procedural deficiencies. Results were announced from polling stations themselves in order to block further avenues for falsification.

On the second polling day, armed men drove through polling stations, ostensibly to maintain order. Incidents of voter intimidation, shots being fired and the destruction of ballot boxes were reported. But radio stations encouraged voters not to be intimidated and urged the security forces to uphold their constitutional duty to protect the citizenry.

The election was saved. The opposition won a relatively free contest against an incumbent perceived to be almost unbeatable. The role of a free media in helping this to happen will always be remembered.

TI-Ghana

The trend should not be exaggerated. Where civil society is beginning to emerge, it does so from a particularly low quantitative base. Across the region, civil society groups are poorly mobilised and have little influence on state action, a status compounded by the presence of conflict, low rates of literacy and the tight rein that governments keep on independent radio and television. Senegal is a rare exception, while Nigeria's media and NGO community has also shown itself to be vigorous and varied.

Religious groups can provide a sturdy platform from which to rally popular disenchantment with existing standards of governance in the region. Both Islamic and Christian groups have sent clear messages condemning corruption, although there is wide variation in the degree to which religious groups are prepared to occupy a political space. Two conferences of the Federation of Christian Councils in West Africa, held in Ghana during the last year, prioritised corruption, and the Roman Catholic church in Cameroon said the problem was destroying the economy and people's consciences.[54] The President of the Seventh-Day Adventist Church in Nigeria decried the high level of corruption in government circles, following the recent Senate scandal.[55] Nigeria's Catholic church attacked the 'tidal wave' of corruption in the country.[56]

NGOs with a governance focus are spreading, mirroring the gradual strengthening of civil society as a whole. This development also reflects the efforts of international donors to find partner organisations outside government. NGO reliance on external support brings further dangers, however, as civil society organisations are often seen by politicians as a questionable form of non-parliamentary opposition.

Soji Apampa of the Nigerian NGO Integrity argued that NGOs that formerly focused on human rights or freedom of expression under military dictatorships, turned to the issue of good governance when the 'freedom fight' was won.[57] The shift reflected the new priorities of donors, he said. In Nigeria, NGOs are actively engaged in the fight against corruption. Under the auspices of the Nigerian chapter of Transparency International, an NGO conference was held in Lagos in May 2001 that explored how new NGOs in the anti-corruption fight might work together as a broad coalition.

In Burkina Faso, there is much less scope for civil society action, though there is a specialist anti-corruption NGO, REN-LAC. Describing the state of affairs in the country, Halidou Ouédraogo, from human rights group Union Interafricain des Droits de l'Homme, confirmed Soji Apampa's remarks: 'At this time we still have basic problems with the system of President Blaise Compaoré, whose policies become more unpredictable and authoritarian. When we have passed this stage, we too will start campaigns for good governance.'[58]

Conclusion

International surveys suggest that West and West-Central Africa may include some of the most corrupt political systems in the world, but political changes over the last year offer some glimmer of hope. With a number of recent transitions to democracy, mechanisms for public accountability are becoming stronger and governments have launched anti-corruption campaigns, though these may be little more than public relations exercises in certain cases.

Public sector reform and privatisation have also moved up on the agenda, promising some improvement in transparency and accountability. However some of the worst corruption cases during the past year were actually facilitated by the process of privatisation.

International donors have played an important role in these developments in the region, but critics cast doubt on how far donors' funding decisions are being driven by a concern to improve governance.

Civil society is gradually gathering some momentum, though it remains unclear how its activities can be incorporated within decision-making processes. Partnerships between civil society and international institutions are growing, but governments remain wary of sharing decision-making and information.

Corruption remains deeply ingrained. Even where official anti-corruption campaigns prove sincere, and civil society becomes still stronger, corruption will continue to take a heavy toll on the poorest. And there is no guarantee that reforms will run smoothly, above all when conflict in Guinea, Liberia and Sierra Leone, combined with the change of regime in Côte d'Ivoire, accentuate the region's underlying volatility.

1   UNDP, *Human Development Report 2001* (New York: Oxford University Press, 2001).
2   *The Economist* (UK), 12 August 2000.
3   AP-Luxembourg, 5 October 2000.
4   *Mail & Guardian* (South Africa), 10 May 2000.
5   *Walfadjri* (Senegal), 19 April 2001.
6   *Expo Times* (Sierra Leone), 26 September 2000.
7   *Fraternité Matin* (Côte d'Ivoire), 25 August 2000.
8   Panafrican News Agency, 7 January 2001.
9   United Nations, 'Report of the Panel of Experts Appointed Pursuant to UN Security Council Resolution 1306 (2000) Paragraph 19 in Relation to Sierra Leone,' S/2000/1195, 20 December 2000.
10 *The Pool* (Sierra Leone), 1 September 2000.
11 *Expo Times* (Sierra Leone), 13–26 September 2000.
12 *Pittsburgh Post-Gazette* (US), 2 April 2001.
13 *The Perspective* (US), 18 January 2001; 28 June 2001.
14 Afrol.com, 8 March 2001; allAfrica.com, 8 May 2001.
15 Afrol.com, 26 October 2000.
16 *Le Front* (Côte d'Ivoire), 3 May 2001.
17 *Africa Confidential* (UK), 20 April 2001.
18 Amnesty International, *Amnesty International Report 2001* (London: Amnesty International, 2001).

19 *Cameroon Tribune* (Cameroon), 16 May 2001.

20 *Fraternité Matin* (Côte d'Ivoire), 26 February 2001; UN Integrated Regional Information Networks (IRIN), 26 February 2001.

21 Agence France Presse, 25 January 2001.

22 Agence France Presse, 25 February 2001.

23 The eight members of UEMOA are: Benin, Burkina Faso, Côte d'Ivoire, Guinea-Bissau, Mali, Niger, Senegal and Togo.

24 *West Africa* (UK), 20–26 November 2000. The 15 members of ECOWAS are: Benin, Burkina Faso, Cape Verde, Côte d'Ivoire, Gambia, Ghana, Guinea, Guinea-Bissau, Liberia, Mali, Niger, Nigeria, Senegal, Sierra Leone and Togo.

25 ECOWAS, press release, 24 May 2001.

26 Interview with author.

27 IRIN, 10 July 2000.

28 Interview with author.

29 Bio-Tchané's assessment of corruption in Benin can be found in Abdoulaye Bio-Tchané and Philippe Montigny, *Lutter contre la corruption: un impératif pour le développement économique du Bénin dans l'économie internationale* (Paris: L'Harmattan, 2000).

30 Agence France Presse, 14 January 2001.

31 Agence France Presse, 4 April 2001; Reuters, 4 May 2001.

32 Agence France Presse, 23 April 2000; 5 December 2000.

33 *Walfadjri* (Senegal), 19 April 2001.

34 *Walfadjri* (Senegal), 21–22 April 2000; *Sud quotidien* (Senegal), 21 April 2001.

35 World Bank, *L'Afrique: peut-elle revendiquer sa place dans le 21ème siècle?* (Washington DC: World Bank, 2000).

36 Jean Cartier-Bresson, 'Les analyses économiques des causes de la corruption,' *Courrier International*, 177, October-November 1999.

37 Civil service reform programmes are discussed in World Bank, 'Civil Service Reform: A Review of World Bank Assistance,' Sector Study No. 19599, April 1999.

38 *The Guardian* (Nigeria), 9 April 2001.

39 Agence France Presse, 26 February 2001.

40 Agence France Presse, 8 December 2000.

41 UEMOA, 'Directive No. 02/2000/CM/UEMOA portant adoption du code de transparence dans la gestion des finances publiques,' 29 June 2000.

42 UEMOA, 'Rapport d'activités de la Commission, Janvier-Novembre 2000,' 14 December 2000.

43 Panafrican News Agency, 23 May 2001.

44 *Vanguard* (Nigeria), 28 March 2001.

45 Panafrican News Agency, 23 May 2001.

46 US Department of State, 'Country Report on Human Rights Practices 2000: Benin,' <http://www.state.gov/g/drl/rls/hrrpt/2000/af/index.cfm?docid=861>.

47 Afrol.com, 26 June 2001.

48 IRIN, 19 February 2001.

49 The 12 countries in the region which have so far reached 'decision point' under the enhanced HIPC Initiative are Benin, Burkina Faso, Cameroon, Chad, Gambia, Guinea, Guinea-Bissau, Mali, Mauritania, Niger, Sao Tome and Principe, and Senegal.

50 Associated Press, 6 June 2000.

51 Reuters, 21 May 2000.

52 Chad's government is involved in onging conflict with rebels in the north. *Le Monde* (France), 22 November 2000.

53 Panafrican News Agency, 8 September 2000.

54 African Newswire Network, 11 October 2000.

55 *The Guardian* (Nigeria), 21 September 2000.

56 *Financial Times* (UK), 30 March 2001.

57 Interview with author.

58 Interview with author.

Middle East and North Africa

Afghanistan, Algeria, Bahrain, Egypt, Iran, Iraq, Israel, Jordan,
Kuwait, Lebanon, Libya, Morocco, Oman, Palestinian territories, Qatar,
Saudi Arabia, Syria, Tunisia, United Arab Emirates, Yemen

By Sa'eda al-Kilani

Introduction

Corruption, sustained by skewed standards of living and a lack of transparent governance across the Middle East and North Africa (MENA), is a major hindrance to the region's economic development. From Yemen, with a per capita income of around US $300 a year, to the United Arab Emirates (UAE), with a per capita income of around US $18,000, all countries are confronted by nepotism, favouritism and profiteering.[1]

Strong networks of leading entrepreneurs and state officials blur the distinction between public and private sectors. In large state bureaucracies, petty corruption among civil servants is widespread, often linked to traditions of *wasta* – the use of connections for personal gain. The state has traditionally dominated the political landscape. In the Gulf, where states are cushioned by oil income or other rents, regimes maintain a large degree of immunity from popular demands for change. But a closed and autocratic flavour to public life is also the norm in other countries in the region.

Egypt, Jordan and Tunisia were in the vanguard of economic reform programmes in the 1980s, but the years leading up to 2000–01 have seen more widespread talk of change. Discussion of political and economic reform is now more common, partly as a result of public disenchantment, but mostly due to rulers' recognition that without addressing reform their countries are in danger of being marginalised in the world economy.

Most regimes remain resistant to dialogue on politically sensitive governance-related issues, however. Information on corruption is notoriously hard to find and research by both local and foreign analysts is hesitant. Attacks on local academics, the media or civil society groups that become too active are frequent. But the rhetoric of change is sweeping the region, accompanied by the emergence of electronic media that foster increased transparency. Governments' control of information and the pace of change is growing less sure.

News review

In January 2001, as part of an anti-corruption campaign launched by new Syrian President Bashar al-Assad, the Syrian People's Assembly lifted immunity from three ruling-party members accused of stealing public assets.[2] The government also revealed that US $52 million had been embezzled from public funds since the beginning of 2000. A number of high-ranking government officials and employees were charged with corruption as a result, including former prime minister Mahmoud el-Zoubi, who committed suicide in May 2000.[3]

In February 2001, Morocco's parliament set up a commission of inquiry to investigate the apparent diversion of more than US $1 billion of state funds over the course of a decade through state bank Crédit Immobilier et Hotelier.[4] This was the first time it had taken such a step, and the move attracted a great deal of attention. The case was seen as a test of the government's willingness to confront members of the traditional political establishment, the *makhzen*, but none of the key subjects of the investigation were taken to court. Meanwhile, several cases related to embezzlement and corruption are pending before the Special Court of Justice, including one against employees at the Caisse Nationale de Crédit Agricole.

Captain Mustapha Adib, who blew the whistle on corruption in the Moroccan army in 1999 and has been in prison ever since, was sentenced to five years' imprisonment by a military court in February 2000. In October 2000, following an overturned appeal, he was given a reduced sentence of two and a half years and suspended from the army. Adib was awarded the Transparency International Integrity Award 2000 for courage in fighting corruption, and his case has been adopted in Morocco and by international human rights organisations.[5]

In May 2000, an Egyptian court convicted four MPs of involvement in a multi-million dollar scandal, sentencing them to 15 years' hard labour. This was the first case against sitting politicians ever prosecuted to the point of imprisonment and, since parliament is perceived as very corrupt, ordinary Egyptians welcomed it. But in a development that illustrated the difficulty of implementing sentences in politically sensitive cases, the High Court ordered the four men's release on bail and set a date for a re-trial.[6]

In May 2001, the Egyptian political scientist Saad el-Din Ibrahim was sentenced to seven years' imprisonment on charges that included embezzlement and receiving unauthorised funds from foreign donors. Twenty-seven of his colleagues were also sent to prison. Ibrahim was working on a project to monitor electoral fraud.[7] While championed by activists as the victim of a corrupt political system, his case was complicated by independent voices casting doubt about his integrity.[8]

Reports of corruption by senior members of the Palestinian Authority (PA) continued to be prominent in 2000–01. In June 2000, after repeated expressions of concern from donors, the PA for the first time published a report with details of its investments and payrolls, announcing it was taking steps towards reform.[9] Despite this welcome development, the PA showed little tolerance of corruption-related accusations. In July 2000, Abdel Sattar Qassem, a political scientist at Nablus al-Najah University, was released following months of imprisonment for his involvement with an anti-corruption manifesto assembled by intellectuals and legislators in 1999.[10] In January 2001, one of the most influential members of the PA inner circle, Hisham Mekki, head of Palestinian Satellite TV, was assassinated. A Palestinian splinter group claimed responsibility for the killing, saying it was punishment for his corruption.[11]

Compared to other countries in the region, Israel has strong institutions and well-established democratic practices, but corruption scandals dominated the year. Former prime minister Ehud Barak and the One Israel party were investigated for campaign funding irregularities, as were the leaderships of the Likud Party, the Centre Party, the United Torah Judaism Party and the Yisrael Beiteinu Party. Former prime minister Benjamin Netanyahu, together with his wife, was charged with fraud, bribery, breach of trust and obstruction of justice.[12] The charges were dropped in September 2000 for lack of evidence. Meanwhile, publisher Ofer Nimrodi was put on trial for allegedly contracting a murder and then bribing senior police officers and other officials to cover it up.[13]

In Iran, the moderate President Mohammed Khatami dismissed the Commander of Security and Chief of Intelligence who was subsequently convicted of corruption. Conservatives meanwhile used their control over state institutions such as the judiciary and the secret services to silence the supporters of greater political freedom. Twenty-five pro-reform independent newspapers and magazines were closed in 2000.[14] But the re-election of Khatami in a landslide victory in June 2001 renewed hopes for political liberalisation, although there are widespread doubts about Khatami's ability to deliver lasting change.

In the UAE, an anti-corruption commission was established after the arrest in early 2001 of the chief of Dubai's customs on corruption charges, a significant development given the country's prominence as a trading centre. In a subsequent campaign, police exposed a network of corruption at Dubai Airport.[15]

In June 2000, the Lebanese government signed an agreement with the United Nations Centre for International Crime Prevention in support of a national strategy to fight corruption. The US $300,000 project will take place over three years.[16] A UN-commissioned report released in January 2001 estimated that the Lebanese state squanders over US $1.5 billion per year through pervasive corruption.[17]

In Yemen, a cabinet reshuffle in March 2001 by President Ali Abdullah Saleh, which included the sacking of the Prime Minister, is thought to have been motivated by the need to give momentum to the country's economic reform pro-gramme. Popular perceptions of high corruption levels within the cabinet were also a factor. In May, the owner and editor-in-chief of the weekly *Al Shoumou* was sentenced to six months in prison for 'defamation' after the newspaper incrimi-nated a government minister in a corruption case.[18]

In Jordan, as part of an anti-corruption campaign led by King Abdullah II, the government of Prime Minister Ali Abul Ragheb took measures in 2001 to limit the privileges accorded to former senior officials. In a case that gripped the coun-try for months, the judiciary released a former consul who had been prosecuted on 86 charges including corruption and forgery.[19] Meanwhile, a parliamentarian alleged that then-premier Abdul Raouf Rawabdeh had received a 15 million dinar bribe (around US $21 million) in exchange for authorisation to construct a tourist village on the airport road in Amman. An investigating commission found Rawabdeh innocent.[20]

From April 2001, rioting in the Berber-speaking region of Kabylia that sub-sequently spread to other parts of Algeria, led to the death of scores of demon-strators when security forces opened fire. The large-scale civil action, which denounced the authorities for corruption, among other things, involved millions of Algerians.[21]

The year saw continued repression of the media in Algeria. Since the Ara-bic-language daily *Al Rai* was founded in 1998, publishing manager Ahmed Benaoum has been prosecuted 70 times for libel. An article implicating a senator in a corruption case landed Benaoum with a two-month prison sentence.[22] Fol-lowing an appeal, the Supreme Court ruled in April 2001 that this sentence would be upheld, although confusingly Benaoum was also informed he had received a presidential pardon. Meanwhile a proposed Penal Code amendment bill included provisions for prison sentences and fines for press offences. Algeria's Minister of Justice defended the bill in parliament saying the Algerian press currently has 'too much freedom'.[23]

News from Iraq and Libya, which suffer from international sanctions and crippling economic embargoes, is particularly hard to obtain, though corruption levels are known to be high in both countries. In May 2001 the Associated Press news agency reported a story based on official sources that President Saddam Hussein had expelled 100 top officials from the ruling Ba'ath party on charges of corruption and incompetence, but no further details were available.[24]

Civil protest in Algeria

Over the course of 2001, between six and seven million Algerians – out of a population of 30 million – took to the streets, demonstrating in the Kabylia region, in metropolitan Algiers and throughout the country. Their slogans included denunciations of government corruption and white-collar crime.

The present-day political context in Algeria is characterised by a total lack of democracy and frequent violations of civil liberties. The press, which is supposed to be independent, nevertheless maintains links with the government. Corruption undermines the capacity of all basic institutions and is enhanced by the total impunity of its perpetrators. It has its roots in the colonial system and subsequent military rule of Algeria. There is now a pressing need to evaluate its scale, understand its mechanisms, and discover the tools to contain it.

Corrupt networks play an excessive role in social, economic and political decision-making. The concentration of power and income from energy sales, as well as vast reliance on borrowing, has fuelled grand corruption at the juncture of a private economy and a state held hostage by a particular class. The recent phase of transition in industry from public monopoly to 'private monopolies' has meanwhile failed to lead to increased transparency. The doubling of Algeria's income from gas and oil exports between 1999 and 2000 served to whet the already voracious appetites of the political and financial elites, who expect to receive the lion's share of this new wealth.

President Bouteflika has frequently been questioned by foreign journalists about corruption since his accession to power in April 1999, and has often changed his tune. The gap between his statements and reality is marked. On 2 June 2001, the Council of Ministers announced that: 'The Head of State has recalled that the fight against corruption is one of the main means for building the rule of law, and it is integrated in the presidential agenda as a priority action.' But the President's manifesto makes no mention of this. Algerians have waited in vain for any concrete measures. Frustration is mounting.

Civil society faces challenges when seeking to organise. At the initiative of journalists, managers of public enterprises, members of liberal professions and NGO activists, the Algerian Association Against Corruption was created in December 1999. However, the group only recently gained recognition from the Minister of Home Affairs. The private sector, though growing in importance, has not yet played a significant role. Apart from an effort in 2000 to see the country's public procurement code modified, the Employers' Association's only lobbying campaign sought fiscal amnesty so as to facilitate access to ever-growing markets.

In the recent popular demonstrations, the denunciation of corruption was written large on the demonstrators' placards. Events in Kabylia and elsewhere testify to the outrage of Algerian citizens. As a result of this mobilisation, political parties, trade unions, professional associations and civil society groups have all adopted corruption as a key issue.

The costs of corruption weigh heavily on the country. The coming months will reveal whether the recent civil mobilisation in Kabylia and elsewhere is sufficiently widespread for change to be achieved.

Djillali Hadjadj

New leaders, new prospects?

The ambitious plans of some of the region's new leaders, and the anti-corruption mantle they have assumed on coming to power, indicate that the language of transparency has become part of the trappings of legitimacy. From Syria to Morocco, the pledge to fight corruption is now a key part of a wider reformist shift in political rhetoric. But though leaders have in some cases taken steps to back their rhetoric with action, their commitment is ultimately uncertain.

The year saw the prosecution and conviction of a number of high-profile figures in corruption cases, as in Syria, and numerous junior officials in other MENA countries. But high-profile figures, including those close to decision-making circles who are known to be corrupt, tended to retain their immunity. Critics argue that the rhetoric of corruption is mostly used as a means of ousting political rivals.

Since coming to power in February 1999, Jordan's King Abdullah II has emphasised the anti-corruption theme. In February 2000, he paid a secret visit to the state-run Bashir Hospital and later demanded an investigation into corruption-related practices there. After several similar visits to government departments, mostly in disguise, the King announced the formation of a special government committee to fight corruption, though it was purely top-level and included no representatives from civil society.[25] Jordan also embarked on an 'e-government' project, designed to increase openness and reduce *wasta*. In addition, the files of certain public companies suspected of corruption were referred to the Prosecutor General.[26] But attempts in 2000 to revive Jordan's Illegitimate Profit Making Law, which is seen as a useful tool for fighting corruption, were rejected by parliament for the fourth time. At the time of going to press, no clear-cut strategy to fight corruption has been outlined in Jordan and the cases that are exposed remain highly selective.

> The language of transparency has become part of the trappings of legitimacy.

Soon after coming to power in July 1999, King Mohammad VI of Morocco dismissed Driss Basri, his father's long-serving interior minister and a pillar of the *makhzen* system, who was widely seen as a key obstacle in the fight against corruption. The public welcomed this important symbolic move. Prime Minister Abdul Rahman Youssoufi had already declared fighting corruption part of the government's programme when he took office in 1998. The Minister of Public Affairs also announced in 2000 that the government had elaborated an anti-corruption programme aimed at improving the business environment.[27]

The Moroccan authorities investigated 129 judges and documented a total of 10,202 cases of petty corruption between 1998 and 2000. Also accused were 433 prison wardens and 423 lawyers.[28] The former administrative and financial director of the official news agency was arrested for mismanagement and allegedly stealing US $1.9 million.[29] And parliament set up the first fact-finding commission to investigate corruption at state bank Crédit Immobilier et Hotelier. But although civil society groups were very active in pushing for the commission, its meetings were closed to the press.

Meanwhile, there is little sign that the anti-corruption programme will be implemented, and institutional obstacles to fighting corruption remain high. The Special Court of Justice authorised to investigate corruption cases can only act on instructions from the Minister of Justice who, in turn, depends on the King. The cases that have been heard in the past few years have had no impact on actual levels of corruption, say activists. Politically sensitive, high-level cases are not addressed. In the light of these piecemeal efforts, concerns are widespread that the new king 'remains a prisoner of an authoritarian system in crisis'.[30]

Syria's leader Bashar al-Assad began his campaign against official corruption before he assumed power. His protest against the status quo was well publicised, raising expectations that he might tackle political as well as economic reform when he became President.[31] But doubts have been aired about his commitment: pressing ahead with anti-corruption measures will implicate close members of his family and an inner political circle. Al-Assad spearheaded a two-year anti-corruption campaign that has so far led to the imprisonment of just two ministers, but he is fond of grandiose rhetoric on the issue: 'There is no escape from bringing the careless, the corrupt and the evildoers to justice,' he said.[32]

Diplomats quoted in a report by news agency Reuters anticipated an easing of al-Assad's commitment to anti-corruption, which has now cleared out some of the political old guard.[33] Exiled opposition groups also criticised his campaign, claiming its real objective was 'to get rid of al-Assad's enemies'.[34] Another group insisted that 'such a programme requires a public national strategy that can only be prepared and carried out in a democratic atmosphere'.[35]

The new Lebanese government of Prime Minister Rafik Hariri has been under pressure to tackle corruption since coming to power in October 2000. In addition to the former government's signing of an anti-corruption plan with the UN Centre for International Crime Prevention in July 2000, the first months of 2001 witnessed the announcement of the furthest-reaching economic and administrative reforms ever attempted in post-war Lebanon. Although the measures taken so far are merely a beginning, observers welcome the developments as a sign of the government's commitment to change.[36]

Citizens of Qatar, where Sheikh Hamad bin Khalifa al-Thani overthrew his father in a bloodless coup in June 1995, witnessed more far-reaching reforms in 2000–01 than any of the other Gulf states. A new satellite channel, *Al-Jazeera* (the

Island), is the first Arabic station to broadcast programmes on sensitive political issues, although coverage of Qatar itself remains cautious. Reports on corruption, mismanagement and nepotism in the region are now regularly broadcast in Arabic to millions of spectators, revealing far more to them than their domestic, state-owned TV services.

Elsewhere in the Gulf, governments introduced important legislation that may have consequences for the strengthening of national integrity systems. The progressive new ruler of Bahrain, Sheikh Hamad Bin Issa al-Khalifa, who succeeded his father in March 1999, introduced a national charter in 2001 that promised wide-ranging reforms including an elected parliament, a constitutional monarchy and an independent judiciary. Bahrainis gave it their wholesale approval in a two-day referendum, and *Mithaq* (charter) has become a popular name for newborn babies.[37] According to Jasim Ajami, a university professor in Bahrain, the atmosphere is now more conducive to the development of an anti-corruption agency than at any other time.[38] The government authorised the establishment of the Bahraini Society for Human Rights in February 2001.

Even in Saudi Arabia the government has tentatively embarked on a reform programme, though civil liberties remain severely curtailed. In late 2000, a Family Council to oversee reform was established under the chairmanship of Crown Prince Emir Abdullah Ben Abdel Aziz and his deputy, Prince Sultan Ben Abdel Aziz. The step surprised observers both inside and outside the kingdom.[39]

Enough new faces have come to power recently, all using anti-corruption rhetoric to help them on the national or international stages, that a major trend can be said to have emerged. However, a former US ambassador cautioned:

'It would be a mistake to overestimate what the new generation can do immediately. Their ideas will take time to implement and they need help to avoid the rending of their political and social fabric if they are to undertake reform. Nor should we forget that these young men are the products of their fathers and their societies. They may be less forthcoming than we would like to think or hope.'[40]

Globalisation and anti-corruption efforts

New anti-corruption campaigns and reform plans in the MENA region are to a large extent motivated by efforts to raise foreign investment. Governments traditionally played a dominant role in managing the region's economies, but MENA countries experienced severe economic stagnation in the late 1980s and early 1990s. Debt servicing alone reached 14 per cent of regional export earnings,[41] and the region's share of world trade contracted to an estimated 3.4 per cent.[42]

'Reform, or risk losing the confidence of foreign investors and international markets,' said a recent report.[43] Even traditionally rich Gulf states such as Saudi Arabia have been pushed to seek foreign involvement to help exploit their oil and gas reserves.[44] This widespread urge to attract foreign investment has had positive implications for increasing transparency and fighting corruption.

In a study carried out by an investment corporation in Jordan, 73 per cent of respondents said that lack of transparency was a primary obstacle facing inward investors.[45] The new king embarked on the Aqaba free trade zone project, an ambitious scheme to turn the Red Sea port into a duty-free economic zone, and a special committee to fight corruption was formed at the same time.[46] Jordan is also working with the World Bank on a series of initiatives to reduce the size of its bureaucracy, which at present acts both as a drain on the budget and as a source of corruption.[47] Syria's reforms are mainly targeted at enticing back an estimated US $50 billion held in foreign banks by the wealthy diaspora.[48] And Morocco is keen to clean up corruption and improve transparency in its import and export customs procedures. The Lebanese government has embarked on reforms to try to contain a national debt of US $23 billion (140 per cent of GDP), and reform what the Associated Press called a 'political system based on religious loyalties and political nepotism that has drained the treasury over the years'.[49] A UN report on corruption found that over 43 per cent of companies in Lebanon 'always or very frequently' pay bribes, and another 40 per cent 'sometimes' do.[50]

Amid all these initiatives, the experience of countries that were among the earliest to push for economic reform in the region sounds a warning note. Algeria, Egypt, Morocco and Tunisia embarked on liberalisation programmes in the mid-1980s, and some observers are sceptical of the results. They argue that privatisation and increased foreign investment did not dismantle the cronyism at the heart of their economies. Rather, they strengthened the rule of elites, which proved to be extremely resistant to economic reforms. 'Despite a recent legacy of legal changes, stock market booms, and free trade agreements, reforms have been selective and the room for governments to wiggle out of or around them has been substantial,' wrote one analyst. Privatisation of key strategic resources was largely avoided until very recently. The analyst added: 'In most of North Africa … privatised assets have often been sold below market value to small groups of investors, increasing their oligarchic control of the market.'[51] Privatisation has also been associated with the rise of informal markets, often involving the connivance of public officials.

It remains to be seen whether the region's new leaders have the commitment to match with action the prominence now being given to transparency and openness. It is also questionable whether economic reform will be accompanied by the more open political culture needed if corruption is to be checked. In the recent past, economic reform through structural adjustment and privatisation programmes has led to increased political repression. In Egypt and Algeria, for instance, structural adjustment triggered rioting and state violence.

Changes in the world economy, including falling energy prices, globalised trade and the increasing poverty of the region, are among the factors compelling leaders to attract foreign investment. The demand for investment in turn motivates a fight against corruption. But whether or not international anti-corruption strategies that challenge the existing networks of financial control by elites can be institutionalised is moot. Certainly these processes will not be as straightforward as the rhetoric of the new wave of leaders seems to imply.

Civil society voices

Governments dominate the dynamic of political liberalisation that underpins the fight against corruption. Even the regimes that seem most determined to introduce reforms will find it difficult to abandon control, while years of repression and suspicion of intellectuals have left civil society weakly organised and vulnerable to penetration by the security services in many instances.[52]

Observers welcome the rise of civil society groups in the region. The number of NGOs increased in the 1990s, particularly in Egypt, Israel, Jordan, the Palestinian territories and Yemen.[53] However, many 'civil' associations have strong links to governments and are unable to fulfil the crucial criterion of independence that is needed if they are to hold governments to account. This is true in Tunisia, where two thirds of all associations emanate from the civil service; in Morocco, where philanthropic associations are traditionally formed by people close to the palace; and in Jordan, where civil society organisations are often run by members of the royal family.[54] In Egypt, an association can only qualify as an NGO if it fulfils restrictive government registration criteria. Egypt's relevant law (no. 153 of 1999), despite being briefly overturned in June 2000, has been emulated in the Palestinian territories and Yemen. In 1996, the Tunisian government identified the NGO sector as a major national security concern and responded with a network of rival 'government' NGOs.[55]

Independent civil society groups are subject to attack by governments and reactionary forces in society alike. Emergency laws are still in place in Algeria, Egypt and Syria, and civil society groups in these countries had a particularly difficult task during 2000–01, which saw high levels of repression, violence and intimidation. Business associations in the region are also weak and unable to promote a transparency agenda. According to a recent report, protest 'remains a risky strategy for North African businessmen. Those who seek to challenge the state apparatus face potential sanctions.'[56]

Most countries continue to suffer from wide-ranging restrictions on freedom of speech and the press. This has grave implications for transparency. In its 2000 annual report, the NGO Freedom House categorised 14 out of 17 Arab countries as 'not free' – the highest proportion of any region in the world. Only Jordan, Kuwait and Morocco were rated 'partly free'.[57] In Algeria, broadcasting is under total state control, but the Arab diaspora press plays a major role in challenging the authorities' propaganda machines.

Compared to the situation a decade ago, however, improvements are visible, with independent activists, writers and human rights advocates becoming ever more vocal. Anti-corruption associations were almost non-existent until recently. Transparency International chapters exist, or are in formation, in Israel, Jordan, Lebanon, Morocco and Yemen, and there are prospects for chapters in Algeria, Bahrain, Egypt, the Palestinian territories and the UAE. Transparency Maroc, the TI chapter in Morocco, is a shining example of how civil society groups can have an impact in the most difficult of circumstances. Despite initial problems gaining official recognition, the group, which works as the focal point of a coalition of 50 domestic organisations, has been active in raising awareness in schools and among public officials, and in lobbying to establish a designated independent anticorruption agency. When the latter failed to materialise, Transparency Maroc founded a National Observatory of Corruption in June 2001, in order to collect independent data on the issue.

> Independent civil society groups are subject to attack by governments and reactionary forces in society alike.

The internet plays a crucial role, reaching universities, schools and homes and making it harder for the strictest of regimes to control information. A street in Irbid, Jordan, dubbed 'Internet Road', recently entered the *Guinness Book of World Records* for hosting the most internet cafes in the world (201).[58] The UAE has the highest proportion of internet users in the Arab world.[59] In North Africa, Morocco has the largest internet market. Even Baghdad, under extreme international sanctions, hosts five internet centres and a fast growing level of internet usage.[60] The internet enables activists on corruption and other issues to share information and network. However, web activities remain subject to severe censorship and monitoring, and the region as a whole still has the lowest penetration of any in the world.[61] The fight against corruption was given a particular boost by the emergence of satellite technology in the late 1990s. It is now possible for viewers in the Arab world to participate in debates on issues that were previously taboo and, with *Al-Jazeera*, to receive independent news on the region, which state-owned terrestrial stations regularly censor or distort.

The increasing transparency stimulated by these technological innovations and the determined efforts of anti-corruption and other civil society activists is beginning to provide an opportunity for citizens' dialogue on corruption. While the anti-corruption drive to date has taken its major dynamic from leaders concerned by the prospect of economic marginalisation in the global economy, civil society is now forcing its way into the debate.

Conclusion

New faces with new visions came to power in the MENA region in 2000–01, bringing with them promises of political and economic liberalisation in varying degrees. Leaders in some countries, even in the Gulf, are competing to amend legislation, introduce reform plans and launch anti-corruption campaigns – though none are pursuing comprehensive strategies for reform. With the Family Council overseeing reform in Saudi Arabia, elections in Kuwait and Qatar, and reforms in Bahrain and the UAE, the landscape for improved governance is very different from that of ten years ago.

The region is gradually changing to keep up with developments in the world economy. Fear of marginalisation is pushing countries forward, and the other dynamics associated with globalisation, such as improved communications, are having a favourable impact on transparency initiatives.

But change brings new opportunities for corruption as well. Despite the rhetoric of economic modernisation and anti-corruption drives, the experience of countries that had a head start with economic reform, combined with signs of national opposition to change, give cause for concern about the prospects for reducing corruption.

Like leaders the world over, the region's rulers have mastered the language of reform and pay lip service to the need to fight corruption. But they are no less determined to maintain control of the pace of change. The rhetoric against corruption will be spurious if it is not accompanied by clear-cut strategies that address the real nature of corrupt practices. Though under heavy pressure and subject to physical attack, the small but growing body of civil society and independent activists are using the rhetoric and new climate to pressure leaders into fulfilling their promises by turning their gestures into action and laws. Civil society must be allowed to develop if reform is to be meaningful. With NGOs and activists restricted or subverted in many countries, programmes and activities that aim to facilitate their free expression and activity are a priority.

1 World Bank, *World Development Report 2000–01* (New York: Oxford University Press, 2000).
2 Arabicnews.com, 30 January 2001.
3 UPI, 31 July 2000.
4 *Al Sharq Al Awsat* (UK), 2 February 2001.
5 His case has been presented to the UN Secretary General's Special Rapporteur on human rights, adopted by Amnesty International and taken up in the international press.
6 *Al Sharq Al Awsat* (UK), 20 March 2001.
7 *Financial Times* (UK), 30 May 2001.
8 *Al-Arab* (UK), 7–8 December 2000.
9 Reuters, 7 June 2000.
10 Associated Press, 29 July 2000.
11 Associated Press, 18 January 2001.
12 Associated Press, 28 March 2000.
13 *Jerusalem Post* (Israel), 6 July 2000.
14 Reuters, 18 September 2000.
15 *Al Sharq Al Awsat* (UK), 18 February 2001.
16 *Al-Safir* (Lebanon), 24 June 2000.
17 *Middle East Intelligence Bulletin*, February 2001.
18 IFEX Action Alert Service, 1 June 2001.
19 TI-Jordan, 'The National Integrity System: Jordan,' presented at The Hague, 28–31 May 2001.
20 *Al Rai* (Jordan), 15 February 2000.
21 Middle East Research and Information Project (MERIP), 11 May 2001.
22 Reporters Sans Frontières, Algeria report, July 2000.
23 Reporters Sans Frontières, 23 April 2001.
24 Associated Press, 7 May 2001.
25 *Al-Dustour* (Jordan), 22 February 2000.
26 TI-Jordan (2001).
27 Arabic News, 24 January 2000.
28 *L'Opinion* (Morocco), 28 February 2001.
29 International Press Service, 16 August 2000.
30 MERIP, No. 218, spring 2001.
31 Human Rights Watch, *World Report 2001* (New York: Human Rights Watch, 2001).
32 Volker Perthes, *Domestic Needs and External Challenges: Political-Economic Variables of Syria after Hafiz al-Asad* (Berlin: Friedrich Ebert Stiftung Foundation, 2001).
33 Reuters, 23 June 2001.
34 Human Rights Watch (2001).
35 Muslim Brotherhood in Syria, based in London, 15 May 2000,
   `<http://www.ikhwan-muslimoon-syria.org>`.
36 TI-Lebanon, interview with author.
37 *The Guardian* (UK), 21 February 2001.
38 Interview with author.
39 *Al-Jazeera* (Qatar), 12 December 2000.
40 Edward D. Walker, Jr, presentation at the Middle East Institute, Washington DC, 20 October 2000.
41 MERIP, No. 213, winter 1999.
42 Miranda Beshara, 'Globalisation and the Middle East,' Middle East Institute, 1999.
43 Reuters, 6 July 2000.
44 Fareed Mohamedi, 'Oil, Gas and the Future of Arab Gulf Countries,' *Middle East Report*, July–September 1997.
45 *Al Rai* (Jordan), 7 June 2001.
47 Though the free trade zone is aimed at attracting massive investment, critics have been quick to argue that it will turn Aqaba into a haven for money launderers. Agence France Presse, 24 July 2000.
47 Amy Henderson and Paul Pasch, *Jordan – Two Years into the Reign of King Abdullah Ibn Al Hussein II* (Berlin: Friedrich Ebert Stiftung Foundation, 2001).
48 *Washington Times* (US), 22 November 2000.
49 Associated Press, 24 October 2000.
50 *Middle East Intelligence Bulletin*, February 2001.
51 Bradford Dillman, 'Facing the Market in North Africa,' *Middle East Journal*, Vol. 55, No. 2, spring 2001.

52 Ali R. Abootalebi, 'Civil Society, Democracy and the Middle East,' *Middle East Review of International Affairs*, Vol. 2, No. 3, September 1998.

53 MERIP, No. 214, spring 2000.

54 Sarah Ben Néfissa, 'NGOs, Governance and Development in the Arab World,' UNESCO Management of Social Transitions Discussion Paper No. 46, April 2001.

55 MERIP, No. 214, spring 2000.

56 Dillman (2001).

57 Freedom House, *Freedom in the World 1999–2000* (New York: Freedom House, 2000).

58 *Al Rai* (Jordan), 10 February 2001.

59 *Al Hayat* (UK), 14 April 2001.

60 *Al Quds Al Arabi* (UK), 10 May 2001.

61 UNDP, *Human Development Report 2000* (New York: Oxford University Press, 2000).

Commonwealth of Independent States

Armenia, Azerbaijan, Belarus, Georgia, Kazakhstan, Kyrgyzstan, Moldova, Russian Federation, Tajikistan, Turkmenistan, Ukraine, Uzbekistan

By Luke Allnutt, Jeremy Druker and Jen Tracy (with Dima Bit-Suleiman, Alisher Khamidov, Sophia Kornienko and Alex Znatkevich)

Introduction

'Do not mistake bribery for corruption,' Russian Minister for the Interior Vladimir Rushailo told journalists in March 2001.[1] Perhaps what Rushailo – who was replaced in a cabinet reshuffle later that month – meant to say was: 'Do not put the policemen who accept bribes for traffic violations on the same level as the oligarchs who line the pockets of key government officials.' Whatever his point, Rushailo's words gave some idea of the many guises that corruption takes in the countries of the former Soviet Union – and hinted at the way it may be tolerated.

Corruption fuelled the political and economic system throughout 70 years of communism. A decade of post-communist transition brought corrupt privatisations and governments unable to provide checks and balances, or to enforce property rights and other legal contracts. As a result, societies across the Commonwealth of Independent States (CIS) now have little more than the shadow of a safety net, and corruption is part and parcel of political, economic and social life.[2] From passing university examinations to acquiring a passport, bribes are the means to get things done.

Though similar in nature, corruption in the countries of the former Soviet Union varies, based in part on the degree to which they have made the transition to a market economy. In Russia and Ukraine, where transition has jolted the system, both elite and petty corruption thrive.[3] Belarus, Turkmenistan and Uzbekistan generally win a better rating in terms of elite corruption, because their transition from communism is less complete.[4] In these countries, the unwillingness to undertake major privatisation and other market reforms means that corruption tends to remain petty and administrative in form. However, electoral fraud and the suppression of information have taken on increasingly dramatic dimensions. In the rest of Central Asia and the Caucasus, religious and ethnic wars, battles over control of oil reserves, and drug smuggling complicate matters further. Clans connected to the government keep society in a stranglehold, siphoning off oil revenues to enrich the elite.[5]

Corruption has imposed one constant across the region: most people are cut off from the economic benefits of their country's resources. Corruption has contributed to stagnating or plummeting standards of living for the majority, while a small class of insiders has amassed enormous wealth.

News review

Pavel Borodin, Secretary General of the Russian-Belarusian Union, was arrested in January 2001 in New York, on charges of having embezzled US $25 million while he was the Kremlin's property manager under President Boris Yeltsin.[6] Swiss investigators accused him of money laundering. In April, Borodin was charged by a Swiss court and then released on US $3 million bail, paid by the Russian federal government. Analysts say his return to Russia, and the fact that the government posted his bail, confirms that the Kremlin was worried about what Borodin could tell investigators.[7]

On attaining office in 2000, President Vladimir Putin made clear his intention to restore law and order and root out corruption. How Putin deals with partially state-owned Gazprom, the world's largest gas company, could be the litmus test. Gazprom has been under increasing fire for asset stripping. In April 2001, board member Boris Fyodorov called on the government to use its share in the company to overthrow Gazprom's corrupt management.[8] Putin heeded Fyodorov's advice and replaced Gazprom head Rem Vyakhirev, a powerful Yeltsin-era insider, at the end of May. Initially, many believed that the government 'didn't have the stomach for a real fight with Russia's richest and most powerful business', but the President, in this case, proved them wrong.[9]

In late 2000 and early 2001, Ukraine was engulfed in a political battle between liberal reformers, responsible for the first signs of economic revival and transparency; communists, who wished to block market reforms; and the oligarchs, who stood to lose from both.[10] Deputy Prime Minister Yulia Tymoshenko was fired in January and later arrested on charges of fraud and natural gas smuggling. Though there are reports that she herself was embroiled in controversy in the mid-1990s, some claim that her proposals to make the energy sector more transparent landed her in hot water with the same oligarchs who later were party to parliament's dismissal of the Yushchenko government in April. In another prominent case, President Leonid Kuchma was allegedly linked in a series of leaked tapes to the disappearance of Georgy Gongadze, an opposition journalist outspoken on the topic of corruption.[11]

In Moldova, where the economy has declined dramatically over the past ten years, the collapse of communism did not lead to any major break with the old bureaucracy, or their traditional system of privileges.[12] The lack of state power continues to allow political clans to act as substitutes for legal norms. The results have been increases in tax evasion, drug trafficking, illegal import/export operations and contract murders. In late 1999, then prime minister Ion Sturza gave some cause for optimism when his government adopted the State Programme for Fighting Crime, Corruption and Protectionism for 1999–2002.[13] But his government resigned shortly thereafter and voters opted for a return to former communist leaders in the parliamentary elections in February 2001. With the communists back in control, parliament is expected to put the brake on reforms, including those related to fighting corruption.[14]

Azerbaijan is ranked by several international organisations as the most corrupt country in the region.[15] An opinion poll in March conducted by the Turan News Agency showed that 72 per cent of citizens surveyed believe that only a change of power would result in progress in the fight against corruption.[16] Electoral corruption keeps many beneficial changes on the back burner. Amid protests of gross fraud, President Heydar Aliev's ruling New Azerbaijan Party swept the November 2000 parliamentary elections. The authorities cancelled the results in 11 constituencies in response to criticism from election observers. Repeat elections in January 2001 were 'marked with some improvement', according to the OSCE, but monitors still reported serious election violations. Azerbaijan was nonetheless admitted into the Council of Europe shortly afterwards.[17]

In Kazakhstan, oil resources provide an opportunity to finance economic development, but they are also a vast source of potential corruption. The discovery in July 2000 of new oil deposits in the Kazakh part of the Caspian Sea boosted possible petro-investment further.[18] Despite this boon to the economy, a diplomat confirmed in early July 2000 that Swiss authorities had frozen bank accounts in Geneva at the request of the US Justice Department, as part of a corruption investigation into a US businessman suspected of funnelling millions of dollars from US oil companies to top Kazakh officials, including the President. The Foreign and Justice Ministries denied any knowledge of the frozen funds. The investigation culminated in no official charges, but the implications for the major oil investors in the country, Mobil, Phillips Petroleum and Amoco among them, are significant, particularly given US laws on the prevention of bribery of foreign officials by US corporations.[19]

In Georgia, President Eduard Shevardnadze and his ruling elite have been busy promoting wide-ranging anti-corruption efforts. Calling corruption a 'mortal danger' to national security, Shevardnadze signed an anti-corruption decree in

March 2001 authorising the creation of a 12-member coordinating council to fight corruption. While some wrote off the move as an empty gesture designed to restore the country's tarnished image, Shevardnadze fired Minister for State Property Mikhail Ukleba several days later, accusing him of failing to curb corruption and other illegal activities in his ministry.[20]

Crony capitalism, CIS-style

With the fall of the Soviet Union and the launch of market reforms, Soviet-era cronyism was given a new lease of life, flourishing under its free market guise of crony capitalism. The presence of crony capitalism across the CIS has meant that weak governments can do little to keep powerful politicians and businessmen from defrauding countries through embezzlement, money laundering and asset stripping. What makes crony capitalism more severe is that the money made by defrauding the state moves out of the country, denying people the chance to increase living standards, according to Vladimir Brovkin, Director of the UN Research Centre on Organised Crime in Eurasia Project.[21]

> The presence of crony capitalism across the CIS means that weak governments can do little to keep powerful politicians and businessmen from defrauding countries.

Examples of crony capitalism abound. In Ukraine, oligarch Igor Bakai resigned from his position as the head of gas giant Neftegaz in March 2000, citing political reasons. An extensive investigation by Radio Free Europe/Radio Liberty in July 2000 claimed to have uncovered evidence that Bakai was forced to resign after the discovery that he had transferred millions of Neftegaz dollars to private offshore accounts.[22] According to Carnegie Endowment senior analyst Anders Aslund, Bakai headed one of the country's most influential clans with close connections to Ukrainian President Kuchma.[23] In Central Asia and the Caucasus, especially in the oil-rich countries of Kazakhstan and Azerbaijan,[24] post-Soviet crony capitalism has meant the siphoning of oil revenues that had the potential to improve the standard of living of millions.

Crony capitalism is changing in nature as time passes. According to Brovkin, the practice of stealing from the state has 'sprouted new criminal wings that are supported by legally sanctioned offshore companies and naive, corrupt or complicit Western institutions'.[25]

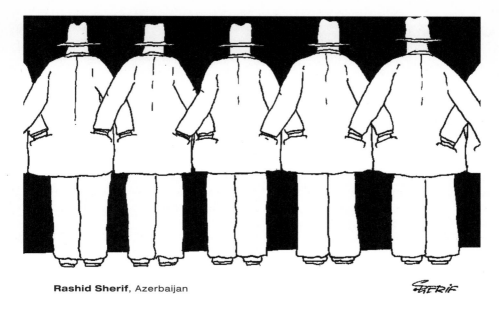

Rashid Sherif, Azerbaijan

State capture

For many states in the CIS, crony capitalism is characterised by 'state capture'. According to the EBRD and the World Bank, state capture occurs when individuals, groups or firms are so powerful that they can influence the formation of laws, rules and decrees; purchase legislation; or gain control of the media or other key institutions.[26] State capture results in state agencies regulating businesses in accordance with private, as opposed to public, interests. Business activity is distorted, investment deterred and the state unable to carry out reforms to which the public is entitled. A key feature of state capture is the weakness of the government in the face of its captors.

According to the World Bank report *Anti-Corruption in Transition*, the most advanced reformist states in the region, such as Armenia, suffer the least from state capture. Similarly low levels are found in countries regarded as post-Soviet dictatorships, like Belarus and Uzbekistan, because society is so rigid there that the entrepreneurial class is still underdeveloped. The worst offenders in the region are those countries that have undertaken only partial reforms, such as Azerbaijan, Georgia, Kyrgyzstan, Moldova, Russia and Ukraine.[27]

Yevgeny Volk, an analyst with the Heritage Foundation in Moscow, agreed that the level of state capture in Russia is dangerously high. 'In Russia today, we can speak of a whole state capture network since no radical barriers were introduced to curb it. Most of the state apparatus members … receive less than US $600 per month in official salary.' There is little incentive on the part of parliamentarians or court judges to reject bribes from businessmen. But levels of state capture differ across the region, Volk said. Ukraine is now where Russia was several years ago, and Ukrainian property division is not yet finished. Furthermore, Volk argued, the situation in Ukraine largely depends on Russia and its oligarchs.[28]

Yury Korgunyuk, with Moscow's Indem Research Centre, said the level of state capture is exaggerated in Russia, at least 'compared to Ukraine and Azerbaijan, where after the fall of the Soviet Union everything was seized by local clans'. According to Korgunyuk, Russia should fare better on current and future corruption indices.[29]

'The stronger the state, the weaker the state capture,' argued Indem's Gregory Satarov. 'Russia today is making an attempt to become a strong state and create a legal foundation for business.' For other CIS countries that are years behind Russia in reform, state capture is only now reaching its peak.[30] There is evidence that state capture is actually on the increase in Central Asia, the Caucasus and Ukraine.

Princes and paupers

The fall of the Soviet Union was followed, to varying degrees across the region, by market reforms that fell prey to a criminal brand of privatisation of state assets, the result of which was the creation of a 'princely' class of former officials with connections to the ruling elite, and a pauper class out of the rest of the population.[31]

Many of Ukraine's communists reinvented themselves before the collapse of the Soviet Union, with the goal of turning their Soviet-era power into tangible wealth. The result was the emergence of a new and powerful oligarchy.[32] In Russia, throughout Yeltsin's tenure as president, powerful businessmen and politi-

In Russian health care, you get what you pay for, even when it's free

When Sasha, a 37-year-old from St Petersburg, tried to help his elderly neighbour receive proper medical care, he witnessed first hand how bribery is truly a matter of life and death.

According to the doctor at the state hospital – where service is 'free' – the elderly woman needed an urgent operation. But the doctor requested a bribe that the woman could never afford. When she didn't pay, the doctor handed her an official medical report that stated her condition as 'inoperable'.

'Everyone believes that free medical care is bad medical care,' says Sasha. 'It's very difficult to get any help for elderly people. No one wants to bother with them.' Many patients view bribery as an acceptable alternative to no health care at all. According to Sasha, 'Everyone has to pay.'

State doctors, earning between US $15 and US $50 per month, feel they have no other choice but to accept bribes for services that should otherwise be free. And the hospitals, with negligible budgets, see bribery as the only way of financing medical supplies.

Svetlana, a 45-year-old neuropathologist at Moscow's Hospital 68, feels uneasy talking about bribery. 'There are medical ethics involved,' she says. 'Of course, patients thank doctors with money. No one can deny that this practice exists. But our attitude never depends on the money patients pay.' Later, she concedes: 'Naturally, if a person does give money, the attitude is a bit more attentive.'

Caught between Soviet socialised medicine and a market economy, the Russian health care system is riddled with corruption. The World Health Organisation's 2000 report ranked Russia among the lowest in terms of health care financing, and pointed to the dangers of governments turning a blind eye to illicit markets in the health sector.

Meanwhile, a form of health care corruption beyond the control of doctors or patients makes the situation even more hopeless.

St Petersburg has been embroiled since 1997 in an ongoing battle against corruption in public procurement of medicines from pharmaceutical companies. In 1997–98, the Public Health Committee conducted an investigation into the sale of expired medicines, unearthing evidence that corruption led to contracts being given to pharmaceutical companies that proposed the highest bids.

Pensioners have a difficult time getting the quality medicines to which they are entitled through the free state system. Anna, 86, used to get a prescription drug for her liver condition called Essential Forte. But when she ran out recently, the doctor refused to give her another prescription and advised her instead to try garlic. 'It's very good for your health,' she remembers the doctor saying.

When asked about corruption in the health care system, the Russian analyst Boris Kargarlitsky said the rules of the health care game are clear: pay with money, or pay with your life.

There is a popular joke about health care in Russia, he recounted. The first question a doctor usually asks a patient is how much they earn. If they earn US $20 a month, the doctor prescribes lots of vegetables and plenty of fresh air.

If they earn less, the doctor just prescribes fresh air.

Jen Tracy and Maria Antonenko

cians acquired lucrative state properties and resources at knockdown prices.[33] According to Yevgeny Volk of the Heritage Foundation, the former communist *nomenklatura* was given the opportunity to manage state property, and most emerging tycoons remained in the government. As a result, privatisation was based less on fair competition and more on political connections that were often corrupt. Moreover, Volk suggested, there was no radical change of authority in Russia – as occurred for instance in the Czech Republic – which could have facilitated a drive toward greater transparency.[34]

Russia and Ukraine have both stated their intentions to rein in the oligarchs. Since President Putin came to power, former Kremlin insider and media magnate Boris Berezovsky lost favour and is now in self-imposed exile in Europe, having escaped a warrant for his arrest. Berezovsky failed to appear for questioning over his alleged role in the illicit transfer of tens of millions of dollars from airline giant Aeroflot to front companies in Switzerland. But his continued freedom abroad leads many to question whether the Kremlin is merely making empty legal threats for the sake of its public image.[35] In Ukraine, reforms in the energy sector hit the oligarchs hard, and they retaliated by using their influence to bring down the government of liberal prime minister Viktor Yushchenko in April 2001. The move was interpreted as a major setback for reform, including anti-corruption and transparency efforts, as well as for the economy in general.

Electoral corruption

The subtle and not-so-subtle art of electoral corruption in the CIS region obstructs the completion of democratic and market reforms. Dirty tricks, such as the removal of opponents from elections, ballot box stuffing, tampering with ballots, and bribing or threatening voters, are some of the more obvious forms of electoral corruption. Manipulating the media and misinforming the voting public is another form, perhaps more subtle and more dangerous in the long run.

In Central Asia, electoral corruption means that the incumbent, who often thrives on a strong cult of personality, will remain in office as long as he desires. In Turkmenistan and Kazakhstan, this can mean becoming president for life. In Russia and Ukraine, it guarantees that the state remains captured by the ruling elite and its kleptocratic oligarchy.

In Kyrgyzstan, the February to March 2000 parliamentary elections and October 2000 presidential elections were marred by allegations of ballot box stuffing, the exclusion of serious opponents, intimidation of the media and other irregularities. Only those loyal to the regime secured seats in the lower house of parliament. Incumbent President Askar Akayev won nearly 75 per cent of the vote.[36] Most local and international observers declared the vote neither free nor fair, and a setback for the development of democracy in the country.[37] 'The authorities stole the victory from the opposition,' said Melis Eshimkanov, editor-in-chief of the opposition *Asaba* newspaper. 'About 60 per cent of the votes were forged.'[38] John

Schoeberlein, Director of the Forum for Central Asian Studies at Harvard University and head of the Central Asia programme for the International Crisis Group, agreed: 'This is a high-profile event that shows that Akayev is not committed to pursuing as democratic a path as possible. It is quite possible – as in the case of any Central Asian elections – that he would have won on the basis of popularity, without fraud. But it seems that the ideal of a clean and fair election is just not flourishing in the minds of the leaders.'[39]

In Russia, the OSCE reported incidents of foul play in the March presidential elections, but overall the vote marked an improvement in the democratic process. Regional elections, especially those for governors, however, have received much lower marks.[40] Regional governors took advantage of a situation that boosted their authority, managing to bring forward elections from their originally scheduled 2000 dates to 1999. Rushing through early elections led to landslide victories for many incumbent governors, who nevertheless resorted to corruption during the voting process, including the questionable banning of opponents from the race, buying votes from beleaguered pensioners, and threatening voters with unemployment or the loss of various social benefits.[41]

The Ukraine parliamentary by-elections held in June 2000 were characterised by numerous dirty tricks. The elections ended in a sweeping victory for the regional ruling elite, and all ten newly elected deputies sided with the pro-presidential, centre-right majority in parliament.[42]

In the region, Belarus takes the prize for electoral malpractice and removing opponents from parliamentary and presidential elections. In 1996, President Lukashenka forced through a referendum that effectively established one-man rule, extending his term in office by two years until 2001. The EU, the US and the country's internal opposition refused to recognise the referendum. With presidential elections due in September 2001, Lukashenka may destroy what few independent voices remain, beginning with the opposition. The executive branch maintains a tight grip on all aspects of the election campaign, from the appointment of election commissions to the court review of appeals by candidates and election observers.[43]

Media coverage of electoral politics

Manipulating the media is one of the most damaging forms of electoral corruption in the region. And it is during campaign time that the real battle is won – influencing the electorate in most cases by eliminating choice. The European Institute for the Media (EIM), which monitors media behaviour in the run-up to elections in the former Soviet Union, had this to say about the Georgian President's re-election in April 2000:

Freedom of the press in Kazakhstan: deceptive appearances

Pick up a newspaper in Almaty and you read story after story criticising the government. A foreign visitor might be forgiven for assuming that Kazakhstan has a robust press operating in a climate free of censorship. But scratch the surface and there are serious limitations to press freedom.

While even the state-owned media publish articles critical of the government, the President is beyond reproach in a country often dubbed a 'supra-presidential' republic. An article in the Criminal Code ensures that any 'insult of the honour and dignity' of the President is subject to criminal prosecution. The result: self-censorship. Critics compare the code with the notorious paragraph ten of Stalin's article 58.

The harsh reality is that reporting on high-level corruption is extremely constrained. Articles typically name only second or third-hand perpetrators. And since investigative journalism has not made much headway, the occasional reports of high-level corruption found in the pages of openly opposition newspapers are usually translations or reprints from Western, or sometimes Moscow-based, media. Even these are sometimes censored.

Reporting on corruption carries risks. Cases of physical assaults on journalists and arson attacks on media offices are well documented. The recent assault on *Respublika 2000*'s editor after the publication of an article about one of the country's 'oil kings' serves as one example. Threats were also made against journalists at *Vremya* who dared to write about corruption and to the television crews of *KTK-TV*, who produced a controversial report at one of the country's military installa-tions. The Prosecutor's Office has failed to investigate these cases.

On top of the threat of physical intimidation, Kazakh journalists are subject to a tangle of legal and administrative constraints. While the constitution guarantees freedom of speech and prohibits censorship, the current Law on the Media, adopted in 1999, is a pale shadow of the 1991 law created on the wave of Mikhail Gorbachev's *perestroika*.

There is common agreement that the rights and freedoms of the media exist only on paper. The cards are stacked: attempts by journalists to appeal to the law, the constitution or the Universal Declaration of Human Rights are, as a rule, unsuccessful, while the provisions of the Law on Media and other legislation used against journalists, editors, publishers and media owners are implemented with fervour. The arbitrary nature of judicial decisions is an obstacle, thwarting attempts by journalists to write about corruption.

Reporting on high-level corruption is further limited by the concentration of media ownership. Although media ownership is regulated by the Civil Code, anti-monopoly legislation and the Law on Media, the mass media is concentrated in the hands of only a few. While there are many newspapers and television stations in Kazakhstan, most media are bought by pro-presidential forces as soon as their public profile and popularity increase.

One of the more influential media companies is owned by the daughter and son-in-law of the president. Even media of secondary importance are bought up by key economic and political players, including the *Kazkommercebank* financial group, the Eurasian Bank Group, local authorities and – unsurprisingly – the President's other son-in-law.

TI-Kazakhstan

'Coverage of the campaign in the broadcast media was dominated by Eduard Shevardnadze, who received around two thirds of the time and space devoted to the candidates on television, radio and newspapers monitored ... The allegiance of the state media to the incumbent, the weak position of the [independent] print media ... combined in this election to frustrate the ability of voters to receive a full, fair and balanced accounting of the choices available to them.'

EIM viewed the Russian presidential elections in a similar light. And, for October 2000 presidential elections in Kyrgyzstan, EIM said that the electorate never had a chance to form its own opinion freely about the candidates. The incumbent Akayev received over 90 per cent of airtime during the campaign.[44]

Government anti-corruption efforts

As far as President Heydar Aliev is concerned, corruption in Azerbaijan is no worse than in any other country.[45] International bodies disagree. Aliev insists that Transparency International, the US State Department and the World Bank are 'biased' in their judgement. In March, he said: 'It is not a novelty that corruption exists in Azerbaijan. We know this fact and are struggling against it. But, regretfully, we could not stop corruption and there has been no result. If I had the opportunity, I could stop corruption within one or two months.' A confusing message, to be sure – but one which makes it unsurprising that few government anti-corruption efforts, apart from firing some officials, have been made to date in Azerbaijan.[46]

Not all anti-corruption initiatives across the former Soviet Union are as hopeless, but most are only moderately effective. This has less to do with any lack of desire to combat corruption and more with the fact that corruption has become institutionalised. Politicians trying to stamp out graft usually find their careers cut short or their efforts rebuffed. Nevertheless, initiatives do continue. In January 2001, Kyrgyzstan adopted a Code of Ethics and Armenia pledged to renew its anti-corruption drive after it was awarded US $300,000 by the World Bank to develop a programme to combat bribery, nepotism and other economic crimes.[47]

In Russia, Putin seems to be acting on pre-election promises to combat corruption, but the jury is still out on whether he is a wolf in reformer's clothing. In one initiative, the government aimed to bring regional legislation and institutions in line with the federal constitution. But what was intended as a grand anti-corruption effort resulted instead in power battles over revenue streams among the new presidential envoys and a wary regional elite.[48] The government also proved ineffective in challenging the regional barons and influencing the corrupt way gubernatorial elections are conducted. When wayward Far Eastern Primorye Governor Yevgeny Nazdratenko was forced to resign early in 2000 – he had controlled industry in his region for years – analysts thought it might be a sign that Putin was serious about cracking down on regional corruption. But Putin did not fire Nazdratenko; instead, he lured him away from his post as governor with the promise of a cushy job in Moscow.

Putin's cabinet reshuffle in March 2001 did result in some radical changes in his security team. Analysts say that Putin aimed to root out corruption in the security forces and the military by filling the security posts in his cabinet with friends and allies. He also appointed former deputy finance minister Lyubov Kudelina to the post of Deputy Defence Minister. This move may signify his recognition of the need to combat corruption in the armed forces by having a former finance official keep a close watch on the defence budget.[49]

Indem analyst Yury Korgunyuk called the reshuffle positive, suggesting that the creation of new teams in the corruption-ridden Interior and Defence Ministries indicated Putin is serious. 'Without bringing order to agencies that are supposed to bring order to the country, it makes no sense to talk about law and order,' Korgunyuk told *The Moscow Times*. The pro-Kremlin daily *Izvestia* was perhaps prematurely triumphant when it declared: 'This is the end of the world for the oligarchy that has ruled the Russian political elite for the last decade.'[50]

Georgia grabbed most of the limelight insofar as national anti-corruption efforts in the region were concerned. With the approval of international donors, President Eduard Shevardnadze signed a groundbreaking anti-corruption decree in March 2001 that promised to introduce maximum transparency in state institutions, define clear distinctions between the functions and duties of public agencies, and identify adequate remuneration for public service employees. The anti-corruption decree was a positive step and was well received by the public, though some Georgian anti-corruption officials were pessimistic.[51]

Georgia's challenge is the challenge to the region. Even if the anti-corruption initiative is sincere, as many experts seem to think, Shevardnadze's hands are tied. A far-reaching campaign would attack members of the ruling elite on whom he relies.[52] Ghia Nodia, head of the Caucasus Institute for Peace, said: 'He is afraid to weaken his power and is not ready to take radical measures.'[53] Shevardnadze cannot sack half of his cabinet. But corruption in Georgia is so pervasive that anti-corruption fighters are often not sure whom to target first.

Many anti-corruption initiatives in the region are rooted in Soviet tradition and have political motivations. In January, Kazakh President Nursultan Nazarbayev berated officials for their excesses abroad and misappropriation of funds. The President said that 865 local officials were sacked last year for misconduct linked to corruption.[54] Fine words and actions, but coming from a president who tolerates little opposition and regularly clamps down on independent media, they are not seen as a sincere commitment to transparency.

The states most resistant to enacting anti-corruption reform remain Azerbaijan, which has still to acknowledge that corruption is a problem, and Turkmenistan, whose leader demonstrates all too clearly how nonchalantly the issue is handled. On 16 April, President Saparmurat Niyazov denounced officials for graft, demanding the country get rid of corruption – in exactly five days.[55]

Conclusion

Corruption across the region continued to keep economic and political reforms from becoming effective in 2000–01. In the short term, the dismissal of the Ukrainian Prime Minister and his cabinet could have signalled an end to reforms aimed at greater transparency in the country. Yushchenko's government was the first to tackle such reforms and to record positive economic growth. In Russia, Putin's first year in office led some to hope that law and order efforts aimed at de-institutionalising corruption are possible. How Putin deals with Russia's enterprise giants will indicate whether the country will be able to tear itself away from the post-Soviet crony capitalism that has strangled the economy and deterred investment for a decade.

In Central Asia and the Caucasus, religious warfare, increased drug smuggling and battles over lucrative oil revenues have resulted in ever-shrinking transparency, a trend made all the more worrying as governments increasingly underplay the seriousness of bribery, nepotism and other abuses of power. Key players are still able to take advantage of partial market reforms and the availability of new offshore outlets for moving money.

In some countries political transparency seemed to be improving, but electoral corruption thwarted major change across the CIS. Anti-corruption efforts, while increasing, often lacked follow-through and proved difficult to implement due to the control state captors have over government institutions.

A primary problem related to corruption has been the weakness of the state. To begin tackling corruption, governments must renew their authority in the face of powerful oligarchs who have ties to leading officials. Stricter legislation against money laundering, asset stripping and bribery must be introduced and implemented. In most cases, such implementation will necessitate major cabinet reshuffles and the ousting of corrupt state managers. Until CIS governments begin to recognise the dangers associated with the conflict of interest between business and state, serious reforms will be difficult to undertake.

The role the West can play in helping post-Soviet countries in their efforts to curb corruption must not be underestimated. One of the most important challenges facing the international community is to monitor more closely offshore banking activities and, in particular, to ensure that banks strictly follow 'know your customer' rules when dealing with money transfers from the region.[56] If it fails in that task, it could be charged with doing little to help the CIS overcome its first anti-corruption hurdles, or even worse, as an accomplice to crony capitalism. The lion's share of anti-corruption work still falls to CIS leaders, who need to strengthen their own governments, but by democratic and transparent means.

1   *RIA Novosti* (Russia), 13 March 2001.
2   European Bank for Reconstruction and Development, *EBRD Transition Report 1999* (London: EBRD, 1999); World Bank, *Transition Newsletter*, Vol. 11, No. 3–4, May-July 2000.
3   Anders Aslund, 'Problems with Economic Transformation in Ukraine,' paper presented at the Fifth Dubrovnik Conference on Post-Communist Economic Transformation, June 1999; Transitions Online, 'Special Report on Corruption,' 2 October 2000.
4   World Bank, *Anti-Corruption in Transition: A Contribution to the Policy Debate* (Washington DC: World Bank, 2000).
5   EurasiaNet, 7 December 2000.
6   Yeltsin-era corruption was acute and institutionalised. Louise Shelly, 'Corruption in the Post-Yeltsin Era,' *East European Constitutional Review*, Vol. 9, No. 1–2, winter-spring 2000.
7   *Argumenty i Fakty* (Russia), 8 November 2000; *Christian Science Monitor*, 17 April 2001; Reuters, 25 January 2001.
8   Fyodorov claimed that the management was transferring prize assets to friends and relatives, thereby cheating the state out of much-needed revenue; and that Gazprom's takeover of Russia's private NTV television station and two other print publications – all belonging to the country's largest independent media group, Media-MOST – was an attempt by Gazprom management to offer the Kremlin media control, in exchange for letting the company structure stand. Bloomberg, 18 and 22 April 2001; Reuters, 31 May 2001; *Business Week* (International Edition), 2 April 2001.
9   *The Economist* (UK), 1 June 2001.
10 CNN.com, 26 April 2001.
11 Ibid.
12 Lilia Carasciuc, 'Fighting Corruption to Improve Governance: The Case of Moldova,' Center for Strategic Studies and Reforms, 1999.
13 Lilia Carasciuc, 'Corruption in Moldova: Macroeconomic Impact,' paper presented at the Princeton University-Central European University Joint Conference on Corruption, November 1999, <http://www.coc.ceu.hu/carasciuc.html>.
14 Transitions Online, 'Week in Review,' 19–25 February and 2–8 April 2001.
15 Azerbaijan's 2001 Corruption Perceptions Index ranking was 84 out of 91 countries, just below Ukraine (83) and Russia (79). See p. 232.
16 Those polled were asked to rank the ministries in terms of their corruption. Customs got the worst ranking, followed by the Health Ministry, the Interior Ministry, the Tax Inspectorate and the State Property Committee. Turan News Agency (Azerbaijan), 6 April 2001.
17 Transitions Online, 7 November 2000; Turan News Agency (Azerbaijan), 6 April 2001.
18 In 2000, the country began to experience economic growth and an increase in living standards from its petro-dollars, with average wages increasing by 20 per cent, making them the second highest in the CIS after Russia. Transitions Online, 'Country Files,' April 2001.
19 According to *Newsweek*, some oil companies allegedly made payments of over US $65 million through offshore shell companies and bank accounts. *Newsweek* (US), 10 and 24 July 2000.
20 Georgian TV, 22 March 2001.
21 Vladimir Brovkin, 'Moving Money, Making Money and Parking Money Overseas: Front Companies in Offshore Jurisdictions,' Transnational Crime and Corruption Center, 2000; P. J. O'Rourke, 'The Godfather Decade: An Encounter With Post-Soviet Corruption,' *Foreign Policy*, November-December 2000.

22 Radio Free Europe/Radio Liberty, 5 September 2000.
23 Anders Aslund, 'State and Governance in Transition Economies: Lessons for the
    Kyrgyz Republic,' Carnegie Endowment for International Peace, October 2000;
    Radio Free Europe/Radio Liberty, 5 September 2000.
24 Jens Christopher Andvig, 'Corruption in Former USSR Countries and International Oil
    Business in Azerbaijan,' Norwegian Institute of International Affairs, 1999; EurasiaNet,
    7 December 2000.
25 Brovkin (2000).
26 World Bank (2000); Joel S. Hellman, Geraint Jones and Daniel Kaufmann,
    'Seize the State, Seize the Day: State Capture, Corruption, and Influence in Transition,'
    World Bank Policy Research Working Paper, September 2000.
27 World Bank (2000).
28 Interview with authors.
29 Interview with authors.
30 Interview with authors.
31 Louise Shelley, 'The Current State of Corruption in NIS,' 2000:
    <http://www.american.edu/transcrime/work/testimony799.htm>.
32 Anders Aslund, 'Problems with Economic Transformation in Ukraine,' Carnegie Endowment
    for International Peace, June 1999.
33 Shelley (2000).
34 Interview with authors.
35 Transitions Online, 'Week in Review,' 13–19 November 2000.
36 Transitions Online, 30 October 2000.
37 The OSCE's report found that both elections had failed to comply with international standards.
    Felix Kulov, a leader of the Arnamys opposition party, was excluded from both campaigns, and
    then sentenced to six years in prison immediately after the elections on charges of abuse of
    power and forgery during the time he occupied the post of national security minister. Other
    strong presidential hopefuls failed to pass a newly instituted Kyrygz language test that was at
    the last minute declared a requirement for participation by the Central Electoral Commission.
    The language test weeded out even several native Kyrgyz speakers, but gave Akayev the
    highest possible score. Transitions Online, 30 October 2000.
38 Interview with authors.
39 Interview with authors.
40 OSCE Office for Democratic Institutions and Human Rights, 'Final Report on 26 March 2000
    Presidential Elections in the Russian Federation,' 19 May 2000,
    <http://www.osce.org/odihr/ election/rus00-1-final.htm>.
41 Transitions Online, 'Country Files,' January 2000; Michael Gray, 'Russia Fights Crime
    and Corruption,' World Bank, *Transition Newsletter,* 29 March 2001,
    <http://www.worldbank.org/html/prdr/trans/n&d95/mgray.htm>.
42 Transitions Online, 'Country Files,' April 2001.
43 OSCE Office for Democratic Institutions and Human Rights, 'Final Report on Belarusian
    Parliamentary Elections,' 30 January 2001; OSCE Office for Democratic Institutions and
    Human Rights, 'Parliamentary Elections 15 and 29 October 2000. Technical Assessment
    Mission. Final Report,' 30 January 2001,
    <http://www.osce.org/odihr/election/be/bel00_efr.html#52>.
44 European Institute for the Media: <http://www.eim.org>.
45 Radio Free Europe/Radio Liberty, 20 November 2000.
46 US Department of State, 'Country Reports on Human Rights Practices 2000,'
    <http://www.state.gov/g/drl/rls/hrrpt/2000/>.
47 *PNA Daily News* (Georgia), 2 May 2001.
48 *The Moscow Times* (Russia), 28 March 2001.
49 Transitions Online, 'Week in Review,' 26 March–2 April 2001.
50 *Izvestia* (Russia), 28 March 2001.
51 President Eduard Shevardnadze, 'Some First Anti-Corruption Measures,' Decree No. 296,
    5 February 2001; EurasiaNet, 30 January 2001.
52 Transitions Online, 'Special Report on Corruption,' 2 October 2000.
53 Interview with authors.
54 Reuters, 30 January 2001.
55 Radio Free Europe/Radio Liberty, 18 April 2001.
56 For more on international efforts to stop money laundering, see p. 204.

Central Europe, Southeast Europe and the Baltic states

Albania, Bosnia and Herzegovina, Bulgaria, Croatia, Czech Republic, Estonia, Hungary, Latvia, Lithuania, Macedonia, Poland, Romania, Slovakia, Slovenia, Yugoslavia

By Luke Allnutt, Jeremy Druker and Jen Tracy (with Kristjan Kaljund, Altin Raxhimi and Daria Sito)

Introduction

Enormous changes have taken place in Central Europe, Southeast Europe and the Baltic states since the collapse of state socialism, but widespread corruption – both petty and grand – lives on. The last decade of post-communist transition to democracy clearly had mixed results. Good intentions to get rid of graft have sometimes fallen foul of obfuscating former communists, inept former dissidents, uninformed foreign advisors or simply corrosion in the system.

Despite a shared legacy, the region is diverse, ranging from war-torn Bosnia, with its dysfunctional economy, to more peaceful and prosperous states, like the technology-savvy Baltic countries who look toward Scandinavia and enjoy a standard of living approaching that of poorer EU members.

The region's relative success stories in terms of prosperity and openness – the Czech Republic, Estonia, Hungary, Poland and Slovenia – have come far in the transition process, witnessing considerable corruption along the way. These countries have learned from experiences in the early 1990s when businessmen and officials took advantage of the collapse of the legal system to siphon money from state companies. Corruption charges make front-page news, and many anti-corruption institutions are now in place. The challenge is to make them work.

In the war-torn parts of the Balkans, corruption charges have more often than not been dwarfed by accusations of war crimes and genocide. In Yugoslavia and Croatia, with former leaders Milosevic and Tudjman gone, the challenge of building the foundations of transparent democracy has only just begun. Even in areas that escaped bloodshed, corruption remains rampant and an integral part of doing business. Countries in Southeast Europe have the opportunity to learn from the mistakes made by their neighbours.

Transition has turned out to be more difficult than expected for many of the countries in the region, but, at the same time, it has speeded up the prospects for some states of joining the EU. In this setting, with mixed results from transition and mixed messages about the future, corruption has become a popular explanation for all that ails societies.

News review

Nothing served as a better indicator of Yugoslavia's desire to end the corruption of President Slobodan Milosevic's regime than his March 2001 arrest on corruption charges, which signalled, in the words of new Yugoslav president Vojislav Kostunica, that no one is above the law.[1] But even with the subsequent deportation of Milosevic to the UN International Criminal Tribunal for the former Yugoslavia in The Hague in June 2001, the hard task of dismantling Milosevic's kleptocracy has just begun. Mafia-state security gangs are still active, and the new President faces the daunting challenge of rooting them out at the risk of his own administration. Kostunica, a constitutional lawyer, repeatedly said that he wants to do things by the book and steer clear of 'revolutionary justice'. But others, both domestically and internationally, accused him of foot dragging and said that, as a nationalist, he lacks the political will to effect real change.[2]

In Bulgaria, despite relative political and economic stability, cleaning up corruption repeatedly rocked the boat of Prime Minister Ivan Kostov's government in its fourth term. Kostov's cabinet narrowly escaped collapse, due to a couple of well-timed foreign policy coups that overshadowed allegations of bribery and nepotism. In April 2000, former interior minister Bogomil Bonev publicly alleged high-level corruption among top officials in the Prime Minister's cabinet, threatening to disclose evidence of misappropriations if Kostov did not step down.[3] In an effort to appease his critics, the premier sacked several high-ranking officials. Several days later, the World Bank disbursed a US $7.5 million loan to Bulgaria to fight corruption.

In June 2000, Bulgaria's chief EU negotiator and former industry minister Alexander Bozhkov was forced to resign after the Prosecutor General's office accused him of corruption. Local media had dubbed Bozhkov 'Mr Ten Per Cent', in reference to his alleged habit of taking a cut of every deal approved. In late August, Prime Minister Kostov's image was soiled again when he admitted that he had taken a US $80,000 'donation' from alleged mafia boss Grigory Luchansky.[4] In June 2001, Bulgarians went to the polls and gave the party of ex-King Simeon 40 per cent of the popular vote. His election manifesto focused on attracting foreign investment, cutting taxes and reducing corruption.[5]

The failure of former Romanian president Emil Constantinescu to achieve success in rooting out corruption was a key factor contributing to his defeat in the November 2000 presidential elections. Discontented with Constantinescu's dawdling on reform, the public elected former communist Ion Illiescu as President for the third time. Illiescu has yet to demonstrate any anti-corruption resolve. Analysts worry that the former president's failure to reform, and the return to power of an ex-communist leader under whom corruption had earlier flourished, may prevent Romania from pulling itself out of poverty and into the EU.[6]

In Poland, an investigation was launched in November 2000 into the tender for consulting services for the privatisation of Telekomunikacja Polska. The Polish Supreme Chamber of Control alleged that the Treasury Minister had violated the Public Procurement Act. And in March 2001, the Treasury Minister annulled a tender that the state gaming enterprise Totalizator Sportowy had closed with the American company G-Tech, on grounds of alleged corruption.[7] On a more positive note, officials and businessmen in Poland recently launched a series of anti-corruption actions, including hard-hitting television and billboard public service announcements against the dangers of corruption.[8]

In the Czech Republic during 2000–01, long-awaited charges were brought against officials and businessmen for corrupt actions in the 1990s. In February 2001, the authorities arrested Frantisek Chvalovsky, the country's top soccer boss and head of the Czech-Moravian Football Association, on charges of credit fraud totalling US $17 million.[9] In December 2000 and early 2001, over a dozen prominent Czech bankers and businessmen were either charged or convicted of bank fraud, insider trading and other corruption-related crimes. Several had close political ties, including contributing funds to some of the country's largest parties.[10] Such connections may have shielded them in the past, but no more.

In Lithuania, nine political parties signed a Pact on Political Honesty and Ethics in August 2000. Signatories committed themselves to ensuring fair elections. An anti-corruption unit exclusively geared to monitoring the public service was also set up. In June 2001, the Financial Action Task Force amended its 'blacklist' of 'non-cooperative' countries in the fight against money laundering to include Hungary.[11]

Reforming public procurement

In the 1990s, corruption scandals in the region tended to focus on privatisation, with politically connected businesses colluding with public officials to purchase state firms at a fraction of their real value. Today, privatisation is mostly complete in the 'success story' countries of Central Europe. Because of past scandals, the sale of remaining assets generally receives enormous media attention, greatly reducing the scope for corruption. In comparison, less attention is paid to

let there be light ...
The National Anti-Corruption Programme
Anna Cechová, Slovakia

corruption in public procurement. This remains a major obstacle on the road toward a transparent and competitive business environment.

Some reformist governments now publish a large quantity of information about tenders, including on the internet. A few Balkan countries have set up central government institutions to monitor procurement. However, such efforts are hindered by an overall lack of resources and qualified personnel. Piotr-Nils Gorecki, an OECD specialist in public procurement, said: 'Most countries have come quite far in setting up institutional and legal frameworks, and have amended, redrafted or introduced laws that have gone quite far toward EU law.'[12] But laws on procurement are still not adequate to prevent corrupt practices.

In the frontrunners for EU membership, the situation is not exactly driving away investors, but continued corruption holds back the economy, provokes public criticism and tarnishes the images of countries trying to impress Brussels.

In Poland, the state Public Procurement Office admits that procurement is one of the areas most susceptible to corruption, a conclusion echoed in recent reports by the World Bank and the Polish Supreme Chamber of Control. Official malpractice includes allowing companies to look into procurement conditions beforehand and to negotiate the prices of contracts after tenders are won. At the local level, where control mechanisms are far more lax, officials have awarded procurement contracts because of family connections, and colluded in the creation of fictitious companies to suit the needs of particular tenders.[13]

Tomasz Chlebowski, deputy head of the Polish Chamber of Information and Telecommunications, commented on IT procurement in a recent article: 'Observing tenders for computer systems, announced by the state administration, leads one to an unnerving conclusion: bidders who do not have "insiders" in tender commissions have absolutely no chance. What's worse, the law itself contributes to such a situation.' He faulted legislation for its failure to address the possibility of some forms of corruption.[14]

The situation in Hungary is equally troubling. After surveying 560 member companies who have invested in Hungary since 1989, the American Chamber of Commerce recently condemned the country's public procurement law for its 'subjectivity'; excessive secrecy, which makes it impossible for losing bidders to review the winner's estimate and for the public to monitor the implementation of the contract; and its low fines for improprieties. André Mecs of the Chamber's legislative and political affairs committee said of the law: 'It serves the interests of the one who is issuing the tender ... and of those people who don't want the process to be transparent.'[15] In November 2000, authorities caught the then chairman of the parliamentary procurement committee red-handed while taking bribes.[16]

The Hungarian government, while paying lip service to public procurement reform, has actually been one of the worst offenders, regularly avoiding competitive tenders. Failure to tender the construction of new motorways was severely criticised by the European Commission, the Hungarian Competition Office and many others. Instead of opening up the estimated US $2 billion project to public bidding, the cabinet allowed the state-owned Hungarian Development Bank (MFB) to choose construction companies and finance the work. Critics charge that firms 'friendly' to the ruling Fidesz-Hungarian Civic Party were chosen by MFB, though Prime Minister Viktor Orban defended the selection process as a way of ensuring that uncorrupt, Hungarian companies came out on top.[17]

With mismanaged privatisation of state utilities and enterprises still commanding media attention in Latvia, corruption in public procurement has not taken centre stage, though procedures are far from transparent. Despite the public's perception that corruption in procurement is high,[18] not a single case of public procurement abuse has come to court since the country regained independence in 1991. In spring 2000 a procurement official at the Defence Ministry was dismissed after ordering uniforms from a company owned by another company of which he was the state trustee – but he was reinstated a few months later.[19]

> With mismanaged privatisation of state utilities and enterprises still commanding media attention, corruption in public procurement has not taken centre stage.

Under the present public procurement law in Latvia the names of the winning and losing bidders are available to the public, but not the sum paid, said Finance Ministry official Edvins Parups.[20] Information about the decision-making process and those responsible for it is restricted to the state auditor. However, a draft law on public procurement aimed at aligning Latvia with EU norms is currently going through parliament. Members of public procurement commissions may in future be obliged to make a statement of their assets to the State Revenue Service, which already publishes information about the assets of other officials. The final form of the new law remains unclear.

While central governments acknowledge the need to make public procurement more transparent, there is much more work to do at the local level. 'The main mass of corruption in Estonia – like elsewhere, probably – remains hidden within local level municipalities,' said Lauri Vahtre, a member of the Estonian parliament.[21] Piotr-Nils Gorecki at the OECD pointed out that flaws in procurement practice cannot always be tied to corruption. 'It's also a question of competence,' he said. 'For many [involved in local government procurement] this is a sideline, since there may be only a few tenders a year. They receive little or no training, and the laws change often.'[22]

Government anti-corruption efforts: fear of stalling

Efforts at fighting corruption by national governments – in part pressured by international agencies – are still adversely affected by widespread political complicity in shady dealings. And the public in many countries, weary of failed reform, continues to associate high-ranking politicians with corruption.

In Hungary, an ongoing oil scam to avoid higher taxes and customs duties has revealed the huge difficulties faced by national institutions investigating and fighting corruption, even in the region's leading countries. A parliamentary ad hoc committee set up to look at oil deals has good intentions but, analysts say, is underfunded and understaffed. More importantly, its role is limited because the case potentially implicates political parties across the board. 'There are people in all parties who are interrelated and their interests are against such a committee,' said Tibor Szanyi, a socialist parliamentary deputy and Vice-Chair of Hungary's Parliamentary Committee on European Integration.[23] 'The impact of such committees is quite limited,' said Janos Bertok at the OECD. 'Of course, they raise the profile of certain valuable sectors and give them publicity. But the real problem is very limited follow-up.'[24]

In the Czech Republic, another of the region's leading countries, a 'Clean Hands' campaign sponsored by the Social Democrat government produced some results. Brady Clough, Vice-Chairman of TI-Czech Republic, said that 'less than two or three cases have been prosecuted. This is alarming when contrasted with the 1,000 or more criminal complaints issued by the government's anti-corruption investigative offices.' But he added that 'the first real victory for the Clean Hands campaign was high-level and bittersweet for the Social Democrats: their Finance Minister, Ivo Svoboda, had to resign along with a colleague on charges of investment and shareholder fraud'.[25]

The Baltic states have perhaps been most creative in their anti-corruption drives. Latvia and Estonia, with well-deserved reputations for embracing information technology and the internet, used this openness to innovation as a way of increasing government transparency. Latvian Finance Minister Gundars Berzins installed a 24-hour web camera in his office to broadcast his every move via the internet.[26] Although gimmicky, the well-publicised venture raised the profile of anti-corruption initiatives.

There have also been more sustainable efforts. At the end of November 2000, Latvian Prime Minister Andris Berzins announced a new campaign designed to inform the public about the problems of corruption and the means to combat it.[27] Estonia, the region's technology leader, last year put government records online. By April 2001, every public official's salary was also published on the internet. 'To most people,' said Daniel Vaarik from the Finance Ministry, 'it is uncomfortable that such data can be read by anyone, but our idea is that the whole financial environment must be transparent. The new system is definitely useful for the state, but perhaps not so comfortable for individuals.'[28] Now the government is looking into online voting for elections.

NGOs get involved

Where governments have faltered, the increasingly influential NGO sector has done much to carry on the fight against corruption. As a recent World Bank report noted, NGOs have demonstrated that civic activists can play a major role in raising public awareness of corruption, devising policies for reducing graft and monitoring governmental anti-corruption initiatives.[29] Promising examples of this trend include the tracking of public auctions by TI-Bulgaria and others; the key role played by Slovak NGOs in lobbying for a new freedom of information law that took effect at the beginning of 2000; and the Polish 'Against Corruption' programme that generated substantial coverage in the press and broadcast media. Several groups have started to spread their net wider, helping to train colleagues in other countries in the region. Coalition 2000, a Bulgarian organisation, is a group that promotes its aims in neighbouring Balkan countries.

Such grassroots initiatives are vital. And organisations such as the Open Society Institute (OSI), with local offices in many countries in the region, have also put the fight against corruption on their agenda. But, across the region, public confidence in bringing the perpetrators of corruption to justice is still low. In Hungary, a survey carried out by Szonda Phone Telemarketing Company revealed that 72 per cent agreed with the statement: 'A few scapegoats will be identified but the real oil mafia will not be revealed.' Seventy-seven per cent said that they believed that politicians were involved in illegal oil deals.[30]

Whirlwind international involvement in fighting corruption

Events of the past year underlined that the international fight against corruption has become much more prominent. Nearly every major international player in the region issued a report on corruption, sponsored a conference or initiated a new programme.[31] Real action seems to have finally caught up with the change in thinking that spread after the collapse of communism. Members of the donor and development community can no longer rationalise their support for 'friendly' but corrupt regimes – an approach that unfortunately carried over into the post-communist era. The race to join the EU is a constant theme, reflecting how deeply the organisation has influenced regional anti-corruption efforts. With

Fighting corruption in Slovakia

The current government – elected in 1998 – recently approved a national programme to fight corruption, based on a proposal developed by TI-Slovakia. Prime Minister Mikulás Dzurinda held public consultations with all major stakeholders, and the programme was approved in June 2000. Ministers were then asked to draw up their own action plans.

Implementation of the programme effectively began before cabinet approved it, since a new Freedom of Information Act was passed in May 2000. A 120-strong NGO umbrella group that united behind the cry 'Everything that is not secret is public!' stimulated public pressure for the Act.

After it came into force, a comprehensive audit was conducted of the public administration. A final report made recommendations to rectify the deficiencies considered most conducive to corruption. The government pledged to implement them: the audit's value ultimately depends on its will to do so.

Corruption is still far too evident in public life in Slovakia, with four members of Prime Minister Dzurinda's cabinet having lost their jobs following corruption-related scandals. Most recently, Deputy Prime Minister for European Integration Pavol Hamžík was forced to resign after failing to disclose the alleged embezzlement of EU funds. Dzurinda sacked Hamžík after he first attempted to cover up the problem and then refused to leave office. Earlier this year, Defence Minister Pavol Kanis also stepped down after failing to explain where he found the funds to purchase a luxury villa. Dzurinda has shown that he means business where corruption in public office is concerned.

A series of new initiatives aims at tackling the many barriers to the transparent conduct of business. The government recently began a review of all licences, concessions, permissions, contributions and grants; and the companies' register was made available to the public by internet. Parliament also adopted an Anti-Money Laundering Act, and began debating transparency in political life. Laws relating to party financing were amended in April 2001.

To give more legal force to the fight against corruption, the institution of *agent provocateur* – a specialised agent to fight corruption – was established. A new judicial code has been adopted, and the creation of an ombudsman is under discussion. The Slovak constitution was amended in February 2001 in order to accommodate these innovations.

Such developments were the subject of wide public debate, which in turn has been informed by the work of NGOs such as TI-Slovakia, currently running a television advertising campaign, as well as a range of educational programmes. Recent polls showed that Slovaks perceived corruption as the third biggest problem in their country.

While gains have been made, some observers were frustrated by the length of time it took to win approval and implementation of the national programme. There are also qualitative shortcomings in the ministry action plans. Other problems remain, such as unskilled officers, a possible lack of commitment to reform in some quarters, non-transparent financing of election campaigns, and continuing links between leaders and various interest groups.

But the commitment of NGOs to fighting corruption is a powerful counterweight to these difficulties. NGO activism in Slovakia played a crucial role over the past months in monitoring and influencing the government's efforts to combat corruption and in raising public awareness of the issue. These efforts show no sign of flagging.

TI-Slovakia

EU accession just around the corner for some, governments desperately want to be seen to achieve 'European' norms as soon as possible. Generally, this has had a positive effect, and the EU has pushed standards higher. But there are concerns that prospective member states are doing no more than ticking off the boxes on the *acquis communautaire* – the body of laws that accession countries must adopt to qualify for admission.

Apart from EU influence, the sea change in international thinking on corruption has snowballed into a series of anti-corruption initiatives by the donor community, often supported by NGOs and other civil society actors. But this flurry of international activity had a downside in some cases. Renewed institutional interest can bring overlapping jurisdictions, a lack of strategy and coordination, and scanty monitoring. Nowhere is this phenomenon better seen than in post-war Bosnia and Herzegovina. Bosnia, of course, is a special case, a country crippled by war that has been a virtual protectorate of the international community since the signature of the 1995 Dayton Peace Accord. Nonetheless, it serves as a useful example of international institutional disorder.

The key anti-corruption agency in Bosnia is the Anti-Fraud Department of the Office of the High Representative (OHR), the West's main oversight body. It has its own budget, investigative powers and a mission to act as a link between local institutions and the international community. In theory, it coordinates the anti-corruption activities and efforts of other international agencies, such as the World Bank, the IMF, the OSCE and the UN International Police Task Force (IPTF). The Anti-Fraud Department has mainly focused on reform of the financial police, together with the European Commission's Customs and Fiscal Assistance Office to Bosnia and Herzegovina, but it has also pushed for and monitored the implementation of customs and tax administration reforms.

Critics charge that the department has largely failed in its coordination role and is far too under-resourced to fulfil its mission. 'They do not have enough staff to make a significant dent in massive and pervasive corruption,' said Tanya Domi, a Balkan specialist who served as former OSCE spokesperson in Bosnia and Herzegovina.[32] The US General Accounting Office concluded that the OHR's coordination strategy had been 'essentially a recitation of existing international efforts and, although the work of the international community is collegial, it is not truly coordinated'.[33]

That view was seconded by a local official working for an international organisation, who blamed lack of coordination more than lack of staff. 'It became obvious a long time ago that OHR's abilities to act and react have been limited by the level of support and coordination among OHR and the rest of Western organisations and countries,' he said. 'The lack of cooperation and different political

International pressure sees results in Slovenia

After a lengthy period in which the government denied the existence of serious corruption in Slovenia, the State Prosecutor and police force finally swung into action this year. Unfortunately, their activities did not result from any systematic anti-corruption programme, or even pressure for change from ordinary Slovenians. Instead, they are the result of international pressure on the government to start fighting corruption.

Like all transition countries in the region, Slovenia is constantly monitored as part of the process of attaining full membership of international organisations such as the EU, NATO and the OECD. In 2000, the states that comprise the Council of Europe's anti-corruption group, GRECO, evaluated Slovenia's legal anti-corruption provisions and the performance of government institutions, agencies, the judiciary, parliament and the Chamber of Commerce.

Inquiries by GRECO revealed corruption by public officials on a grand scale. There is also evidence of corruption inside Slovenia's system of state subsidies to the private sector. Police investigations exposed the bribery of state prosecutors by international criminal organisations, as well as misuse of a political party official's influence to gain advantage in municipal administrative procedures. Legal cases are still pending.

Government perception of the importance of fighting corruption has increased dramatically since GRECO's evaluation report, which was made public in March 2001. This repre-sents the most significant boost to efforts to tackle the problem in Slovenia.

The report recommended that Slovenia create a mechanism to coordinate departments involved in corruption prevention, in order to set up an integrated anti-corruption strategy. A major priority was the creation of a body to collect data and information on the frequency and types of corruption in the country.

Other recommendations included increasing the number of police officers in the anti-corruption division; strengthening the role of the public prosecutor in pre-trial proceedings; the recruitment and promotion of public prosecutors on the basis of objective criteria alone; and the provision of training on corruption and its detection for officials involved in public tenders and revenue collection.

By the end of March 2001, the government had taken preliminary steps towards establishing a governmental anti-corruption office and an inter-governmental anti-corruption coordination body.

The authorities have also expressed interest in acceding to the OECD Anti-Bribery Convention, and made a formal application to participate in the OECD Working Group on Bribery in International Business Transactions. A decision regarding Slovenian participation is awaited.

The Slovenian parliament adopted a law based on the OECD Anti-Bribery Convention in 1999. Inclusion in the Working Group would mean further international monitoring of Slovenia. This would result in more positive steps towards reducing corruption.

TI-Slovenia

and economic agendas of Western agencies and embassies prevent the creation of any serious long-term, or at least medium-term, anti-corruption strategy.'[34]

In Albania, the relative stability that has prevailed since the widespread anarchy that followed the collapse of pyramid investment schemes in 1997 has allowed international organisations and the government an opportunity to create a new framework – albeit, perhaps, a superficial one – against widespread corruption. On the advice of the World Bank, Albania formed a commission on corruption in January 1998 that focused chiefly on legal reform. In October 2000, a three-year anti-corruption project was launched, sponsored by USAID, implemented by Management Systems International and supported by Albanian NGOs.[35] The project will help in the formation of civil society organisations and the promotion of public-private partnerships.

> Bosnia ... serves as a useful example of international institutional disorder.

One problem that inhibits the fight against corruption is the lack of continuous monitoring. 'There is no periodical check on the situation, while the methodology used in various surveys is also different,' said Auron Pasha, Executive Director of the Tirana think-tank Institute for Research and Development Alternatives. He added that discussion on corruption had missed its target, since it focused on big scandals, and not on curbing insidious petty corruption.[36] According to figures from the Albanian courts, there were only three investigations of 'abuse of duty' in the first half of 2000. One highly publicised case involved Idajet Beqiri, leader of the small left-wing National Unity Party, who was caught taking a bribe to bring about the release of an arrested official. Beqiri's was the first case in Albania's recent history of a politician being prosecuted for corruption.[37]

Critics of the international community say that limited resources, as well as support for non-nationalist politicians no matter how dirty, prevent headway being made. A local official in Bosnia cited the example of a leading Bosnian Serb politician, widely thought to be engaged in corrupt activities, who managed to avoid investigation because he was a Western ally in the battle against Bosnian Serb hardliners. 'These double standards, which are quite obvious and visible to the local community, harm Western anti-corruption efforts,' he said.[38]

But international agency involvement in the region has also had positive results. In Bosnia, a new electoral rule introduced by the OSCE in February 2000 bans elected officials from joining privatisation agencies and the boards of public enterprises. It has had a major impact. 'These rules reduced the level of corruption in Bosnia by clearly defining the rules of behaviour of a public official,' said Kristina Hemon, analyst in the Sarajevo office of International Crisis Group.[39] The OSCE rule led to investigations and audits of public enterprises, whose funds were believed to have been used to finance political parties, such as the state-owned power company Elektroprivreda BiH and the Mostar-based Hercegovacka Banka. In the latter case, the UN High Representative introduced provisional administration in April 2000 because of alleged misuse by the Croatian Democratic Union party.

'All of this has created a momentum that is still underway,' said Hemon. 'It indicates that changes introduced to fight corruption have been effective. Their full implementation depends on the political will of the governments.'[40] As a positive sign, Hemon cited the importance of a July 2000 political party financing law passed by the Federation parliament. Long-term capacity and willingness to fight corruption at the national level must accompany international efforts for meaningful change to occur.

Conclusion

In the countries of Central Europe, Southeast Europe and the Baltic states, there are both striking similarities and wide discrepancies in the fortunes of the anti-corruption movement. Cleaning up public procurement in the Baltic states contrasts sharply with rooting out kleptocracy in former Yugoslavia. While increased international involvement in the area has had a positive impact on standards, it runs the risk of faltering due to overlapping jurisdictions and lack of coordination. And across the region, to varying degrees, governments' will to fight corruption, and their publics' confidence in their ability to do so, is low.

Countries on the verge of accession to the EU have more incentive to combat corruption, yet even they face enormous challenges. There is concern that the momentum to eradicate graft will falter in the region's laggard countries, notably Romania, which has only an embryonic anti-corruption strategy. Or, even when the incentive is there, that frequent changes of government will fragment anti-corruption efforts. This could happen in Slovakia, which has made considerable progress after the crony capitalism of the Meciar era. A political switch away from reform, as publics tire of slow progress, would be a major obstacle for the region's anti-corruption effort.

International organisations and foundations have actively recruited and funded civil society groups, but many initiatives originate with local NGOs. Government officials realise that they must show positive gains from the battle against corruption not just to the international community, but also to the wider society at home. They have begun to engage with civil society organisations to this end. There is a long way to go, but this sense of the growing accountability of politicians to their citizens was unthinkable only a few years ago and represents real progress.

Another worry is that with new NGOs popping up all over the region, particularly in Southeast Europe, the benefits of diversity and pluralism could be overtaken by the flaws of poor coordination, overlapping mandates and, ultimately, the very lack of accountability and transparency that NGOs seek to address. A self-serving NGO sector, with inconsistent standards but a dedication to promoting transparency, would be one of the region's more troubling ironies.

1 Transitions Online, 'Week in Review,' 26 March–1 April 2001; 2–8 April 2001.
2 Democratic Opposition of Serbia, 'Contract With Serbia,' <http://www.dos.org.yu/english/documents/contract.html>; *The Guardian* (UK), 28 March 2001.
3 Radio Free Liberty/Radio Europe, 20 April 2000.
4 Kostov claimed he was unaware of the source at the time. Centre for the Study of Democracy, 'Corruption Assessment Report 2000,' <http://www.csd.bg/news/law/car.htm>; Transitions Online, 'Country Files,' April 2001; Agence France Presse, 10 November 2000.
5 *International Herald Tribune* (US), 18 June 2001.
6 Transitions Online, 'Country Files,' April 2001; 'Diagnostic Surveys of Corruption in Romania,' prepared by the World Bank on the request of the Romanian government, 2000, <http://www.worldbank.org.ro/eng/data/publications.shtml>.
7 Polish Supreme Chamber of Control (NIK), 'Information on the Results of the Control of the Privatisation of Telekomunikacja Polska,' Report No. 175, 2000.
8 *Rzeczpospolita* (Poland), 1 March 2001; *Gazeta Wyborcza* (Poland), 22 March 2001.
9 Transitions Online, 'Week in Review,' 26 February–4 March 2001; Transitions Online, 5 March 2001.
10 Transitions Online, 5 March 2001.
11 Financial Action Task Force on Money Laundering, press release, 22 June 2001, <http://www.oecd.org/fatf>.
12 Interview with authors.
13 Polish Public Procurement Office Report, 'Pathological Occurrences in Public Procurements,' April 2000.
14 *Rzeczpospolita* (Poland), 25 January 2001.
15 *Budapest Business Journal* (Hungary), 27 November 2000.
16 Transitions Online, 5 February 2001.
17 *Budapest Business Journal* (Hungary), 7 May 2001; 14 May 2001; 28 May 2001.
18 World Bank, 'Anti-Corruption in Transition: A Contribution to the Policy Debate,' September 2000.
19 Radio Free Europe/Radio Liberty, 'Baltic States Report,' Vol. 1, No. 27, 7 August 2000.
20 Interview with authors.
21 Interview with authors.
22 Interview with authors.
23 Interview with authors.
24 Interview with authors.
25 Interview with authors.
26 BBC World Service, 24 October 2000.
27 Radio Free Europe/Radio Liberty, 'Newsline,' 29 November 2000.
28 Transitions Online, 2 April 2001.
29 World Bank (2000).
30 Poll by Szonda Phone Telemarketing Company, 29 August 2000.
31 For example USAID Bureau for Europe and Eurasia, 'A Strategy for Combating Corruption,' draft paper, January 2001.
32 Interview with authors. Also *Washington Post* (US), 9 November 2000.
33 Harold J. Johnson, associate director, International Relations and Trade Issues, United States General Accounting Office, testimony to the US House of Representatives on 19 July 2000.
34 Interview with authors.
35 Anti-Corruption Network for Transition Economies, November 2000, <http://www.nobribes.org/CH_Archive/Eng/ch_november00.shtm>.
36 Interview with authors.
37 *Albanian Daily News* (Albania), 6–7 May 2000.
38 Interview with authors.
39 Interview with authors.
40 Interview with authors.

West Europe and North America

Austria, Belgium, Canada, Cyprus, Denmark, Finland, France, Germany, Greece, Iceland, Ireland, Italy, Liechtenstein, Luxembourg, Malta, Netherlands, Norway, Portugal, Spain, Sweden, Switzerland, Turkey, United Kingdom, United States

By Paul Lashmar

Introduction

West Europe and North America include many of the world's most economically powerful countries, with close and well-established economic and cultural links. Together they contribute nearly 70 per cent of world exports. But the responsibility to the rest of the world that such power brings, not least in the area of preventing bribery, is often not fulfilled. And at home too, corruption afflicts many countries, not least in political party funding.

The extent of public sector corruption, particularly common in the contracting and execution of public works, varies markedly between countries and institutions. In Scandinavia and Canada, it appears to be negligible. Observers report much higher levels of corruption in a number of other countries, including Belgium, Greece, Italy and Portugal.[1] But recent cases of corruption involving senior politicians in Germany and prosecutions of police and state officials in the US reveal corruption in countries that had a relatively clean reputation in the past. Turkey, where democracy is fragile, has set about the task of tackling corruption, but, as was evident in its 2001 economic crisis, it has a long way to go.

Private sector companies from right across the region have been identified with the bribery of foreign officials, usually in developing or transition countries. Until recently many governments in West Europe and North America implicitly condoned bribery for foreign contracts, the US being a notable exception since the passage of the Foreign Corrupt Practices Act in 1977.

Approaches are changing in both the public and private sectors. Some intergovernmental institutions and their member states are emerging as leaders of international anti-corruption efforts. According to the OECD, 'corruption has moved to the top of the global political agenda and its dramatic impact on economic development and its corrosive effect on political stability and democratic political institutions has become increasingly obvious'.[2] Business leaders are also increasingly taking steps to prevent bribery as part of a wider trend to incorporate ethical standards in corporate codes of conduct. But it is clear that the increasing attention given to corruption is only a beginning, as more stories emerge of corruption by politicians and public officials within West Europe and North America – and of bribery abroad by companies from the region.

News review

Eva Joly is one of a group of active investigating magistrates in the recently created financial unit of the Paris tribunal. She has run the investigation into perhaps the most prominent and far-reaching corruption case in the region – the Elf Aquitaine affair. With its allegations of corruption at the highest levels of French political life, the case has been at the centre of media attention in France over the last 18 months. Some US $350 million of the then state-owned oil company's funds were reportedly diverted for corrupt purposes.[3] Judge Joly has shown great determination in seeing that those involved are brought to justice. This year Roland Dumas, French foreign minister under the late president François Mitterrand and later head of the Constitutional Council, was found guilty of taking bribes. Released on bail to appeal against his sentence, Dumas made sweeping public allegations against the political establishment, and said that French justice was 'protecting those still in power'.[4]

Numerous corruption cases in France received heavy media coverage in 2000–01. Allegations against President Jacques Chirac were rekindled after a property developer said in a video recording that he had handed over illicit payments in Chirac's presence when he was mayor of Paris.[5] Mitterrand's son, Jean-Christophe, was meanwhile investigated for money laundering and illegal arms trafficking to Angola while serving as his father's African affairs advisor in the early 1990s. The investigation snared several senior politicians close to the late president.[6] In March 2001, the voters of Paris handed the city administration over to the Socialist Party for the first time, partly because the administration of outgoing mayor Jean Tiberi had become embroiled in allegations of corruption.[7]

In the latest twist in a long tale of party financing scandals linked to Germany's Christian Democratic party (CDU), former chancellor Helmut Kohl escaped prosecution in March 2001 but was forced to pay a US $142,000 fine. Kohl admitted accepting US $1 million from secret benefactors for his party while he was chancellor, breaking rules on the funding of political parties, but he denied accusations that his political decisions were affected by the donations.[8] Kohl continues to refuse to identify the donors.

The election of Silvio Berlusconi as Prime Minister of Italy raised the vexed question of just how important corruption is to Italian voters. Berlusconi was elected in May 2001 with a comfortable majority in spite of numerous spent or pending legal actions concerning the media magnate's business and political probity. Elsewhere in Italy, while direct mafia activity has receded since the spectacular *Mani Pulite* ('Clean Hands') trials of the 1990s, public sector corruption continued to be rife. In September 2000 Massimo Guarischi, Chairman of the Lombardy regional assembly budget committee, was charged with rigging public contracts, along with eight businessmen.[9]

Privatisation and public-private finance initiatives are key sources of high-level corruption in the region. Spanish anti-corruption public prosecutors began an investigation in March 2001 into the allegedly fraudulent sale of the telephone installation company Sintel. The action was taken after unions accused the former management of embezzling millions of pesetas from the sale.[10]

Evidence has been mounting that Cyprus has evolved into a money laundering centre for both Russian mafia and Balkan despots. Much of the US $4 billion allegedly diverted from Serbia by the family of the former dictator Slobodan Milosevic is reported to have passed through Cyprus.[11] Concern also arose about the role of Greek banks in channelling money sent abroad by Milosevic.[12]

Corruption remains a pervasive problem in Turkey, hindering attempts at economic reform and entry into the EU. In February 2001, the government of Prime Minister Bulent Ecevit came under attack when he was accused by President Ahmet Necdet Sezer of 'dragging his feet' in the fight against corruption.

While petty corruption among the police in most developed countries has diminished, the massive amounts of money involved in the narcotics trade are a prime cause of corruption in many police forces. The head of the UK's National Crime Squad revealed that 61 officers were expelled from the elite crime fighting squad in the first three years of its existence. Seven were accused of corruption, including taking bribes and dealing in drugs.[13] Although the UK's new Freedom of Information Act, passed in November 2000, was criticised by campaigners for not going far enough, it may have some impact in limiting the scope for corruption across the public sector.[14]

There are few reports of public sector corruption in Scandinavia, but in April 2001 the World Bank put seven Swedish companies and one Swedish individual on its blacklist of entities disbarred from tendering for World Bank-financed contracts. The bans are linked to the sacking of several employees of the World Bank in December 2000 after it was alleged they took kickbacks for steering contracts in the direction of firms paying bribes.[15]

Regional institutions are playing an increasing role in the fight against corruption. Within the Council of Europe, which links West and East European countries, the anti-corruption strategies of a number of states are being examined in a

From corruption to crisis: a turbulent year in Turkey

Recent events in Southeast Asia and Russia underlined one basic rule of the globalised economy: economic crisis is often bound up with corruption. Now Turkey has shown that it is no exception.

A package of IMF monetary reforms was introduced in Turkey on 1 January 2000. It did not include the structural changes needed to end irresponsible public spending, but observers at the time were upbeat. There was optimism that Turkey might see an end to 20 years of high inflation.

As inflation and interest rates fell, the issue of corruption was far from the public's mind. The warning signs came in November 2000, when several banks declared bankruptcy and were taken over by the government. Investigations revealed that the capital of at least five of them had been 'drained' by the owners and deposited in offshore accounts.

Turkey's economic woes intensified in February 2001 and were still not over as the *Global Corruption Report 2001* went to print. Perceptions of a crisis in government led to massive investor withdrawal, followed by a currency devaluation and liquidity crunch. A key factor in this was public awareness of the government's difficulties in the fight against corruption.

Prime Minister Ecevit declared during a press conference on 19 February that there was a crisis at the highest level of the state. He was reporting on a confrontation at a National Security Council meeting in which President Sezer had pushed for an intensification of the fight against corruption.

The Prime Minister had argued that the fight against corruption was not his responsibility. President Sezer apparently responded by throwing the constitution at the Prime Minister (literally, according to news reports), arguing that in fact he could and should take action against corruption with the agencies under his control.

This incident crystallised a divide in public life on the issue of reform. Some institutions and individuals are struggling for the change in political attitudes needed to fight corruption. President Sezer is one of them. A handful of ministers, the majority of the army command, and sections of the business community that promote integration within the global economy are also calling for serious anti-corruption measures.

The role of civil society in the fight against corruption was given greater prominence with the publication in February 2001 of a survey of corruption in Turkey carried out by the Turkish Economic and Social Studies Foundation (TESEV).[1]

Pressure from the international community is strengthening. The World Bank, the IMF, the US and the EU have all called for far-reaching changes to Turkey's political and administrative structures. The government announced a new economic programme on 19 March 2001 to meet the conditions set by the countries that are lending currency through the IMF.

The measures include making the central bank independent of government, an accelerating programme of privatisations (notably of Turkish Airlines and Turk Telecom), and deregulating key industries, including electricity distribution.

Turkey's candidacy for membership of the EU also provides pressure for reform. For negotiations to open on Turkey's accession to the EU, it must first carry out a series of reforms, many of which correspond to the conditions of the IMF loan.

**Turkish Economic and
Social Studies Foundation (TESEV)**

---

1 TESEV, 'Corruption in Turkey,' February 2001, <http://www.tesev.org.tr/eng>.

programme of evaluations undertaken by GRECO (the Group of States against Corruption), one of the Council's principal anti-corruption initiatives.[16] The Council has a range of legal instruments against corruption. The Criminal and Civil Law Conventions on Corruption define common principles and rules and seek to improve international cooperation in the fight against corruption. Signing is optional for member states.[17]

On the issue of corruption the EU showed little leadership until recently. It failed to take all possible regulatory measures to curb trans-border corruption, relying rather on the work of the OECD. But under the presidency of Romano Prodi, the EU put transparency and the elimination of corruption in its own institutions at the top of its agenda, following the collective resignation in 1999 of the European Commission in the wake of a series of accusations of nepotism and mismanagement. The European Anti-Fraud Office (OLAF), first established in 1999, is currently being expanded through a major recruitment drive, although in a newspaper interview in early 2001 Franz-Hermann Brüner, its Director General, said that the limited independence of OLAF from the Commission was a constraint on its effectiveness.[18] The EU is also giving the fight against corruption greater prominence in external relations, through the Cotonou Agreement, for example, that governs relations with African, Caribbean and Pacific (ACP) countries.[19] The Agreement includes articles that specifically address the fight against corruption. These reflect a growing concern among EU governments that aid should work to strengthen governance in developing countries. New procurement rules have been introduced into EU aid, which include the exclusion from future EU-financed contracts of companies convicted on bribery charges.

Concern with corruption abroad is shared by the US government. The International Anti-Corruption and Good Governance Act, signed into US law by former president Bill Clinton in October 2000, introduced a new formal goal to US foreign development policy: 'the promotion of good governance through combating corruption and improving transparency and accountability'. Under the Act, anti-corruption programmes will be integrated as a component of US aid to developing countries.[20]

Public sector corruption continues to rear its head within the US, often in local administrations. In April 2001 the long-standing mayor of Providence, Rhode Island, was indicted on federal corruption charges as part of a major FBI investigation into Providence City Hall that had already resulted in a number of convictions.[21] In another investigation, the mayor of Camden, New Jersey, was convicted of fraud and soliciting bribes from figures in organised crime.[22] Meanwhile, a vast network of corruption has been exposed in the Los Angeles Police Department (LAPD). Although a high-profile trial of police officers ended in

Fighting corruption as a priority for international development

I welcome this first *Global Corruption Report*. To those already involved in the fight against corruption, I hope it provides fresh inspiration. Among those who are not yet engaged, I hope it promotes a conviction that action is necessary and feasible. Too often, corruption thrives because of a climate of despondency, because people believe nothing can be done. The experiences documented in these pages provide the evidence that strategies to tackle corruption can be implemented successfully.

Corruption casts a long shadow, but it is the poor of the world – the one in five of humanity who live in abject poverty – who pay the highest price. Poor people are most directly affected by petty corruption – the dishonest policeman, the official who will not provide a service without a 'tip'. But they also suffer the consequences of grand corruption, which diverts substantial resources away from the public good and into the pockets of the corrupt few.

Of course, corruption is not confined to the developing world and it is clear that businesses in developed countries often fuel corruption overseas. Developed countries have a responsibility to root out sources of corruption in their jurisdictions, and to be ready partners in assisting the tracking and reclaiming of funds looted from developing countries.

I do not have any illusions about the scale of the task in bearing down on corruption. But the prospects for progress have never been better. Poor people are demanding action. Governments are increasingly aware of the costs of corruption to trade and investment. Corrupt leaders are being exposed and chased from office. Many players are now engaged: international organisations, business, governments and civil society all have contributions to make.

Helping build the systems for effective management of public finances, law enforcement and democratic accountability is essential to enabling developing countries to crack down on corruption. Too often in the past, OECD governments were ready to blame governments for the fact that they lacked the capacity to do what was needed. The reality is that there are those who abuse positions of power in all political systems. In all our countries there has been a history of corruption. The difference between industrialised and developing countries is not moral commitment, but systems that constrain, catch and punish corrupt behaviour. Development agencies must be more committed to help put such systems in place and to enter into long-term partnerships to help build such capacity as a potential for successful development.

Transparency International was the first and loudest voice to challenge corruption in international development and trade and to demand action from governments. I applaud its achievement. Never has the challenge of corruption been so openly debated. Never have we better understood how to tackle it. We must all commit ourselves to action to curb this corrosive force for which the poor of the world pay the biggest price.

The Rt Hon Clare Short, MP
UK Secretary of State for International Development

acquittal in December 2000, the original investigations led to a series of reviews of previous arrests and prosecutions and to the appointment of an independent monitor to oversee the LAPD for a five-year period.[23]

Political donations and corruption

During 2000–01, many of the allegations of corruption in West Europe and North America centred on donations to political parties. France, Germany, the UK and the US were among the countries affected. In some cases the scandals dated back to the 1980s, but that in no way diminished their significance.

Efforts have been made in a number of countries to reform legislation so as to reduce the potential for corrupt political donations, but incidence of this problem is expected to rise, rather than fall.[24] In the TV age, where advertising is the key to campaigning, the cost of standing for election has been rising rapidly. There has been a fall in individual contributions to parties as a result of the declining role of the traditional activist. Parties seek more funding from taxes, but there will always be constraints on this source. So parties turn to rich donors and corporations, who often see their contributions as a means of securing political influence.

The Elf Aquitaine investigation was the most prominent case during 2000–01 of corruption linked to political funding. According to political scientist Dominique Moisi, political corruption worsened in France in the 1980s under Mitterrand, as a result of both decentralisation and the steeper funding required by the 'Americanisation of political campaigning'.[25] The Elf Aquitaine affair spread from France to Germany where it was alleged that millions of dollars were paid by Elf in 'commissions' relating to the privatisation of the Leuna refinery in eastern Germany in the early 1990s.[26]

Meanwhile, also in Germany, a series of party financing scandals has gripped the Christian Democratic party (CDU) in the last few years. A presidential inquiry into reform of Germany's party funding laws, the Rau Commission, was established in January 2000 in response. Most political parties submitted recommendations to the Commission, but TI-Germany described them as 'piecemeal and full of loopholes' and submitted its own set. As of May 2001, Chancellor Gerhard Schröder's Social Democratic party had yet to come forward with proposals of its own. Major reform is unlikely to occur before the 2002 federal elections.[27]

In Ireland, in January 2001, journalists watched parliamentarian Liam Lawlor light a bonfire in his back garden to burn allegedly confidential financial documents.[28] Lawlor had just spent a week in Mountjoy Prison for refusing to cooperate with the Flood Tribunal, which investigated the planning process relating to land in County Dublin and improper payments made to politicians. Lawlor was allegedly at the centre of a web of bribery involving politicians that stretched back 20 years. Meanwhile the Moriarty Tribunal, running since 1997, continued its investigation of illegal payments allegedly made to former prime minister Charles Haughey and former minister Michael Lowry.

In the UK, the Labour government suffered from repeated allegations that

Elf Aquitaine: grand corruption goes to court

The investigation into the activities of French oil company Elf Aquitaine had far-flung international ramifications in 2000–01. The year saw Elf's former chairman in court, along with former foreign minister Roland Dumas. Allegations relating to the company emerged from Angola and Germany, shedding more light on the role played by multinational corporations in perpetuating corruption abroad.

Political and oil industry officials were incriminated in illegally profiting from the company's public status and through its overseas subsidiaries; covering their tracks with banking secrecy; and using slush funds to achieve political ends.

The complex trial opened in Paris in January 2001 amid intense media attention. The accused included Dumas, his former mistress and Elf lobbyist Christine Deviers-Joncour, former Elf chairman Le Floch-Prigent and his close associate, Alfred Sirven. The first two were accused of taking bribes and, in the case of Dumas, misuse of public funds; the latter two with misuse of corporate funds. On 30 May, Dumas was sentenced to six months in prison and a fine of FFr1 million (US $130,000). The other defendants all received prison sentences and fines.

The court refused on technical grounds to include additional allegations about Elf's supposed intervention to secure the purchase by Taiwan of six French frigates.

The German Leuna refinery affair revealed further evidence of Elf's unscrupulous activities. In June 1991, the Treuhandanstalt – the body in charge of privatisation in former East Germany – announced its intention to privatise the network of Minol service stations and the refinery. The final agreement, signed in July 1992 between the Treuhandanstalt, Thyssen (an intermediary registered in Liechtenstein) and Elf's refinery management division, involved an investment of more than €2.59 billion (US $2.19 billion). But in a report of 14 September 2000, investigating

Swiss judge Paul Perraudin said that the deal was based on political rather than economic factors.

A third area of intrigue concerned Elf's African activities. The investigation showed that between 1990–97 more than €91.4 million (US $ 77.1 million) was transmitted to the Swiss accounts of the Elf Aquitaine group's 'Mr Africa'. The sums, entered into balance sheets under the rubric 'execution of Elf group commitments', appear to have been used as secret payments to presidents in francophone Africa and Angola.

The tangle of clandestine bank accounts that investigators had to sift through, and the plethora of secret funding protocols, meant that it took ten years for the Elf affair to come to trial. Judicial cooperation with Switzerland, the single most important destination of the illegal money, was crucial. After international requests for assistance, the judges identified several recipients of transfers from the Swiss accounts of Alfred Sirven. Since September 1997, Judge Perraudin has been responsible for an investigation into 'unfair management and money laundering' relating to capital distributed by Elf between 1989–93.

The quest for the truth about Elf's activities encountered many obstacles. Sirven avoided arrest for five years and was only placed on Interpol's 'wanted' list after 1999. Vital documents disappeared from the premises of the financial squad in charge of the investigation in April 1997, and computer memories were also 'visited'. Meanwhile, the investigating judges have still not been able to convince customs authorities to send them archives that contain the record of Elf commissions paid abroad between 1989–93.

As for Leuna, German prosecutors have been far from zealous. Law officers in Magdeburg, which has jurisdiction in the case, have still not launched an official investigation, and the German authorities waited until March 2001 before suing for damages.

Yves-Marie Doublet

political donations had resulted in improper influence despite its early promises of transparency. Legislation was passed in 2000 that introduced new restrictions on party funding and that required greater transparency from parties in declaring the source of their donations.[29]

There have been continuing attempts to reform the US campaign financing system, with a range of options advocated. Critics liken the current system to a legal 'money laundering' operation that exchanges cash for influence. Its defenders argue that limits on political donations violate free-speech rights and endanger political parties. According to academic Michael Johnston, while the influence of individual campaign donations is often 'too small to draw much attention', the volume of funds in the system may 'collectively add up to a corrupting influence upon American politics'.[30]

> Perceived political corruption has contributed to growing popular disillusionment with the established parties and with 'money-driven' political systems.

Of particular concern are the unlimited 'soft money' donations from corporations, unions and wealthy individuals to national parties that circumvent the spirit of campaign laws. The escalating scale of soft money donations has led to calls for change from many quarters. In March 2001, Senators McCain and Feingold proposed a bill to reform US laws on political donations. At the core of the McCain-Feingold bill is a ban on 'soft money' contributions. As the *Global Corruption Report 2001* went to print, the Senate had passed the bill, and the House was preparing to consider it.[31]

With political corruption exposed as never before, the issue of political donations has emerged as one of the most controversial areas in the democratic process. Unless major reforms in laws affecting political funding are undertaken, politics will remain vulnerable to accusations that undue influence can be wielded by wealthy individuals and corporations. Perceived political corruption has contributed to growing popular disillusionment with the established parties and with 'money-driven' political systems. Declining levels of voter turnout are eloquent testimony to this.

Outlawing bribery of foreign officials

In the past, the extent of bribery of foreign officials by companies based in West Europe and North America seeking to win contracts in other parts of the world was a matter of pure speculation. Recently that has begun to change, as court cases and surveys make clear that Western companies have long been a key source of corruption in developing countries.

The US Department of State wrote in a June 2000 report that it had a list of 'foreign firms on which credible information exists indicating that they have been engaging in activities that would be prohibited by the [OECD Anti-Bribery] Convention'.[32] In a typical year, 1998, the US intelligence community found that some 60 'major international contracts' valued at US $30 billion went to the biggest briber, according to then secretary of commerce William Daley. 'This was in just 12 months,' said Daley. 'Corruption, obviously, is big business.'[33]

Recently, a number of prominent court cases caught the public's attention. One allegation that emerged from the Elf Aquitaine case is that the company paid bribes to senior African politicians and officials over a 25-year period.[34] In Lesotho, the case of a government official charged with receiving bribes put the spotlight on the international construction companies alleged to have paid the bribes to win contracts in the multi-billion dollar dam project. Accusations were made against a dozen of the world's leading construction companies – from Canada, France, Germany, Italy, South Africa, Switzerland and the UK – though the companies denied paying the bribes.[35]

Since 1977, the Foreign Corrupt Practices Act (FCPA) has exposed US businesses to prosecution when they bribe foreign officials. Under the FCPA, the US Justice Department considers some 25–40 cases a year. Many of the largest US corporations have developed detailed FCPA compliance programmes that include staff training. However views differ as to the efficacy of the FCPA and the adequacy of resources available for investigations. In Transparency International's Bribe Payers' Index, which measures perceptions of the frequency with which bribes are paid by companies from the 19 leading exporting countries, the US appears in the middle of the ranking. And of the world's leading exporters, the US government is perceived to be the most likely to engage in 'unfair practices' to benefit its businesses.[36]

Since the OECD Anti-Bribery Convention came into force in 1999, most West European countries have made the bribery of foreign public officials a criminal offence, and the US too has had to adapt its legislation to come into line with the Convention. In part because of the Convention, most Western governments have now also eliminated the practice whereby companies were able to claim tax deductions on bribes paid abroad. Fifteen countries that signed the Anti-Bribery Convention previously allowed tax deductibility, but 13 of those have since revised their legislation.

But OECD members differ in the speed with which they have introduced corrective legislation and effective enforcement systems: it will be some time before the full effect of the Convention is felt.[37] Furthermore, the Convention contains a major loophole. It does not bar multinational companies from making contributions to foreign political party officials, and that may prove to be a key means to gain influence.

There is also pressure for change in the area of export credit insurance. These funds insure companies against some of the political risks of operating abroad – and are provided either by the state, or privately but with state support if losses are made. Hidden bribes or semi-legal commissions have traditionally been covered, with the illegal commission quotient sometimes reaching as high as 30 per cent. In response to a Transparency International initiative, OECD member states announced in Paris in December 2000 that they agreed to measures to deter bribery in this area. The measures called for export credit agencies in all OECD countries to obtain written statements from companies applying for coverage, that they had not and will not engage in bribery.

These legislative changes are having a perceptible impact. Western companies, increasingly conscious of their public image, have incorporated anti-bribery mission statements and compliance procedures into their company codes and regulations. But a dramatic change of corporate practices is unlikely to occur unless anti-bribery legislation is supported by determined investigation and vigorous prosecution.

Curbing money laundering

Last year saw notable developments in the crackdown on money laundering.[38] Although it is the war against drugs that propels this campaign, rather than corruption, money laundering is also essential to the bribery process. In almost all cases of international corruption, those bribed need to deposit the proceeds in offshore financial centres or in countries with relaxed banking regulations.

Offshore centres that act as money laundering conduits cannot work effectively without the cooperation of banks in major financial centres that are able to reinvest the cash. In February 2001, a report was published by the minority staff of a US Senate committee that highlighted a number of money laundering cases and accused major financial institutions of absorbing large sums through correspondent relationships with foreign banks without due diligence on the real owners of the cash.[39]

Investigations into the accounts of the family of former Nigerian president Sani Abacha by the Swiss Federal Banking Commission and the UK Financial Services Authority revealed that a large share of the money travelled through private accounts in British retail banks.[40] This confirmed a suspicion, heightened by the 1999 Bank of New York scandal, that the reporting of suspicious transactions is still poor in the City of London. In March 2001, the UK government published a Proceeds of Crime Bill that will broaden existing anti-money laundering legislation and establish an agency for the recovery of criminal assets.[41]

The most encouraging signs of change occurred in Switzerland, where the heads of the big Swiss banks have come under pressure to open their books if accounts are suspected of being connected to serious crime. The impetus for greater transparency came from the belief that large sums of money, deposited in accounts by Holocaust victims, were being withheld from their heirs by Swiss banks hiding behind secrecy laws. In 1995, the government overcame its longstanding reluctance and allowed these allegations to be investigated. Pressure on the banking system mounted over the money stolen by the late president Ferdinand Marcos of the Philippines. Though some funds were returned, campaigners say the bulk is still secreted in accounts in Switzerland or Liechtenstein.[42] The Swiss government extended the Holocaust precedent and now requires banks to act where there are clear moral and legal issues at stake. The decision in the case of Sani Abacha was encouraging. Crédit Suisse, the main bank involved, faces a probe from the authorities. But the Swiss have so far promised to return only about 10 per cent of this money.[43] Switzerland also froze US $80 million tied to Vladimiro Montesinos, former head of Peru's secret service, after investigators launched a probe into money laundering.[44]

> The OECD and the Financial Action Task Force have recently put strong pressure on the more notorious tax havens.

The OECD and the Financial Action Task Force have recently put strong pressure on the more notorious tax havens to overhaul their laws in order to make themselves more transparent and cooperative. Blacklists have put those centres with lax regulation in the spotlight, but pressure from other quarters may weaken this initiative. With the arrival of the Bush administration in the White House, there have been conflicting messages on the issue. In May 2001 the US Treasury Secretary Paul O'Neill indicated that he 'had cause to re-evaluate' US participation in the OECD working group that targets 'harmful tax practices', but Attorney General John Ashcroft seems to have taken a more supportive stand.[45]

There is also a growing realisation within the banking sector that self-policing must be seen to work if the big banks want to enhance their credibility and avoid tough new regulations. In October 2000, Transparency International and 11 of the world's largest commercial banks announced an agreement to establish a set of global anti-money laundering guidelines.[46] Known as the Wolfsberg Principles, they are designed to encourage banks to ensure that they have deeper knowledge of their private banking customers.

Conclusion

Most surveys of bribery in government suggest that corruption is relatively low in West Europe and North America, but the picture is far from uniform. There is a significant level of public sector corruption in many countries, often in local government, and sometimes in political party funding. But the form of corruption that appears everywhere in the region is usually exposed only in other parts of the world: the bribery of foreign public officials. Bribery by West European and North American companies of public officials in developing countries has long existed, but its extent is only now being recognised and documented. Legislative changes to combat the practice are spreading, but their impact will only be felt if they are backed by determined investigation and prosecution.

A spate of scandals related to the funding of political parties and politicians demonstrates only too well that where there is power and influence to be gained, there is also money to corrupt. As the cost of political campaigning rises, payments to political parties to influence political decision making are also on the rise. This is a dangerous trend that undermines democratic institutions.

Corrupt money, wherever it is from, needs to be laundered and it seeks out weak points in networks of financial control. A number of these weak points are in West Europe and North America, including some of the most important financial centres in the world, such as Zurich and the City of London. But pressure is growing to tighten controls, and also to return corrupt funds when they have been identified.

The capacity of the private sector to reform itself must be noted. In the fight against the bribery of foreign officials, there is a growing tendency of businesses to introduce and enforce codes of ethics. In the fight against money laundering, the Wolfsberg Principles are an important step. The key to future progress in fighting corruption may be the power of consumers to influence corporate behaviour.

1 See TI's 2001 Corruption Perceptions Index, on p. 232.
2 OECD, *No Longer Business as Usual: Fighting Bribery and Corruption* (Paris: OECD, 2000).
3 *Guardian Europe* (UK), 31 May 2001.
4 *The Guardian* (UK), 19 June 2001; BBC News, 18 June 2001.
5 *Financial Times* (UK), 29 March 2001; Reuters, 20 June 2001. Allegations against Chirac have not been taken to court because of the high degree of legal immunity enjoyed by the office of the presidency in France. However, in June 2001 a bill was passed in the National Assembly (the lower house) seeking to limit this immunity in future. Reuters, 20 June 2001.
6 *The Guardian* (UK), 21 April 2001.
7 CNN.com, 19 March 2001.
8 BBC News, 2 March 2001.
9 *The Guardian* (UK), 2 December 2001.
10 *El País* (Spain), 14 March 2001.
11 *La Repubblica* (Italy), 26 June 1999.
12 *Financial Times* (UK), 27 March 2001.
13 *The Independent* (UK), 30 April 2001.

14 The Act will not come into force for central government departments until April 2002.
15 In all, 68 firms and individuals were on the blacklist by May 2001. The complete list is available at <http://www.worldbank.org/html/opr/procure/debarr.html>.
16 Evaluation reports are at: <http://www.greco.coe.int>.
17 As of June 2001, the Criminal Law Convention on Corruption had been ratified by nine countries – of which only Cyprus and Denmark are in the West Europe region – and the Civil Law Convention by three. The conventions have been open for signature since 1999: <http://www.legal.coe.int/economiccrime>.
18 *Süddeutsche Zeitung* (Germany), 1 March 2001.
19 The Cotonou Agreement, signed in June 2000, replaces the Lomé Convention.
20 US Microenterprise Self Reliance and Good Governance Act of 2000.
21 *The Washington Post* (US), 4 April 2001.
22 *The Washington Post* (US), 22 December 2000.
23 Associated Press, 7 November 2000; *Philadelphia Inquirer* (US), 24 December 2000.
24 For more on efforts to address corruption in political party financing, see p. 186.
25 *Washington Post Foreign Service* (US), 25 March 2001.
26 *The Economist* (UK), 27 January 2000; BBC News, 24 January 2001.
27 TI-Germany: <http://www.transparency.de/html/09dokumente/dok0.html> and <http://www.transparency.de/html/09dokumente/vorschl_rau.html>.
28 *Irish Independent* (Ireland), 24 January 2001.
29 UK Political Parties, Elections and Referendums Act 2000.
30 Michael Johnston, 'International Corruption via Campaign Contributions,' paper presented at a TI workshop on corruption and political party funding, La Pietra, Italy, October 2000: <http://www.transparency.org/working_papers/country/us_paper.html>.
31 *Washington Post* (US), 26 June 2001.
32 US Department of State, Bureau of Economic and Business Affairs, 'Battling International Bribery 2000,' June 2000: <http://www.state.gov/www/issues/economic/bribery_index.html>.
33 NBC News, 21 July 2000.
34 Global Witness, press release, 17 February 2000.
35 *Business Report* (South Africa), 10 June 2001; *The Guardian* (UK), 19 June 2001. The companies alleged to be involved include: Acres International of Canada; Alstom, Dumez, Spie-Batignolles of France; Lahmeyer International of Germany; Impreglio of Italy; Group Five of South Africa; ABB of Switzerland; Kier International, Sterling International, Sir Alexander Gibb & Co. and Balfour Beatty of the UK.
36 For details of the Bribe Payers Index, see p. 237 in the data and research section.
37 For a report on the state of implementation of the Anti-Bribery Convention, see p. 197.
38 For more on the subject, see the report on money laundering, p. 204.
39 Minority Staff of the US Senate Permanent Subcommittee on Investigations, 'Report on Correspondent Banking: A Gateway to Money Laundering,' 5 February 2001.
40 BBC News, 9 March 2001.
41 *Financial Times* (UK), 6 March 2001.
42 See the 'Missing Marcos Billions' website: <http://www.marcosbillions.com>.
43 BBC News, 21 July 2000.
44 BBC News, 20 April 2001.
45 *The Washington Times* (US), 11 May 2001.
46 The participating banks are ABN AMRO Bank, Barclays Bank, Banco Santander Central Hispano, S.A., Chase Manhattan Private Bank, Citibank N.A., Crédit Suisse Group, Deutsche Bank AG, HSBC, J.P. Morgan, Société Générale, and UBS AG.

Central America,
the Caribbean and Mexico

Bahamas, Belize, Costa Rica, Cuba, Dominican Republic, El Salvador,
Guatemala, Haiti, Honduras, Jamaica, Mexico, Nicaragua, Panama,
Trinidad and Tobago, and other Caribbean island states

By Miren Gutiérrez

Introduction

After years of political and economic disruption, the region including Central America, the Caribbean and Mexico is engaged in efforts to consolidate its democratic transition. Public sector reforms are common in almost every country. Governments are inviting, or at least accepting, civil society participation in transparency and accountability initiatives. The region seems to be finally coming to grips with the fact that its long history of corruption hinders development.

After the notorious *piñatas*[1] of the 1980s and 1990s that accompanied the sale of public property, said Salvadoran analyst Alberto Arene, 'new winds of change are blowing in Central America with new privatisation and free market laws, a fresh criticism of lack of efficiency and independence, ... new projects by international organisations geared to strengthen and modernise [these countries], and some media prepared to investigate and inform about impunity'.[2]

A host of international, regional, national and sub-national actors are participating in the campaign against malfeasance in governance. But the panorama in the region is mixed. Overall, practical institutional and normative development is positive, but the results are modest.

Mexico is currently the region's shining star. President Vicente Fox, the first opposition leader to be elected in more than seven decades, called for a break from corruption as 'the favoured instrument of control'. In Central America, 2000–01 brought further natural disasters and, with them, challenges to the fight against corruption. Several financial centres in the region, particularly in the Caribbean, came under concerted international pressure to clean up their lax approach to money laundering, often linked to the narcotics trade.

Weak regard for the rule of law, unfair judicial systems, the lack of independent control institutions, poor access to information, and the politicisation of media ownership remain widespread. Civil society groups are making notable efforts to monitor public affairs, but there is concern at the impact corruption has on citizens' faith in the power of democracy.[3] Indeed, one major obstacle is that societies in the region tend to view corruption – almost fatalistically – as an intrinsic part of their lives.

News review

The most welcome news for the region was the election in July 2000 of former Coca Cola executive Vicente Fox, who defeated one of the oldest political organisations in the hemisphere, the Institutional Revolutionary Party, through pledges to modernise and revolutionise the way that Mexico operates. In view of the country's prominent role in the region, the Fox administration will have an impact far beyond its borders if it lives up to voters' expectations.

In February 2001, two months into the new administration, the government signed a National Pact on Transparency and Fighting Corruption, and the Secretariat of Audit and Administrative Development (SECODAM), the agency charged with fighting corruption, created a unit with special responsibility for involving civil society in its work. Similar watchdog units are being created to ensure transparency in federal agencies and monitor government spending. In a bid to tackle pervasive petty corruption, the government launched an operation to purge corrupt officers from the Customs Agency. In February 2001, Director José Guzman fired 45 of the agency's 47 supervisors around the country in what signalled the beginning of a top-to-bottom overhaul.[4]

El Salvador introduced an ethics code for civil servants in December 2000, through an agreement with USAID. 'El Salvador is including anti-corruption measures in its process of modernising the state,' said Gregorio Ernesto Zelayandia, Director of the Instituto Salvadoreño para la Democracia (Salvadoran Institute for Democracy), 'but there is still a lack of political will, especially in the administration of institutions such as the Comptroller's Office.'[5]

El Salvador's Attorney General Belisario Artiga was the driving force behind an attempted clean up of his office. He investigated public prosecutors under a special permit granted by Congress and discovered cases that ranged from simple incompetence to abuse and bribery. 'We have to determine which are unacceptable and which are tolerable,' he said, in order to 'purge' the institution.[6] As a result of Artiga's initiative, 60 of a total of 550 public prosecutors were indicted, 60 judges were investigated and a further 50 officials were dismissed from their posts. But Artiga had mixed results beyond the confines of his own office. Though he prosecuted several cases through the courts, he failed in 2000–01 to secure a single conviction. 'He created a lot of expectations,' said Luis González, a sociologist from the University of Central America, 'but has not lived up to them.'[7]

El Salvador's Finance Secretary Miguel Lacayo, was accused of granting zero import tariffs to sectors containing his own companies.[8] He was subsequently charged with tax evasion, conflict of interest and lack of ethics. Lacayo was to appear before the Economic Commission of the Legislative Assembly in January 2001 to explain how his companies had profited from his position. But the earthquakes that shook El Salvador in early 2001 led to his hearing being postponed and, to the dismay of the public, he was entirely exonerated. 'He was neither prosecuted nor investigated,' said Jaime López of *Probidad* magazine. 'The only thing that happened was that he was asked to testify before legislators about the irregularities reported in the press.'[9]

In Honduras, cases of corruption were endemic throughout the police and military during the year. High-ranking military officers are being investigated on a number of charges related to misappropriation of state resources.[10] Meanwhile Minister of Security Gautama Fonseca began to tackle the Preventative Police Force. Over a hundred agents and officers were dismissed under a decree issued by Congress for negligence, illegal enrichment and theft. All told, the government has fired more than 3,000 officers for alleged corruption since 1999.[11]

Guatemala is usually considered one of the most opaque countries in Central America, and reports of misuse of public funds and human rights violations are common. But activist organisations and opposition parties applauded the decision in March 2001 to strip former general Efraín Ríos Montt, a leader in the ruling party, of his parliamentary immunity, along with 23 of his colleagues. Ríos Montt was charged with tampering with the text of a law after it passed in Congress in 2000.[12] But his loss of immunity was welcomed less for alleged law-tampering, and more because allegations implicate Ríos Montt in human rights violations during Guatemala's 36-year civil war. The decision to lift his immunity could have led to Ríos Montt's prosecution, but a judge exonerated him in April 2001 and his immunity was restored.

The situation in Nicaragua also continued to be bleak. President Arnoldo Aleman faced a major crisis in confidence when chief tax collector Byron Jérez was accused of issuing US $500,000 worth of undocumented tax credits and illicitly using funds. The allegations, by Comptroller General Agustín Jarquín, were made public days before a donor meeting to discuss a US $6.6 billion aid and debt relief package. In July 2000, the Comptroller General himself resigned, claiming he was the victim of a plot to discredit him – a plot that began with his arrest on alleged fraud charges in November 1999. In January 2000, Comptroller General Jarquín accused State Treasurer Esteban Duquestrada and two former high-ranking civil servants of corruption. He also sanctioned the president of the country's telecommunications monopoly for contractual irregularities involving a

The plague of corruption: overcoming impunity and injustice

Corruption is a serious problem that affects all countries. Today, rather than decreasing, it seems to be increasing, especially in countries where the power of the military still prevails, as in Guatemala.

I maintain that the main source of corruption is the abusive exercise of power, be it economic, political or military. In countries such as mine, gaining office (whether by popular election or by appointment) is akin to political plunder: the position offers a blank cheque, and the guarantee of great personal enrichment. This is a rule tacitly accepted by all those who call themselves 'politicians'.

The history of corruption in Guatemala shows how the use of political and military power enabled the accumulation of huge fortunes under the protective wing of the state. And what has happened in Guatemala is repeated throughout the whole world. Endemic corruption is a complex system that pervades nearly all state institutions. Powerful groups, with strong political and economic interests, actively nurture it. Recently, there was a clear instance of the way such groups are able to make laws work in their favour. Despite all the evidence brought to light, and enormous efforts to achieve justice, the principal political actor, the President of Congress, General Efraín Ríos Montt, was declared innocent.

Corruption contributes to the weakening of the justice system. When acts of corruption that involve high-ranking officials of the government or the state are denounced, the institutions charged with prosecuting them either do not investigate or make an acquittal.

There is another factor that contributes to the growth of corruption: the weakness of institutions that exercise control over public administration. In Guatemala the office of the Comptroller General has demonstrated that it is deficient and ineffective in the face of the power of the corrupt. Further, civil society is not equipped to fight corruption and curtail the activities of public officials on its own, even in cases of clear and flagrant corruption.

Without strong watchdog institutions, impunity becomes the very foundation upon which systems of corruption are built. And if impunity is not demolished, all efforts to bring an end to corruption are in vain. Nothing is more encouraging to those who corrupt than to see themselves reflected in the same mirror of impunity that has been utilised by thousands of public officials, military commanders, businessmen and politicians all over the world.

Finally, and I intentionally make this my last remark, I am convinced that the absence of ethics is at the core of the corruption phenomenon. And although one can discuss what is understood by ethics, ethics must constitute more than a code – it must be a way of acting, behaving and doing. The features that define or should define ethics, as far as public administration is concerned, are responsibility, honesty and a good conscience in the use of state resources to serve the collective public interest.

There are two major priorities for all citizens and institutions committed to building the rule of law: promoting an effective democracy and enabling citizen participation in the control of public officials; and supporting stronger control mechanisms and an empowered judiciary. These are the measures with which impunity – the cancer that constitutes the basis and the sustenance of corruption – can be overcome.

Rigoberta Menchú Tum
Nobel Peace Prize Laureate and
UNESCO Goodwill Ambassador

company with connections to President Alemán's son.[13] In a separate case, Dutch assistance to Chinandega municipality was suspended in early 2001 after a case of misuse of public funds was reported.[14]

Costa Rica continued to live up to its reputation as one of the bright spots in an otherwise murky region, but corruption may well be on the rise by some accounts.[15] In January 2001, the Supreme Court imposed large fines on journalist Mauricio Herrera Ulloa and the daily *La Nación* for articles they published about a diplomat's financial dealings in Europe, based on stories in the German and Belgian press.[16] However, the World Press Freedom Committee reported that President Miguel Angel Rodríguez is now committed to reforming Costa Rica's colonial-era defamation law.[17]

Panama is indicative of both the progress and the problems in fighting corruption in the region. The government is introducing measures and new institutions to foster transparency, including an anti-corruption office opened in early 2000. While the office has limited powers and narrow goals, the Office of Social Security seems to be committed to creating an island of public service integrity. The social security director started by making the purchase of medical drugs more transparent.

But Panama and some of the Caribbean island states protested in June 2000 at their inclusion on the Financial Action Task Force's (FATF) 'blacklist' of countries that were failing to cooperate in the fight against money laundering. Although Panama came off the list in June 2001, the domestic anti-corruption authorities have not prosecuted – much less jailed – a single person for laundering illicit money.[18]

In early 2001, the Dominican Republic's anti-corruption department, which reports to the Office of the Comptroller, announced that it would investigate past activities of the Ministry of Public Works after allegations of major fraud and misuse of public funds in the construction of several large-scale projects. The investigation is expected to include other state institutions, including the department responsible for state property.[19]

The former government of Leonel Fernández is accused of diverting around US $90 million in funds earmarked for the employment generation scheme, Programa de Empleo Mínimo Eventual. The money may have been used to stave off civil unrest by making payments to citizens' leaders.[20] Fernández denied corruption but publicly acknowledged that he 'preferred paying to punching', according to Adriana del Conte, journalist at the *Listín Diario*.[21] Two civil servants are currently in prison and Fernández had to testify personally in court. However, according to another observer, 'the case is already falling into the thick soup of political influence and back-scratching practices'.[22]

In Haiti, Jean Léopold Dominique, the owner of independent Radio Haiti Inter and a prominent civil rights activist, was murdered in June 2000. This 'had a trickle-down effect on the media', according to Deborah Kirk of the International Centre for Journalists. 'Haiti is probably the most dangerous country in the region for journalists. People don't want to speak out. There is an atmosphere of corruption.'[23]

Limits to official anti-corruption measures

Many governments in the region have launched well-publicised anti-corruption programmes, though some are piecemeal. In Mexico, government efforts offer the possibility of real change in a society that has been mired in corruption for generations. In other countries, such as Panama and Honduras, the powers of the offices charged with investigating corruption are circumscribed by political or legal constraints. Where no national plans exist, it is left to civil society, the press and the international community to expose corruption and push for new strategies to be adopted.

Mexico launched the region's most comprehensive anti-corruption plan in 2001. On taking office, President Fox took an ethics pledge and disclosed his personal assets – an unprecedented gesture in Mexico. Other first-time developments were plans for the revenue administration service to audit political parties, and for the Universidad Nacional Autónoma de México to provide a budget accountability report to Congress. There are dissenting voices that argue that Fox has taken on too much too quickly, but the developments generally represent a welcome prioritisation of the fight against corruption.

However, the anti-corruption effort pre-dated Fox's arrival. The Senate approved the OECD Anti-Bribery Convention in April 1999. According to one corruption watcher, former president Ernesto Zedillo also had important achievements to his credit, particularly using technology to improve transparency.[24]

Other governments are trailing behind the Mexican example. José Vega, a lawyer specialising in property rights and commercial law, pointed out that Costa Rica, Guatemala and Panama all passed laws that prevent the smuggling of goods and that make it easier for companies to recover their merchandise quickly, or to instigate legal action against smugglers. But Vega complained about the lack of enthusiasm from public officials for enforcing these measures.[25]

An anti-corruption office was created in Panama in 2000, but there were serious limitations to its remit. The head of the office had to report to the Finance Minister, one of the public servants he was employed to monitor, while his office was totally under-resourced and lacked full autonomy. It remained rudderless for

Corruption and change in Mexico

'Change' was the mantra that brought down a 71-year-old one-party system in Mexico at the end of last year, a system that was visibly corrupt and lacking in accountability. And widespread change is expected from the new Vicente Fox administration that took office in December 2000. But the new anti-corruption 'tsar' Francisco Barrio said uprooting corruption in Mexico could take 30 years.

'Emphasis will be given to making things work better from here onwards,' he said. 'What we are interested in is lowering the level of corruption rather than getting people [from past administrations] into jail.'[1]

The Fox government's interest is in building the legal and institutional architecture needed to curtail future corruption. On 30 January 2001, the administration established the Comisión Intersecretarial para la Transparencia y el Combate a la Corrupción (Commission for Transparency and Combating Corruption). Headed by Barrio, the task-force includes representatives of the Ministry of the Interior, the army, the Attorney General's office and the National Security Agency. It has three specific areas of focus: prisons, the police force and customs. Other objectives are the prevention and punishment of corrupt practices and the promotion of citizens' participation in anti-corruption efforts.

Barrio's office has been most active in dismantling corrupt mechanisms in the customs service. He has also announced a proposal, due to be sent to Congress by September 2001, to overhaul the civil service, toughen punishments for corrupt public officers, and introduce greater government transparency. Though the details of the latter have yet to be elaborated, any legislation is likely to fall short of a genuine freedom of information act.

As part of the Commission's work, President Fox launched a marketing campaign inviting citizens to join the fight against corruption – though he has not persuaded all the members of his cabinet to come clean about their own personal finances. While Fox himself pushes for more transparency, others in government are more ambivalent.

The new administration's performance remains uneven in one crucial realm – the convergence of organised crime and public officialdom. Mexico's police and armed services are known to be contaminated by multimillion dollar bribes from the transnational narco-trafficking business.[2] Though the problem is not as pervasive in the military as it is in the police, it is widely considered to have attained the status of a national security threat. The Fox administration's preliminary decision was to strengthen the military presence in the office of the Attorney General. The results have been mixed. While one army general, allegedly protecting a drug ring, has been detained with his deputy, several important drug dealers have escaped prison.

Whatever the administration's limits, it has ushered in an era in which change seems possible after generations of one-party rule. Interestingly, however, it was legislators, not the executive, who laid the foundations of the anti-corruption drive in Mexico. Under the previous administration, Congress established the Entidad de Fiscalización Superior de la Federación (EFSF), or General Accounting Office, which was granted far-reaching powers to supervise the budgets and expenses of each of the three branches of government. The EFSF now conducts 'efficiency supervisions' to assess whether the funds disbursed by public officials have been spent on the best possible goods and services available. Previously, pay-offs were frequent and big business took turns to exploit large government contracts. The EFSF goes some way toward correcting these practices.

Remaining hurdles
The World Economic Forum and Harvard University *Global Competitiveness Report* stated in September 2000 that organised crime, police inefficiency, paybacks to judges or other civil servants, and a general lack of transparency were clear disincentives to

investing in Mexico.[3] Mexico's private sector also remains under-scrutinised when it comes to corruption, a problem that still needs to be addressed.

Another area of resistance to accountability is Mexico's political parties. 'Corruption in political parties could attack the fragile legitimacy of the democratic institutions,' warns Alonso Lujambio of the Instituto Federal Electoral (IFE), which supervises parties. The public money allocated to the electoral process is rarely accounted for. In half of the country's 32 states, legislation prevents the IFE from supervising party expenses in local and municipal elections, opening up vast potential for political corruption. The IFE is seeking to eliminate the secrecy provision that obscures party bank accounts, and to persuade the Ministry of Finance to supervise expenditure during elections. At present, procurement expenses related to elections can be scrutinised only five months after polling day.

Meanwhile, decentralisation of the budget has inadvertently opened a door to diminished transparency as the allocation of state expenditure becomes more discretional. The lack of appropriate mechanisms to ensure local government accountability is a growing problem. Fundar, a multidisciplinary NGO, proved in late 2000 that federal funds granted to local poverty reduction programmes in the states of Nuevo Léon and Yucatán in 1999 were not supervised. The supposed beneficiaries were unaware both of the funds' existence and the fact they were entitled to participate in determing how they should be spent.[4] Federalism complicates the fight against corruption. The official supervisory body, the Consejo Federal de la Judicatura (the Federal Judicial Council), for example, is incapable of real supervision since it is prohibited from requesting additional information on legal rulings at the state level.

At stake in the fight against corruption in Mexico is nothing less than the country's economic and political future, for there is a real danger that the public will get frustrated, either with unfulfilled promises, or with democracy itself.

**Rossana Fuentes Berain and
Jorge Carrasco Araizaga**

1   *El Universal* (Mexico), February 2001.
2   Jorge Fernández Meléndez, *Narcotráfico y Poder* (Mexico: Rayuela Editores, 1999). Also John Bailey and Roy Godson, *Crimen Organizado y Gobernabilidad Democrática* (Mexico: Grijalbo, 2000).
3   Harvard University and World Economic Forum, *Global Competitiveness Report 2000* (New York: Oxford University Press, September 2000).
4   Fundar y Allianza Civica, 'Análisis de Presupuestos Publicos y Generación de Propuestas Ciudadanas,' 2000.

months, prosecuting not a single official. In March 2001, prominent lawyer César Guevara was appointed anti-corruption 'tsar' and took over the reins of the anti-corruption fight in Panama. Meanwhile, efforts by TI-Panama and other activists to persuade President Mireya Moscoso to pass a new freedom of information act were unsuccessful.

Government efforts to stamp out corruption come to nothing in some countries. In Nicaragua last year, accountability and anti-corruption efforts collapsed. No serious attention was paid to allegations of corruption against revenue director Byron Jeréz although President Alemán admitted that Jeréz had misappropriated 6 million córdobas (US $500,000).[26] Possibly more damaging for institutional capacity was the dismantling of the Comptroller's Office and its division into a five-headed political organisation after Comptroller General Jarquín left office.[27]

A committee that includes four politicians from the two most powerful parties now runs the agency. Nicaragua has a progressive anti-corruption plan, but the government failed at every juncture to put it into action.

The Dominican Republic government established a Department for the Prevention of Corruption as long ago as July 1997 and has since set up auditing committees for individual government offices. Despite these institutional improvements, Javier Cabreja, who is Executive Director at the NGO Participación Ciudadana, said: 'Where we have advanced less is in the passing of a comprehensive law that would allow us to fight against corruption.'[28] Other anti-corruption measures are still in the pipeline: the creation of an anti-corruption investigation office; new rules for public bidding; legal requirements for officials to declare their assets before taking office; and the improvement of access to information. But activists such as Cabreja argue that the lack of an all-embracing anti-corruption law fundamentally weakens these institutions' powers to investigate freely and prosecute official wrongdoers.

Another problem occurs when officials turn a blind eye to a narcotics trade that looms large in the region. 'Central America has become the meat in the sandwich' – as a trans-shipment point, storehouse and money laundering centre – in the drug traffic from Colombia to the US, said Costa Rican parliamentarian Belisario Solano.[29] The Costa Rican Defence Ministry estimates that between 50 and 70 tonnes of cocaine travel through Costa Rica to the US every year.

While there is evidence that governments are moving forward on some issues, there is ample room for stronger measures, including the implementation of existing legislation, the creation and/or implementation of national plans, and the establishment of specific anti-corruption institutions.

One promising common feature of recent anti-corruption efforts in Costa Rica, Honduras and Nicaragua was the invitation to civil society groups to participate, usually by means of a civic commission. Composed of professionals and civil society representatives, these commissions can play a watchdog role by monitoring government activities. Though semi-statal and funded by the government, Probidad Administrativa in Honduras conducts investigations into illicit enrichment by public officials. Other methods of facilitating a citizen's right to denounce corruption are currently being explored.

International efforts: raising the bar?

Globalisation – in this case, the globalisation of information and the exposure it affords – has shown how local patterns are out of tune with the higher standards promoted internationally. The region is now in the process of making its practices conform to those advocated by international donors and financial institutions. In certain cases, reforms in reaction to international input have come quickly and with significant effect.

In June 1999, the OAS launched a project, co-sponsored by the IDB, designed to help strengthen anti-corruption laws in 12 Latin American nations. Technical support was provided to institutions in each participating country with the aim of helping them to implement the Inter-American Convention Against Corruption.[30] The most recent to ratify the OAS Convention was Guatemala. In Central America, the OAS project focused on broad, society-wide reforms.

Both the OAS and the IDB opened their doors to civil society participation. The positive impact of these changes was evident during preparations for the Third Summit of the Americas, held in Quebec City, Canada, in April 2001. In response to the OAS invitation for input, broad consultations were held involving close to 900 civil society organisations, including delegates from Barbados, Belize, the Dominican Republic, Grenada, Guatemala, Honduras, Jamaica, Mexico, and Trinidad and Tobago.[31]

> Globalisation has shown how local patterns of governance are out of tune with the higher standards promoted internationally.

The heads of state and government from Latin America and the Caribbean who met in Quebec agreed that 'corruption undermines core democratic values' and pledged 'to reinvigorate our fight against corruption'.[32] Delegates also supported the establishment of a follow-up mechanism to the Convention. The need for specific monitoring and evaluation was forcefully argued in the proposal made by civil society groups.

In 2000–01, international efforts to clamp down on tax havens forced several Caribbean nations to change their banking secrecy laws and close down fly-by-night financial institutions. The OECD's tax haven list, followed by the FATF 'blacklist', named countries suspected of making life easier for money launderers, prompting several to take swift action to tighten up banking legislation and supervisory regulations. Others protested vociferously, but took little action to stop the laundering wheels grinding. The Bahamas, Cayman Islands and Panama were taken off the list in 2001, while Dominica, St Kitts and Nevis, and St Vincent and the Grenadines still need to bring their standards into conformity with international criteria.[33]

The US Treasury and other institutions took note of the impact of the lists, issuing financial advisories against several islands. 'The change has been amazing,' said David Marchant, editor of the financial bulletin *Offshore Alert*. 'As soon as the so-called hit list came out, islands which generally move at less that one mile an hour fast-forwarded to 500 miles an hour with respect to passing laws to appease the international community.'[34] Within hours of the US Treasury issuing a financial advisory against St Vincent, the island closed down about half a dozen banks, he said.

Unfortunately, international pressure did little to improve anti-corruption efforts in Haiti, the hemisphere's poorest country. There are allegations that aid was diverted to corrupt ends in the September 2000 elections and that impropriety during the elections showed the limits of international influence.[35] According to Aryeh Neier, President of the NGO Open Society Institute: 'Most international donors are wary of Haiti, in part because of corruption.'[36]

Punished by one earthquake after another, El Salvador is a special case – high levels of international aid put the government's integrity to the test. 'The majority of Salvadorans are worried at the apparent lack of adequate strategies for bringing humanitarian assistance to the people, and the excessive red tape involved in the reconstruction process and distribution of water and food,' said a report by *Probidad*.[37]

OAS, IDB, OECD and FATF initiatives appear overall to have had a positive impact on the anti-corruption effort in the region, while donor involvement in Haiti and El Salvador proved more problematic. The journalists' organisation Periodistas Frente a la Corrupción (Journalists Confront Corruption) argued that international anti-corruption measures tended to fail in El Salvador, as elsewhere in the region, when they were instances of global prescriptions being imposed without consideration of specific local problems.[38] Ultimately, international efforts to fight corruption are necessary, but not sufficient. Throughout the region, however, a slow standardisation of norms against corruption is evolving. International actors must continue to be engaged and to find constructive points of entry into local initiatives.

Civil society's 'anti-corruption eruption'

Civil society played a vital role in the fight against corruption in Central America, the Caribbean and Mexico. Jim Wesberry, Director of the Americas' Accountability/Anti-Corruption (AAA) Project, said 'the corruption eruption, and the anti-corruption eruption' are both common trends sweeping the region. The former refers to the coming to light of a number of grave cases of corrupt practices; the latter is 'the spontaneous reaction of revulsion, rejection and repudiation of the fruits of corruption'.[39]

In the Dominican Republic, Honduras, Mexico and Nicaragua, civil society has exerted increasing pressure for the introduction of anti-corruption legislation.

The Mexican anti-corruption agency SECODAM relies on TI-Mexico to foster Transparency International's 'Integrity Pact' approach in the procurement process of several agencies. Also in Mexico, Alianza Civica leads a group of civil society organisations that signed an accord with the Secretariat to serve as watchdog and ensure full transparency in all the agency's activities. The NGO Fundar concentrates its efforts on public scrutiny of the nation's budget by determining, for example, how much of the money put aside for the fight against poverty is actually spent on poverty alleviation projects.

Manfredo Marroquín of the TI chapter in formation in Guatemala observes that four NGOs that promote democracy have begun working together to exert greater leverage over the government.[40] Supported by USAID, these NGOs have rather different agendas, but aim to produce a national strategy on how to achieve greater transparency. Their proposals for action also vary, but include a joint study of legal changes needed to improve the transparency of state bodies and to prevent corrupt practices.[41]

The role of USAID in promoting civil society cooperation in Guatemala is not unique. Experience in the region indicates that fighting corruption works most efficiently when several civil actors come together. Public awareness campaigns organised by civil society are bringing citizens' attention to the corrosive impact of government corruption, particularly in the delivery of services.

Focus on the press

The news media is a crucial part of civil society. Journalists help expose corruption where governments fail to, and their ability to write and publish freely and to access information is a strong indicator of transparency. In El Salvador, for instance, efforts are underway to secure greater media openness.

But the independence and activism of journalists is not strong everywhere in the region, due partly to a history of dictatorial government. When weak reporting is combined with monopoly media ownership, the results are devastating for transparency. 'A major unrecognised problem in Latin America is corruption in the journalism field, not only involving the working press but also ownership of the media,' said Jim Wesberry of AAA.[42]

In Costa Rica, Grupo La Nación owns *La Nación* and *Al Día*, which together monopolise 80 per cent of the local media market. In Honduras, magnates with close links to power or politicians themselves own the media: the powerful Canahuati family owns *La Prensa* and *El Heraldo*, *La Tribuna* belongs to President Carlos Flores, while businessman and former presidential candidate Jaime Rosenthal owns *Diario Tiempo*. Deborah Kirk of the International Centre for Journalists, who spent several months training journalists across the region,

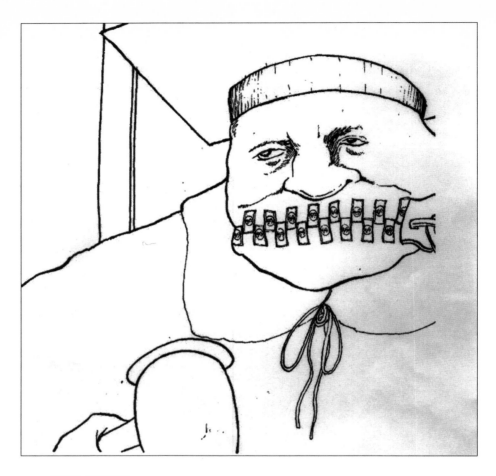

Bonil, Ecuador

found it 'absolutely shocking' that all four main newspapers in Honduras are linked to presidential candidates or have political ties.[43]

In the Dominican Republic, four of the six biggest newspapers belong to banks, and another financial institution is setting up a new paper. In addition: 'Five newspapers have their capital mingled, which is a very dangerous concentration for press freedom,' wrote *Estrategia & Negocios*. 'It is a risk for democracy, not only politically, but also in terms of a free market. In a country that lacks working institutions and where public influence is bought and sold, concentration within the media is highly counterproductive.'[44]

Judging by recent events at *La Prensa*, Panama's only fully independent newspaper, experts are right when they forecast rocky days ahead for local press freedom. Ricardo Alberto Arias, a former foreign affairs secretary in the administration of ex-president Ernesto Pérez Balladares, who has made clear his intention of running for president, took over as a chairman of *La Prensa's* board of directors in March 2001. Gustavo Gorriti, associate director of the paper and a highly respected investigative journalist known for his work exposing corruption during Pérez Balladares' term, was squeezed out of *La Prensa* shortly before the take-over.[45]

Just as discouraging was the news that when the government began a serious discussion about abolishing the country's 'gag laws', the Panama Journalists Union publicly supported their retention. These laws allow civil servants to imprison journalists without trial if they feel they have been 'disrespected': 70 journalists currently face criminal defamation charges under 'crimes against honour' laws.[46]

On a more positive note, El Salvador's Periodistas Frente a la Corrupción (PFC) and *Probidad* magazine are good examples of how reporters and anti-corruption activists can cooperate in exposing corruption. PFC was set up as a non-profit organisation in 2000, funded by the Centre for International Private Enterprise. Through its website, it facilitates more and better investigation and corruption reporting.[47]

Although the region's news media operates under difficult circumstances, its role in promoting transparency should not be underestimated. Journalists have contributed to the campaign against corruption in two distinct ways: by uncovering cases of corruption and abuses of power; and by forming organisations to lobby for transparency more effectively. But newspapers and the media in general are not always objective observers due to the massive concentration of ownership. To safeguard the role of the media as an advocate for transparency, independence must be guaranteed.

> Journalists have contributed to the campaign against corruption in two distinct ways: by uncovering cases of corruption and abuses of power; and by forming organisations to lobby for transparency.

Conclusion

Efforts to tackle corruption have strengthened across the region. National anti-corruption initiatives are now common, either as overarching plans or as piecemeal offerings, sometimes installed at the behest of international donors. In the era of globalisation, policy-makers acknowledge that corruption adds costs to doing business in the region and is a disincentive to investors and aid donors. The normative change that such a realisation entails is significant.

In Mexico, in particular, a real opportunity to improve transparency now exists. However, official anti-corruption efforts in other countries still remain low priority. The Dominican Republic seems inclined to meet civil society demands for reform half way, but Haiti's ongoing instability does not fare well for any serious initiative. Transparency initiatives in the English-speaking Caribbean are modest, primarily geared toward countering the threat of international sanctions for assisting in money laundering. On this front, however, there was progress in 2000–01.

International initiatives to promote an anti-corruption agenda have been instrumental in spurring change. In a region beset by regular humanitarian emergencies, donors are increasingly linking the delivery of post-disaster reconstruction and relief to concrete measures by governments to introduce transparency in the way funds and relief supplies are disbursed.

And, across the region, civil society is reacting as never before. People speak with increasing freedom about corruption cases and dishonest officials. They have also formed myriad organisations dedicated to pushing for greater transparency. The press, where it enjoys editorial independence, increasingly finds that rooting out corruption not only improves society, but also sells newspapers. It is now time for the business community to take a more active role.

In a paper released in May 1999, Ian Bannon of the World Bank concluded that most of the liberalisation reforms that the World Bank had proposed for the region's economies were complete or substantially advanced. 'Efforts to combat corruption therefore must necessarily focus on building stronger institutions to improve governance and increase transparency, and ensure the competitive functioning of markets.'[48] Programmes to reform and modernise institutions and procedures result in a reduction of bureaucracy and red tape, increasing transparency and decreasing opportunities for bribes and other corrupt practices. But without far-reaching changes in watchdog offices such as the attorney general and the comptroller, anyone seeking to take the fight against corruption to another level faces a Sisyphean task.

Despite the changes, bribery remains widespread across the region. Public administration is bureaucratic and inefficient, stimulating 'back-door' tactics. Access to political power continues to ensure access to economic privilege. But anti-corruption offices have sprung forth across the region, and are being pressured by activists to do more to fulfil their mandates, however limited. The progress of the past year is just a beginning.

1   A *piñata* is a common child's party toy in Latin America – usually an animal shape made of papier-maché and filled with sweets that children try to break open with a stick, while blindfolded. When it breaks, the treats fly out for all to grab.
2   Alberto Arene, 'Derrotemos la Corrupción en Centroamérica,' extracts from the Central America Anti-Corruption Forum, 6–7 April 2000.

3   *Washington Post* (US), 13 March 2000.
4   *San Jose Mercury News* (US), 2 February 2001.
5   Interview with author.
6   Interview with author.
7   Interview with author.
8   *La Prensa Gráfica* (El Salvador) and its investigative magazine *Enfoques* (El Salvador) published a series of articles on Lacayo's actions, 17–23 December 2000.
9   Interview with author.
10 *Sun Sentinel* (US), 19 February 2001.
11 *Miami Herald* (US), 26 March 2001.
12 *El País* (Spain), 8 March 2001.
13 *El Nuevo Diario* (Nicaragua), 19 April 2000.
14 *La Prensa* (Panama), 16 January 2001.
15 *Tico Times* (Costa Rica), 2 January 2001.
16 *La Nación* (Costa Rica), 24 May 2001.
17 World Press Freedom Committee, press release, 20 February 2001.
18 See Minority Staff of the US Senate Permanent Subcommittee on Investigations, 'Report on Correspondent Banking: A Gateway to Money Laundering,' 5 February 2001.
19 Dominican Republic News and Information Service, 9 April 2001.
20 *El Nuevo Herald* (US), 28 November 2000.
21 Interview with author.
22 Author's interview with Dominican journalist Ernesto Pascual.
23 Interview with author.
24 Interview with author.
25 Interview with author.
26 *La Prensa* (Panama), 18 January 2001.
27 Reuters, 3 May 2000.
28 Interview with author.
29 Interview with author.
30 This joint OAS-IDB project was called 'The State of Criminal Legislation vis à vis the Interamerican Convention Against Corruption': <http://www.summit-americas.org/corruption/corruption.htm>.
31 Fecha y Temas de las Consultas Nacionales, Citizen Participation for the Summit of the Americas: <http://www.sociedadcivil.org/eng/portada.pl.cgi>.
32 OAS, 'Declaration of Quebec City,' Third Summit of the Americas, Quebec City, Canada, 20–22 April 2001. Summit of the Americas Information Network: <http://www.summit-americas.org>.
33 Financial Action Task Force on Money Laundering, press release, 22 June 2001.
34 Interview with author.
35 International Human Rights Organisations joint statement on Haiti, 5 February 2001.
36 Interview with author.
37 *Probidad* (El Salvador), 13 February 2001.
38 Interview with author.
39 Interview with author.
40 Interview with author.
41 Acción Ciudadana, 'Draft Report on the National Integrity System in Guatemala,' 2001.
42 Interview with author.
43 Interview with author.
44 *Estrategia & Negocios* (Costa Rica), December 2000.
45 *El País* (Spain), 24 March 2001.
46 Committee to Protect Journalists, 16 May 2001.
47 Periodistas Frente a la Corrupción: <http://www.probidad.org/pfc>.
48 Ian Bannon, 'The Fight Against Corruption: A World Bank Perspective,' paper presented at the Central America Country Management Unit workshop, Stockholm, Sweden, 25 May 1999.

South America

Argentina, Bolivia, Brazil, Chile, Colombia, Ecuador, Guyana, Paraguay, Peru, Suriname, Uruguay, Venezuela

By Telma Luzzani[1]

Introduction

Corruption in South America is fuelled by inadequate laws, irreverence for the law even when it is adequate, and the impunity of those who are corrupt. In many countries in the region, public administration controls are weak and politicised, and the capacity of law enforcement and the judiciary are uneven. This translates into low credibility of institutions and the perception that 'anything goes'. According to the Colombian scholar Alvaro Camacho Guizado, Latin America has yet to end the double curse whereby institutional weakness serves as a cover or conduit for corruption while, at the same time, 'corruption contributes to the deterioration of the institutional, legal and ethical basis of the state'.[2]

The struggle against corruption in South America emerged with the end of the Cold War, when communism ceased to be the overarching political concern on the continent. Corruption did not necessarily worsen in the 1990s, Professor Juan Gabriel Tokatlian of the University of San Andrés in Buenos Aires pointed out,[3] but it certainly became more visible, as both democracy and corruption captured news headlines as never before.[4] Another crucial factor that has motivated the fight against corruption is the growing awareness that corruption perpetuates poverty. The Secretary General of the Organisation of American States (OAS) César Gaviria asserted that 'in those countries with increasing levels of poverty, corruption is certainly getting worse and running rampant'.[5]

New research has documented the costs of corruption. Government estimates placed the cost to Colombia at 1 per cent of its annual GDP, or around US $6,100 per head of population.[6] A study by economists in Brazil estimated the yearly losses due to corruption at US $6,000 per capita.[7]

With corruption now prominent on both policy and public agendas, expectations are high that improvements are on the way, though scepticism lingers. The state institutions established in South America to counter corruption have to overcome this scepticism. With greater resources, an active network of NGOs and a vigorous independent media, the fight against corruption showed signs of progress in 2000–01, though results varied from country to country. Prominent cases of corruption – and there were many – still result in public apathy and short-term political fixes, threatening the capacity to achieve lasting change.

News review

A number of cases of political corruption in 2000–01, reported widely in the media, dealt body blows to the governments of Peru and Argentina. In Peru, corruption toppled President Alberto Fujimori. Fujimori began a controversial third term in office after elections that were contested on the grounds of voting irregularities and fraud. Shortly after his victory, a video emerged showing Vladimiro Montesinos, head of the National Intelligence Agency, apparently offering a congressman a US $15,000 bribe to endorse Fujimori's re-election. Thousands of similar episodes of Montesinos allegedly bribing or coercing ministers, judges, police, military bosses and business leaders, were captured on tape, with some subsequently leaked to the media and broadcast to Peruvians.[8] Montesinos fled the country, but was captured in Venezuela and extradited in June 2001. Fujimori successfully sought asylum in Japan in November 2000.

Revelations of high level corruption also shattered the ruling coalition in Argentina. In July 2000, seven months into the new administration, bribes were allegedly offered to a number of senators to secure the passage of a highly unpopular reform of the country's labour law. The episode was played down by the judiciary, despite extensive attention in the media, but the government's popularity suffered badly in opinion polls.

The Argentinian judiciary set an important precedent in 2000–01 by placing former president Carlos Menem under house arrest in June 2001 on charges of illegal trade in weapons during his administration from 1989–99. According to the daily *Clarín*, some US $60 million of a total US $100 million dollars spent on 6,500 tonnes of arms went on bribing Argentinian and foreign officials.[9]

Brazil has experienced a new era of economic growth and stability since the start of President Fernando Henrique Cardoso's administration in 1995, but the government has made only hesitant efforts to fight corruption. In April 2001 the President announced the creation of a cabinet-level anti-corruption bureau, but it is limited in scope, activists say, due to political pressure.[10]

The Brazilian government started investigating Sudam, the agency responsible for development of the Amazon region, in March 2001. Though incomplete at the time of going to press, the investigation is reported to have discovered that around US $1 billion was diverted from state reserves to finance election campaigns and enrich high-ranking politicians – the new Senate President among them – over a period of 25 years.[11]

'I want to tell you that you are the only sensible man to have denounced the government's greedy zeal to privatise; to have discovered the cut-rate deals that were made and the forced bankruptcies. As a result, on behalf of the whole group, I say ... you're fired!'

Bonil, Ecuador

According to Karen Flores, chief coordinator for Bolivia's National Plan for Integrity (the country's anti-corruption bureau), 'judicial security is limited in Bolivia, the credibility of the political leadership is very low and the public administration is plagued with corruption'.[12] A powerful example of the challenges faced by Bolivia was the country's recent flooding, which left 150,000 people without shelter. In January 2001, the government raised several million dollars for the victims, but there was never full disclosure of how the funds were spent. There is suspicion that only a fraction actually benefited the homeless.[13]

In Colombia, the government faced a number of high-profile scandals with corruption implications. The case of TermoRío, still unresolved, concerned an allegedly corrupt arrangement between businessmen and the state-run electricity company. In another development, the Supreme Court charged Armando Pomárico, former president of the House of Representatives, with procurement irregularities during his term in office. Pomárico's parliamentary immunity was suspended, showing some welcome political will.[14] In April 2001, the government proposed the creation of a National Commission of Integrity, intended to foster social awareness of integrity-related issues.[15]

Venezuelans heard revelations of a major loss to corruption of public funds derived from oil revenues. In March 2001, President Hugo Chávez, who won office in December 1998 under a populist campaign banner of anti-corruption, also admitted that there had been irregularities in Plan Bolivar 2000, a US $113 million social welfare and poverty eradication programme managed by high-ranking military officers.[16] Fraud, largely committed through inflated invoices, consumed as much as 40 per cent of the Plan's expenditures, according to analysts. Another serious set of accusations involved the country's Fondo Unico Social.[17]

In Paraguay, corruption remains systemic. The Comptroller General investigated fraud in the Instituto de Previsión Social, the organisation responsible for the country's main pension fund, over a six-year period. Allegations against the agency included improper loans to companies, dubious payments to officials as bonuses and rewards, and unwarranted payments to contributors on retirement.[18] The Comptroller General also examined the National Electricity Authority following accusations of currency purchasing irregularities.[19]

Ecuador witnessed the disclosure of high levels of corruption in its public administration. Ninety-five per cent of reports approved by the Comptroller General showed signs of severe irregularities in the handling of public funds.[20]

Most analyses show Chile as having the lowest levels of corruption in South America. However, Comptroller General Arturo Aylwin pointed out in 2000 that there was corruption in Chile's municipal administration and state purchasing. One case involved the compensation of former officials at the end of the administration of former president Eduardo Frei. The Spanish daily *El Mundo* estimated the over-payments in the case at more than US $86 million.[21]

President Jorge Batlle of Uruguay sent a draft law to Congress last year that will criminalise money laundering with sentences of up to ten years.[22] An important feature of the law, which passed in March 2001, is that it also applies to Uruguayans living abroad.

Political corruption

Democracy in South America, still young in many countries, is often vulnerable and unstable. Corrupt practices at the heart of the democratic process – in party funding and election campaigning – are all too often compounded by a lack of transparency, the abuse of power and impunity. Political corruption in much of the continent results from the need of all politicians – from the lowest office-holder to the head of state – to secure the financial pipeline necessary to guarantee election.

Peru and Argentina saw the unravelling of complex networks of political corruption in 2000–01, reaching into the highest levels of power. In Ecuador, a corrupt network of money and political influence was exposed in a recent case of illegal campaign contributions that highlighted the ongoing conflict between the public and private spheres, and the need to enforce stricter controls on campaign and party funding.[23]

In Peru, disclosures of bribery in electoral politics led to the downfall of President Fujimori and his strongman, Vladimiro Montesinos. Montesinos was the chief architect of Fujimori's power, designing the threats, blackmail and bribery needed to keep his master in power. So strong was his influence that Montesinos was able to deliver the constitutional reform required for Fujimori to stand for a third, controversial term of office.

The interim government of Valentín Paniagua that followed Fujimori's downfall launched a tide of investigations that laid the groundwork for new institutional structures to prevent political corruption on such a scale ever recurring.[24] The reconstruction of the traditional parties and institutions, shattered by the hurricane of *fujimorismo*, is now underway and brings some hope of democratic renewal during the administration of Alejandro Toledo.

In Argentina, allegations of bribery in the Senate in 2000–01 revealed details about the illegal financing of politicians; an impressive list of officials who cashed a monthly salary without working; and evidence of how bribery is used to approve or speed up the passage of laws in Congress.[25] Bribe-takers included senators in the opposition party, as well as secretaries of state, advisors, and close personal friends of President Fernando De La Rúa. Roberto de Michele, Director of the Anti-Corruption Bureau, explained that 'the damage produced should not be assessed in terms of the quantity of bribes taken by officials, but, rather, by the motives that triggered the bribe and the means that facilitated them'.[26]

> Corrupt practices at the heart of the democratic process – in party funding and election campaigning – are all too often compounded by a lack of transparency.

The administration undoubtedly lost credibility following the revelations, but the political bodies reacted by trying to shield themselves from scrutiny. The fate of Vice-President Carlos Alvarez, who emerged from dissident Peronism in the 1990s and was the driving force behind the ruling coalition, is telling. As head of the Senate, Alvarez flooded the media with statements against bribery and corporate malpractice in the wake of the Senate bribery allegations. His message was clear: the country would never reverse its stagnation unless transparency was re-established in Congress. The party factions involved in the case rapidly isolated Alvarez, and he resigned in October 2000.[27]

In Ecuador, former banker Fernando Aspiazu, currently detained on corruption charges, was ordered by the Supreme Electoral Tribunal to pay a fine of

US $ 6.2 million for the illegal financing of former president Jamil Mahuad's election campaign. Aspiazu acknowledged that he had contributed US $ 3.1 million to Mahuad's campaign while he had business pending with the Ecuadorian state. The Tribunal also ordered Mahuad's campaign committee and his party, Democracia Popular, to pay back the same amount to the state.[28]

In a recent report on corruption, Argentina's Attorney General Rafael Bielsa stressed the links between 'the illegal appropriation of public funds and the illegal financing of political parties'. He argued that party finance is often linked to the access party members are able to secure to positions in the public administration or to business opportunities that they can exchange for favours. 'We cannot object to the discretional handling of funds by the parties,' he said, 'if we do not allocate them the necessary means.' Bielsa also strongly advocated a society-wide debate on the subject.[29]

Political corruption has numerous negative consequences. It undermines the legitimacy of democratic institutions and the justice system. And while legitimate debates about the extent of public funding and private donations to political parties continue, it is encouraging that the topic is gaining widespread attention across South America.

Corruption in the public sector

The theory that bribery makes public administration work more smoothly is, astonishingly, quite prevalent in South America. A case study in Colombia by Confecámaras, the country's Confederation of Chambers of Commerce, recently illustrated how the private sector accepts corruption as part of the process in public works bids and contracts. Other research shows, however, that public sector corruption results in higher costs, limits foreign investment, reduces overall investment and causes overspending on public infrastructure. 'It hinders trade, growth and economic development,' said César Gaviria of the OAS.[30]

Transparency and oversight are necessary to counter the multiple opportunities for corruption in public works projects, yet despite some recent initiatives, these elements are all too often lacking in South America.[31]

Although Paraguay's dictator Alfredo Stroessner was overthrown in 1989, a long tradition of corrupt administration is still alive and well in the country. Research carried out in conjunction with the country's anti-corruption plan, with assistance from the World Bank, identified that two main areas of corruption are linked to public administration: customs and public works.[32]

A World Bank report in April 2001 revealed gross mismanagement of a Paraguayan public roads project, part of the ongoing Programme for the Admin-

Brazil's new fiscal responsibility law

Congress passed a new Fiscal Responsibility Bill into law in May 2000, and so established strict budgetary limits for managers of all public offices and agencies at the three levels of Brazilian government – federal, state and municipal. The law also applies to the legislature, the judiciary and the prosecutors' offices.

Only New Zealand boasts a similar law, but it doesn't have the same scope as Brazil's. The law addresses areas of the administration that are regularly subject to mismanagement and corruption, particularly at a municipal government level. Under the new law, mayors will no longer be able to spend more than their projected revenues, as they have long been able to do.

The new law limits payroll expenditure, forbids the accumulation of new debt without the expectation of increased revenue, and establishes fiscal goals based on three-year budgets by which administrators must abide. Non-compliance results in penalties both to the administrative units – loss of rights to federal transfers, loss of federal guarantees for financial operations and other measures – and to the officials responsible.

If expenditures exceed the legal limit, the administrator must correct the problem within a given period. Excessive indebtedness must be reduced by at least 25 per cent within four months of being identified.

Every four months, senior administrators must publish detailed fiscal reports encompassing all offices and agencies under their responsibility on the internet. Simplified accounts must be published bi-monthly.

Restrictions are tougher in election years. For example, it is no longer legal for an administration to take on new debt or launch unbudgeted projects that have to be paid for after the election results are in. This tactic was a favourite of incumbent mayors seeking either to project a more dynamic campaigning image or simply to make things difficult for their successors.

From a managerial point of view, the new law forces administrators to enhance their control mechanisms in order to ensure better use is made of public money. Moreover, administrators found guilty of intentional mismanagement are held personally liable. The requirements of transparency, in the form of publication of detailed reports, provide for more effective monitoring both by responsible departments and also civil society organisations.

The nature of coalition politics in Brazil means that the government has consistently refused to sponsor a strategic anti-corruption programme, because a serious assault on corruption would jeopardise members of the current coalition. In most cases, the government only acts after facts have forced it to do so. The fiscal responsibility law, together with other initiatives aimed at strengthening internal financial controls, is thus part of a rather mixed signal from the Brazilian government regarding the fight against corruption.

Transparência Brasil (TI-Brazil)

istration of Natural Resources.[33] The report suggested that the Minister for Public Works and Communication altered contracts in order to increase project costs. As a result, the price of improving 445 kilometres of rural roads went from an original estimate of US $13 million to US $24 million.

Meanwhile in Venezuela, 700 ghost employees were found on the payroll of the Fund for Urban Development. With less than 40 per cent of the Fund's planned programme complete, some construction works have already collapsed. The head

Foul play in Brazilian football

Increased scrutiny of the underbelly of the world's most popular sport is bringing to light a host of shady dealings.

With weekly audiences in the hundreds of millions, football is a high-powered commercial activity whose financial dimensions have long remained opaque. This is beginning to change. Cases of corruption in the sport have recently been reported in France, Italy, Portugal and Spain, as well as a number of African countries.

The changing climate is also affecting Brazil, the world's football superpower. Four times world champion and the biggest exporter of players to all parts of the globe, Brazilian football is now in the limelight because of corruption and other financial irregularities.

During 2000–01, a number of Brazilian players were found to hold Portuguese passports, obtained under false pretences, which enabled them to circumvent EU quotas on the number of foreign players allowed on club rosters.

Age falsification is also a common phenomenon. It allows underage players to be sold to foreign clubs or 'older' players to qualify for tournaments that are subject to age limitations. At least 16 Brazilian players have been implicated since 1999. In one case, a player had used the documents of a dead person. In almost all recorded cases, false birth certificates had been obtained in the northern state of Maranhão, one of Brazil's poorest. The vice-president of the Maranhão football federation has since been charged with falsifying players' ages and the diversion of funds. Former national coach Wanderley Luxemburgo was convicted of the same crime. One high-profile case involved Luis Oliveira, who gained Belgian citizenship and played on the Belgian national team and was in fact four years older than his documents stated.

In mid-2000, Congress set up two special investigative commissions to examine the Brazilian Football Confederation (CBF). Particular attention was paid to its contract with sports marketing firm Traffic, which negotiates all CBF marketing contracts, including the US $160 million deal with Nike which allows the sports equipment giant to influence Brazil's international game schedule.

Nike's influence with the national team's management was so strong, some say, that it was able to insist that star player Ronaldo play in the 1998 World Cup Final even though he had suffered unexplained seizures just before the game. Ronaldo went on and Brazil lost 3–0 to France. Nike denies any such interference.

Although the commissions' findings did not go as far as had been anticipated, they did reveal the following:

- CBF funds to the tune of US $250,000 were used to finance political campaigns, including one candidate for governor in the state of Piauí, and one Worker's Party representative for the state of Rio de Janeiro.[1] Though not strictly illegal, the findings illustrated just how far into politics football finance can reach.
- Lack of transparency in club finances had opened up wide opportunities for fraud, allowing bureaucrats to get rich while clubs stayed poor.
- As some state football federations cannot survive without financial help, CBF provides it. But, in some such cases, these transfers disappeared.
- Dealings between marketing firms, intermediaries and clubs include illicit transfers of money to foreign accounts through tax havens. Even Brazilian football hero Pelé's marketing firm came under suspicion.

One result of the investigations has been increased pressure for a reform of laws governing the game, including the way clubs are managed. Two different proposals are now being discussed, one put forward by the special commissions and the other co-sponsored by the government.

Juca Kfouri

1 *Estado de S. Paulo* (Brazil), 12 April 2001.

of the Fund, Victor Cruz Weffer, who is close to President Chávez, publicly stated that he 'objected' to open bids and preferred the discretionary allocation of public works, in open contradiction to Venezuelan regulations.[34]

The major challenges to cleaning up public sector corruption are to counter the politicisation of tender awards, cronyism and a tradition of advancement based on favours rather than merit. South American officials – and their critics – are well aware that transparency and efficiency are enshrined in public law, but putting these principles to work is a major challenge.[35]

Illegal drug trade and money laundering

Money laundering has devastating social consequences. It threatens security because it provides the fuel for drug and arms dealers, terrorists and other criminals to operate and expand their criminal enterprises. Unchecked, money laundering erodes the integrity of financial institutions, and together with corruption and the narcotics trade, forms a tangled web of illegality in some South American countries.

The Presidential Programme Against Corruption in Colombia specifically addresses 'narco-corruption'.[36] Colombia, with a capacity to produce 580 tonnes of pure cocaine in 2000,[37] is particularly poisoned by the interplay of narcotics and violence, with an estimated one million people internally displaced as a result of battles for territorial control by rebel groups and paramilitary forces. 'The corruptive effect of this kind of profit is devastating, since it has penetrated to perverse levels in the judiciary and the political system,' the official report of the Presidential Programme concluded, adding that the rapid accumulation of wealth from illegal drugs 'has fostered codes and behaviours which promote corruption, fast money and the predominance of private welfare over general interest'.

A parliamentary commission led by Representative Moroni Torgan is investigating the scale of drug money laundering in Brazil, which has been estimated to total US $25 billion a year. According to a report presented to Congress, corruption leads to the laundering of a further US $25 billion a year, or roughly 10 per cent of the total amount laundered globally. The commission suggested that one third of this sum goes to government officials and the private sector, including banks, to oil the laundering chain.[38]

Illegal drugs are not the only source of funds washing through the banking sector. The large-scale bribes paid to politicians from the proceeds of crime (including narcotics sales) also need laundering services. According to Argentinian politician Elisa Carrió: 'Until now, money laundering was understood as the cleansing of illegal revenues, mostly from the drug trade. But what do we call it when the money laundered stems from corruption and tax evasion?' Carrió led an aggressive public campaign in Argentina against money laundering, pointing to officials from Menem's administration.[39] It remains difficult to bring money laundering of the proceeds of crime, including corruption, to justice. But the problem may be gaining more attention from governments across the region, in conjunction with the fight against corruption.[40]

Anti-corruption efforts

The fight against corruption continues at varying speeds in South America. Without doubt, there is growing official concern, but success depends on three key requirements: strong political will and the capacity to execute reform; a high level of awareness and social involvement; and follow-up by the authorities of steps taken by officials and private corporations.

The government is actively campaigning against corruption in Colombia. As referred to above, President Andrés Pastrana established a Presidential Programme Against Corruption, headed by Vice-President Gustavo Bell. Both private sector and civil society groups (including the TI chapter Transparencia por Colombia) were invited to contribute. As a result, President Pastrana's plan included a component that called on all public sector departments to use TI-Colombia's innovative 'Integrity Pacts' to make public contracting and investment transparent, equitable and sustainable.[41]

The government also created a Unit for Investigation and Sanctions and, within it, a group to tackle federal cases. Since it started work in August 1999, the Unit has investigated hundreds of cases: the most striking involved irregular contracts that led to the arrest of 30 senators.[42] The government

> Success depends on three key requirements: strong political will, a high level of awareness and social involvement, and follow-up by the authorities.

also set up an Elite Division Against Corruption, headed by the Attorney General, to conduct public hearings on allegations of corruption in the civil service.[43] Other initiatives included educational programmes on ethical values for officials; advertising campaigns; and mechanisms to certify compliance with transparency regulations in public contracts. In 2000–01, the UN chose Colombia as a pilot country for the creation of a National System of Integrity as part of its Global Programme Against Corruption.[44] Despite these measures, the government acknowledged the limited capacity of its control mechanisms.

In Argentina, Fernando De La Rúa established the Bureau Against Corruption after winning the presidency on a transparency ticket. The Bureau's first task was to investigate the previous administration, which had been plagued by allegations of financial impropriety and crime. By December 2000, over 1,000 allegations of corruption were reported to the Bureau, but only one official was arrested. The Bureau Against Corruption promoted cooperation with Argentina's neighbours, via organisations such as the OAS, Mercosur and the Free Trade Area of the Americas. It also pushed for public disclosure of assets by officials and a system to determine conflicts of interest.

The interim president of Peru, Valentín Paniagua, embarked on a crusade against corruption. His successor, Alejandro Toledo, 'publicly backed up the efforts of the National Anti-Corruption Initiative (INA), which has made a diagnosis of the problem, established an agenda of tasks and an outline to carry them out', said Santiago Pedraglio, responsible for technical affairs at the INA.[45] The interim government sought to institutionalise the process of fighting corruption to the greatest extent possible, even before Toledo took office.

Peru's Special Prosecutor against corruption, José Ugaz, is heading the investigation of Montesinos, Fujimori and others, under special legislation that allows for reduced sentences in exchange for 'honest confession'. The programme has had considerable success: 137 investigations into 532 individuals are underway and US $153 million worth of suspect money has been frozen in foreign accounts. A number of senior military officers, businessmen and public officials are currently under arrest.

The Peruvian Ombudsman is working on a law designed to improve citizens' access to information. 'Although the law is not new,' said Roberto Pereira of the Ombudsman's office, 'there were no clear mechanisms of application and there was a general tendency to withhold information.'[46]

In 1999, Paraguayan President González Macchi signed an agreement with the World Bank that established the National Office Against Corruption, a joint civil society and government office. The Inter-American Development Bank (IDB) announced in May 2001 that it would provide Paraguay US $605,000 in assistance for its anti-corruption plan. In spite of the agreements, there were few results and the public remains sceptical.[47] According to a report by José Antonio Bergues of TI-Paraguay, corruption over the last decade has, ironically, become 'more democratic', and now pervades the entire spectrum of power. During the Stroessner era, corruption was more of an elite monopoly.

In Venezuela, the government's failure to get to grips with corruption has proven to be a bitter irony for President Chávez, who won office on his anti-graft messages. Expert Alfredo Ramos Jiménez pointed out that 'Venezuelans voice their criticisms to the press. In practice, the media has become a substitute for justice. We certainly have freedom of expression, but this does not translate politi-

Cleaning up corruption on Peru's roads

Jorge Lopez is a 54-year-old retired policeman. To support his family of four, he drives a taxi around the streets of Lima, Peru's capital. Like most taxi drivers, he usually settles the price with a customer before letting them in to his car – typically this is less than US $2 for a ten-mile ride, depending on the time of day.

His encounters with traffic policemen are frequent, and have made his frugal earnings even smaller. 'One time, at three o'clock in the morning, I was ordered to pull over by a patrol car with the siren on. I got out of the car, as I knew I had gone through a red light. Two officers came up and started implying that I was drunk or on drugs. "You know how much this will cost you if we report the incident?" they said. I knew they were asking for money. Only when I showed them my police ID did they back down.'

The force's dark side

Unfortunately, this is one of many similar stories in this city of eight million people. 'It's basically a pyramidal problem,' explained Manuel Piqueras, senior counsellor on urban security in the mayor's office. 'When the boss participates in corruption, or even just allows it, it spreads throughout the force.'

Not surprisingly, Lima is a scared city and has been so for some time. In a study conducted by survey company Apoyo, fear rather than reassurance was the feeling evoked in the public at the sight of a police officer. Not once in ten years has the percentage of people that trust the force outnumbered those who don't. And since August 2000 those who distrust the police have led by a 19-point margin.[1]

'I was in the force for 23 years,' said Jorge Lopez, 'and saw police corruption at every level. I know cab drivers who always carry a 20 or 50 soles bill in case they are pulled over. It's that widespread.'

In an attempt to address the situation, former president Alberto Fujimori announced in September 1998 that most traffic regulation issues would be controlled by women officers, a measure initially proposed by Lima's Mayor Alberto Andrade. The decision was based on the popular perception that women are stricter, fairer and less corruptible. Many doubted it would work, but the results have been promising.

During the trial period, Colonel Eduardo Perez Rocha, head of Lima's traffic department, said: 'In a recent poll, 70 per cent answered that female officers are effective and that traffic control has improved.' This was particularly impressive considering that, only two years earlier, the police effectiveness approval rating was as low as 13.6 per cent.[2]

The head of traffic control for Lima's south-side, Commanding Officer Roberto Lujan Jara, agreed the programme has been a success. 'In the past, we used to handle 40 to 50 tickets per day. Now the number has increased by 200 per cent.' More traffic tickets doesn't necessarily mean drivers are now caught more often, but it does support the theory that a bribe is no longer the standard way out of police trouble. Lujan said: 'Women stand by their reputation of incorruptibility, and that is the key to this plan.'

Despite these developments, corruption on the streets of Lima is far from disappearing. Lopez acknowledged some degree of change, but said much more needs to be done. 'Women have definitely made a difference, but that hasn't stopped corruption in other areas of police work. And no one is tackling that.'

Carolina De Andrea
Gabriel Chávez-Tafur

1 Apoyo, Opinión y Mercado S.A., August 2000.
2 Instituto Nacional de Estadística e Informática, February 1998.

cally into action.'[48] Jiménez said that the concentration of power in the executive hindered anti-corruption efforts.

The role of international organisations and NGOs in the fight

The fight against corruption does not stand or fall on the actions of governments. International and regional organisations, in addition to local NGOs, play a decisive role in tackling the corruption pandemic. The World Bank, IDB and bilateral donors have been important and at times controversial forces behind reform in the region.

The WBI aimed to design local anti-corruption reforms based on comprehensive surveys of individual countries that have to date been conducted in Bolivia, Colombia, Ecuador, Paraguay and Peru.[49] These diagnostics form the foundation of action plans, which are then promoted among representatives from civil society, political parties, professional associations and others. But non-governmental participation in the design of action plans has been uneven so far, and their implementation incomplete.

The IDB announced in March 2001 that, in order to stiffen commitment to anti-corruption measures, future loan arrangements would extend to civil service reform, providing support to structures that promote sound administration and improved accounting and auditing standards. Programmes against money laundering that utilise the internet are also eligible for support under its new criteria. 'The access to electronic information on administrative activities, such as public purchasing, public finance and the legislative process, can effectively reduce the chances of corruption,' said IDB head Enrique Iglesias.[50]

The main OAS involvement has been in winning government ratification of the Inter-American Convention Against Corruption (CICC). The general consensus is that the Convention provides a valuable framework, but that implementation will be a challenge.[51] The General Assembly of the OAS, meeting in Costa Rica in June 2001, agreed to create a follow-up mechanism to the CICC, one that focuses on monitoring the implementation of the Convention in each country.[52] Twenty-two of the 34 OAS countries have so far ratified.

Meanwhile a wide array of civil society organisations involved in the fight against corruption has begun to establish networks at the national and international levels. The proliferation of NGOs is a sign of South American societies' growing impatience with institutionalised graft.[53] The private sector is beginning to see the potential advantage to its own interests of underwriting activities that target more transparent business practices, business ethics and corporate social responsibility.[54]

In Colombia and Venezuela, networks of *veedurías* (citizens' watchdog groups) share information on good practices. In Colombia, *veedurías* oversee public procurement, election campaigns and various aspects of administration. In Peru, a number of civil society organisations came together in the wake of Fujimori to coordinate efforts to build a national alliance against corruption, known as Proética (Pro-Ethics).[55] Proética collaborated with the Justice Ministry in setting up a major national anti-corruption conference, held in June 2001. It focused on diagnosing the nature of Peruvian corruption and formulating a plan that could be adopted by the Toledo government.

The consolidation of TI chapters in a network known as TI-LAC (Transparency International in Latin America and the Caribbean) increased their individual capacity to monitor public sector practices and engage the private sector in anti-corruption activities, particularly in Argentina, Brazil, Colombia, Ecuador and Paraguay. Another initiative, the Red Interamericana para la Democracia (Inter-American Network for Democracy), links up a range of civil society organisations. One of its activities, the Visible Congress project, provides background information on election candidates in Argentina, Colombia and Ecuador. In Ecuador, the Visible Congress project is tied to another project monitoring political programmes. And the Lima Agreement, established in late 2000, created a network of NGOs interested in monitoring elections and political financing.[56]

Civil society campaigning against corruption is supported by a vibrant press, although the concentration of media ownership tends to shield high office holders from scrutiny, and some countries retain laws on the statute book that empower officials accused of wrongdoing to go to court and sue journalists for 'disrespect of office' or 'dishonour' as soon as their propriety is questioned. In Colombia, the profession of journalist is a high-risk venture. A dozen journalists were murdered in 2000 for attempting to expose the links between drug traffickers and the corruption of provincial or municipal politicians. Despite years of persecution under Fujimori's administration, however, the Peruvian media has proved highly resilient. And new networks of investigative journalists have taken root in Paraguay, supported by international freedom of expression organisations.

Civil society and the independent media still face a number of daunting challenges. For NGOs, these include the maintenance of funding, achieving institutional development, and strengthening their own governance structures. Activists admit that they need to reach out to other sectors of society, in order to use their advocacy to help the disadvantaged, who are corruption's main victims.

Conclusion

The main sources of corruption in South America are non-transparent structures of government with long traditions of exemption from the law; the escalating need to finance political careers; and the enmeshed problems of the illegal drug trade and money laundering.

Corruption in party funding is a major challenge, given the spiralling costs of election campaigns, and this corruption trickles down through the system to pervade all levels of official service provision. Official anti-corruption programmes provide little palliative, although recent developments in Peru have created a popular momentum that should ensure that the most flagrant abuses of the Fujimori administration are not repeated. Increasingly, international and regional organisations are providing a source of innovation, with civil society actors playing an important role, as weather vanes for local perceptions of corruption and as advocates of anti-corruption initiatives.

'Studies show that there is a demand to curb corruption in Latin America,' said Argentinian lawyer and Poder Ciudadano activist Luis Moreno Ocampo. 'The process of democratisation clearly resulted in improvement since what used to remain under wraps is now in the open. Steps are being taken ... to ensure that regulations are more than just ink on paper.'[57]

South American analysts agree that further awareness of the corruption problem needs to be promoted among citizens. Increasing the availability of information can lead to more effective evaluation of anti-corruption efforts. Mechanisms are needed that optimise civil society involvement: civic participation councils; accelerated systems for denouncing corruption; and the appointment of anti-corruption ombudsmen. 'Besides a consistent state policy to fight corruption,' argued Juan Tokatlian of the University of San Andrés, 'it also takes strong civic involvement, to control, curb and warn against corruption before it takes place. Without active citizenship, corruption will be even more widespread.'[58]

1   The author would like to thank Matilde Sanchez and Héctor Pavón for their assistance in the preparation of this report.
2   Alvaro Camacho Guizado, 'Democracia, Exclusión Social y la Construcción de lo Público en Colombia,' *Nueva Sociedad*, 171, January–February 2001.
3   Juan Gabriel Tokatlian, *Globalización, Narcotráfico y Violencia: Siete Ensayos sobre Colombia* (Buenos Aires: Grupo Editorial Norma, 2000).
4   *Probidad* (El Salvador), May–June 2001.
5   César Gaviria, opening message at a workshop on the application of the OAS Anti-Corruption Convention to Chilean law, Santiago, Chile, October 2000.
6   Office of the President of Colombia, 'Presidential Programme Against Corruption,' May 1999.
7   Marcos Fernandes Gonçalves da Silva, Fernando Garcia and Andrea Camara Bandeira, 'How Does Corruption Hurt Growth? Evidence about the Effects of Corruption on Factor Productivity and Per Capita Income,' supplied by TI-Brazil.
8   *The Economist* (UK), 8 February 2001.
9   *Clarín* (Argentina), 5 April 2001.

10   *O Globo* (Brazil), 10 April 2001.

11   *O Globo, Folha de S. Paulo, O Estado de S. Paulo* and *Correio Braziliense* (all Brazil),
     9–15 April 2001.

12   *Probidad* (El Salvador), March–April 2001.

13   *La Razón* (Bolivia), 10 February 2001.

14   *El Tiempo* (Colombia), 26–27 March 2001.

15   Office of the President of Colombia, press release, 3 April 2001.

16   The plan aimed to subsidise popular market fairs, improve school buildings and housing,
     and address other social needs.

17   *Tal Cual* (Venezuela), 14 April 2001.

18   *Ultima Hora* (Paraguay), February 2001.

19   *ABC* (Paraguay), April 2001.

20   Ecuador's Commission for the Civic Control of Corruption, 'Report for the Period
     March 2000–February 2001,' March 2001.

21   *El Mundo* (Spain), 4 October 2000.

22   *La Nación* (Argentina), 8 April 2001.

23   For more on corruption in political party financing, see the report on p. 186.

24   Until the interim government's reforms, Peru did not have a law regulating political party
     financing, although such a law was foreseen in the country's 1993 constitution. Instituto Apoyo,
     'Country Report on Peru's National Integrity System,' draft report, May 2001.

25   The case was widely reported in the second half of 2000 in *Clarín, La Nación*, and *Página*
     (all Argentina).

26   *Probidad*, (El Salvador), May–June 2001.

27   *Clarín* (Argentina), 6 October 2000.

28   *El Comercio* (Ecuador), 9 March 2001.

29   *Probidad* (El Salvador), May–June 2001.

30   Gaviria (2000).

31   Devices such as Integrity Pacts (Colombia), internet bidding (Chile) and reference pricing,
     which allows price comparison of goods and services by different providers (Argentina),
     are now being put in place in some countries of the region.

32   *ResponDabilidad*, No. 29, January 2001.

33   *ABC* (Paraguay), 3 April 2001.

34   *Tal Cual* (Venezuela), 19 March 2001.

35   *Probidad* (El Salvador), May–June 2001.

36   Office of the President of Colombia, 'Presidential Programme Against Corruption,' May 1999.

37   US Department of State: <http://www.usembassy.state.gov/posts/col/wwwhncpe.html>.

38   *Clarín* (Argentina), 30 November 2000.

39   Interview with author.

40   For more on the issue of money laundering and corruption, see the report on p. 204.

41   'Change toward the Building of Peace,' Colombian National Development Plan for the
     1998–2000 period, Article 4, Chapter 2. An Integrity Pact is a contract in which bidders in a
     given public procurement process explicitly promise each other and the respective government
     not to offer bribes or pay bribes, and to subject themselves to specific fines if they fail to live
     up to these promises. Thus far, TI-Colombia has successfully implemented 13 Integrity Pacts
     at different administrative levels involving various contracting processes. For more on the
     Integrity Pacts (in Spanish), see <http://www.transparenciacolombia.org.co>.

42   Office of the President of Colombia, press release, 23 March 2001.

43   Office of the President of Colombia, press release, 30 March 2001. The division includes
     officials specialised in facilitating in corruption cases. As of March 2001, it had already heard
     from more than 20,000 citizens and received 3,422 accusations.

44   Office of the President of Colombia, press release, 30 March 2001; *El Tiempo* (Colombia),
     3 April 2001.

45   Interview with author.

46   Interview with author.

47   *ResponDabilidad*, No. 29, January 2001.

48   Interview with author. Jimenez also pointed out that allegations of corruption in the
     Venezuelan government have seldom been scrutinised by prosecutors, as prosecutors
     themselves are appointed by the National Assembly and at present side with President Chávez.

49   The surveys target public officials, households and enterprises, and measure the prevalence and
     costs of corruption, <http://www.oas.org/juridico/english/sigs/b-58.html>.

50 IDB, 'Successful Strategies for Combating Corruption,' Seminar on Transparency
    and Development, 19 May 2000.
51 The OAS fight against corruption emerged in 1992. At the Summit of the Americas in Miami
    in 1994 a multilateral effort was agreed that resulted in the adoption of the Inter-American
    Convention Against Corruption, signed in Caracas in March 1996.
52 Transparency International, 'TI Chapters in the Americas Endorse the OAS Follow-up
    Mechanism to the Inter-American Convention Against Corruption,' press release, Costa Rica,
    5 June 2001.
53 A recent survey carried out by Latinobarómetro showed the growing concern of Latin
    Americans about corruption. In 2000, 82 per cent of Latin Americans said that corruption
    'had increased significantly', compared to 70 per cent in 1997. See p. 312.
54 In Brazil, such activities have been undertaken by Instituto Ethos and in Chile by Acción
    Empresarial and the Chilean-American Chamber of Commerce.
55 Proética consists of the Asociación Civil Transparencia (Civil Transparency Association),
    Instituto Prensa y Sociedad (Institute for Press and Society), Asociación de Exportadores
    (Exporters Association) and the Comisión Andina de Juristas (Andean Commission of Jurists).
56 Civil society organisations involved include Poder Ciudadano (Argentina), Transparencia (Peru)
    and Momento de la Gente (Venezuela).
57 Interview by Héctor Pavón for the author.
58 Tokatlian (2000).

Global issues

Corruption in party financing: the case for global standards

By Keith Ewing

Introduction

Preventing corruption in the funding of political parties is crucial to the quality of democracy. Crude electoral bribery and political malpractice, the 'capture' of the political process, whether by commercial or criminal interests, and the absence of independent institutions all mar the democratic process.

A particular concern in contemporary politics is the rising costs of elections and campaigns, a factor that is now partly responsible for corruption in party financing. A related concern is the large donations that are given to finance campaigns, sometimes in brazen disregard of the law.

The nature and scale of the problem[1]

Although the rules and traditions governing party politics vary the world over, basic patterns of illegal party funding and campaigning clearly emerge. These include setting up 'front' organisations, through which funds can be channelled in excess of legal limitations,[2] or smuggling hidden 'slush' funds into party coffers. In some instances, funding operates through legal loopholes, and is thus not hidden or in any way criminal, as is the case with 'soft money' in US political campaign financing. But there are critics of the latter nonetheless.

Transparency laws related to party funding were fatally evaded across the globe during 2000–01. In Germany, Chancellor Kohl was forced to resign as honorary chairman of the Christian Democrat Union (CDU) following revelations of illegal donations to his party during his chancellorship. In Southeast Asia, the rising costs of elections were cited as being partly responsible for the different forms of corruption that were exposed in Indonesia, the Philippines and Thailand. In Ecuador, large, illicit donations were discovered to have been made to the campaign of the former president, leading to the arrest of a prominent banker.[3]

Even countries that claim to have tough regulatory bodies and independent courts do not escape censure – as Germany's recent history testifies. Paradoxically the 'independence' or 'relative autonomy' of courts can present another set of problems for those wishing to clean up politics. Many party funding problems in the US are a direct result of the 1976 decision of the Supreme Court to strike down spending limits introduced after Watergate – limits that were established to eliminate electoral corruption by reducing campaign costs. The Court invoked the First Amendment (which guarantees freedom of speech) and delivered the opinion that money is speech. It ruled that it was unconstitutional to reduce the spending of wealthy candidates to enhance the relative voice of the less wealthy.

Global standards: the seed is sown

What can be done? Many countries have identified campaign financing and the funding of political parties as serious problems and have taken steps to deal with them.[4] These include bans or limits on private political contributions; state subsidies for parties and/or candidates; controls over political expenditures; and rules securing transparency of contributions and expenditures. Such measures are applied in varying combinations in different political systems. But the global nature of this problem raises questions about whether there is at least a global response that might be contemplated, if not yet a global solution.

International initiatives

Recent initiatives by the OECD confirm the possibility of international standards. The OECD Anti-Bribery Convention provides that countries that sign it shall take measures to ensure that it is a criminal offence to bribe a foreign public official. A foreign public official is defined as any person holding legislative, administrative or judicial office, but this does not include the officials of foreign political parties. This last omission needs to be addressed in order to close an important loophole in the Convention.[5]

Meanwhile, if an international convention prohibiting bribery of foreign government officials is possible, why not a convention prohibiting corporate donations to foreign political parties? This is a question that demands broader analysis and discussion.

Also significant at an international level are the revised OECD Guidelines on Multinational Enterprises, which were adopted by 29 member states (as well as non-members Argentina, Brazil, Chile, and now-member Slovakia) in June 2000. Although these voluntary guidelines will be difficult to enforce, they nevertheless make encouraging reading. They are wide-ranging and far-reaching, dealing with issues such as the environment and workers' rights. They also exhort multinationals to 'abstain from any improper involvement in local political activities'. A section on 'combating bribery' clearly states that enterprises should 'not make illegal contributions to candidates for public office or to political parties or

Soft money and what it buys

Common Cause believes that the integrity of US democracy is gravely compromised by the arrangements that currently govern the financing of campaigns for federal office. The corrupting feature is 'soft money'. This is money that private interests donate to political parties, evading legal restrictions on contributions.

The 1999–2000 election cycle, which saw presidential candidates George W. Bush and Al Gore fight to the last inch of victory, was fuelled by US $463 million of soft money, about evenly split between the two parties. This represents more than 90 per cent more money than either party had raised during the previous presidential election cycle. The bulk of this money (over US $360 million) was given by corporate interests.[1]

Since 1907, corporations have been prohibited from donating to federal office candidates, and labour unions have been subject to the same rule since 1947. But in recent years, the two major parties have come to depend more and more heavily on television advertising – while television broadcasters continue to refuse to give candidates free or even reduced-rate time for their campaign messages.

Both Republicans and Democrats now pretend that television advertising fulfils legal requirements, provided that it avoids certain prohibited expressions such as 'vote for', or 'vote against'. As an election cycle approaches, the parties and their candidates frantically solicit soft money contributions that both donors and recipients know are intended to pay for campaign advertising. Meanwhile, efforts to raise support at the grassroots level have declined.

When in 1978 the Federal Election Commission (FEC) ruled that unlimited and unregulated contributions could be made to national political parties for grassroots campaign efforts for state and local candidates, they opened up a huge loophole. Although parties did not begin taking full advantage of

it until the mid-1990s, by the 1996 presidential election, the loophole had completely swallowed up the law's prohibition of corporate and union money. The parties did not use this unlimited money for local, party building efforts, but to influence federal elections, eroding the efficacy of laws enacted in the wake of the Watergate scandal, which limited individuals' contributions to US $1,000 per candidate per election.

The implications are serious. According to a survey of US business executives conducted by the think-tank Committee for Economic Development, some of the contributors who volunteer donations actually acknowledge that they do so in hopes of special treatment in legislative or regulatory matters. The result is that federal campaigns have come to resemble auctions, in which candidates and parties sell what they disingenuously call 'access'.

Common Cause, founded in 1970, began pursuing the campaign finance issue during the scandals that erupted in the Nixon administration, and as a civil society actor has had a major impact on the subsequent drive for reform. Since 1988, its commitment to the issue has intensified. Some 80 volunteers help mobilise the 200,000 Common Cause grassroots members, who lobby elected officials and maintain pressure for reform. In Washington, Common Cause lobbies both incumbents and challengers, documents the accelerating sale of 'access', and feeds the results to both national and local news media.

Common Cause has worked on reform legislation with both the Senate and the House of Representatives since these were first mooted in 1997. In April 2001, a Senate bill passed after grassroots pressure helped Senator John McCain frighten opponents into allowing a fair vote. By that time the movement had won new allies, some of them from unexpected quarters, as public revulsion at the soft money scandal grew.

Diversity is now a striking feature of the reform coalition. It has come to embrace not only those whose material and political interests are damaged by soft money, but also people and corporations whose selfish interests would be served by continuing to play the game. Many Fortune 500 corporations have stopped making soft money contributions out of frustration with what one former CEO, Ed Kangas of Deloitte Touche Tohmatsu, flatly called 'extortion'. Successful investor Warren Buffett and other individuals have publicly called for reform, saying that if money cannot be eliminated from US politics, tough legislation will at least 'minimise the amount that arrives via the sewer system'.[2]

Recognition of prevailing corruption is also seeping into the parties themselves. 'The political parties have become nothing more than money machines,' lamented Paul Kirk, former head of the Democratic National Com-mittee, in 2000. And William Brock, former chair of the Republican National Committee, argued that 'parties were stronger and closer to their roots before the advent of this [soft money] loophole'.[3]

In mid-2001, reform legislation is still being considered in the US House of Representatives. Even if it is not enacted into law by the time the current House session ends, the growing size and breadth of the reform movement gives reason to expect eventual success.

Common Cause

1 Figures from Common Cause:
  <http://www.commoncause.org>.
2 *The Buffalo News* (US), 25 March 2001.
3 *The Hill* (US), 29 April 1997.

to other political organisations. Contributions should fully comply with public disclosure requirements and should be reported to senior management.'[6]

Regional initiatives

Initiatives of a different kind have been taken at regional level, with the Council of Europe and EU taking the idea of international standards even further. The Council of Europe has established a Working Group on the Funding of Political Parties and a study was undertaken by the Political Affairs Committee of the Parliamentary Assembly. The report of the latter was given in the Assembly's Spring Meeting in Istanbul in May 2001. It focused on the need for transparency in party funding, the need to regulate the source and size of donations, the role of the state in the funding of political parties and the need to control campaign costs in an era of expensive media. It seems possible that a recommendation will be made for a standard-setting legal text based on the report.

The Council of Europe is not alone in being poised to intervene with an international standard. The EU took powers at Nice in 1999 to introduce Community-wide legislation to govern political parties at the European level, in particular rules regarding party funding. This will inevitably lead to some form of regulation by the Community, though any such initiative will clearly have limitations, and measures developed as a result will be confined to the operation of the EU itself. At the same time, it is not certain whether any legislation on 'funding' would extend to the related issue of 'spending', which seems crucial if the law is to have impact.

In 1998, Organisation of American States (OAS) member-state governments proposed 'to promote cooperation and consider measures to prevent organised crime and drug traffickers from making financial contributions to electoral campaigns'.[7] Other regional political organisations, such as the Southern African Development Community (SADC), have adopted standards relating to fighting corruption, but have not yet addressed the issue of corruption in party financing. But given the prevalence of the problem, it is now time the issue was addressed in other forums as well.

The challenges

The idea of global standards in an era of globalisation, establishing a benchmark by which all might be assessed and judged, is an attractive possibility. But is it far-fetched? There are serious problems to overcome. The first is that democratic systems are different. Is it possible to have common standards that could apply equally to developed and developing countries, to democratic and non-democratic regimes, and to presidential and parliamentary systems of government? Does it make a difference that some countries are federal and that others are unitary states? And what about differing electoral systems?

A second problem is that constitutional structures are different. Constitutions provide a framework of restraint within which party funding law may be developed and applied. Not all countries are as permissive as others, with similar rights being applied in different ways in different countries.

Related to this framework for rights, one reform strategy may be to fund political parties in part by the state, while another may be to reduce the levels of permitted campaign expenditure, thereby dousing the demand for money. The former approach has run into difficulties in Germany, while the latter has encountered serious problems in the US and Canada. In Australia, restrictions on political advertising as a way of reducing costs were ruled unconstitutional.

In less developed democracies, weaker bureaucratic, judicial or constitutional arrangements further complicate the issue. Parties in Russia, for instance, play a restricted role because of vast presidential power. The Russian party funding model is based on tax exemptions for political donations, among other subsidies. While there are rules to ensure fair party financing processes, these have tended not to be enforced.[8]

Apart from such systemic variations, there is a third problem for consideration. To be universally acceptable, any international standards would have to take into account the different models for political parties themselves. The typical character of a political party is one of an association of individuals bound together voluntarily in a common cause. But not all parties conform to this type: across the globe a range of differing organisational characteristics are found.

The content of global standards

Notwithstanding the scale of the challenge, something is beginning to stir. The threat to democratic government and the fear that public confidence in democracy is being undermined by lax political funding regimes are generating concern not only within nations but also between nations. The problem of political funding is a global one, and there is a case for universal standards that establish a framework of principle to which all can be encouraged to subscribe and apply, and by which all can be judged.

How might such a framework be constructed? Most agree that the starting point is transparency. There is a need above all for a regulatory standard that requires political parties and candidates for political office to account for their funds. This includes a requirement in particular to account for the size and source

Polyp, UK

Changing incentives in Argentinian politics

Come election time, Argentina was once a perfect place for candidates and political parties with self-interest in mind. The particular combination of legal, political and institutional factors in the country created both incentives and opportunities for the illegal financing of electoral campaigns.

In political and institutional terms, Argentina has high levels of corruption, low levels of accountability, weak rule of law and low respect for institutions. Current campaign finance law imposes no limits on donations, no limits on campaign expenditure and no limits on campaign duration. With regard to the control of private funds, Article 41 of the Political Parties Law enables donors to require candidates to withhold donors' names for at least three years.

The informal economy also represents a serious problem in Argentina. According to a recent study, annual income tax evasion could amount to as much as US $1.8 billion, an evasion rate of between 45–50 per cent. Meanwhile, annual VAT evasion could be US $9.1 billion, an evasion rate of 35 per cent.[1]

This feature of economic life in Argentina indicates the existence of a large and uncontrolled flow of illegal funds, some of which may turn into financing not reported on the parties' balance sheets.

How is it possible, in this context, to monitor political parties' election fund raising?

Poder Ciudadano's model

Poder Ciudadano, Argentina's TI chapter, has developed a model that seeks to change political parties' incentives from below. Politicians are first encouraged to sign a 'transparency agreement' (TA). As part of this agreement, they pledge to inform Poder Ciudadano on a monthly basis of their expenditures, and to allow the NGO to review their campaign budgets. For comparison, Poder Ciudadano also compiles its own data on campaign financing and spending, in collaboration with an outside private sector company. Complete monitoring should include all party expenditure, but, given limited resources in terms of money and time, this is generally not feasible. Poder Ciudadano's research focuses instead on monitoring expenditure in media advertising – on the assumption that spending in this one vital campaign area can be taken as indicative of parties' funding and expenditure patterns as a whole.

In short, the Poder Ciudadano model produces highly relevant, reliable and easily understood data on the expenditures incurred by parties and candidates during elections. By widely publicising this information in the media, and putting it at the disposal of all citizens, the model set forth in Argentina is a tool that encourages collective action and generates pressure from civil society by correcting deliberate information asymmetries.

With this pressure, it has now become more costly for politicians not to sign the TA than to sign it. Once the TA is signed, it is similarly costly for the parties not to honour its terms.

Poder Ciudadano has been monitoring campaign expenditures since the 1997 elections, including the 1999 presidential elections and the 2000 municipal elections for Buenos Aires. This experience has been very encouraging. For example, while it was possible to access only very limited information on candidates' campaign expenditure during the 1996 elections, during the 1999 presidential elections all three main presidential candidates (Domingo Cavallo, Fernando De la Rúa and Eduardo Duhalde) and their respective parties committed themselves to cooperating with Poder Ciudadano to fulfil the demands for disclosure of expenditures. This unprecedented experience marked a turning point in government-civil society relations in Argentina.

In the May 2000 elections for the legislature and mayor of the city of Buenos Aires, this success was repeated. All candidates agreed to the monitoring and signed a TA. The monitoring results were highly publicised and resulted in extended controversy in the media.

The monitoring of campaign expenditures has also begun in Peru where the NGO Asociación Civil Transparencia applied the model in the first round of the 2001 presidential elections.[2]

As the Argentinian case shows, increased public debate and pressure from civil society can change politicians' incentives and actions. The high level of public debate on the topic has led to an increased involvement of civil society in politics generally. The model is a powerful tool for empowering citizens and increasing transparency in campaign expenditure. Now the challenge in Argentina, and elsewhere, is to extend this commitment to transparency and integrity to party funding and politics more generally. By combining greater public information with collective action, the rules of the political game can and must be changed for the better.

Poder Ciudadano (TI-Argentina)

1 Fundación de Investigaciones Económicas Lati-noamericanas (FIEL), *La Economía Oculta en Argentina* (Buenos Aires: FIEL, 2000).
2 Poder Ciudadano has trained other NGOs across Latin America to use this model of monitoring party spending. For a discussion of such NGO networks, see p. 180.

of contributions above a prescribed *de minimis* limit. People in any political system are entitled to know who is funding their parties and candidates, in order to be fully informed of the interests they are likely to serve.

Options for reducing costs

The greatest need is for measures that control spending. This strategy has been grievously underestimated and overlooked thus far. Until steps are taken to control the demand for money, it will be impossible to regulate its corrupt use. Of course this will be difficult, since neither the independently wealthy nor the corrupt will like having their influence restrained or their current role diminished. But it remains the case that high spending is the engine of corruption, and large contributions its fuel. Unless spending is kept under control in an era of escalating media costs, attempts to reform corrupt party-funding systems will ultimately be futile.

Containing the costs of elections can be justified on a number of grounds. It is not simply a way of controlling the demand for dirty money, soft money or any other money; it is a way of responding to fundamental democratic principles. Politics should be conducted on the basis of the quality of a message, not its volume. The spoils of office should not go to those with the ability to shout loudest. These aphorisms reflect the first principle of democratic self-government, which is the principle of political equality: those representing major sections of opinion within a community should not be excluded from office because of the wealth of their opponents.

There are in fact several cost-reducing options available. The first would be to require a limit to be imposed on the amount of money that candidates and parties can spend on a campaign. This would have to be set low enough to be meaningful, but high enough to allow candidates and parties to be heard and to prevent the election being dominated by the institutional press and its proprietors.

The second option, for states where freedom of expression is an obstacle, would be to outflank it by creating a regime of public funding of elections as a whole, or in part (say for broadcasting costs). The underwriting of costs by the state in this way has the double advantage of further reducing the demand for money by parties themselves.

Options for addressing the problem of donations

When addressing the challenge of financial contributions to a political party, one first has to grapple with the question of who should be permitted to donate. Arguably, a general rule could be that contributions from foreign individuals or corporations should not be permitted. Political parties should represent the interests of local people and not foreign companies. An exception might be made for donations from permitted foreign sources (such as political foundations). Such provision needs to be made with extreme caution, in order to ensure that it does not become a laundry for foreign money.

But it is more difficult to say who within a particular jurisdiction should be permitted to donate, and how much. A requirement that only individuals may donate could lead to a critical funding crisis in some parties and could seriously affect party structure and organisation in others. A limit on the amount that individuals or others may donate could have similar consequences. This means that it would be necessary to meet the shortfall by one of a number of methods of public funding (such as tax relief for political donations or annual block grants). It is, however, not clear that it would be prudent in a transnational instrument to seek to compel governments to fund political parties in this way.

All of which is to suggest that the problem of the source and size of contributions could again best be addressed in a transnational standard by a menu of options from which each state could select to accommodate best their own domestic circumstances. Option one would be to require a restriction on the size of donations (no big contributions) and the source (natural persons only). The *quid pro quo* would be an obligation to ensure that parties had enough funding from public sources, if necessary, to enable them to meet their needs. Option two would be to accept the legitimacy of funding from legal persons, but to impose a requirement that companies and trade unions could donate only with the authority of their shareholders and members, who ought to be consulted on a regular basis. But it may be difficult to resist the case for a limit on the size of contributions.

Setting and enforcing global standards

Who should set these international standards and how could they be enforced? It is not enough that this matter should be left to specialist bodies. Political corruption is a subject ripe for the UN, which has a responsibility to develop standards that in turn can be a source of inspiration for regional bodies such as the EU, the Asia Pacific Economic Cooperation (APEC) forum, the Organisation of African Unity (OAU) and the OAS. These standards could be sufficiently flexible – while remaining meaningful – to accommodate the rich variety of different political systems.

The UN is already doing important work on corruption in related political fields.[9] But there is a sense that more could be done to promote better standards relating to the funding of political parties. These include programmes of support to promote and consolidate new or restored democracies. The Global Compact is a missed opportunity to address the issue of political corruption.[10]

The case for a transnational standard for the funding of political parties is a strong one, based on a number of principles of universal application. These principles need to be sufficiently flexible to be relevant to all democracies. And, in addition to strategies based on transparency, controlling costs and regulating the source and size of contributions, there is also a need to address the question of enforcement. Without an independent regulatory body with strong powers and a proper budget to monitor standards backed by tough sanctions, the utility of standards becomes dubious. In many countries of the world there is no tradition of an independent judiciary, and in others there are regimes in which the law enforcement agencies are part of the problem of corruption, rather than its solution. How realistic is it to look for genuinely independent electoral commissions in these regimes?

It is at this point that we confront the reality that the funding of political parties is part of a wider problem, not only about electoral politics, but about the nature of civil society and its institutions on the one hand; and about constitutional government on the other. Control of spending and standard setting in party funding is one vital aspect of a multi-dimensional effort in the fight against corruption. Global standards would play a crucial role. Such standards would ultimately have to be enforceable and effective at the national level – but the possibility of international pressure to enforce them ought not to be ruled out.

1 Research for this section contributed by Kevin Casas-Zamora.
2 In 1999, the One Israel Party of then premier Ehud Barak allegedly evaded spending limits in his campaign by using monies raised by supposedly independent non-profit organisations. Michael Pinto-Duschinsky, *Handbook on Funding of Parties and Election Campaigns* (Stockholm: IDEA, forthcoming 2001), overview available at <http://www.idea.int./publications/funding_parties/funding_overview.pdf>.

3   Both the banker and the former president's party were required to pay back the funds in this case. *La Hora* (Ecuador), 8 March 2001.

4   Recent examples include the UK's comprehensive Political Parties, Elections and Referendums Act of 2000; the Rau Commission in Germany, established in 2000 in response to the CDU party donation scandal to examine existing party funding methods; and the Federation Parliament in Bosnia, which passed a new party funding law in July 2000.

5   For more on the OECD Anti-Bribery Convention see the following report.

6   Available at: <http://www.oecd.org/daf/investment/guidelines/>.

7   OAS, Summit of the American Information network: <http://www.summit-americas.org/corruption/corruption.htm>.

8   Daniel Smilov, 'Structural Corruption of Party Funding Models,' contribution to the Joint Conference on Corruption, Budapest 1999, <http://www.coc.ceu.hu/smilov.html>.

9   UN work on corruption is undertaken by UN DESA, UNICRI and UNDP PACT.

10 Kofi Anan's 1999 'Global Compact'challenges world business leaders to change corporate practices and support public policies in line with a number of principles that relate to human rights, labour and environment, but not explicitly to corruption in party funding: <http://www.unglobalcompact.org>.

Implementing the Anti-Bribery Convention: an update from the OECD

By Enery Quinones

Introduction

In 1997, 34 of the world's largest exporting countries agreed to ban corruption in international business transactions by adopting common rules to punish companies or individuals that engage in bribery. Bribery of domestic public officials has long been illegal in member countries, but the OECD Convention on Combating Bribery of Foreign Public Officials in International Business Transactions (the Anti-Bribery Convention) is testimony to a larger trend to improve public and private sector governance globally. The Convention categorically makes it a crime to bribe a foreign public official in order to obtain or retain international business.[1]

Four years after this historic event, ratification of the Anti-Bribery Convention is almost complete. Thirty-three of the original 34 signatories have deposited instruments of ratification with the OECD Secretary General (see table). Ireland was expected to complete ratification imminently, as the *Global Corruption Report 2001* went to print. Twenty-nine countries have meanwhile implemented legislation to bring national law into accordance with the Convention.

The Anti-Bribery Convention is part of a growing international arsenal against bribery and corruption. The OAS, the Council of Europe and the EU – among others – all have legal instruments binding their member states to take anti-corruption measures. These instruments need to be monitored internally among the parties to the agreements and scrutinised publicly to ensure that governments are living up to their obligations. In this regard, the Anti-Bribery Convention is one of the more effective of the anti-corruption agreements.

When a country ratifies and adopts legislation to implement the Convention in national law, the OECD Working Group on Bribery in International Business Transactions then undertakes a two-phase monitoring process. Phase One, detailed below, assesses whether new legislation meets the standards set by the Convention. Phase Two, scheduled to begin in November 2001, examines application of the Convention in practice.[2] It will involve looking at the structures and institutional mechanisms that are in place in the different countries to enforce leg-

	Country	Date of deposit of instrument of acceptance, approval or ratification
1	Iceland	17 August 1998
2	Japan	13 October 1998
3	Germany	10 November 1998
4	Hungary	4 December 1998
5	United States	8 December 1998
6	Finland	10 December 1998
7	United Kingdom	14 December 1998
8	Canada	17 December 1998
9	Norway	18 December 1998
10	Bulgaria	22 December 1998
11	Korea	4 January 1999
12	Greece	5 February 1999
13	Austria	20 May 1999
14	Mexico	27 May 1999
15	Sweden	8 June 1999
16	Belgium	27 July 1999
17	Slovak Republic	24 September 1999
18	Australia	18 October 1999
19	Spain	14 January 2000
20	Czech Republic	21 January 2000
21	Switzerland	31 May 2000
22	Turkey*	26 July 2000
23	France	31 July 2000
24	Brazil*	24 August 2000
25	Denmark	5 September 2000
26	Poland	8 September 2000
27	Portugal	23 November 2000
28	Italy	15 December 2000
29	Netherlands	12 January 2001
30	Argentina	8 February 2001
31	Luxembourg	21 March 2001
32	Chile*	18 April 2001
33	New Zealand	25 June 2001

Status of ratification of the
OECD Anti-Bribery Convention

*As of 12 July 2001, these countries had
not yet enacted implementing legislation.*

islation, including in the private sector. Input from civil society will also be invited.

Findings of Phase One

So far, almost all of the countries that have implemented laws in order to meet the Convention's standards have been reviewed.[3] Most of the countries have done a satisfactory job, and overall compliance with standards is underway. There were, however, significant deficiencies, and OECD ministers have asked some countries to take remedial action. Legal loopholes or provisions that might lead to inconsistent application have been identified, most of them relating to indirect bribery through intermediaries, or bribes paid to third parties for a public official's benefit. Because the Convention works within a country's existing legal system, such differences are to be expected. Nevertheless, the Working Group's role is to ensure that there are no major discrepancies that would undermine the goal of equal application.

Responding to the Group's recommendation, Japanese authorities recently informed the OECD that the Diet (parliament) has adopted an amendment to its law, which will broaden the scope of its foreign bribery offence. In the UK, the government will soon submit to

parliament new legislation that will specifically apply to bribery of foreign public officials. Meanwhile other countries either have already eliminated, or are in
the process of eliminating, the application of certain domestic bribery defences
(such as 'provocation', or 'effective regret') to cases of foreign bribery. The expectation is that this will forestall attempts to bypass liability.

A key provision of the Convention is that both 'natural' (physical) and 'legal'
persons (including companies) should be held responsible for bribery acts. But in
their domestic law, some countries can impose criminal liability on legal persons,
while others cannot. In order to bridge this difference, the Convention allows parties to provide either for criminal or non-criminal liability, as long as the sanctions are effective. Nevertheless, the monitoring process has shown that this is an
area where many countries will have to make greater efforts, and some are considering introducing legislation to this end.

In terms of punishments, the Convention does not actually specify what the
sanctions for bribery should be, leaving this to be determined by each country's
penal system. Generally, countries have provided for imprisonment penalties
ranging from one to ten years. A country is not evaluated in the monitoring process
solely on the basis of its penalties, but there are concerns that weak sanctions may
have an adverse impact on the ability to provide effective mutual legal assistance
and extradition. Some countries have taken the opportunity to review their sanctions, and some, like Iceland, have removed any limits on fines for legal persons.
In addition to fines and imprisonment, the Convention requires seizure and confiscation of the bribe itself, as well as of any other illegal gains from bribery.

Meanwhile, in order to pursue cases of international bribery effectively, a
broad interpretation of territorial jurisdiction is required to reflect the reality of
today's international business transactions. Many countries in the Convention
have provided that some form of connection to the territory, be it by fax,
e-mail or telephone, is sufficient to establish territorial jurisdiction over a given
bribery-related offence. The Convention also encourages those countries that can
prosecute their nationals for crimes committed abroad, without territorial connection, to extend this jurisdiction to foreign bribery offences. At least 24 countries have now provided for such nationality jurisdiction for foreign bribery, usually on condition that the act is also a crime in the place where it was committed
('dual criminality'). Still, Phase One reviews showed that there might be different
interpretations of dual criminality among countries, as well as certain special
requirements that can undermine the effectiveness of this basis of jurisdiction.

The Working Group looks closely at the conditions or requirements for instituting prosecutions. The Convention respects legal regimes of prosecutorial discretion, but does not permit concerns of a political nature to influence prosecuto-

rial decisions. Phase Two monitoring will carefully examine whether, in practice, the statutes of limitations relating to foreign bribery offences allow an adequate time period for investigation and prosecution to take place.

To put a stop to bribery in international business transactions, OECD countries have also agreed to end the practice of allowing tax deductions for bribes to foreign public officials. Almost all countries now prohibit these. The effectiveness of this change will also be assessed in Phase Two.[4]

Conclusion

Overall, the results of two years of monitoring are very encouraging. To ensure a level playing field for companies from all states that are party to the Convention, it is important that the remaining countries ratify and adopt implementing legislation as soon as possible.

Governments' commitment to stamping out bribery in international business transactions must be strictly enforced and, in this regard, there are many aspects of the Anti-Bribery Convention that will be judged by how they are applied in practice. It is too early to look for actual prosecutions under the Convention's auspices, but Phase Two will reveal what indictments are pending. Phase Two of the monitoring process will also keep up the pressure on signatory states, both to continue modifying domestic law in order to meet the Convention's standards, and to realise fully the effort to combat bribery abroad.

1 The Organisation for Economic Cooperation and Development (OECD) is an inter-
governmental group of 30 member countries which provides governments with a forum
for discussion and development of economic and social policy. All 30 OECD countries signed
the Convention as well as four non-members (Argentina, Brazil, Bulgaria and Chile).
2 Rules of procedure and the questionnaire for Phase One and Phase Two evaluations are at:
<http://www.oecd.org/daf/nocorruption>.
3 Twenty-one countries were reviewed between April 1999 and May 2000 and an additional
seven countries were reviewed between May 2000 and May 2001. Individual country reports
are available on the OECD website.
4 In New Zealand, the tax amendment to deny deductibility is pending in parliament.
The Netherlands has introduced a bill proposing to remove the requirement of a prior
criminal conviction as a condition for denying tax deductibility.

TI keeps up the pressure

Most major multinational enterprises have their headquarters in OECD countries and, from its earliest days in 1993, Transparency International (TI) recognised that OECD action to prohibit bribery of foreign officials could sharply curtail the supply side of international corruption.

The OECD also provided the right forum to overcome the 'prisoner's dilemma' which had long prevented action to stop bribery. Many business leaders recognised the damage done by corruption, not least to the public image of their companies. But they were concerned about the loss of business that would result if they stopped bribing, while their competitors continued.

Steps to the Anti-Bribery Convention

Although discussions began several years earlier, in 1994 the OECD recommended that its member countries consider a list of possible actions to curb corruption. While there was little support for prohibiting foreign bribery, there was less opposition to ending the tax deductibility of bribes, about which the OECD duly issued a recommendation in 1996. In 1997, OECD ministers decided that a convention to prohibit foreign bribery should be negotiated. There was concern that adopting a convention, rather than using the OECD's more common approach of a recommendation, would result in long delays. To meet that concern, a deadline was set to complete the negotiation of a convention by the end of 1997. The Anti-Bribery Convention was signed on 17 December of that year.

The Convention reflected a sea change in public attitudes about corruption in both developing and industrialised countries that in turn influenced the attitudes of business leaders and government officials. TI's efforts to raise awareness of the damage done by corruption and to build coalitions to promote reforms played a major role in overcoming decades of apathy, cynicism and denial. The achievement was also testimony to the effec-

tive leadership of the OECD's Working Group on Bribery in International Business Transactions, chaired by Professor Mark Pieth.

TI and the International Chamber of Commerce collaborated in spring 1997 to bring together 20 leading European business leaders who addressed a joint letter to the OECD, urging prompt action to prohibit foreign bribery. The letter helped overcome perceptions that the European business community opposed such action.

Through its national chapters in key OECD countries, TI played a further role in galvanising support by promoting the ratification of implementing laws in many countries. TI also provided the OECD Working Group with its own evaluation of these laws. A few examples deserve mention:

- TI-UK played a key role in disproving the contention of the UK government that no new legislation was needed because existing laws could be applied to foreign bribery.
- TI-Germany took issue with the German government's plan to terminate tax deductibility of bribes only in cases where there had been criminal convictions. This would have continued the deduction of most bribes. As a result of TI-Germany's criticism, an effective prohibition of tax deductibility of bribes was adopted.
- When the Canadian government failed to take action to secure ratification of the Convention, TI-Canada led the effort to gain support from all major parties for expedited action by parliament. Canada became the eighth country to ratify.
- TI-France worked successfully to delete a provision from French implementing legislation that would have broadly 'grandfathered' all bribe commitments made before the effective date of the French law. This would have permitted the continuation of bribe payments indefinitely.
- TI-USA testified before the Senate Foreign Relations Committee and helped persuade the Committee's chairman, Senator Jesse Helms, to overcome his scepticism about

the usefulness of international conventions. Senator Helms persuaded the Senate leadership to schedule the Convention for prompt action, and it received unanimous approval. TI-USA also played an active role in securing swift US implementing legislation.

- TI-Italy helped secure approval for the Convention and the implementing law in the Italian parliament. This required much sustained effort because of the weakness of the governing coalition at the time, while opposition efforts to bring down the government made it difficult to motivate parliament to take action.

Looking ahead

Beginning in November 2001, the OECD Working Group will monitor the enforcement of the Convention by national governments. The plan is to send review groups to about eight countries per year with the goal of reviewing all signatories by the end of 2005.

Many business people remain to be convinced that governments will really enforce the Convention. Some governments may be reluctant to take strong action until they are convinced that other governments are doing so. Only when enforcement actions are brought will there be a clear signal that the bribery of foreign officials must stop. The review of enforcement programmes is the critical test of whether the Convention will really change the way international business is conducted. This process will be more difficult than Phase One. It is not yet clear whether the OECD Working Group will be able to obtain sufficient staff and budget to be effective.

Another concern is the role of civil society and the private sector. TI has taken the position that obtaining objective, non-governmental assessments of the adequacy of enforcement programmes is essential to the effectiveness and credibility of the review process. However, this is a controversial issue. Concerns have been expressed that it could lead to public confrontations similar to those that occurred in Seattle. In TI's view, a more open process is likely to defuse confrontations. Efforts are underway to develop a reasonable basis for consultation.

Making the Convention effective, in its present form, must continue to have the highest priority. However, looking ahead, consideration should also be given to several amendments. The most important change would be to cover the bribery of political parties and party officials, since presently only bribery of public officials is covered. This is a dangerous loophole that will grow in importance as the Convention is enforced.

A second issue to be considered is coverage of bribery of corporate officials, sometimes referred to as 'private-to-private' bribery. At a time of increasing privatisation, it is hard to maintain that bribing a minister of telecommunications should be prohibited, but that there is no need to prohibit bribing the same individual when s/he becomes the CEO of the privatised telephone company. Bribery of public, party and corporate officials has taken on transnational dimensions in a global economy, and there is a similar need for international action to combat each effectively.

Thirdly, foreign bribery should become a predicate offence under anti-money laundering laws. Such action was recommended by OECD ministers in 2000. It is time to change the present language of the Convention, which obligates countries to make foreign bribery a predicate offence only if domestic bribery is treated as such. This makes little sense, as money laundering is much more likely to occur in cases of foreign bribery.

Finally, it should be noted that the next TI Bribe Payers Index (BPI) will be published in 2002. The BPI measures the propensity of companies from the 19 leading exporting states to pay for foreign bribes. The first BPI was published in October 1999 and was based on surveys conducted shortly after the OECD Anti-Bribery Convention became effective. The next BPI will provide a report card on the Convention's impact.

Transparency International

Building civil society coalitions

For the battle against corruption to be successful, a multi-stakeholder approach is required. Governments, businesses and specialists in the field recognise that without the involvement of civil society, it is impossible to establish an effective coalition against corrupt practices in the state and corporate sectors.

States draw their strength from their authoritative decision-making powers; the market from its economic influence. Civil society's legitimacy rests on its defining characteristic as citizens acting collectively in the public interest. To ensure recognition as a legitimate public actor in the fight against corruption, civil society itself has to embrace the highest standards of transparency and accountability.

The malpractice of a small number of NGOs, as well as the general backlash from senior government officials who accuse civil society leaders of being largely self-appointed 'do-gooders', unaccountable to anyone other than themselves, are factors that have led civil society organisations to make these issues a priority. 'Downward accountability', or developing and retaining links to grassroots' constituencies, as well as trust among the greater public, are crucial in this respect.

The experience of Transparency International and other groups working in the field of combating corruption has shown that 'anticorruption campaigns cannot succeed unless the public is behind them'.[1] Civil society is uniquely placed to raise awareness about the negative consequences of corruption for democracy and development, and to create a readiness to act against corrupt practices in state bureaucracy and the private sector.

There are many success stories of citizens taking action in fighting corruption at all levels, individually and collectively. Just as important as high-profile cases, such as the overthrow of President Estrada's corrupt regime in the Philippines earlier this year, are the day-to-day activities of the many anticorruption groups and organisations around the world working to pull out corruption by its roots.

Civil society is able to bring together a range of societal stakeholders in a joint effort to combat corruption. In the context of globalisation, crucial tasks ahead for civil society in its fight against corruption are to build transnational coalitions and to share knowledge on both effective anti-corruption strategies and internal civil society accountability initiatives. Here, transnational civil society networks, such as CIVICUS: World Alliance for Citizen Participation and Transparency International, have a crucial role to play as clearing-houses, convenors and information-providers on the pertinent issues surrounding corruption and accountability in the world today. The *Global Corruption Report* is a welcome contribution to this endeavour.

Transparency International is an important member of CIVICUS. Since joining the World Alliance for Citizen Participation, it has highlighted the urgent interventions needed in combating global corruption at several CIVICUS events. CIVICUS is interested in supporting TI in generating a broader debate both within civil society and at large, promoting the idea that all civil society groups need to address the issue of corruption.

Kumi Naidoo
Secretary General and CEO
CIVICUS: World Alliance
for Citizen Participation

1 Jeremy Pope (ed.), *The TI Source Book* (Berlin: Transparency International, 1997).

Money laundering: private banking becomes less private

By Michael Levi

Introduction

Criminals, whether narcotics dealers or corrupt heads of state, have long used secret accounts, trusts in false names and other devices to launder the proceeds of their crimes. An estimated US $500 billion to US $1.5 trillion are laundered through banks each year[1] – though these figures include huge transaction costs and consumables and do not represent net criminal savings. Now, as national and international regulators start to enforce new banking rules and the banking industry is beginning to respond with its own voluntary efforts, there are fewer places where the proceeds of crime can be hidden without risk of exposure.

Prominent cases have demonstrated just how recent these changes are. In the late 1980s, Citibank in London accepted as clients two young 'commodity and oil dealers', Ibrahim and Mohamed Sani Abacha. Bank files recorded the brothers as the sons of Zachary Abacha, 'a well-connected and respected member of the northern Nigerian community', but no mention was made that Abacha senior (later head of state) was a general in the Nigerian army and chairman of the country's Joint Chiefs of Staff.[2] By 1998, the Sani Abachas had deposited US $60 million with Citibank.[3]

The Sani Abachas and other members of the Abacha circle allegedly stole an estimated US $4.3 billion over a number of years – about half of it from the Nigerian central bank. The web of banks and jurisdictions implicated in these thefts is wide and tangled. So far, more than US $1.4 billion has been found and frozen in banks in Liechtenstein, Luxembourg and Switzerland.

In September 2000, the Swiss Federal Banking Commission 'named and shamed' leading banks in Switzerland, including Crédit Suisse, for 'serious failures' in allowing the Abacha clan to amass US $660 million. Numerous middle-ranking employees left the industry, sending the signal to others that this kind of laxity could affect them personally. Further, Swiss investigators found US $123 million of the funds had originally come from the UK – some allegedly as bribes from UK companies. Investigators also discovered that a further US $219 million had been transferred out of Switzerland again to British banks.

In March 2001, the UK Financial Services Authority (FSA) determined that, though some suspicious transaction reports had been made by various banks to the National Criminal Intelligence Service, 15 of the 23 banks dealing with the Abacha family funds had 'significant' control weaknesses.[4] None of the banks was named, as the FSA did not then have the legislative provision to do so.[5] At the time of going to print, it remained to be seen what the follow-up would be.[6]

How seriously should the ramifications of the Abacha affair be taken, or those that have emerged around Benazir Bhutto, Ferdinand Marcos, Mobutu Sese Seko, or Papa Doc and Baby Doc Duvalier? What will be the result of investigations into the African bribery aspects of the French Elf Aquitaine affair? What are the implications for private banking, for the corporations and high net-worth individuals who are traditional private banking clients, and for the governments that need to regulate an industry that is notoriously secretive and yet global in scope? What do these cases, and the recent responses to them, mean for the worldwide fight against corruption?

Money laundering and its links to corruption

Money laundering typically evokes images of major international financial manipulation, with a depositor using myriad offshore bank and trust company accounts in places resistant to investigation. Legally, however, money laundering can consist of nothing more than depositing the proceeds of crime in a domestic bank account. The difficulty of recognising funds as the proceeds of crime is compounded by the vast sums involved: trillions of dollars move around the world daily, and banks and others do no more than technically process these.[7]

A review of money laundering conducted for the UN illustrates the use of trusts, international business corporations and free trade zones for laundering schemes.[8] Proceeds of corruption can be laundered to avoid exchange control restrictions, and these overseas funds can then be loaned to international business people to facilitate their legitimate trade. Devices such as 'walking trust accounts' – accounts that move automatically to another jurisdiction when inquiries or mutual assistance requests are made – clearly facilitate crime. They also inhibit responses, by making it much more difficult and expensive to pursue suspected offenders for either evidence or recompense.

Money laundering (like organised crime) is more often associated with drugs than with elite crime, such as the theft of state assets or inter-corporate bribery. But while the war on drugs has dominated international legal and practical changes in money laundering and in the confiscation of assets, cases of grand corruption have also been important in shaping regulatory efforts. Since the 1970s, for instance, grand corruption has influenced Swiss measures for due diligence.

Without money laundering, there would still be corruption, but bribes would have to be paid (and held) in cash or readily movable valuables such as gold, diamonds and art. Not all bribes received have to be laundered: some cash can be redistributed as 'grease' payments or simply spent. Corrupt public and corporate officials, as well as other criminals, often use laundering agents, relying on them to show discretion in handling funds – and to be uncooperative in any criminal investigations that might arise.

Unfortunately, laundering only needs to be good enough to defeat the capacity of financial investigation skills and the burden of proof in any of the jurisdictions along its economic path. But though financial investigators may not be able to find out where assets are, or who owns them, they can at least make it hard for traffickers and launderers to collect the money.

Evidence suggests that it is now more expensive than ever to launder money. The costs of laundering are thought to have risen from 6 to 8 per cent of transaction values at the beginning of the 1980s, to as much as 20 per cent by the mid-1990s.[9] According to a US law enforcement source, costs rose substantially again by 2000–01, at least in the drugs sector.[10] Unfortunately, these higher costs do not indicate whether the actual amount of laundering has changed, or whether more 'rent' is being demanded by bankers or others for taking greater risks.

In the case of grand corruption, far less is known about laundering costs. Generally speaking, such costs are not marginal, but they are built into the operations of corporate actors for whom the payment of a few million dollars is routine. As regards corporate actors, the key regulatory role is played by internal and external audit controls – and by penal and reputational risks.

Global initiatives to stop money laundering

Since 1999, pressure to control money laundering has come from all quarters, including international agencies; regulators (the main thrust of regulatory efforts has been to stop dirty money entering the banking system, and to make sure it is traceable if it does); prosecutors, acting as the world's financial policemen; and private sector multinationals acting voluntarily, influenced by concern about reputational risk and the desire to avoid tough regulatory and criminal powers.

FATF, OECD and other international organisations

A major actor has been the Financial Action Task Force on Money Laundering (FATF), an intergovernmental, policy-making body established in 1989 to guide the implementation of anti-money laundering measures in the aftermath of the 1988 UN Drugs Convention.[11] One FATF initiative in June 2000 represented a

Making legislation work in Switzerland

The head of the Money Laundering Reporting Office Switzerland (MROS) resigned in frustration at the end of 2000, followed by all of his colleagues. He had sought in vain government permission to strengthen the power and personnel of the office. The episode illustrated the difficulties encountered in implementing the new Swiss law against money laundering, which came into effect in April 1998.

The law is one of the toughest pieces of anti-money laundering legislation in the world. It aims to tighten cooperation between the private sector and government, through a mandatory but strictly confidential, exchange of information in instances when corruption or criminality is suspected.

The law covers not only banks, but also all financial intermediaries. In the interest of better controls, all banks and financial intermediaries must now register either as members of a recognised self-regulatory organisation, or with a special federal government control office. They are forced by law to declare all suspicious funds to the MROS, which will launch criminal proceedings when necessary.

The law has been difficult to implement. The volume of assets held by Swiss financial institutions is estimated at around US $4,000 billion, yet declarations to the MROS last year only amounted to US $364 million. The 311 declarations made last year since the law came into force amount to less than one declaration per bank. Only 25 per cent of the declarations stem from financial intermediaries, pointing to a possible lack of cooperation.

The obligation to make a declaration to the MROS under the law exists only if a business relationship has been established between a financial institution and the suspect, and then only if there are 'founded suspicions'. This is not a well-defined notion and allows for many omissions. With regard to the definition of 'financial intermediaries', the law is broad, but it omits consideration of certain categories of agent, such as traders in primary goods.

Violation of the obligation incurs a fine of up to US $114,000, and/or penal and administrative sanctions.

Another problem lies in the mutual legal assistance procedures, providing for cooperation between states. The entire procedure can be held up at three points if a party 'objects' to the way it is being handled. Judicial reform due to be implemented in 2002 should resolve at least one of these problem points.

Meanwhile, the MROS is dramatically under-staffed when faced with the powerful Swiss financial sector, and compared to equivalent bodies in other countries. MROS has a staff of only six, while bodies in France and Italy have over 30 and 60 respectively.

Some of these factors are recognised by the Swiss authorities. But French parliamentarian Arnaud de Montebourg has accused Switzerland of tackling the money laundering issue solely for the sake of appearances. A more benign view might recognise that the difficulties encountered by the law are inevitable teething troubles.

The political structure of Switzerland creates its own set of obstacles. Many different actors are involved in the legal procedures, both at federal and cantonal levels. Among the cantonal authorities, the degree of commitment to cooperate varies from one authority to the next. Upcoming judicial reform will centralise prosecution of money laundering cases at the federal level. But it is not yet clear how this increased demand for federal resources will be met – whether the government will be able to attract former cantonal civil servants (who already have the know-how), or whether it will have to train new personnel.

Given the characteristic of consensus that governs the Swiss political system and the influence of the private sector in parliament, self-regulation may be the only realistic solution. It is too early to determine if this system will be successful.

TI-Switzerland

1 'La lutte contre le blanchiment des capitaux en Suisse: un combat de façade,' Documents d'information de l'assemblée nationale française, 2001.

major shift in efforts to tackle the problem, focusing efforts on country by country review instead of general international pressure and mutual evaluation. After a review by FATF, 15 jurisdictions were declared to be sufficiently 'uncooperative' as to merit economic sanctions if they failed to reform their money laundering laws and procedural implementation by June 2001.[12] One outcome was that the G7 issued formal advisories to these countries' domestic financial institutions to ensure that all transactions from, for example, Israel and Russia (on the so-called FATF 'blacklist'), were legitimate.[13] This led to an enormous effort by some of those countries to reform their laws and, to some extent, their banking practices. Such reform has involved financial regulators as well as legislators and police.

A subsequent FATF meeting in June 2001 focused on criteria for removing jurisdictions from its sanctions list, and reviewing its 40 'principles', such as 'know your customer'. FATF decided to remove some countries from its blacklist (but will closely monitor future developments) but added others.[14] It further recommended that its members apply countermeasures after September 2001 to Nauru, the Philippines and Russia unless their governments enacted significant legislation that addresses FATF-identified money laundering concerns. In future, FATF ought also to address measures against laundering of corruption proceeds.

Due to pressure from FATF and the OECD's Anti-Bribery Convention, corruption and fraud have increasingly been criminalised as money laundering predicates. This is a welcome development, but can be problematic. Although corruption and fraud normally have to be proved in order to sustain a conviction for laundering, mutual legal assistance from certain governments may be hard to obtain where key suspects still exercise local power. Even when financial institutions make a 'suspicious transaction' report, financial investigators may not be able to obtain further information from the overseas jurisdiction. However, the creative interpretation by prosecutors and investigating judges in France, Italy, Spain and Switzerland has meant that, where substantive and evidential rules allow laundering as a separate offence, it is possible for proceedings to take place in another country outside the sphere of influence of the corruption, where there may be some legal protection for suspected offenders. And this in turn can mean the freezing of assets, though – as with the Marcos millions – these assets will generally only finally be confiscated if there is a legal determination of guilt.

Treaties, conventions and regulatory agreements set out a framework, but do not indicate the levels of actual activity against money laundering. Internationally, the favoured anti-laundering strategy to supplement such legal agreements has been that of 'mutual evaluation', which was recently extended to include mutual legal assistance and the proceeds of crime confiscation, both by FATF and by the Council of the EU.[15] Peer evaluation is intended to draw countries into greater compliance, not least by enabling them to begin developing consistent standards. There is of course a danger of duplication or conflict in such evaluations, as the work of the Council of Europe, FATF, OECD and, potentially, the UN increasingly overlap.[16]

Until recently, the problem with this approach has been that mutual and expert evaluations have failed to focus on the laundering of transnational bribery, since it does not feature in conceptions of 'organised crime'. However, there is now a greater focus on the laundering of corruption proceeds. Evaluations by the joint OECD and Council of Europe Group of States against Corruption (GRECO) are one instance.[17]

Bank for International Settlements

The Bank for International Settlements (BIS), owned by the world's leading central banks, proposed much tougher rules for bank customer identification in a Basel Committee for Banking Supervisors consultation document in January 2001.[18] Stressing that its initiative was wider than the FATF guidelines, the BIS said that voluntary industry codes of conduct were to be encouraged, though 'they are not in themselves sufficient to ensure market integrity or sound risk management'. Further, the BIS argued that if banks did not exercise 'adequate due diligence' on all customers, they could become subject to 'reputational, operational, legal and concentration risks, which can result in significant financial costs'.[19]

The Basel Committee added that 'special attention' should be exercised in the case of non-resident customers who channel their funds through offshore centres: 'The bank should always ask itself why the customer has chosen to open an account in a foreign jurisdiction.'[20] Notwithstanding these bold statements, however, clear guidelines to identify money laundering risks are underdeveloped.

Capital flight and its effects on the stability of the world banking system have always been of concern to the BIS. In recent years the connection between capital flight and the proceeds of crime has generated additional motivation for action because of the relationship between integrity and stability.

Wolfsberg Principles

One of the aims of anti-laundering measures is to encourage bankers and others to know their clients sufficiently well to be able both to identify and report suspicious transactions. Few bankers know what types of crime – if any – their customers may be engaged in. If clients fool bankers or lawyers into believing that, at most, their deposited funds constitute 'merely' tax avoidance, then no suspicious transaction report on corruption will be made.[21] A crucial step is that all crimes need to be included within the obligation to report suspicious funds.

Tax havens, corruption and poverty[1]

It has been estimated that the equivalent of one third of one year's global GDP is held in tax havens. Much of this wealth is undisclosed and untaxed. The 'offshore' world provides a safe haven for the proceeds of political corruption, illicit arms dealing, illegal diamond trafficking and the global drug trade. Governments everywhere are increasingly concerned about the tax loss and money laundering associated with tax havens. This has led to a proliferation of initiatives designed to tackle different aspects of the problem.

Oxfam's view is that while these initiatives are useful up to a point, they primarily reflect the concerns of northern governments and, consequently, lack a poverty perspective. The OECD crackdown, for instance, has principally focused on tax havens in developing countries. But financial havens are part of a wider problem extending beyond the offshore activity of small island states to 'onshore' activity in major financial centres such as London and New York.

Tax havens may seem far removed from the problem of poverty, but they are intimately connected. Corruption, and the secretive system that facilitates it, denies people in developing countries the right to just public policies, with devastating implications for the very poor.

Tax havens provide companies and wealthy individuals with a way of escaping their tax obligations, thereby limiting the ability of governments to raise revenue and make vital investments.

The secrecy space provided by the 'offshore interface' between criminal activity and the world of legitimate financial transactions has become a crucial element of modern crime and a vital enabling mechanism for corruption.[2] The use of financial havens to launder the proceeds of corruption is an important issue for both national and global governance.

Money laundering facilitates public corruption. In the developing countries, some of the most notorious clients of the international private banking industry are those in or close to political office. In 1999, *The Economist* estimated that African leaders had accumulated US $20 billion in Swiss bank accounts alone over the decades.[3] To put this in context, this is nearly twice the amount that Sub-Saharan Africa spends servicing its debt annually.[4]

Research to discover workable policy options is a vital part of Oxfam's advocacy programme to increase finance for development.[5] To tackle money laundering, Oxfam recommends that a multilateral agreement to share information on tax matters would help countries, especially poorer ones, to stem tax evasion and illicit activities.

The international community should also support the proposal for an international convention to facilitate the recovery and repatriation of funds illegally appropriated from national treasuries. African, Caribbean and Pacific heads of state and government adopted such a proposal in November 1999 as part of the Santo Domingo Declaration.[6]

Oxfam

1 This is an updated extract from the Oxfam briefing paper 'Tax Havens: Releasing the Hidden Billions for Poverty Eradication,' June 2000. Available on the Oxfam website <http://www.oxfam.org.uk>.
2 Mark Hampton, *The Offshore Interface: Tax Havens in the Global Economy* (Basingstoke: Macmillan, 1996).
3 *The Economist* (UK), 14 January 1999.
4 According to the campaign group Drop the Debt, Sub-Saharan Africa spends US $13.6 billion per year on debt-servicing: <http://www.dropthedebt.org>.
5 For a broader discussion on policy options addressing problems associated with tax havens and offshore centres, see Oxfam (2000).
6 More recently, in March 2001, TI chapters in 11 African countries signed the Nyanga Declaration, aimed at spearheading an international campaign for the tracing, recovery and repatriation of Africa's stolen wealth.

In 2000, a group of international private banks, with the participation of Transparency International, engaged in a voluntary effort to control money laundering by cutting across the multiplicity of jurisdictional issues and addressing the serious reputational damage they were suffering in the media because of money laundering. Eleven banks (two have since merged), accounting for at least one third of the world's private banking funds, agreed at Wolfsberg, Switzerland, to establish a common global standard for their private banking operations.

The Wolfsberg Principles include common due diligence or 'know your customer' procedures for opening and keeping watch over accounts, especially those identified as belonging to 'politically exposed persons' (i.e. potentially corrupt public officials). In the case of individuals, if doubt exists as to whether the account holder is the beneficial owner, 'the bank will establish the capacity in which, and on whose behalf, the account holder is acting'. In the case of companies and trusts, 'the private banker will understand the structure of the company [or trust] sufficiently to determine the provider of funds, principal owner(s) of the shares and those who have control over the funds'. A key part of the 'know your customer' review process is to establish the source of funds being placed. The Wolfsberg Principles state that if there is no plausible, legitimate explanation for transactions, a decision will be made to continue the business relationship with increased monitoring; to cancel the business relationship; or to report the business relationship to the authorities. Assets may be blocked and transactions made subject to approval as required by local laws and regulations, which is the case in Germany, Liechtenstein and Switzerland.

The application of these principles retrospectively is a key question for banks. Several have argued that questionable accounts were opened long before due diligence rules were tightened. One way forward is the compilation of a list of public officials, former officials and their families. Yet even if such a 'risk list' was created and carefully maintained, a stronger compliance culture and appropriate account oversight technology is required to ensure suspicious funds are not missed or underreported.

The Wolfsberg signatory banks are in any case subject to supervision by their lead host regulators, but their public commitment to the principles produces a powerful reputational incentive for compliance. The fact that other banks now wish to sign up to the Wolfsberg Principles underlines the extent to which reputational issues have become central to international banking.

Conclusion

It is tempting to be dismissive of the rhetoric of politicians and banking sector leaders. Certainly, the direct, short-term impact of money laundering reporting has been modest in terms of prosecutions and confiscations. This is particularly true with regard to corruption cases, with the partial exception of Switzerland. Arguably, the results from suspicious transaction reporting are not illustrative of the potential of reporting systems. Rather, they reflect the limited resources at present put into such systems by bankers, financial investigators and prosecutors, as well as the difficult legal framework which, as discussed, requires proof of the predicate offence.

Nevertheless, the non-transparent world for financial services is undeniably shrinking: private banking is becoming a little less private. This affects individuals or mafia networks more than it does large corporations, accountants and law firms. The very global spread of the latter does, however, make them more vulnerable to loss (though not yet, it should be noted, to closure), through reputational damage and regulatory sanction. There are some signs that key corporate actors are willing to engage in a Wolfsberg-style commitment to good practice.

Anti-money laundering policies, combined with expanding criminalisation of transnational bribery, have made bribery riskier both for corporate actors and the intended recipients. Such policies also significantly enhance the international transparency of financial transfers, at least after the fact, if not always at the preventive stage.

One of the unintended benefits of recent high-profile cases is that they have pointed to corruption (and the capital flight that sometimes hides corruption), rather than illegal drugs, as a core problem of international crime control. Furthermore, such cases have thrown a spotlight on the private banking sector, where the assets of the richest people typically end up.

The pressures of measures against all-crimes laundering, transnational bribery, transnational organised crime and 'harmful tax competition', and in favour of transparency in offshore finance flows, have eroded national sovereignty in these domains. Less progress has been made to curb the use of corporations, trusts or other devices as secrecy vehicles. This will be the main thrust of future international efforts to curb money laundering. Here, enhanced corporate governance, supported both by external and internal audits is needed, as is the development of warning indicators. It is also crucial to review prominent cases of money laundering with a view to developing realistic guidelines for banking staff and others. Importantly, any guidelines will have to anticipate new countermeasures by those seeking to place corrupt funds. In the battle against money laundering, the continuing shift towards evaluating practice, rather than developing laws and regulations, will be helpful. However, vigilance against 'evaluation fatigue' – leading to resentment rather than reform – must also be maintained.

1 IMF estimates cited in *The Economist* (UK), 21 June 2001.
2 *The Guardian* (UK), 7 October 2001.
3 Citibank London facilitated the opening of new accounts to handle funds from the Sani Abachas' airline with Citibank New York. The Sani Abachas continued to operate the New York account long after the airline stopped trading.
4 FSA press release, 8 March 2001. The FSA investigation identified 42 personal and corporate account relationships linked to Abacha family members and close associates in the UK, held at 23 banks (both UK banks and branches of banks from both inside and outside the EU). Between 1996 and 2000, total turnover on the 42 accounts amounted to US $1.3 billion – not necessarily proceeds of crime – ending up in the UK, of which some 98 per cent went through the 15 banks with significant control weaknesses.
5 The Financial Services and Markets Act 2000 is due to come into force shortly, and will allow the organisation to name banks in future.
6 In June 2001, the Abacha family won the right to a judicial review of the UK Home Secretary's decision to cooperate by freezing funds. The family argued that it had already repaid US $800 million to Nigeria in exchange for the lifting of civil and criminal liability, and that the Nigerian government was seeking to recover funds that were not owed to it, without issuing civil proceedings. *Financial Times* (UK), 6 June 2001.
7 The scale of laundering from corruption and other crimes is vast. In the US, the headline figures of forfeitures (almost US $1 billion annually) – much of it from laundering prosecutions – are larger than for the rest of the world combined. Even there, the sums confiscated are very small compared with actual crime proceeds.
8 Jack Blum, Michael Levi, R. Tom Naylor and Phil Williams, 'Financial Havens, Banking Secrecy and Money Laundering,' Issue 8, UN Office for Drug Control and Crime Prevention (UNDCP) Technical Series, 1998.
9 Cost assessments here relate directly to the laundering of organised crime assets. UNDCP, *World Drug Report* (Oxford: Oxford University Press, 1997).
10 Interview with author.
11 FATF was originally convened by G7 Heads of State and the President of the European Commission; it is now comprised of 29 countries and two regional organisations.
12 The FATF list comprised Bahamas, Cayman Islands, Cook Islands, Dominica, Israel, Lebanon, Liechtenstein, Marshall Islands, Nauru, Niue, Panama, Philippines, Russia, St Kitts and Nevis, and St Vincent and the Grenadines.
13 G7 Finance Ministers, 'Actions against Abuse of the Global Financial System,' report to Heads of State and Government, Okinawa, 21 July 2000.
14 Bahamas, Cayman Islands, Liechtenstein and Panama were removed, while Egypt, Guatemala, Hungary, Indonesia, Myanmar and Nigeria were added.
15 The EU has been actively facilitating international cooperation against organised crime through its new 'Eurojust' mechanism, established after the Tampere European Council.
16 For example, the 2001 Council of Europe evaluation of anti-corruption measures in the UK is largely favourable, whereas the 2000 Phase One evaluation by OECD is quite negative. Of course, different criteria can be used, but there is potential for confusion and 'evaluation shopping' here. At an even broader level of involvement, there are a number of organisations taking steps to combat money laundering and financial crime that need to coordinate efforts, including Interpol, the IMF and the World Bank. The latter two produced a joint paper in April 2001, 'Enhancing Contributions To Combating Money Laundering,' available at <http://www.imf.org/external/np/ml/2001/eng/042601.htm>.
17 GRECO states include those who have signed the Council of Europe's 1999 Criminal Law Convention on Corruption and agreed to the mutual evaluation process.
18 The Basel Committee lays down rules for regulators internationally and is part of the BIS.
19 Basel Committee on Banking Supervision, 'Customer Due Diligence by Banks,' consultative document, January 2001; *Financial Times* (UK), 1 February 2001.
20 *Financial Times* (UK), 1 February 2001.
21 Only if there are 'objective' legal liabilities will a suspicious transaction report need to be made.

Transparency in the international diamond trade

By Nicholas Shaxson

Introduction

It is now widely known that so-called 'blood diamonds' have allowed brutal rebel movements such as Sierra Leone's Revolutionary United Front (RUF) and Jonas Savimbi's National Union for the Total Independence of Angola (UNITA) to buy arms, sustain protracted conflicts and terrorise millions of the world's poorest civilians. Diamonds have also fuelled recent conflicts in the Democratic Republic of Congo (DRC) and Liberia.

Dealers in these gems have hidden networks that reach deep into an underworld of arms merchants and international organised crime, with links to government officials and, sometimes, presidents. These corrupt, diamond-funded patronage networks have corrosive effects on the political economies of diamond-producing countries and raise serious issues of industry and consumer ethics.

The diamond industry initially dismissed a challenge by activists to curb the trade in goods that are so easy to smuggle. But a new set of initiatives is now having a tangible effect on both rebel finances and industry transparency. These changes are testimony to the ways in which industry can be pushed to greater accountability by civil society protest.

Diamond output (US $ million)		
	1999	2000
Angola	600	750
Of which: UNITA	*150*	*75*
South Africa	800	900
Namibia	400	500
Botswana	1,800	2,200
Russia	1,600	1,600
Canada	400	400
Australia	400	300
Other	800	900
Of which: RUF	*70*	*70* (estimates range from 35–100)
DRC rebels (Kisangani)	35	35
World total	**6,800**	**7,500**

Table 1: World diamond output

Source: De Beers
Note: Diamond statistics vary enormously. For both 1999 and 2000, the De Beers estimates for UNITA output are roughly half that suggested by the UN (see table 2).

Diamonds, conflict and corruption

Diamonds are usually found in two types of place. Primary kimberlite deposits cover compact locations and can be defended and monitored relatively easily. But rivers running over these deposits for millions of years have carried diamonds across huge swathes of land that are ideal for exploitation by dispersed rebel groups. Dug with buckets and spades, these more accessible gems not only fund rebel armies, but lie close to the very causes of armed rebellion.

'It is the feasibility of predation which determines the risk of conflict,' said a recent World Bank report that analysed links between resources and conflicts worldwide.[1] Corruption in the management of diamond resources sows the seeds of the socio-economic decay that can lead to conflict and, once conflict has begun, fuels it with an income that has financed some of Africa's most destructive wars.

In Angola, diamond areas have for years been part of a complex patchwork of shifting fiefdoms, in which official companies often mined next to UNITA, or other illegal diggers, under local non-aggression pacts. Different groups make money not only from diamond sales, but from access to a comprehensive, diamond-based economy in the production areas. The involvement of government security forces in mining influences the military dynamic and has undoubtedly helped UNITA. 'Diamonds have resulted in the fragmentation and criminalisation of the conflict as military units shifted their activities from politico-military objectives to economic ones,' according to author Philippe Le Billon.[2]

Commenting on the conflict in Sierra Leone, a January 2000 report by the Canadian NGO Partnership Africa Canada (PAC) concluded: 'The point of the war may not actually have been to win it, but to engage in profitable crime under cover of warfare. Only the economic opportunity presented by a breakdown in law and order could sustain violence at the levels that have plagued Sierra Leone.'[3] State weakness encouraged Sierra Leone rebel leader Foday Sankoh's insurgency, which started in 1991 and flourished as his forces pushed into the diamond fields near Kono, providing a new financial platform for its spectacularly brutal campaigns. Under severe threat, the government of the time made Faustian bargains with foreign private security companies, which offered military help in exchange for diamond concessions.[4]

'Diamond vice' is not constrained by national borders. Sierra Leone's conflict was fanned by President Charles Taylor of neighbouring Liberia, at the helm of what many consider to be a diamond and timber-based criminal state. Taylor not only armed Sierra Leone's RUF, he used his office to shield its illegal diamond activities. 'By the end of the 1990s, Liberia had become a major centre of diamond-related, criminal activity, with connections to guns, drugs and money laundering,' according to PAC.

Author William Reno explains that, in countries like Liberia, the regime's survival depends upon its leader's ability to let officials exploit opportunities in diamond or drug trafficking and money laundering. 'It points to a basic dilemma: What can reformers do if a government has a vested financial interest in shielding illicit transactions?'[5] A shift in officials' interest away from public service and toward personal profit damages governments' ability to provide services, erodes states' structure and legitimacy, and has a critical impact on democracy.

In the DRC, foreign armies, including Zimbabwe's, acted as private security companies, providing military support in exchange for mining concessions. Zimbabwe's President Robert Mugabe used the lure of personal gain in the DRC to consolidate control over his own domestic governance structures. Angola, Namibia, Rwanda and Uganda found similar inducements in the DRC conflict, though they had vital strategic concerns to pursue as well. Senior government officials in Togo and Burkina Faso also benefited from the illicit trade in UNITA and RUF diamonds, according to UN and NGO reports.

The networks extend beyond Africa, with arms dealers in Bulgaria, Lebanon, Ukraine and other countries exploiting lax international controls to seal covert arms transactions, often directly bartered for diamonds. Significant amounts of money are also laundered through the diamond trade by organised criminal groups, according to one expert.[6]

Amid this chaos, otherwise reputable companies have for years sent dealers to African war zones to buy stones – hiding behind international and local apathy and an attitude that, by not inquiring too deeply, they would not be incriminated by the stones' illegality. Lack of transparency in the diamond industry and corrupt management of resources in the countries of origin fed on each other in this lucrative trade.

The world starts to notice

A 'conflict diamonds' campaign, initially launched in December 1998 by the London-based NGO Global Witness, highlighted the complicity of the world's diamond trade in flouting UN sanctions against UNITA, and the links between the diamond industry and the Angolan conflict.[7] 'There is dangerous acceptance among the international community that the mechanics of the trade in diamonds, particularly from UNITA-held areas, are beyond any real controls,' its report said. It criticised the complacency at the summit of the industry, notably at De Beers and at the Diamond High Council (HRD) in Antwerp. Belgium has long played a key role in the diamond trade and 50 per cent of world production still passes through Antwerp.[8]

Advocacy in the case of conflict diamonds

In the wake of Global Witness's efforts to draw international attention to corruption in Cambodia's logging industry, the UK Environmental Investigation Agency commissioned the NGO to carry out preliminary research in 1996 into diamond mining in Angola and its links to conflict and human rights abuses.

The research was aimed primarily at documenting De Beers' diamond trading relationship with the UNITA rebel movement – which maintains a stranglehold on the country's most diamond-rich territories – and assessing the role of the diamond trade in financing a military conflict that, despite the peace process, continues today. De Beers held nearly 80 per cent of the world diamond market at the time and was shown to have openly bought smuggled diamonds from rebels. Investigations also proved that foreign governments had flouted the UN Security Council embargo on unofficial Angolan diamonds.

A report published in December 1998 on the findings, 'A Rough Trade: The Role of Companies and Governments in Angola's Civil War,' criticised the UN and governments with significant diamond interests – notably Belgium, Israel, the UK and the US – in addition to De Beers and other key players in the Angolan industry. 'A Rough Trade' was followed in May 2000 by a second report, 'Conflict Diamonds: Possibilities for the Identification and Certification and Control of Diamonds,' which detailed how an international system of certification could be applied to the trade in conflict diamonds.

Global Witness also sought to raise consumer awareness through a campaign called 'Fatal Transactions', in collaboration with the Netherlands Institute for Southern Africa (NIZA), the Netherlands Organisation for International Development (NOVIB) and Medico International in Germany. Fatal Transactions is an educational campaign that highlights the role played by natural resource exploitation in funding conflicts. The campaign focused initially on conflict diamonds, but intends to move to other primary resources such as oil, timber and coltan, a mineral compound commonly used in the manufacture of cell phones. The fact that many natural resources that fuel conflicts end up as consumables makes such consumer initiatives crucial aspects of international campaigns aimed at stemming their illicit trade.

Fatal Transactions did not call for a general boycott, since the bulk of the diamond trade in Australia, Botswana, Canada, Namibia, Russia and South Africa is 'clean'. However, given the impact of the campaign at the multilateral and consumer levels, diamond companies quickly recognised that a failure to take action was untenable and that self-regulation was unavoidable. The diamond industry conducted several polls to discover whether consumer buying patterns had been affected. Marketing and research group MVI Marketing found that, although consumers were largely unaware of the issue of conflict diamonds (9 per cent in a May 2000 survey), 73 per cent said they would not buy a diamond if they knew it came from a conflict source.

Taken at face value, the industry has implemented some far-reaching changes in response to the campaign but, in the view of Global Witness, these fall far short of true self-regulation. One indication of the industry's ambivalence toward greater transparency is that, while it continues to hold information on who deals in conflict diamonds, it will not divulge any names.

Despite these and other continuing problems, the conflict diamonds campaign showed that civil society groups can achieve a remarkable amount in a very short space of time with a minimum of resources. To tackle issues of natural resource exploitation, conflict, corruption and human rights abuses, Global Witness is now committed to a strategy of state and industry-level lobbying, backed by more intensive, consumer awareness-raising efforts.

Global Witness

Industry players, reassured that this had always been the way to do business in Africa and believing it was the UN's job to enforce its own embargo, scorned the activists at first. One Belgian diamond official described Global Witness as 'a bunch of well-intentioned hooligans'. He pointed out that a high-profile consumer campaign threatened poor but peaceful producer nations, such as Botswana, Namibia and South Africa, as well as India, where the cutting industry employs hundreds of thousands of people.[9] Since rebel-mined stones formed only a small fraction of the US $7.5 billion annual trade in rough diamonds, many argued it was impossible to prevent them being smuggled or to work out where they were mined, especially if different parcels were mixed.

Contempt turned to fear as the term 'blood diamonds' crept into Western consumers' consciousness, threatening the carefully manicured image of the diamond itself, a prospect that shook the industry to its foundations. To the industry's standard quality criteria, known as the 'Four Cs' – carat, colour, clarity and cut – another was being added: conflict. (A sixth 'C', standing for the corruption in the trade, might also be noted.) Campaigners suggested that the diamond industry's reputation, and its relationship with consumers, could soon go the way of the fur trade.

The 'conflict diamonds' campaign coincided with a new and bloody phase in Angola's long conflict that helped focus international attention. UNITA had used the 1994 Lusaka peace accords with the Movement for the Popular Liberation of Angola (MPLA) government as a shield behind which to hide and re-arm, mining over US $2.5 billion worth of diamonds before war erupted again in December 1998.[10] It quickly captured huge swathes of territory, shelling the islands of government control to which terrified civilians were fleeing, and threatening US, French and other interests in Angola's fast-growing oil industry (now running at 750,000 barrels per day). A strong coalition of Western governments and international organisations joined the effort to curb UNITA diamonds, which now accounted for a large proportion of Angola's diamond output. A parallel campaign on Sierra Leone, led by PAC and reinforced by new UN sanctions, added to the pressure for change.

Diamond output (US $ million)

	1999	2000
Ascorp (Angolan state monopoly) total	650	746
Official mines	*330*	*398*
Unofficial output	*320*	*348*
Non-UNITA smuggled	n/a	250+
UNITA smuggled	300+*	100+
Angola total	**n/a**	**1,100+**

Table 2: Angola's diamond output

*Source: *UN Security Council addendum, 18 April 2001. Other figures are government or unofficial estimates.*
Note: '+' means 'at least'

Diamond industry response

The multinational De Beers saw the threat early and in October 1999 said it would stop buying Angolan diamonds except for those under contract from a single, official mine. In February 2000, it then announced that it would no longer sell African gems originating in zones controlled by forces rebelling against legitimate governments.[11] These were the first moves in an attempt to forge a new regulatory architecture for the world diamond trade.

At the heart of today's efforts is the government-initiated Kimberley Process, launched in May 2000 with South Africa taking the lead, but including about 20 other countries. It aims to create a workable global tracking system of export certification and import verification, based on national certification schemes. A parallel initiative by the diamond industry, the World Diamond Council (WDC), pledged to help implement this system and favours legislation that ensures diamonds will only be imported from countries with certified import and export controls.[12] These measures are aimed principally at rough diamonds, though elements of the polished trade may later be affected. It is proposed that rough diamonds traded internationally will be in sealed, tamper-proof containers accompanied by documents certifying their origin. Transactions will be recorded in a unified, government-operated system with credible registration controls.

A 'chain of warranties', yielding a verifiable audit trail linking every diamond back to its mine of origin, underpins the system promoted by the Kimberley Process and the WDC. A stone moving from one stage of the chain to the next will require a 'conflict-free' warranty, which may be given legal force, making it a criminal offence to falsify a diamond's origin. 'If reputable dealers on the open market take the view this is not a business they want to be involved in, we think that will make a difference,' said De Beers director Tim Capon.[13]

The controls also seek to close the loophole whereby national laws make no distinction between the country of a diamond's origin and its country of provenance – the place from where it was shipped. In recent years, Belgium has recorded imports from Liberia far in excess of its mining capacity, with much of the balance assumed to have originated from areas mined by Sierra Leone's RUF.[14] Such circumstantial evidence will be crucial to monitoring compliance in the event that an international certification system is put in place, and it played an important role in the UN's decision to impose sanctions on Liberia, which is now also accused of fomenting conflict in neighbouring Guinea.[15]

The first legally binding national controls have been implemented in Angola and Sierra Leone, both of which developed 'certificate of origin' schemes with Belgian help. In April 2001, Belgium also agreed a bilateral certification scheme with the DRC. In the US, which accounts for around half of world diamond sales,[16] efforts to control imports with a chain of warranties system were initiated by Congressman Tony Hall. A Clean Diamonds bill was later proposed to the Senate in June 2001. Other countries are working to see how domestic legislation meshes with the proposed changes. Officials at a recent Kimberley Process meeting said they hoped to agree on minimum common rules for certification by November 2001 before presenting them to the UN.

Implications and limitations of the conflict diamonds campaign

The campaign still faces many hurdles – not least the need to find political solutions to the conflicts in question. But the moves to mitigate the diamond trade's contribution to conflicts, which have also been shaped by the corrupt and unaccountable management of resources at a national level, are testimony to the private sector's ability to respond when confronted with a sufficiently robust challenge from consumers.

The speed with which the campaign changed the world's diamond trade suggests possible ramifications elsewhere. 'I cannot think of any industry that has gone through this kind of process, and at such a speed,' a diamond industry official said. 'You could translate this to other industries ... the fact it can be done is the exciting bit.'[17] The 'chain of warranties' idea, in fact, is already being applied in more limited forms in the timber industry, enabling consumers in some Western countries to choose to buy wood only from sustainable sources. Comparable coalitions of interests have started to tackle changes in other fields, for instance with regard to labour conditions in the production of primary commodities, notably coffee and cocoa, as well as in some manufacturing sectors.

The broader corruption issues surrounding the diamond trade, however, are generally not addressed by the campaign, which focuses on 'conflict diamonds' – those under UN sanctions – rather than the wider definition of 'illicit diamonds' that are mined and traded outside recognised official channels, though not necessarily under UN embargo. 'The industry would like not to have to address the bigger issue, but they are flipsides of the same coin,' said PAC's Ian Smillie.[18] It is clear that in the affected countries rebel successes were partly the result of state failure, which reflects diamond-related and other forms of corruption. Sanctions and the conflict diamonds campaign do little to address these root causes.

Despite a shake-up in Angola's diamond industry in early 2000, through licensing informal diggers and creating a single-channel buying monopoly, the government has not convincingly demonstrated that it has eliminated UNITA gems from certified official channels. 'The President and his retainers used the international outcry against dirty diamonds to restructure Angola's diamond economy to suit their needs,' said expert Christian Dietrich, adding that the shake-up was primarily aimed at bringing parts of the informal economy into the Luanda patronage network.[19] 'Ascorp [the state marketing monopoly] was not established to spurn diamonds, but to push licensed competitors out.'

By pushing down overall prices in the diamond areas to boost its own profitability, the state monopoly may have cut into UNITA's finances – thereby meeting one objective of the conflict diamonds campaign – but the problem of state corruption has been avoided.

If official diamonds are not 'clean' in spite of certificate of origin schemes, there arise serious doubts about the evolving international architecture for the diamond trade. Unscrupulous dealers could launder dirty diamonds by smuggling them across poorly controlled African borders and inserting them into the output streams of mines in peaceful countries. Participants in the Kimberley Process appear to be playing down the importance of controls in this regard, perhaps because 'clean' producer governments are afraid that the origins of their diamonds will be called into question.

The solution to both issues lies in more openness, with publication of clear and verifiable production data by mines and companies, checkable against exports. The chain of warranties concept will go some way to help. If the source of diamonds is questionable, despite official certification, the audit trail could form part of a 'branding' process whereby consumers may express their preference for diamonds from specific companies or countries. There is no sign yet that 'guaranteed' diamonds command any retail price premium, though there is evidence that rebels are suffering discounts on their stones. This may be due to the UN sanctions, as some claim – but it could be a result of the more opaque operations now conducted by bodies such as Ascorp.[20]

Outlook

Even if a new architecture emerges soon, controls will have to be ratified in a number of countries, a process littered with obstacles. And, after an initial period of rapid action, there are signs of apathy, particularly at government level. 'The whole Kimberley Process is in danger of unravelling,' said a group of NGOs after meeting in Brussels in April 2001.[21] 'Despite strong South African and Belgian leadership, many government representatives said they had come to the meeting with no mandate to agree to anything.' Russia and the US were singled out for particular criticism.

Tackling the problem needs the long-term commitment of governments,

NGOs, companies, journalists and others to investigate and publish abuses and to promote consumer awareness of the issue. The role that wealthier societies can play in contributing to the problems of conflict and corruption in Africa is still insufficiently acknowledged. The highly corrosive effects of the illicit trade in diamonds – and the international criminal networks it nourishes – must also be addressed more forcefully if efforts to tackle these are to have lasting results.

1 Paul Collier, 'Economic Causes of Civil Conflict and their Implications for Policy,' World Bank report, 1999: <http://www.worldbank.org/research/conflict/papers/civilconflict.pdf>.
2 Philippe Le Billon, *A Land Cursed by its Wealth? Angola's War Economy 1975–1999* (Helsinki: UNU/WIDER, 1999).
3 Ian Smillie, Lansana Gberie and Ralph Hazelton, 'The Heart of the Matter: Sierra Leone, Diamonds and Human Security,' Partnership Africa Canada, January 2000.
4 Ibid.
5 Correspondence with author. William Reno is author of *Corruption and State Politics in Sierra Leone* (Cambridge: Cambridge University Press, 1995) and *Warlord Politics and African States* (Boulder: Lynne Rienner Publishers, 1998).
6 Author's private correspondence with Christian Dietrich.
7 Global Witness, 'A Rough Trade – The Role of Companies and Governments in the Angolan Conflict,' 1998.
8 According to the HRD: <http://www.diamond.be>.
9 Interview with author.
10 Global Witness estimate.
11 De Beers press releases, February 2000.
12 World Diamond Council: <http://www.worlddiamondcouncil.com>.
13 Interview with author.
14 Ian Smille et al. (2000).
15 The UN imposed an embargo on all Liberian diamonds from 7 May 2001.
16 *The Economist* (UK), 21 June 2001.
17 Interview with author.
18 Correspondence with author.
19 Christian Dietrich, 'Power Struggles in the Diamond Fields,' in Jakkie Cilliers and Christian Dietrich (eds.), *Angola's War Economy: The Role of Oil and Diamonds* (Pretoria: Institute for Security Studies, 2000).
20 Richard Ryan, chairman of the UN sanctions committee on Angola, quoted in UN Integrated Regional Information Network (IRIN), 2 April 2001.
21 'Kimberley process stalled? Concern at lack of progress towards a conflict diamond certification system,' press release, 27 April 2001, by a group of over 70 NGOs including PAC, Global Witness and Oxfam. The meeting in Brussels was followed by other Kimberley Process meetings in June 2001 in Moscow and planned for November 2001 in Botswana.

Data and research

Overview

By Fredrik Galtung

Corruption hardly lends itself to measurement. It tends to be hidden from view, and the parties to a successful corrupt transaction seldom have an incentive to be open about their dealings. Until the mid-1990s, most empirical findings on corruption in the academic literature were of an incidental or anecdotal nature. Aggregated analyses, whether across time for a given business sector, or in cross-country comparisons, were speculative and theoretical, often citing 'impression-istic evidence' as their basis.[1] In a methodological essay, entitled 'What Cannot be Analysed in Statistical Terms,' corruption was cited as the classic example of an observable phenomenon that was not quantifiable since 'there cannot be statis-tics on a phenomenon which by its very nature is concealed'.[2]

Transparency International's (TI) Corruption Perceptions Index (CPI), first published in 1995, changed these assumptions. In subsequent years, there has been a remarkable growth in empirical research on corruption, fuelled to a great extent by growing international interest in finding the means to curb it. It has been bolstered by support and interest from multilateral organisations, founda-tions and researchers at universities in a host of countries.

This section of the *Global Corruption Report 2001* reviews some of the cur-rent comparative empirical studies of corruption undertaken by international organisations, aid agencies, research centres, NGOs and private companies. The studies range from opinion polls and composite indices to regression analyses, focus groups and diagnostic studies. They can be divided into three sub-sections: surveys and polls on a variety of aspects of corruption; recent secondary analysis of corruption data; and studies of public integrity and institutions.[3]

Surveys and polls

Opinion surveys are now the most frequently used diagnostic tool in the assessment of corruption levels. Survey samples include polling of the general population, the private sector and segments of public administrations.

Business people are a frequently used sample since they are thought to be knowledgeable in this area. TI's CPI (p. 232), for example, is a composite index that largely uses private sector surveys, or surveys produced for the private sec-tor. Another helpful recent effort is the World Business Environment Survey

(p. 249), an initiative of the World Bank Group, which surveyed over 10,000 enterprises in 80 countries. Respondents in East Asian developing countries reported the highest incidence of 'irregular additional payments to government officials' (over 60 per cent). At the other extreme, only 28 per cent of respondents in Latin America and 12 per cent in OECD countries reported such payments. Significant differences were found between small, medium and large enterprises.

PricewaterhouseCoopers (PwC) conducted a private sector survey of chief financial officers of major companies, equity analysts, bankers and PwC employees in January 2001 that estimated the adverse effects of public sector 'opacity' on the cost and availability of capital across several dozen countries (p. 276). The final results will be available at the end of 2001. Preliminary findings revealed that opacity has a significant negative effect on foreign direct investment rates and is a major additional 'tax' on private enterprise.

A Control Risks Group survey of 121 companies in the US and Northern Europe found that the number of companies deterred from investing in high-corruption countries has increased in recent years (p. 279). It also found that the number of companies with anti-corruption codes was rising. But the Dow Jones Sustainability Group Index of private sector 'sustainability leaders' – major companies that perform particularly well against a variety of environmental, economic and social indicators – demonstrated that there are still significant differences from region to region (p. 282). Whereas 82 per cent of US-based companies in the survey had explicit codes prohibiting employees from offering items of value to government officials, only 66 per cent of Japanese companies and 50 per cent of South American-based companies had similar rules. A study by The Conference Board (p. 285) used a combination of interviews, focus groups and working group discussions with executives from 151 companies from all major industries and regions. It found that the single most powerful stimulus to the development of a corporate anti-corruption strategy is the leadership and commitment of senior management, far ahead of any moral, legal or risk management concerns.

TI's Bribe Payers Index (BPI), prepared in the summer of 1999, was an effort to capture a snapshot of the supply side of international bribery (p. 237). Intended as a complement to the CPI, the BPI ranked 19 leading exporting countries according to the degree to which their companies were perceived to be paying bribes in order to win business abroad. Researchers sampled the views of 779 business professionals in 14 leading emerging markets.

Comparative samples of public officials are more difficult to obtain. A study by Court of bureaucracies and corruption in Africa drew on the assessments of five senior officials in each of the 20 countries surveyed (p. 296). The survey showed mixed results on the propensity to bribe, but elicited subjective evidence that corruption now adds considerably more to bureaucrats' salaries than it used to. In a more comprehensive effort, the World Bank PREM Network conducted a survey of 7,011 public officials in 16 countries that appeared to confirm that where political patronage is low, organisational performance tends to be high (p. 252). The survey also found that the reward or recognition of individual staff performance by senior staff leads to increased productivity and loyalty even in high-patronage environments.

Randomised nationwide samples of adult populations are particularly useful in assessing first-hand experiences of petty corruption. The Latinobarómetro survey of 17 South and Central American countries showed that, while there may be an overwhelming consensus that corruption constitutes a 'very serious' problem in a particular country, this view does not necessarily correlate with the actual or verifiable levels of corruption (p. 312). Whereas 61 per cent of Mexicans polled in 2000 considered corruption to be 'very serious', a greater percentage of respondents held the same view in Chile, a country with notably lower levels of corruption. The Afrobarometer of seven Southern African countries established that there are wide variations in perceptions of the level of government corruption. It also found that personal experiences of corruption are generally lower than perception levels, and that corruption does not uniformly figure among citizens' most significant problems (p. 307).

The International Crime Victims Survey showed wide variations in the number of people with first hand experience of corruption, with 60 per cent of respondents in Tirana claiming to have encountered corrupt officials, 8 per cent in Prague, and insignificant levels in most Western European countries (p. 266). The New Europe Barometer (p. 310), conducted in Eastern Europe and the former Soviet Union, showed how the readiness to pay bribes also varies. Miller, Grødeland and Koshechkina (p. 303), who carried out a study of four post-communist countries, found that large numbers of respondents admitted to having paid bribes or offered other favours for public services, while the majority of officials sampled also confessed to having accepted 'presents' from clients.

Taking the findings of these surveys together, a consensus seems to emerge across Latin America, Eastern Europe and the former Soviet Union that corruption has significantly increased in recent years. Nearly 90 per cent of Ukrainians said that corruption has 'increased', and 91 per cent of Hondurans that it has 'increased a lot'. Interestingly, respondents in five countries in Southern Africa – Botswana, Lesotho, Namibia, South Africa, and Zambia – took a different view, saying that the current government was 'the same' or 'less corrupt' than the previous one. Since no comparable data is included for Asia, Western Europe or North America, it is not yet possible to determine a global trend. In 2001–02

Transparency International will begin to gather such data through in-country diagnostic surveys in more than 70 countries. The aim is to produce a more comprehensive assessment of changes in corruption levels around the world.

Secondary analysis of corruption data

A.T. Kearney/*Foreign Policy* suggested that countries that rank highly on their Globalization Index™, which measures levels of cross-national economic, social and technological integration, are also the least corrupt (p. 287). Wei provided further nuance, positing that corruption reduces the benefits of globalisation while raising its risk elements (p. 289). What seems to be clear from these studies is that the benefits of globalisation accrue to those countries that are least tolerant of corruption. Neither study confirmed the suspicion – held by some – that increases in corruption may be due to increased globalisation.

The World Bank and IMF have studied the macro-economic and social implications of corruption in depth, publishing dozens of working papers, journal articles and books on the phenomenon over the last five years. The IMF has provided a useful summary of its research in table form for this volume (p. 255). Four IMF studies of whether corruption damages per capita GDP growth found that public-private wage differentials are a major causal factor. Less surprisingly, corruption was found to have a negative impact on infrastructure maintenance. Kaufmann, Kraay and Zoido (p. 244) have presented the diagnostic tools used by the World Bank. These include what they describe as qualitative, relatively imprecise measures of governance; the Bank's quantitative data based on private sector selfassessment; and detailed surveys that triangulate the responses of households, enterprises and public officials.

Levy compared the recently developed Environmental Sustainability Index (ESI) with levels of corruption, using the World Bank's aggregated governance indicators (p. 300). He found that corruption is the variable with the highest correlation with the overall E S I. Adserà et al. (p.293) found that corruption is a function of the degree to which citizens are empowered to hold officials accountable, with the frequency of news access a significant explanatory variable.

Assessing national integrity systems and governance

Several recent studies have explored the workings of what TI calls the National Integrity System (NIS), moving on from researching the causes of corruption to assessing the institutional framework needed to curb it and enhance governance. With a focus on the private sector, USAID designed 'Investors

Roadmaps' for 40 countries, highlighting the existing administrative barriers to investment, and exploring how these might be reduced (p. 272).

The OECD used a checklist approach to assess the quality of implementation of its 1998 Recommendation on Improving Ethical Conduct in the Public Service (p. 269). The survey covered 29 OECD countries, tabulating the number of countries with such factors as their rules on the use of official information, work outside the public service, and whether ethics is a consideration in recruitment. Only six OECD member countries were found to have dedicated government offices with responsibility for ethics in public service. UN DESA conducted a similar study in ten African countries, with a focus on 'ethics infrastructure' (p. 262).

Two sets of multi-country studies provide a qualitative and in-depth approach: the 20 NIS country studies conducted by Doig and McIvor with TI (p. 240); and collaborative studies by the UNDP and the OECD Development Centre of five national anti-corruption programmes (p. 259). Though employing different methodologies, both groups of studies aimed not just to enumerate the presence or absence of formal institutional provisions for corruption prevention and control, but also to assess their effectiveness within specific national contexts. They used a combination of literature reviews and desk studies, government reports, high-level interviews, field missions and focus groups. These efforts form the basis for ongoing evaluations that can be replicated in other countries, whether at the initiative of governments, NGOs or international organisations.

Conclusion

The question is no longer whether corruption can be measured or analysed empirically. The questions are: How? With what level of accuracy? And to what effect? The picture that emerges from this review is of the wide diversity and scope of the recent literature on the causes and consequences of corruption and on possible strategies of corruption prevention.

The scope of survey work has expanded exponentially in the past few years. In terms of quantitative research, 'macro' assessments like TI's CPI and numerous socio-political analyses by academic researchers are now available. But there is also a growing trend in the direction of qualitative research, such as the NIS country studies and surveys of public sector ethics. Some of these studies have a clear focus on corruption, while others examine the institutional frameworks in which corruption continues to thrive. There is also considerable variation in the types of audience for which these studies have been prepared: some are geared towards policy makers or the news media; others are intended for the private sector.

Not all approaches are equally robust: some use small samples; some are self-

Reviewing the literature on corruption (1990–99)

In August 2000, a database was assembled of books and scholarly articles on corruption that had been published in the 1990s, drawn from 12 specialised social science archives. Over 4,000 books and journals with corruption as a main or leading theme were identified during the search.[1] All items were classified according to a variety of criteria, including theme, geographical focus, language and year of publication.

According to the study, the total number of publications on corruption peaked in the mid-1990s, but the number of publications with an anti-corruption focus continued to grow. While only 5 per cent of the literature had an anti-corruption focus in 1990 – that is, a focus on methods to fight corruption – this rose to 14 per cent by 1999.

When all the publications in the database were classified by theme (see figure 1), it was found that 74 per cent addressed 'politics and public administration', and were mostly descriptions and analyses of the state of corruption or of a specific political scandal.[2]

A different thematic breakdown was discovered when the analysis was confined to books and articles with a primary focus on anti-corruption (see figure 2). While 48 per cent were in the area of 'politics and public administration', 44 per cent were in the area of 'law and judiciary'.

Only a very small proportion of anti-corruption articles were classified under economics, history or ethnography. Most notably, whereas 10 per cent of the total literature on corruption was historical, this was true of only 1 per cent of anti-corruption literature – there has been little explicit analysis of the genesis and history of low-corruption states.

The literature on corruption is global in both its subject matter and its origin. In terms of subject matter, it is evenly divided between addressing the industrialised world and developing or transition countries. Fifty per cent of the publications explored corruption in developing and transition countries, 43 per cent were studies in industrialised countries. Four per cent had a global reach, and 3 per cent were purely theoretical.

The books and articles in the database appeared in more than 44 languages. About half were published in English, 13 per cent in French, 11 per cent in Spanish, 5 per cent in Italian, 4 per cent in Chinese and 17 per cent in other languages.

Figure 1: **Main subject area of publications on corruption**

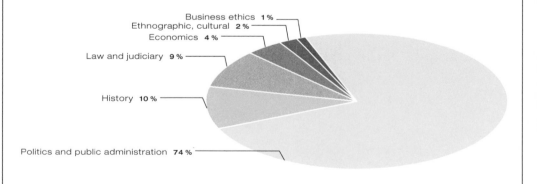

Business ethics 1%
Ethnographic, cultural 2%
Economics 4%
Law and judiciary 9%
History 10%
Politics and public administration 74%

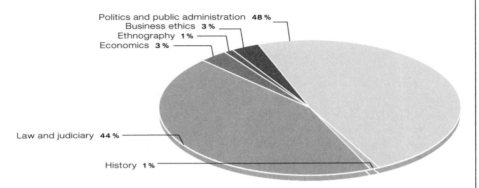
selective and cannot, therefore, be seen as fully representative of any given sector. Others are so large and costly that the surveys are unlikely to be repeated, reducing their value as diagnostic tools.

The more robust investigations can play a crucial role in raising awareness and deepening understanding of the developmental, social, political and environmental repercussions of corruption. As tools for concrete policy reform, however, these diagnoses have limitations. A minister of health cannot derive policy recommendations from the knowledge that corruption affects child mortality rates. A minister of finance will not know what to do with the information that corruption has a negative impact on real per capita GDP growth or foreign direct investment. This is where detailed, more targeted investigations into the public and private sector can provide valuable new insights. At an institutional and strategic level, quantitative research is complemented by qualitative, in-depth research into integrity systems and ethics institutions.

With increasing awareness of corruption and lower tolerance of it, a window of opportunity is now open for significant anti-corruption reform. The research challenge is to combine more specific qualitative and quantitative micro indicators so as to assess continually the quality of public and private institutions and the effectiveness of reforms.

The major development of the past few years is that evaluations are no longer only carried out by public institutions, a situation that would clearly be inadequate, since these are often the very institutions under investigation. Today, such evaluations are as likely to be initiated by academics, NGOs or corporations. A leading goal in the coming years will be for researchers to pool their findings so as to maximise their value as awareness-raising, diagnostic, accountability and policy tools. With this compilation, the *Global Corruption Report 2001* takes a step forward in this direction.

1 S.P. Huntington, *Political Order in Changing Societies* (New Haven: Yale University Press, 1968).

2 M. Dogan and A. Kazancigil, *Comparing Nations: Concepts, Strategies, Substance* (Oxford: Blackwell, 1994).

3 *Editor's note: The research contributions included in this section of the* Global Corruption Report 2001 *were selected using the following criteria: 1) studies had to show findings that measured corruption, the effectiveness of anti-corruption systems, transparency of governance, or the relationship of corruption to other socio-economic phenomena; 2) research results had to provide comparisons across at least three countries, or use comparative data. As a result of these criteria, this selection of empirical studies does not include a great deal of qualitative or case-study based research. It is therefore not comprehensive, nor does it try to reflect the current breadth of research. Contributions are only brief excerpts from the original studies, but full research papers and data sets are often available from authors. Contact details are given.*

Transparency International 2001 Corruption Perceptions Index

Johann Graf Lambsdorff
(University of Göttingen and Transparency International)

Since it was first published in 1995, Transparency International's annual Corruption Perceptions Index (CPI) has changed worldwide perceptions regarding corruption. By putting countries on a continuous scale, the CPI has shown that country comparisons can be made by assessing perceptions of the extent of corruption (see table). The CPI has also facilitated academic research. Using a cross-section of countries, it has become easier for researchers around the world to investigate the causes and consequences of corruption.[1] This has increased our knowledge in an area where research was long considered impossible.

The CPI methodology has been constantly improved since its inception. Since no methodology exists to collect meaningful hard data on actual levels of corruption, the CPI collects what is available: the perceptions of well-informed people. It provides a snapshot of the views of decision-makers in the areas of investment and trade. This year's CPI used data collected between 1999 and 2001.

The CPI is a composite index. The CPI 2001 draws on 14 data sources were used in the 2001 CPI, from seven different institutions: the World Economic Forum, the World Business Environment Survey of the World Bank, the Institute of Management Development (in Lausanne), PricewaterhouseCoopers, the Political and Economic Risk Consultancy (in Hong Kong), the Economist Intelligence Unit and Freedom House's *Nations in Transit*. One condition for inclusion of a source in the index is that it must provide a ranking of nations. Another is that it must measure the overall level of corruption, not forecast changes in corruption or risks to political stability.

Unlike last year's index, the 2001 CPI did not include surveys of the general public. Since these surveys are scarce, a strategic decision was taken to base assessments only on perceptions of business people and risk analysts. With the exception of three data sources that relied on expatriates' perceptions, the sources mostly sampled residents, who provided local estimates of the degree of corruption, given the meaning of the term in their own cultural context. The robustness of the CPI findings is enhanced by the fact that residents' viewpoints were found to correlate well with those of expatriates.

The sources generally define corruption as the misuse of public power for private benefit, which includes the bribing of public officials, kickbacks in public procurement and the embezzlement of public funds. The term 'level of corruption' includes at least two aspects: the frequency of corruption, and the total value of bribes paid. These two tend to go hand in hand; in countries where bribes are frequent, they also tend to represent a large proportion of firms' revenues.

The strength of the CPI lies in the combination of multiple data sources in a single index, which increases the reliability of each country's score. The benefit of combining data in this manner is that erratic findings from one source can be balanced by the inclusion of other sources, which lowers the probability of misrepresenting a country's level of corruption.

Equally important, the CPI leaves out countries if fewer than three reliable sources of data are available. This excludes those countries that would otherwise be measured with an unsatisfactory level of precision.

The high correlation that was found between the different sources used in the CPI also indicates its overall reliability. However, the sources do vary in the rankings they give. Transparency International addresses this issue by publishing the standard deviation of each country's score. The lower the standard deviation, the more agreement there is between the sources. In addition, the high-low range is reported in the table, depicting the range of assessments obtained for a country. Combining the CPI score with these items, as well as with the number of sources used for each country, provides a comprehensive picture of the extent of perceived corruption in different countries.

Contact: Johann Graf Lambsdorff (jlambsd@gwdg.de).

1   An overview of such research is provided in Johann Graf Lambsdorff, 'Corruption in Empirical Research – a Review,' TI Working Paper, November 1999: <http://www.transparency.org/working_papers/thematic/lambsdorff_eresearch.html>.

2001 Corruption Perceptions Index

Country rank	Country	2001 CPI score	Number of surveys used	Standard deviation	High-low range
1	Finland	9.9	7	0.6	9.2–10.6
2	Denmark	9.5	7	0.7	8.8–10.6
3	New Zealand	9.4	7	0.6	8.6–10.2
4	Iceland	9.2	6	1.1	7.4–10.1
	Singapore	9.2	12	0.5	8.5–9.9
6	Sweden	9.0	8	0.5	8.2–9.7
7	Canada	8.9	8	0.5	8.2–9.7
8	Netherlands	8.8	7	0.3	8.4–9.2
9	Luxembourg	8.7	6	0.5	8.1–9.5
10	Norway	8.6	7	0.8	7.4–9.6
11	Australia	8.5	9	0.9	6.8–9.4
12	Switzerland	8.4	7	0.5	7.4–9.2
13	United Kingdom	8.3	9	0.5	7.4–8.8
14	Hong Kong	7.9	11	0.5	7.2–8.7
15	Austria	7.8	7	0.5	7.2–8.7
16	Israel	7.6	8	0.3	7.3–8.1
	United States	7.6	11	0.7	6.1–9.0
18	Chile	7.5	9	0.6	6.5–8.5
	Ireland	7.5	7	0.3	6.8–7.9
20	Germany	7.4	8	0.8	5.8–8.6
21	Japan	7.1	11	0.9	5.6–8.4
22	Spain	7.0	8	0.7	5.8–8.1
23	France	6.7	8	0.8	5.6–7.8
24	Belgium	6.6	7	0.7	5.7–7.6
25	Portugal	6.3	8	0.8	5.3–7.4
26	Botswana	6.0	3	0.5	5.6–6.6
27	Taiwan	5.9	11	1.0	4.6–7.3
28	Estonia	5.6	5	0.3	5.0–6.0
29	Italy	5.5	9	1.0	4.0–6.9
30	Namibia	5.4	3	1.4	3.8–6.7
31	Hungary	5.3	10	0.8	4.0–6.2
	Trinidad & Tobago	5.3	3	1.5	3.8–6.9
	Tunisia	5.3	3	1.3	3.8–6.5
34	Slovenia	5.2	7	1.0	4.1–7.1
35	Uruguay	5.1	4	0.7	4.4–5.8
36	Malaysia	5.0	11	0.7	3.8–5.9
37	Jordan	4.9	4	0.8	3.8–5.7
38	Lithuania	4.8	5	1.5	3.8–7.5
	South Africa	4.8	10	0.7	3.8–5.6

Country rank	Country	2001 CPI score	Number of surveys used	Standard deviation	High-low range
40	Costa Rica	4.5	5	0.7	3.7–5.6
	Mauritius	4.5	5	0.7	3.9–5.6
42	Greece	4.2	8	0.6	3.6–5.6
	South Korea	4.2	11	0.7	3.4–5.6
44	Peru	4.1	6	1.1	2.0–5.3
	Poland	4.1	10	0.9	2.9–5.6
46	Brazil	4.0	9	0.3	3.5–4.5
47	Bulgaria	3.9	6	0.6	3.2–5.0
	Croatia	3.9	3	0.6	3.4–4.6
	Czech Republic	3.9	10	0.9	2.6–5.6
50	Colombia	3.8	9	0.6	3.0–4.5
51	Mexico	3.7	9	0.6	2.5–5.0
	Panama	3.7	3	0.4	3.1–4.0
	Slovak Republic	3.7	7	0.9	2.1–4.9
54	Egypt	3.6	7	1.5	1.2–6.2
	El Salvador	3.6	5	0.9	2.0–4.3
	Turkey	3.6	9	0.8	2.0–4.5
57	Argentina	3.5	9	0.6	2.9–4.4
	China	3.5	10	0.4	2.7–3.9
59	Ghana	3.4	3	0.5	2.9–3.8
	Latvia	3.4	3	1.2	2.0–4.3
61	Malawi	3.2	3	1.0	2.0–3.9
	Thailand	3.2	12	0.9	0.6–4.0
63	Dominican Republic	3.1	3	0.9	2.0–3.9
	Moldova	3.1	3	0.9	2.1–3.8
65	Guatemala	2.9	4	0.9	2.0–4.2
	Philippines	2.9	11	0.9	1.6–4.8
	Senegal	2.9	3	0.8	2.2–3.8
	Zimbabwe	2.9	6	1.1	1.6–4.7
69	Romania	2.8	5	0.5	2.0–3.4
	Venezuela	2.8	9	0.4	2.0–3.6
71	Honduras	2.7	3	1.1	2.0–4.0
	India	2.7	12	0.5	2.1–3.8
	Kazakhstan	2.7	3	1.3	1.8–4.3
	Uzbekistan	2.7	3	1.1	2.0–4.0
75	Vietnam	2.6	7	0.7	1.5–3.8
	Zambia	2.6	3	0.5	2.0–3.0
77	Côte d´Ivoire	2.4	3	1.0	1.5–3.6
	Nicaragua	2.4	3	0.8	1.9–3.4

Country rank	Country	2001 CPI score	Number of surveys used	Standard deviation	High-low range
79	Ecuador	2.3	6	0.3	1.8–2.6
	Pakistan	2.3	3	1.7	0.8–4.2
	Russia	2.3	10	1.2	0.3–4.2
82	Tanzania	2.2	3	0.6	1.6–2.9
83	Ukraine	2.1	6	1.1	1.0–4.3
84	Azerbaijan	2.0	3	0.2	1.8–2.2
	Bolivia	2.0	5	0.6	1.5–3.0
	Cameroon	2.0	3	0.8	1.2–2.9
	Kenya	2.0	4	0.7	0.9–2.6
88	Indonesia	1.9	12	0.8	0.2–3.1
	Uganda	1.9	3	0.6	1.3–2.4
90	Nigeria	1.0	4	0.9	−0.1–2.0
91	Bangladesh	0.4	3	2.9	−1.7–3.8

Notes:
1. The '2001 CPI score' ranges between 10 (highly clean) and 0 (highly corrupt).
2. 'Standard deviation' indicates differences in the values given by the sources: the greater the standard deviation, the greater the differences.
3. 'High-low range' provides the highest and lowest values given by the different sources. Since each individual source has its own scaling system, scores are standardised around a common mean. As a result, it is possible in rare cases that the highest value exceeds 10 and that the lowest is lower than 0. Only the aggregate final country scores are restricted to the reported range of 0 to 10.

1999 Bribe Payers Index

Transparency International

The Transparency International (TI) Corruption Perceptions Index captures one specific dimension of the international corruption equation: the demand side. To measure the supply side – the relative propensity of international companies to pay bribes – TI commissioned Gallup International (GIA) to conduct surveys for a Bribe Payers Index (BPI) in 1999. TI published the first BPI in October 1999, ranking the 19 leading exporting countries of the world in terms of the degree to which their companies were perceived to be paying bribes abroad.[1] The second BPI survey is planned for the end of 2001.

GIA conducted in-depth interviews with 779 private sector leaders in 14 major emerging market economies that account for over 60 per cent of all imports into non-OECD countries. The countries were Argentina, Brazil, Colombia, Hungary, India, Indonesia, Morocco, Nigeria, the Philippines, Poland, Russia, South Africa, South Korea and Thailand. Approximately 55 people were interviewed in each country, including senior executives at major national and international companies, chartered accountancies, foreign chambers of commerce, national and foreign commercial banks and senior partners at commercial law firms.

Of the 19 leading exporting countries that were evaluated, Chinese companies were perceived to bribe most frequently and Swedish companies least frequently (see table 1). It is notable that while several countries scored almost corruption-free in the CPI, none of the exporters in the BPI were seen to be completely ethical.

The BPI was intended as a benchmark for an assessment of the implementation of the OECD Anti-Bribery Convention. It was found that the countries that fared worst on the BPI were also the countries least likely to have signed or ratified the Convention (see table 1). Awareness of the Convention was generally low: only 6 per cent of respondents expressed 'familiarity' with it, while 13 per cent said they 'know something about it'.

At the same time, TI asked respondents to identify the sectors in which bribery most commonly occurs. As indicated in table 2, bribery was perceived to occur most often in public works contracts and construction, followed by the arms and defence industry. Bribery was perceived to be much less frequent in banking, finance and agriculture, though even here the scores point to its existence.

Table 1: **1999 Bribe Payers Index (BPI)**

Rank	Country	Score (0 – high bribery, 10 – low bribery)	Compliance with OECD Anti-Bribery Convention, as of 26 October 1999
1	Sweden	8.3	Ratified
2	Australia	8.1	Ratified
	Canada	8.1	Ratified
4	Austria	7.8	Ratified
5	Switzerland	7.7	Signed but not ratified
6	Netherlands	7.4	Signed but not ratified
7	United Kingdom	7.2	Ratified
8	Belgium	6.8	Ratified
9	Germany	6.2	Ratified
	United States	6.2	Ratified
11	Singapore	5.7	Not signed
12	Spain	5.3	Ratified
13	France	5.2	Signed but not ratified
14	Japan	5.1	Ratified
15	Malaysia	3.9	Not signed
16	Italy	3.7	Signed but not ratified
17	Taiwan	3.5	Not signed
18	South Korea	3.4	Ratified
19	China	3.1	Not signed

Notes:
1. The standard error in the results was 0.2 or less.
2. GIA asked: 'In the business sectors with which you are familiar, please indicate whether companies from the following countries are very likely, quite likely, or unlikely to pay bribes to win or retain business in this country.'

One of the more controversial aspects of the survey focused on the role of the governments in leading exporting countries. Respondents were asked what 'other means' governments used to give their own companies 'unfair' business advantages over companies from other countries.

A range of practices was reported, including: diplomatic and political pressure, commercial pressure, dumping, financial pressure, tied aid, official gifts, and tied defence and arms deals. The US government was perceived to be by far the most likely to engage in such 'unfair' practices. After the US, the governments most likely to use unfair practices were France, Japan, China, Germany and Italy.

Table 2: **Bribery in different business sectors**

Sector	Score (0 – high bribery, 10 – low bribery)
Public works contracts and construction	1.5
Arms and defence industry	2.0
Power (including petroleum and energy)	3.5
Industry (including mining)	4.2
Health care/social work	4.6
Telecommunications, post (equipment and services)	4.6
Civilian aerospace	5.0
Banking and finance	5.3
Agriculture	6.0

Note:
1. The standard error in the results was 0.2 or less.
2. GIA asked: 'Which are the sectors in your country of residence where senior public officials would be very likely, quite likely, or unlikely to accept or extort bribes?'

Contact: Fredrik Galtung,
Transparency International (galtung@transparency.org).

---

1 The reason for looking at only 19 countries was that, in other countries, either commodities make up a relatively high proportion of exports, or export levels are so low that the countries' roles in international bribery cannot be adequately assessed.

Evaluating the National Integrity System

Alan Doig and Stephanie McIvor (University of Teesside)

The National Integrity System (NIS), developed by Transparency International (TI), is a set of objectives, which, supported by key strategies or approaches (elements), are delivered by, or through, key institutions, sectors or specific activities (or 'pillars'). TI and others widely use the NIS as a conceptual and practical tool in developing anti-corruption programmes and projects around the world.

Collectively, the NIS is proposed as a system that, when operating both interactively and effectively, addresses two goals: combating corruption as part of a larger struggle against misconduct and misappropriation; and creating efficient and effective governments working in the public interest.

The ultimate goal of the NIS is to promote good governance: 'The aim is not complete rectitude, or a one-time cure or remedy, but an increase in the honesty or integrity of government as a whole.'[1] One of the features of the NIS and its constituent parts and activities is that it provides audit criteria both for NIS elements and the NIS as a whole.

In 2000–01, a project was undertaken to assess the pillars of the NIS in 19 countries, chosen to reflect regional and developmental variety.[2] The project evaluated the effectiveness and credibility of the NIS in combating corruption.

The research was based on a framework and questionnaire devised by TI and the Centre for Fraud Management Studies, then at Liverpool John Moores University. Outputs include country reports; an overview that summarises the NIS concept and raises issues concerning the NIS in practice; and a report on the themes raised by the country reports.

The findings

Most countries have nearly all the pillars necessary for a functioning NIS (see table). But a conclusion repeated throughout the reports is the need for the pillars – particularly those involving politicians – to implement self-pro-claimed regulations and procedures. To quote from the report on Colombia: 'The problem is practical rather than formal: in other words, it is not the absence of regulations, but their management and the ways in which existing instruments are used.'

Existing pillars – the formal practice

	Primacy of parliament	Peaceful transfer of power	Active party choice	Rules on party funding	Rules governing conduct of public officials	Parliamentary oversight of budget and accounts	Office of Auditor General	Anti-corruption agency	Ombudsman	Formal judicial independence	Rules on procurement	Independent media	Active civil society	National anti-corruption plan
Trinidad and Tobago	P	Y	Y	N	Y	Y	Y	P	Y	Y	Y	Y	Y	N
South Korea	P	Y	Y	Y	Y	Y	Y	N	Y	Y	Y	Y	Y	Y
Senegal	P	Y	Y	N	Y	Y	Y	N	Y	Y	Y	Y	P	Y*
Netherlands	Y	Y	Y	Y	Y	Y	Y	N	Y	Y	Y	Y	Y	N
Nepal	P	Y	Y	N	Y	Y	Y	P	N	Y	Y	P	P	N
Mongolia	P	Y	Y	P	Y	Y	Y	Y*	N	Y	Y	P	P	Y*
Mexico	P	Y	Y	Y	Y	Y	Y	Y*	Y	Y	Y	Y	Y	Y*
Lithuania	Y	Y	Y	Y	Y	Y	Y	Y	Y	Y	Y	Y	Y	Y
Kazakhstan	N	P	P	P	Y	Y	Y	N	N	N	Y	P	P	P
Jordan	P	P	P	P	Y	Y	Y	Y	N	Y	Y	P	P	P
Ghana	P	Y	Y	P	Y	Y	Y	Y	Y	Y	Y	Y	Y	N
Fiji	N	N	Y	–	Y	Y	Y	N	Y	Y	Y	P	Y	N
Colombia	P	Y	Y	P	Y	Y	Y	N	Y	Y	Y	Y	Y	Y
Canada	Y	Y	Y	Y	Y	Y	Y	N	N	Y	Y	Y	Y	N
Bulgaria	P	Y	Y	P	Y	Y	Y	P	N	Y	Y	P	Y	Y
Brazil	P	Y	Y	Y	Y	Y	Y	N	N	Y	Y	Y	Y	N
Botswana	P	Y	P	N	Y	Y	Y	Y	Y	Y	Y	Y	P	N
Bangladesh	N	Y	Y	P	Y	Y	Y	Y	Y	Y	Y	P	P	N
Argentina	P	Y	Y	P	Y	Y	Y	P	Y	Y	Y	Y	Y	N

Y In existence (Y* = proposed)
N Not in existence
P Only partially in existence, or not with full functionality (for example, a minority independent press or an anti-corruption agency without investigative powers)

In a number of countries, the pillars' impartiality, credibility and effectiveness are limited by a range of countervailing influences that include lack of commitment, self-interest, skewed formal or constitutional arrangements, failings in other pillars and, above all, the primacy of political influence. The results of the survey confirm the belief, expressed in the *TI Source Book*, that the NIS approach must be inter-dependent, moving away 'from a system which is essentially top down' to a system of 'horizontal accountability'.[3]

The country reports also note that the corruption confronting the pillars is pervasive – present, practised and not particularly concealed – in most of the countries surveyed. But the nature and extent of corruption varies and, for a number of states in transition, anti-corruption is only one among a range of issues on reform agendas.

The emphasis on democratisation noted by the various reports contains inherent threats. Democratisation provides the opportunities and incentives for both existing and new forms of corruption. In other words, democracy as a process may not be intrinsically more honest than any other political system.

The 'new' areas of corruption that emerge with democratisation include corruption through party funding, electoral misconduct and the development of new patronage networks to sustain electoral support. For some authoritarian states, a veneer of democracy is being cemented over the old political systems and power relationships that continue to operate beneath the surface.[4]

Decentralisation, often seen as complementary to democratisation in that it allows political engagement at district or local levels, offers existing elite groupings opportunities to colonise reform or selectively misuse their new constitutional powers. The continuity of centralised networks of control persists because the means of horizontal accountability have not been developed at the same rate, or with a sufficient level of support, to offer a counterbalance to the corruption opportunities opening up to local elites.[5]

Further developing the NIS

Support for the NIS is reflected in a number of the country reports. A range of institutions and agencies carrying out country assessments have now adopted the NIS as a concept and working methodology.

The country reports suggest that the NIS offers a means to measure performance and delivery. As audits, the reports provide a level of information that allows assessments to be made, fleshing out the skeleton which is often all that quantitative data can provide. Significantly, each country report is prepared within the country concerned. The reports demonstrate the relevance and application of a uniform approach that can be used by countries and donors as the basis for national anti-corruption plans and wider reform.

Contact: Alan Doig (R.A.Doig@tees.ac.uk).

1   Jeremy Pope (ed.), *The TI Source Book* (Berlin: Transparency International, 1997). See also the new, expanded edition: Jeremy Pope, *The TI Source Book 2000: Confronting Corruption, The Elements of a National Integrity System* (Berlin: Transparency International, 2000).
2   The countries surveyed were: Argentina, Bangladesh, Botswana, Brazil, Bulgaria, Canada, Colombia, Fiji, Ghana, Jordan, Kazakhstan, Lithuania, Mexico, Mongolia, Nepal, Netherlands, Senegal, South Korea, and Trinidad and Tobago. The report from Bangladesh was not published because government approval of the survey was not secured in time.
3   Pope (2000).
4   For a discussion of corruption and democratisation, see the country reports from Brazil, Bulgaria, Colombia, Fiji, Ghana, Jordan, Kazakhstan, Nepal, Senegal, and Trinidad and Tobago.
5   For a discussion of corruption and decentralisation, see the country reports from Colombia and Botswana.

Approaches to measuring governance

Daniel Kaufmann (World Bank Institute), Aart Kraay
(World Bank Institute) and Pablo Zoido (Stanford University)

Governance and the control of corruption are closely related. Indeed, corruption is a particularly relevant indicator of weak governance. Two approaches to measuring governance are presented here – cross-country indicators and regional surveys of entrepreneurs.[1]

Cross-country indicators

Governance is here defined as the traditions and institutions by which authority in a country is exercised.[2] A wide variety of cross-country indicators sheds light on the various dimensions of this broad definition.[3] Primarily measured in qualitative units, these indicators are produced by a range of organisations (commercial risk-rating agencies, multilateral organisations, think-tanks and NGOs). They include the perspectives of diverse observers (experts, businesses and citizens) and cover a wide range of topics (perceptions of political stability and the business climate, views on the efficacy of public service provision, experiences with corruption).

This qualitative data is relevant for measuring governance. For many aspects of governance, particularly corruption, only qualitative data is generally available. Moreover, stakeholders' perceptions of the quality of governance, as reflected in these qualitative ratings, matter at least as much as objective data and are often a more accurate reflection of *de facto* outcomes. For example, the perception among enterprises that courts do not effectively enforce property rights may lead them to look for other, less efficient, means of enforcing contracts.

An important result that emerges from this work is that, for many countries and many aspects of governance, cross-country differences are not very precisely measured. The figure illustrates this by ordering 155 countries according to their rating on the aggregate 'control of corruption' indicator.[4] The range of statistically likely values of this indicator is shown as a vertical line for each country, with the mid-point indicating the best estimate. While control of corruption varies widely across countries, the statistically likely range for each country is also very large.

Control of corruption

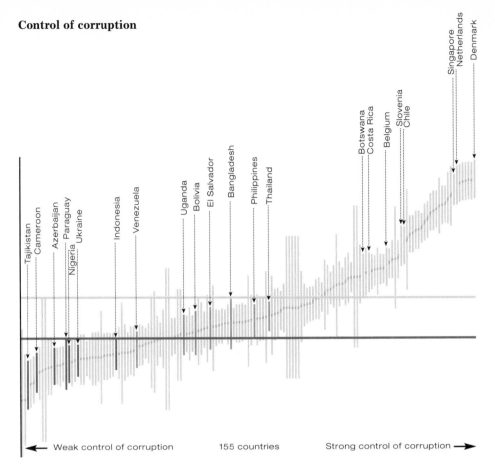

Note: This chart shows estimates of control of corruption for 155 countries during 1997–98, with selected countries indicated for illustrative purposes. The vertical bars show the likely range of the indicator, and the midpoint of each bar shows the most likely value for each country. The length of these ranges varies with the amount of information available for each country and with the extent to which different sources' perceptions of corruption coincide. Countries with dark red (or the opposite, pale red) vertical bars are those for which the indicator is statistically significant in the bottom (or the opposite, top) third of all countries. Countries with medium red bars fall into neither of the two previous groups. Countries' relative positions are subject to significant margins of error and reflect the perceptions of a variety of public and private sector organisations worldwide. Countries' relative positions in no way reflect the official views of the World Bank or the IMF.

Sources: Daniel Kaufmann, Aart Kraay, and Pablo Zoido-Lobatón, 'Aggregating Governance Indicators,' World Bank Policy Research Department Working Paper No. 2195, 1999; and Daniel Kaufmann, Aart Kraay, and Pablo Zoido-Lobatón, 'Governance Matters,' World Bank Policy Research Department Working Paper No. 2196, 1999.

This illustrates that even efficient aggregate indicators are relatively imprecise, since many countries' likely ranges of governance overlap.

This imprecision indicates that it may be less appropriate to compare precise rankings on governance than simply to group countries into broad categories along various governance dimensions, using a 'traffic light' approach. The figure illustrates this approach by highlighting selected countries in three broad categories: countries in 'governance crisis' (dark red); 'at risk' countries (medium red); and countries 'not at risk' (pale red).

Does the imprecision of these aggregate indicators imply that they have limited value? Not at all. Although imprecise, they can identify the group of countries facing major governance challenges. Furthermore, they can be used to assess systematically the benefits of good governance for a large sample of countries. For example, additional research found that a reduction in corruption from the very high level prevalent in Indonesia to the level in Korea leads to between a two and fourfold increase in per capita incomes, a decline in infant mortality of similar magnitude, and a 15-25 percentage point improvement in literacy levels.

Regional surveys of entrepreneurs

One effort to improve the quality of internationally comparable governance indicators is the World Business Environment Survey (WBES). This survey asked detailed questions on various dimensions of governance and probed quantitatively into issues typically considered to be qualitative. For example, it elicited specific information about the share of bribes paid in businesses' total revenue, and the percentage bribe 'cut' in public procurement projects.

While a separate contribution on the WBES follows, the table shows some early findings on transition economies, unbundling the notion of corruption into distinct components. The table focuses on the contrast between conventionally measured, administrative corruption and 'grand' forms of corruption, such as the 'purchase' of decrees and parliamentary laws. The latter approach of measuring the extent to which the policies, laws and regulations in a country are being shaped by 'captor' firms allows for arriving at an estimate of 'state capture' in each transition economy.

The results of this collaborative work between the World Bank and the European Bank for Reconstruction and Development point to the need for anti-corruption strategies to address the incentives firms have to capture state laws and policies.

State capture and administrative corruption

Country	State Capture Index and its components (% of firms affected by illicit purchase of:)						Capture index (average)	Capture classification	Administrative corruption Level of bribery (as % of firm revenues)
	Parliamentary legislation	Presidential decrees	Central bank	Criminal courts	Commercial courts	Political party finance			
Albania	12	7	8	22	20	25	16	Medium	4.0
Azerbaijan	41	48	39	44	40	35	41	High	5.7
Bulgaria	28	26	28	28	19	42	28	High	2.1
Croatia	18	24	30	29	29	30	27	High	1.1
Czech Rep	18	11	12	9	9	6	11	Medium	2.5
Estonia	14	7	8	8	8	17	10	Medium	1.6
Georgia	29	24	32	18	20	21	24	High	4.3
Hungary	12	7	8	5	5	4	7	Medium	1.7
Kyrgyzstan	18	16	59	26	30	27	29	High	5.3
Latvia	40	49	8	21	26	35	30	High	1.4
Lithuania	15	7	9	11	14	13	11	Medium	2.8
Moldova	43	30	40	33	34	42	37	High	4.0
Poland	13	10	6	12	18	10	12	Medium	1.6
Romania	22	20	26	14	17	27	21	High	3.2
Russia	35	32	47	24	27	24	32	High	2.8
Slovakia	20	12	37	29	25	20	24	High	2.5
Slovenia	8	5	4	6	6	11	7	Medium	1.4
Ukraine	44	37	37	21	26	29	32	High	4.4
Overall	24	21	25	18	20	20	21		3.0

See note on following page

Note: Selected countries in transition, 1999 data. The first six columns provide the estimate of percentage of 'capture' from each sub-component. The seventh and eighth columns show the overall State Capture Index (average of the six previous components) and whether the country falls into the medium or high capture category. In contrast with all previous columns, the last column provides the estimate of administrative corruption. Note that countries may exhibit a particularly high incidence of state capture but lower administrative corruption, or vice versa (with different policy implications). The individual estimates are subject to a margin of error, thus care ought to be exercised in the use of each individual estimate or in inferring precise rankings. Countries' relative positions in no way reflect the official views of the World Bank or the IMF.

Source: J. Hellman, G. Jones, and D. Kaufmann, 'Seize the State, Seize the Day: State Capture, Corruption and Influence in Transition Economies,' World Bank Policy Research Working Paper No. 2444, 2000: <http://www.worldbank.org/wbi/governance>.

Other approaches to measuring governance

A wealth of cross-country indicators of various aspects of governance now exist and point to the strong impact of governance on development. But even the best of these remain imprecise and say little about the specific institutional failures that underlie weak governance in a particular setting.

A key tool for addressing specific institutional challenges are in-depth, country-specific surveys of thousands of households, enterprises and public officials, carried out by domestic NGOs. Such surveys gather experiential and quantifiable information about specific vulnerabilities within a country's institutions. The responses of the three groups of stakeholders can be compared for consistency and pooled for in-depth analysis and the identification of priorities for action. Diagnostic studies have already identified key priorities for reform, such as the legal system and judiciary, customs, police and the sub-national level of government, and they provide empirical insights into the governance-poverty nexus.

Among others, the World Bank Institute has been involved in diagnostic studies in Eastern Europe (Albania, Georgia, Latvia, Romania and Slovenia); Latin America (Bolivia, Colombia, Ecuador, Honduras, Paraguay, Peru, Campo Elias in Venezuela, and São Paulo in Brazil); in East Asia (Cambodia, Indonesia and Thailand); and in Africa (Ghana, Nigeria and Tanzania).

---

1 The findings, interpretations and conclusions expressed in this paper are entirely those of the authors. They do not necessarily represent the views of the World Bank, its Executive Directors or the countries they represent.
2 This includes: (1) the process by which governments are selected, held accountable, monitored and replaced; (2) the capacity of governments to manage resources efficiently and formulate, implement and enforce sound policies and regulations; and (3) the respect of citizens and the state for the institutions that govern economic and social interactions among them.
3 See Daniel Kaufmann, Aart Kraay and Pablo Zoido-Lobatón, 'Governance Matters,' World Bank Policy Research Department Working Paper No. 2196, 1999: <http://www.worldbank.org/wbi/governance>.
4 A new update of the governance indicators, comprising data for 2000 and 2001, should be available in 2001.

World Business Environment Survey

World Bank Group

How can we assess and compare the environment for doing business in countries around the world?[1] Enterprise surveys provide an important means of generating consensus around a credible, locally-derived information source – that of entrepreneurs and managers who deal daily with the institutions, policies and practices of the local business environment. The World Business Environment Survey (WBES) is an initiative of the World Bank Group, which, in partnership with other institutions, has to date assessed the state of the enabling environment for private enterprise in 80 countries.[2]

The WBES assesses how conditions for private investment are shaped by: local economic policy; governance; regulatory, infrastructural and financial impediments; and services to businesses. One of its purposes is to measure the quality of governance and public services, including the extent of corruption. It also provides the World Bank with better information on constraints to private sector growth and stimulates systematic, public-private dialogue on business perceptions. The WBES generates indicators that allow comparisons across countries and, if repeated, over time.

The WBES builds on the start made in a survey carried out for the World Bank's *World Development Report 1997*, but substantially broadens coverage on a number of issues, expands the sample and the number of countries covered, and harmonises methodology across countries. The steering committee for the survey worked in collaboration with its partners in different regions and countries, to apply the core questionnaire, to develop regional modules to capture in detail issues judged important to those regions, and to implement the survey. To ensure adequate representation of firms by industry, size, ownership, export orientation and location, minimum quotas were set for different categories of firm, while sectorally the number of manufacturing versus service and commerce enterprises was allocated roughly according to their contributions to national GDP.

The survey was implemented by the Gallup Organization in East Asia, Pakistan, Latin America and OECD countries; by AC Nielsen in Eastern Europe and Turkey; by the Confederation of Indian Industries in India; by the Harvard Center for International Development in Africa; and by a number of national partners in other countries. The survey enumeration was carried out between late 1998 and mid-2000. Data was collected though personal interviews at senior managerial level in enterprises in most regions, with the exception of Africa where surveys by mail predominated. Response rates were generally high, with the exception in some countries of responses to questions on corruption.[3] By region, response rates were lowest in Africa. Globally, 10,090 enterprises responded to the core questionnaire.

Table 1 distinguishes responses to corruption-related questions by size of firm, where a small firm is one with fewer than 50 employees, and a large firm is one with more than 500 employees. It suggests that smaller firms are more likely than larger ones to find it necessary to make irregular payments to government officials. And in dealing with official misconduct, larger firms can get correct treatment more frequently without recourse to unofficial payments.

Table 2 suggests that small and medium firms pay a larger proportion of their revenues in unofficial payments to public officials.

Table 1: **Firms' experience of the need to make unofficial payments (%)**

	Irregular additional payments to government officials	If government official acts against rules, firm can go to a superior and get correct treatment without recourse to unofficial payment
Small firms	40.4	38.4
Medium firms	34.0	48.2
Large firms	30.9	53.2
All firms	36.0	44.8

Note: Table indicates the proportion of firms that state each event occurs 'always', 'mostly' or 'frequently'.

Table 2: **Proportion of firms' revenues in unofficial payments to public officials (%)**

Proportion of firms' revenues	0%	<1%	1–1.99%	2–9.99%	10-12%	13–25%	>25%
Small firms	32.3	21.3	13.7	17.6	9.4	3.7	2.0
Medium firms	37.6	26.9	11.7	14.0	5.9	3.0	1.0
Large firms	58.2	20.9	6.8	8.0	3.7	1.5	0.9
All firms	38.6	23.4	11.8	14.6	7.1	3.1	1.4

Table 3 suggests that, by region, informal payments to public officials occur most frequently in 'developing' East Asia, in South Asia and in Africa, where over half of responding firms report the necessity of payments. Of regions where data is available, appeals against official misconduct are most difficult in East Asia – both 'developing' and 'newly-industrialised'. Only around a quarter of firms in East Asia feel they can get correct treatment by appealing to a superior in case of official misconduct (although initial incidents of irregular payments are relatively rare in newly-industrialised countries in East Asia).

Table 3: **Firms' experience of the need to make unofficial payments (%)**

	Irregular additional payments to government official	If government official acts against rules, firm can go to a superior and get correct treatment without recourse to unofficial payment
East Asia, developing	61.8	26.3
South Asia	53.0	42.5
Africa	52.4	n/a
MENA	35.7	n/a
CEE	33.5	35.7
CIS	29.3	38.3
Latin America	28.2	69.3
OECD	11.9	44.9
East Asia, newly industrialised (excluding China)	10.7	25.0

Note: Table indicates the proportion of firms that state each event occurs 'always', 'mostly' or 'frequently'.

For more information on the WBES, please visit the website:
<http://www1.worldbank.org/beext/resources/ assess-wbessurvey-alt.htm>.

1 This contribution reflects the views of the authors, Andrew Stone, Geeta Batra and Daniel Kaufmann, and should not be attributed to the World Bank, its Board of Directors, management or any of its member countries.
2 The WBES began with substantial seed capital from the Innovation Marketplace and the support of World Bank President James D. Wolfensohn. The steering committee of the WBES comprised the authors and Guy Pfeffermann, Luke Haggarty, Shyam Khemani and Homi Kharas. External partners included the EBRD, the IDB, Harvard CID and the Egyptian Centre for Economic Studies.
3 Questions on corruption could not be asked in China.

Pragmatic approaches
to patronage

Nick Manning, Ranjana Mukherjee and Omer Gokcekus
(World Bank Poverty Reduction and Economic Management Network)

During 1999–2001, some 7,011 public officials in 16 countries were surveyed to map the strengths and weaknesses of the public sector and to model the potential benefits from reform interventions.[1] The surveys and analyses were undertaken by the World Bank and financed under the Bank-Netherlands Partnership Program (BNPP). BNPP-funded surveys of public officials have been completed in Albania, Argentina, Bangladesh, Bolivia, Bulgaria, six East Caribbean states, Guyana, Indonesia, Kenya, Macedonia and Moldova. Surveys are in preparation for Russia. The programme also provided funds for data analysis of a separate survey of public officials in Armenia.

Local researchers using an agreed methodology surveyed public officials at all levels and in a range of government agencies. The surveys were based on a model designed in collaboration with Professor Bert Rockman of the University of Pittsburgh. World Bank staff working on a particular country tailored the approach to the country-specific background and issues in public sector reform.

The surveys offer insights for reform interventions in many areas. The framework used for analysing the survey data offers an approach for understanding how accountability is linked with both bad performance and good, and for presenting the results to policy-makers in a format that leads to more informed choices about public sector reform. The reforms discussed include: strengthening the credibility of rules for evaluation, record management, training and recruitment; ensuring that staff support government policy; preventing political interference or micro-management; and making government policies consistent.

Patronage is common in many developing country public sectors, violating principles of merit and competition in civil service recruitment and promotion. A small number of patronage appointments are justified as a means for political leaders to fashion a circle of government policy-makers and managers who share a common agenda. Patronage is clearly a problem when such appointments pervade the public administration. On a large scale, it is associated with poor performance and other forms of corruption. Patronage itself can be a form of corruption to the extent that it entails selling positions that are formally merit-based.

Patronage can vary significantly between agencies within the same country. The surveys indicated unambiguously that performance deteriorates in agencies with high levels of patronage. Political patronage and organisational performance indicators can be constructed for each agency. Figure 1 shows agencies divided into two groups on the basis of their degree of political patronage relative to the country's average.[2] Organisational performance is expressed as standard deviations from the country's average.

Figure 1: **Political patronage and organisational performance**

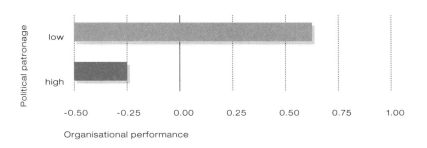

Organisational performance

Patronage is a peculiarly well-entrenched institutional phenomenon. It responds to the demand-side pressures of politicians and others looking to recruit officials who will owe them trust and loyalty. It also provides protection for public officials who fear – often with justification – that without it, arbitrarily applied rules will be used to prevent their career advancing. If patronage is hard to remove, it is also hard to live with. There are difficulties in enforcing disciplinary rules in high-patronage environments because of resistance from complicit and occasionally corrupt public sector unions and other bodies.

The research findings suggest that local managers can take actions that mitigate the impact of patronage. Recognising that the larger problem cannot be easily resolved, even in high-patronage countries, agency managers who take action to improve rewards and recognition get better results from their staff. Such action could take the form of an out-of-turn promotion or an award or other recognition, publicised in the official's local area.

In a high-patronage environment, managers who publicly recognise their staff are likely to see a distinct improvement in performance, perhaps even more than in low-patronage environments. This is seen in figure 2, where public sector organisations have been divided into two groups on the basis of average level of political patronage, and both low and high-patronage groups have then been subdivided into groups with either weak or strong rewards and recognition.[3]

Figure 2: **The impact of strong rewards and recognition on organisational performance**

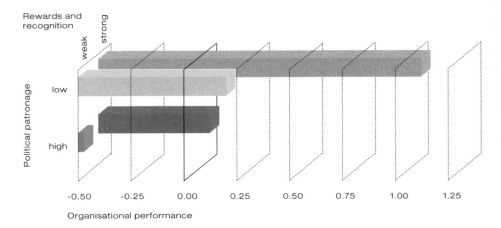

Organisational performance

Other survey results indicated that staff themselves see the value of this approach. The surveys showed that many staff consider recognition more important than increased remuneration.

The conclusions are clear. In an environment of low accountability, steps to reduce political patronage are as productive as banging heads against the proverbial brick wall. Managers can still make a difference, however, by the simple expedient of recognising good behaviour. Carrots work better than sticks.

Findings to date are available at the website:
**<http://www1.worldbank.org/publicsector/
civilservice/surveys.htm>.**

1   This contribution presents some summary findings. It reflects work in progress and should not be taken as any indication of World Bank policy.
2   Ranjana Mukherjee and Omer Gokcekus, 'Civil Service Reform Options when Patronage Cannot be Eliminated Immediately,' draft World Bank Working Paper, 2001. See also the following papers: Omer Gokcekus, Nick Manning, Ranjana Mukherjee and Raj Nallari, 'Institutional Environment and Public Officials' Performance in Guyana,' World Bank Technical Paper, 2001; Nick Manning, Ranjana Mukherjee and Omer Gokcekus, 'Public Officials and their Institutional Environment: An Analytical Model for Assessing the Impact of Institutional Change on Public Sector Performance,' World Bank Policy Research Working Paper No. 2427, 2000, <http://econ.worldbank.org/view.php?type=5&id=1182>; and Ranjana Mukherjee, Omer Gokcekus, Nick Manning and Pierre Landell-Mills, 'Bangladesh: The Experience and Perceptions of Public Officials,' World Bank Technical Paper, 2001.
3   Ranjana Mukherjee and Omer Gokcekus (2001).

IMF research on corruption

International Monetary Fund (IMF) Fiscal Affairs Department

In recent years, the IMF has increasingly recognised the adverse impact of corruption and poor governance on economic performance and on the success of economic reforms in IMF-supported programmes.[1]

In parallel with this recognition, empirical research at the IMF has highlighted the causes of corruption, its impact (on economic growth, public finances, poverty, income inequality and the provision of social services) and the effect of anti-corruption strategies. The IMF has published 11 such empirical studies since the mid-1990s, mostly relying on measures of corruption developed by Business International, International Country Risk Guide and Transparency International.

The findings of each study depend on: the choice of the corruption measure; consideration of other factors besides corruption that may affect economic performance; countries sampled; and the statistical technique used for estimating the relationship between corruption and each measure of economic performance. Tables 1 and 2, which contain a summary of these studies, provide a range of estimates of the likely impact of corruption and of the causes of corruption.

Four studies identified the negative impact of corruption on economic growth (see table 1). One study found that increasing corruption by one unit (on a scale of zero to ten) would lower real per capita GDP growth by some 0.3 to 1.8 percentage points,[2] while others reported a narrower range. In the four studies, corruption was shown to lower growth by reducing private investment,[3] by attracting talented individuals to unproductive activities,[4] by poor management of rich natural resources[5] and as a proxy for the postponement of growth-enhancing structural reforms.[6] The last of these studies argued that structural reforms aimed at rationalising the role of the state, increasing the reliance on market-based pricing and creating a sound regulatory environment should contribute to growth directly and indirectly by lowering the incidence of corruption. It provided supporting empirical evidence from the experiences of countries of the former Soviet Union and Eastern Europe.

A large number of IMF studies found that corruption distorts the composition of public expenditures in favour of sectors where the collection of bribes is easier. Corruption shifts spending away from routine maintenance and repair[7] and education and health[8] to excessive and inefficient physical public investments[9] and higher military spending.[10] Higher corruption was also found to have adverse consequences for social indicators such as child mortality rate, student dropout rates,[11] and income inequality and poverty.[12] These studies imply that policies aimed at reducing corruption will improve the composition of government spending in favour of more productive outlays.

Table 1: **Impact of increasing corruption by one unit**[1]

Author(s)	Impact on	Finding
Mauro (1996)	Real per capita GDP growth	−0.3 to −1.8 percentage points
Leite and Weidmann (1999)	Real per capita GDP growth	−0.7 to −1.2 percentage points
Tanzi and Davoodi (2000)	Real per capita GDP growth	−0.6 percentage points
Abed and Davoodi (2000)	Real per capita GDP growth	−1 to −1.3 percentage points
Mauro (1996)	Ratio of investment to GDP	−1 to −2.8 percentage points
Mauro (1998)[2]	Ratio of public education spending to GDP	−0.7 to −0.9 percentage points
Mauro (1998)[3]	Ratio of public health spending to GDP	−0.6 to −1.7 percentage points
Gupta, Davoodi and Alonso-Terme (1998)	Income inequality (Gini coefficient)	+0.9 to +2.1 Gini points
Gupta, Davoodi and Alonso-Terme (1998)	Income growth of the poor	−2 to −10 percentage points
Ghura (1998)	Ratio of tax revenues to GDP	−1 to −2.9 percentage points
Tanzi and Davoodi (2000)[4]	Measures of government revenues to GDP ratio	−0.1 to −4.5 percentage points
Gupta, de Mello and Sharan (2000)[5]	Ratio of military spending to GDP	+1 percentage point
Gupta, Davoodi and Tiongson (2000)[6]	Child mortality rate	+1.1 to 2.7 deaths per 1,000 live births
Gupta, Davoodi and Tiongson (2000)[7]	Primary student dropout rate	+1.4 to 4.8 percentage points
Tanzi and Davoodi (1997)[8]	Ratio of public investment to GDP	+0.5 percentage points
Tanzi and Davoodi (1997)[9]	Per cent of paved roads in good condition	−2.2 to −3.9 percentage points

1. *Corruption is measured on a scale of 0 (highly clean) to 10 (highly corrupt).*
2. *Three other measures of education spending are also reported in this study.*
3. *Three other measures of health spending are also reported in this study.*
4. *This study covers 15 types of government revenues.*
5. *Three additional measures of military spending are also reported in this study.*
6. *Four additional indicators of health are reported in this study.*
7. *Four additional indicators of education are reported in this study.*
8. *Two additional measures of public spending are also reported in this study.*
9. *Four additional indicators of infrastructure are used in this study.*

Corruption was also shown to reduce government revenue because it contributes to tax evasion, improper tax exemptions or weak tax administration, thereby limiting the ability of the government to provide quality public services.[13]

Several studies investigated the causes of corruption (see table 2). These range from weak rule of law and the availability of natural resources[14] to the public-private wage differential,[15] a country's past political history and its propensity to embark on structural reforms.[16] Future research at the IMF will most likely include further analysis of the causes of corruption and analysis of the role of standards and codes of conduct in promoting good governance.

Table 2: **Causes of corruption**[1]

Author(s)	Impact of	Impact on corruption
Van Rijckeghem and Weder (1997)[2]	Doubling civil service wages relative to manufacturing wages	−1.9 to −2.1 points
Leite and Weidmann (1999)[2]	Increasing ratio of fuel and ore exports to GDP by one percentage point	+2.7 to +4.2 points
Abed and Davoodi (2000)[2]	Increasing pace of structural reforms by one unit	−1 to −1.2 points
Abed and Davoodi (2000)[2]	Increasing years lived under central planning by 10 to 20 years	+0.5 to +1 point

1. Corruption is measured on a scale of 0 (highly clean) to 10 (highly corrupt).
2. See these studies for additional causes of corruption.

Contact: Hamid R. Davoodi, economist, IMF (hdavoodi@imf.org).

1 In 1997 the IMF issued a guidance note on governance issues, <http://www.imf.org/external/np/sec/nb/1997/nb9715.htm>, and, on 14 February 2001, the IMF's Executive Board reviewed experiences with governance issues in IMF-supported programmes, <http://www.imf.org/external/np/sec/pn/2001/pn0120.htm>.
2 Paulo Mauro, 'Corruption and Composition of Government Expenditure,' IMF Working Paper 96/98, 1996. Also published in *Journal of Public Economics*, No. 69, June 1999.
3 Ibid.
4 Vito Tanzi and Hamid Davoodi, 'Corruption, Growth and Public Finances,' IMF Working Paper 00/116, 2000. Also in Arvind K. Jain (ed.), *The Political Economy of Corruption* (London: Routledge, forthcoming).
5 Carlos Leite and Jens Weidmann, 'Does Mother Nature Corrupt? Natural Resources, Corruption and Economic Growth,' IMF Working Paper 99/85, 1999.
6 George Abed and Hamid Davoodi, 'Corruption, Structural Reforms and Economic Performance in the Transition Economies,' IMF Working Paper 00/132, 2000.
7 Vito Tanzi and Hamid Davoodi, 'Corruption, Public Investment and Growth,' IMF Working Paper 97/139, 1997. Also published in T. Shibata and T. Ihori (eds.), *The Welfare State, Public Investment and Growth* (Tokyo: Springer Verlag, 1998).
8 Sanjeev Gupta, Hamid Davoodi and Rosa Alonso-Terme, 'Does Corruption Affect Income Inequality and Poverty?' IMF Working Paper 98/76, 1998; Mauro (1996).

9   Tanzi and Davoodi (2000); Mauro (1996).
10 Sanjeev Gupta, Luiz de Mello and Raju Sharan, 'Corruption and Military Spending,'
    IMF Working Paper 00/23, 2000. Also forthcoming in *European Journal of Political Economy*.
11 Sanjeev Gupta, Hamid Davoodi and Erwin Tiongson, 'Corruption and the Provision of Health
    Care and Education Services,' IMF Working Paper 00/116, 2000. Also in Jain (forthcoming).
12 Gupta, Davoodi and Alonso-Terme (2000).
13 Dhaneshwar Ghura, 'Tax Revenue in Sub-Saharan Africa: Effects of Economic Policies and
    Corruption,' IMF Working Paper 98/135, 1998; Vito Tanzi and Hamid Davoodi, 'Corruption,
    Growth and Public Finances,' IMF Working Paper 00/116, 2000. Also in Jain (forthcoming).
14 Leite and Weidmann (1999).
15 Caroline Van Rijckeghem and Beatrice Weder, 'Corruption and the Rate of Temptation:
    Do Low Wages in the Civil Service Cause Corruption?' IMF Working Paper 97/73, 1997.
16 Abed and Davoodi (2000).

Fighting corruption in developing countries: what can we learn from recent experiences?

UN Development Programme (UNDP) and the Organisation for Economic Cooperation and Development (OECD) Development Centre

The UNDP Programme for Accountability and Transparency (PACT) and the OECD Development Centre jointly undertook a research project to compare the experiences of anti-corruption efforts in five developing countries. All five are countries in which political leaders had launched anti-corruption programmes with support from the international community: Benin, Bolivia, Morocco, Pakistan and the Philippines.

The methodology combined fact-finding case studies entrusted to experts, with field missions and literature reviews by the authors. This qualitative approach allowed the researchers to test anti-corruption models such as the National Integrity System and sets of recommendations such as the Arusha Declaration.[1] It provided a detailed, objective and intimate account of the character of corruption practices, the forces at work for and against reform, and the outcome of the different initiatives undertaken in the countries studied.

The first component of the project studied the national anti-corruption programmes. This is still work in progress, although the first results have been published.[2] The second component focused on the problem of corruption in one specific area of administration, that of customs, in three countries only: Bolivia, Pakistan and the Philippines. Findings have recently been published and there are three main conclusions of the research.[3]

First, while all acts of corruption by definition involve the use of public office for private gain, they vary in nature. In the customs environment, three types of corrupt practice can be distinguished: routine, fraudulent and criminal. These are driven by different 'logics of action' (i. e. different rationales) on the part of the private actors involved, and they call for different solutions. This observation leads to a simple framework of analysis that distinguishes between the opportunity for corruption and the rationale of the actors who seize that opportunity (see figure). The opportunity for corruption stems from defects in the organisation of an administrative unit (such as customs). The logic of action refers to the broader social environment.

Revisiting the analysis of corruption

CORRUPTION = OPPORTUNITIES + LOGICS OF ACTION

OPPORTUNITIES in the operational environment of the customs administration:

- Discretionary interface and
- Lack of efficient controls and
- Networks of accomplices

LOGICS OF ACTION stemming from the broader environment:

For public actors:
- Contrast between remuneration level and personal expectations
- Functioning of the political system
- Criminal logics of action

For private actors:
- Growth in the volume of trade
- High level of taxes and tax structure perceived as unfair
- Criminal logics of action

Second, in a context of entrenched corruption, an approach based on 're-engineering' the structure of the administration is more likely to bear fruit than measures more strictly limited to changing incentives. Purges of staff, reinforced controls and mechanisms to secure spontaneous compliance all aim to modify incentives for those working at each station of the 'customs chain'. It is more effective to rethink the customs chain, in order to reduce the need for controls and positive incentives, or to facilitate those controls and incentives still necessary.

Third, the relative success in the Philippines, compared to the serious setbacks observed in Bolivia and Pakistan, can be explained by astute implementation of reforms and by the existence of a facilitating environment.[4] The table compares the processes of implementing reform using three criteria: the actors involved, the management of change and the monitoring of the process.

Comparing three experiences of reform in customs administration

	Philippines	Bolivia, Pakistan
Actors involved	Real will of government expressed. Strong personal commitment of the President, and close collaboration with the Director of Customs.	Real will of government expressed.
	Transparent design and implementation process.	Lack of transparency in the design and implementation process.
	Close involvement and support of business associations.	Failure to involve private sector associations.
Management of change	Progressive implementation of reforms.	Design of a radical reform programme, arousing different sources of opposition, which converged to make the project fail in Pakistan.
	Changes in management combined with re-engineering measures.	Disputed staff selection measures in Pakistan.
Monitoring of progress	Indicators set up by Customs Commissioner to monitor progress.	Belated monitoring of reform effort in Bolivia.

*Contact: Pauline Tamesis, UNDP (pauline.tamesis@undp.org) or
Irène Hors, OECD (irene.hors@oecd.org).*

1 Declaration of the Customs Cooperation Council Concerning Integrity in Customs, adopted in Arusha, Tanzania, in July 1993.
2 Irène Hors, 'Fighting Corruption in Developing Countries,' *OECD Observer*, No. 220, April 2000; Irène Hors, 'Les difficultés de la lutte contre la corruption: l'expérience de quatre pays en développement,' *Revue Tiers Monde*, XLI, No. 161, January-March 2000; and Irène Hors, 'Dealing with Corruption in Developing Countries,' in *No Longer Business as Usual: Fighting Bribery and Corruption* (Paris: OECD, 2000).
3 Irène Hors, 'Fighting Corruption in Customs Administration: What Can We Learn From Recent Experiences?' OECD Development Centre Technical Paper No. 175, 2001, <http://www.oecd.org/dev/publication/tp1a.htm>.
4 Assessment based on private sector testimonies.

Public service ethics in Africa

UN Department of Economic and Social Affairs (UN DESA)

Between 1999 and 2001, the Division for Public Economics and Public Administration of the UN Department of Economic and Social Affairs (UN DESA) conducted a comparative study on public service ethics in Africa, funded by the Regional Bureau for Africa of the UNDP.

The study involved ten countries: Cameroon, Gabon, Ghana, Kenya, Madagascar, Namibia, Nigeria, Senegal, South Africa and Uganda. These countries were chosen to ensure broad representation of the cultural and linguistic diversity in Sub-Saharan Africa. The selection was based on a consultation process between UN DESA, UNDP country offices and national governments.

The overall aim of the study was to help African governments improve the management of ethics and conduct in public services. For this purpose, comparative information on current legislation, policies, programmes and practices was compiled to highlight gaps and practices that can serve as a basis to introduce new, or improve existing, ethics policies and programmes at the national level.

Methodology

The conceptual framework of the study was the description of the specific 'ethics infrastructure' in each country: the set of rules, institutions and practices that are in place to guide, manage and enforce good conduct in the public sector. The OECD initially developed the concept, but it was modified by UN DESA in order to reflect the African context.

The research design for the study was a combination of expert interviews and document analysis. The research process at the country level, conducted by national consultants, was supported and guided by a detailed standardised questionnaire and research guidelines developed by UN DESA. The questionnaire focused mostly on publicly available statistics, administrative data and legal documents. In order to ensure the validity and reliability of the data gathered, as well as the participation of regional and national stakeholders in the research process, the project was advised by a project steering group.

Current status

- Internet website **<http://www.unpan.org/ethics>** with overviews, downloadable project documents and links.
- Project report in two volumes: Volume 1, with comparative overview, has been published; and Volume 2, containing individual country reports, is currently being finalised.
- Database on survey data available upon request.
- Consultative meetings on possible follow-up action at the country level scheduled for 2001.

Contact: Elia Yi Armstrong, Project Coordinator (armstronge@un.org) or Stefan Lock, Associate Expert (lock@un.org).

Synopsis of findings and recommendations

Findings	Recommendations
Government employment • Access to public service employment data is highly limited in many countries.	• Strengthen capacity to collect basic public service statistics.
Public sector salaries • Lowest and highest nominal income are often very close to each other. • Seven countries reported that salaries have been paid regularly. Only South Africa reported that public service salaries kept up with inflation and in parity with private sector salaries.	• Improve public sector salary structures, where appropriate, by introducing decompression, inflation adjustment and competitiveness with the private sector.
Identification and provision of values and standards • All ten countries reported having public service-wide statements of core values. The most common values are: impartiality/neutrality/financial disinterestedness; honesty/integrity; equality; fairness/justice; selflessness; accountability; dedication/diligence; discretion; efficiency; and transparency.	

Findings	Recommendations
Communication of values and standards	
• Few countries offer continuous training and regular reminder activities for their public servants in this area. • Only three countries indicated that the values and standards relevant to the work of their public servants are given to them individually and in printed form.	• Continuous communication of values and standards, and continuous training in public service ethics.
Restrictions on conduct	
• Restrictions regarding the conduct of members of the public service are in place for most countries. • The acceptance of gifts, fees or payments, unauthorised use of official property or use of official information and political engagement are usually covered. • Some traditional concerns like inappropriate employment and/or supervision of family members are insufficiently addressed.	• Inappropriate employment and/or supervision of family members need to be addressed more explicitly. Inappropriate employment of family and friends should be important targets for reform in many participating countries. • Current standards in many countries do not sufficiently address new areas of concern such as official travel, movement to the private sector, post-employment and lobbying. It is recommended that national governments in Africa observe further developments in these areas and prepare appropriate regulations.
Integrity strategies	
• Six countries indicated the existence of a specific national integrity strategy. • Less than half of the countries were able to indicate whether they had established routines for risk assessment, systematic policy analysis, and evaluation mechanisms in their coordination of ethics and anti-corruption measures.	• More policy and impact analysis in the field of management activities for the enhancement of ethical values and standards in the public sector.
Human resources management	
• While appropriate regulatory provisions seem to be in place, they are often not translated satisfactorily into daily action. • Relevant management tools, such as the identification and reporting of conflicts-of-interest in various areas, service standards and anti-corruption provisions in bidding procedures, are usually provided.	• Disciplinary measures and sanctions need to be enforced in daily administrative practice. • Appropriate training of managers and supervisors in disciplinary procedures and measures should be encouraged.

Findings	Recommendations
Disclosure requirements	
• All countries reported that previous employment has to be declared. • Less than half of the participating countries reported that loans and outside positions are covered by disclosure requirements.	• Need to strengthen and expand disclosure systems.
Internal reporting procedures	
• Nine countries indicated that public servants have an obligation to report or 'blow the whistle' on wrongdoing. • Six countries indicated the availability of protection for those public servants reporting wrongdoing.	• Need to simplify reporting procedures, both internally for public servants and externally for the general public. • Governments should provide sufficient protection for public servants willing to report misconduct.
Public complaints mechanisms	
• Seven countries confirmed that they have public complaints procedures. • The institution of ombudsman, public defender, or the inspector general was the most frequently mentioned agency.	• Need to simplify reporting procedures, both internally for public servants and externally for the general public. • Need to strengthen capacity of external agencies, such as the ombudsman or the inspector general.
Role of non-governmental actors	
• Transparency in sharing information about public sector activities is acknowledged to variable degrees in most countries. • In many countries the press is still not entirely free to express its views or operate without government interference.	• Governments need to enhance their transparency and disclosure requirements. • The private sector and civil society should be included as partners in ethics and anti-corruption policies. • Public administrations need to accept the public reporting and oversight function of private media.

Full documentation is available at the website:
<http://www.unpan.org/ethics>.

The International Crime Victims Survey

United Nations Interregional Crime and Justice Research Institute (UNICRI)[1]

The International Crime Victims Survey (ICVS) looks at households' experience of crime, policing, crime prevention and feelings of unsafety across countries and large cities in both developed and developing countries. One of the crimes recorded by the ICVS is corruption by government officials, as directly experienced by citizens.

The ICVS is the most far-reaching programme of standardised sample surveys to look at households' experience of crime and policing. The project started in 1989 with surveys in 14 industrialised countries. To date, over 140 surveys have been carried out in more than 70 countries. The surveys were equally distributed between industrialised countries, large European cities and large cities in developing countries. The next round of surveys is scheduled for 2004.

The programme was created for a number of reasons. First, police records of offences are inadequate for comparing crime across countries because of different definitions of crimes, different recording practices and differences in reporting to the police by victims. In a number of developing countries, there is no reliable recording of crime by police at all. Secondly, there was no alternative standardised measure. Thirdly, the programme was intended to stimulate research in the fields of crime and criminal justice in non-industrialised countries. In some countries, the ICVS is the only source of information on crime and victimisation.

The surveys involved questioning a random sample of the population about their experiences with 13 types of victimisation, policing, fear of crime and crime prevention. In general, surveys in industrialised countries were nationwide. Surveys in non-industrialised countries were largely city-based, though some were national. Two methodologies were applied: one, by telephone interviews, used in industrialised countries; and one by face-to-face interviews, used in city surveys in non-industrialised countries. All aspects of the surveys were standardised, including questionnaires, sampling methodology, interview techniques, as well as procedures for handling and analysing data.

Responses to questions about corruption provided a measure of its actual incidence, rather than the perception of corruption measured in many other studies. Respondents who reported having been confronted with a corrupt official were also asked whether the incident was reported to the police or another authority. The 2000 version of the face-to-face methodology included additional questions on the reporting of crimes to the police and the perception of changes in corruption over the last few years.

The figure shows the percentage of the population with direct experiences of a corrupt official in 1999. Two groups of surveys are presented: data from 17 mainly European cities and data from 17 national surveys in industrialised countries. Since urbanisation is a major factor in crime, the responses from the national surveys for cities of over 100,000 inhabitants are also included in the graph for comparison. Also included are the results of an *ad hoc* survey in Lebanon.

The survey shows a huge gap between East and Central Europe and other former socialist countries on the one hand, and the industrialised countries on the other. Portugal and France are the only two countries in the latter group with corruption figures of slightly over 1 per cent. By contrast, between 8 and 22 per cent of inhabitants of the capital cities in East and Central Europe were confronted with a corrupt official in 1999. Tirana (Albania) stands out with almost a 60 per cent experience of corruption. Corruption in Lebanon is also very high, especially considering that the data applies to the whole of Lebanon, not just the capital.

The ICVS is an important research and policy/management tool for screening and evaluating the present situation in crime and corruption and for identifying directions for future work. Because it focuses on experienced, rather than perceived corruption, the ICVS has been selected as one of the assessment tools of the UN Global Programme Against Corruption, currently being conducted in several countries across the world.

Contact: icvs@unicri.it

---

1   The principal researchers and institutes involved are: Anna Alvazzi del Frate (UNICRI, Turin), Pat Mayhew (Home Office, London), Jan J.M. van Dijk (CICP, Vienna), John van Kesteren (UNICRI, Turin), Paul Nieuwbeerta (NSCR, Leiden), plus national coordinators in each of the participating countries.

Experience of corruption in industrialised countries and large European cities

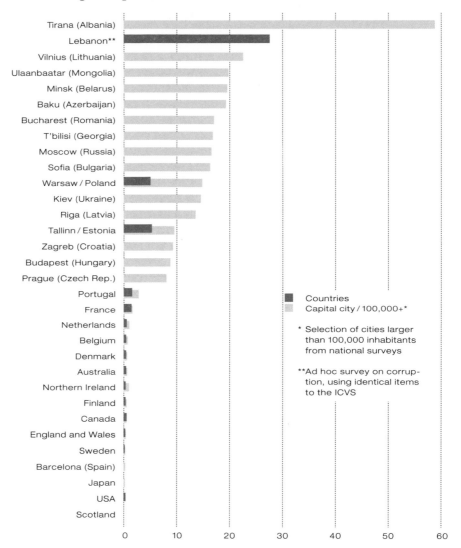

% of population confronted with bribery in the year preceding the interview

A database of integrity measures: lessons from OECD countries

OECD Public Management Service (PUMA)

In summer 1999, the Public Management Service (PUMA) of the OECD launched a survey on the implementation of the OECD 1998 Recommendation on Improving Ethical Conduct in the Public Service. The overall objective was to support the development of modern anti-corruption and ethics strategies by providing analysis of common trends, and a framework for assessment and identifying promising practices – what works and how, in different national environments – on the basis of the first comprehensive database of integrity measures in the public service of 29 OECD countries. The report was presented to the OECD Council Meeting at ministerial level in June 2000.

The survey reviewed the public service environment in OECD countries to examine the arrangements/mechanisms – including regulations, institutions and procedures – used to:

1. Redefine, communicate and inculcate core values and ethical standards for public servants and provide clear guidance to help solve ethical dilemmas.
2. Monitor compliance and reward ethical conduct through career development, and prevent situations prone to conflict of interest.
3. Report, detect, investigate, prosecute and punish misconduct.

With regard to the first, a visible shift in values clearly indicates that OECD countries have re-emphasised 'traditional' values, while giving them a modern content and combining them with 'new' values to mirror the increasingly results-based public service culture. Impartiality, legality and integrity are the three most frequently stated core public service values in OECD countries, and they determine the distinct characteristics of the public service. But they have been complemented by 'new' principles, such as efficiency and transparency, reflecting the evolving social demands and changes in public management. Furthermore, OECD countries have developed a more detailed description of the standards expected of all public servants. Figure 1 indicates the areas of concern where OECD countries provide standards for public servants.

Putting values into practice starts with communicating them and creating a working environment that promotes integrity in daily operations. For example,

Figure 1: **Areas of concern where OECD countries provide standards for public servants**

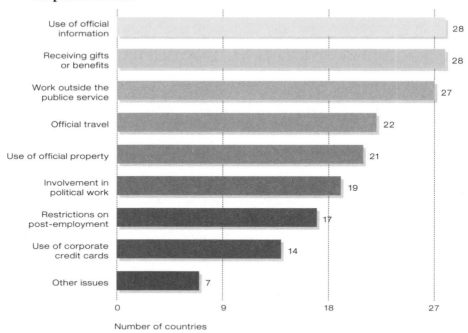

Number of countries

Figure 2: **Human resource management measures used by OECD countries to ensure transparency, accountability and integrity**

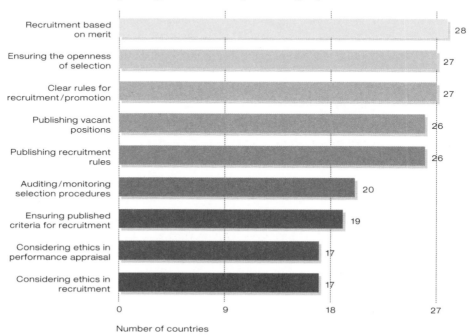

Number of countries

figure 2 shows which human resource management measures OECD countries employ to ensure transparency and accountability and to reinforce integrity.

The experience of OECD countries proves that sound ethics management not only sets standards of behaviour, but also monitors compliance with these standards. Internal control is used to detect individual irregularities and systemic failures, while independent scrutiny keeps public servants accountable – ultimately to the public – for their actions. Figure 3 indicates the combination of independent institutions exercising external scrutiny of the administration.

Figure 3: **Independent institutions exercising external scrutiny of the administration**

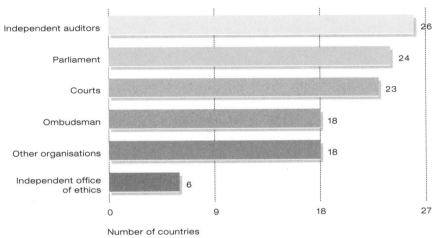

The full survey report, *Trust in Government: Ethics Measures in OECD Countries*, can be viewed and/or ordered from the website of the Public Management Service (PUMA) of the OECD:
<http://www.oecd.org/puma/ ethics/index.htm>.

Contact: János Bertók, Principal Administrator,
Public Management Service, OECD (janos.bertok@oecd.org).

Investors Roadmap

United States Agency for International Development (USAID)

The Investors Roadmap is a comprehensive, in-depth diagnostic study of the individual steps required for an investor to become legally established and operational (up to the commencement of production) in a specific country. It addresses the procedural and administrative barriers to investment and business operations.

The delineation of the Investors Roadmap identifies many kinds of inefficiencies that may relate directly or indirectly to corruption. In general, where the steps in the Investors Roadmap process are time-consuming, costly and complicated, there is the opportunity and, most likely, the actuality of high levels of corruption. Sometimes delays and extra steps stem from poorly functioning institutions and allow opportunities for massive petty corruption. In other cases, individuals, internal or external to the institutions, are able to manipulate institutions for personal gain on a grander scale. On still other occasions, legislation has been poorly conceived from the outset or subsequently corrupted, indicating that corruption is more widely spread in the political system.

From a research perspective, the 40 experiences of the Investors Roadmap have probably been the largest effort in the developing world to estimate systematically the transaction costs to investing.[1] It is only now, however, that this resource is becoming available to larger research efforts on transaction costs.

Looking at the Investors Roadmap experiences across all 40 countries, a few commonalities stand out. First, in any given country there is broad variation in the strengths and weaknesses of the range of institutions involved. Across countries in the same region, there is little predictability as to patterns of strength or weakness in the institutions of most concern to investors. Second, the strength or weakness of an institution appears to depend on the individual at its head. If a dynamic, pro-investment leader is in charge, the institution will reflect those characteristics in dealing with investors. The random variation in quality of leadership within institutions may be due to the absence of strong central governments that maintain consistent quality across the institutional landscape. Third, the nature of the bureaucratic treatment of investors relates closely to the origin of a country's legal framework. Countries whose law is based in common law tend to have fewer steps, less bureaucracy and greater transparency.

The Investors Roadmap was discovered inadvertently.[2] The first was made in Ghana in 1995. President Jerry Rawlings had been calling for more foreign investment and requested USAID-Accra to produce a step-by-step guide for prospective investors. To carry out the exercise, Services Group, a private contractor based in the US, proceeded as any foreign investor who had just arrived in Ghana to start a business. The findings were worse than expected: everyone in the country knew that administrative red tape was a nuisance, but no one realised that it frequently amounted to the complete frustration of a projected investment. In the end, this first roadmap proved less a 'how to' guide than a catalogue of cumbersome procedures.

As a result, President Rawlings set up a special inter-ministerial committee to oversee the streamlining of procedures by the different agencies involved and for their respective areas of authority. Thus the first Investors Roadmap report resulted in a number of efforts to reform the actual situation.

In its most fully developed form, the Investors Roadmap involves a three-phased process. First, it charts the red tape and administrative barriers to investment. Second, it helps government officials examine how these barriers can be reduced. Third, it assists officials in the reform of institutions, regulations and laws that stand in the way of foreign and local investment. The Investors Roadmap, in fact, benefits foreign and local investors alike.

In some countries, USAID missions have worked with the government to complete reform in the three-phase process described above. For example, in Tanzania (see the figure), the Investors Roadmap led to the following results:
- Customs clearance reduced from 15 days to as few as two days
- Introduction of random inspection, with only 30 per cent of goods inspected (before, there was no random inspection and over 80 per cent of all goods were inspected)
- Issuance of work permits for expatriates decreased from six months to one week
- Application forms provided in both English and Swahili, instead of just Swahili.

Other countries, like Malawi and Mozambique, have pursued reform in the wake of the roadmap exercise and are now developing a second round of roadmaps to see how the picture has changed after five years. Investors Roadmaps have also been examined comparatively for the Common Market for Eastern and Southern Africa (COMESA) group of countries to assist in further trade integration. Geographically diverse countries like Russia and Kazakhstan have also undertaken multiple Investors Roadmaps at the regional level.

Investors Roadmap of Tanzania, August 1997

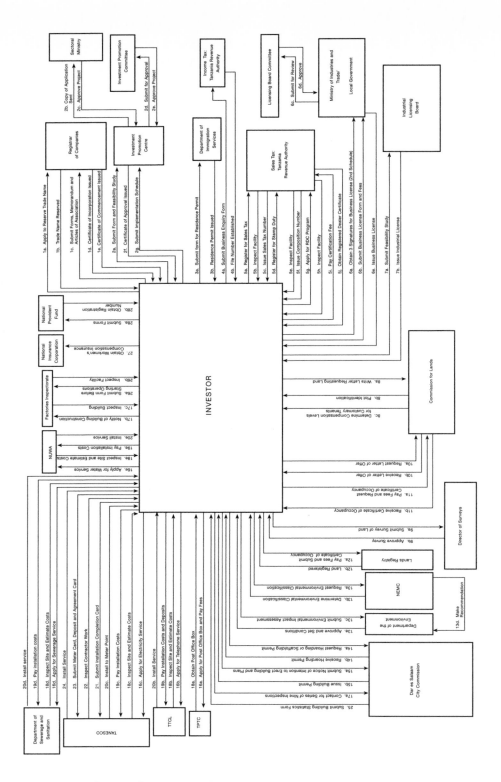

The Investors Roadmap demonstrates to all concerned – but, above all, to governments – the kinds of administrative barriers that discourage both foreign investors and domestic investment. In this way, the Investors Roadmap is not only a study, but, when successfully implemented, a very cost-effective means of promoting administrative reform.

Contact: Grant Morrill, Bureau for Global Affairs, Center for Economic Growth and Agricultural Development, USAID (gmorrill@usaid.gov).

1   The 40 countries for which a roadmap has been prepared are: Algeria, Armenia, Bolivia, Bosnia, Bulgaria, Chile, Croatia, Djibouti, Dominican Republic, Ghana, Guyana, Hungary, Jamaica, Jordan, Kazakhstan, Kenya, Laos, Latvia, Lithuania, Madagascar, Malawi, Malaysia, Mali, Mauritius, Mongolia, Morocco, Mozambique, Namibia, Nigeria, Russia, Senegal, Slovakia, Slovenia, South Africa, Tanzania, Tunisia, Turkey, Uganda, Zambia and Zimbabwe. Some, but not all, roadmaps are available from USAID.
2   The intellectual antecedents of the roadmap can be found in Hernando De Soto, *The Other Path: The Invisible Revolution in the Third World* (New York: Harper & Row, 1989). Years of researching the informal sector in Peru from the perspective of the micro-entrepreneur led De Soto to conclude that the informal sector was forced to stay informal because the administrative burdens that it faced were virtually insurmountable. The basis for the argument was a step-by-step map.

The Opacity Index

PricewaterhouseCoopers

The Opacity Index is a new measure of the effects of 'opacity' on the cost and availability of capital in countries worldwide. 'Opacity' is the lack of clear, accurate, formal, easily discernible and widely accepted practices in the world's capital markets. While the topic of opacity has ethical, political and cultural aspects, this research focuses on a new question: how much do certain behaviours cost? The first release provided estimates of the adverse effects of opacity on the cost and availability of capital in 35 countries.

Launched in January 2001, the Opacity Index will be expanded and updated at regular intervals. Supplementary releases appeared in April and May, and a fully updated, expanded release is scheduled for September. The Opacity Index is a project of the PricewaterhouseCoopers (PwC) Endowment for the Study of Transparency and Sustainability.[1]

The Index offers a composite 'O-Factor' score for each country, based on opacity data in five different dimensions that affect capital markets: a) corruption, b) legal system, c) economic policies at the government level, d) accounting standards and practices (including corporate governance and information release), and e) regulatory regime. These five dimensions of opacity generate, as indicated, a useful acronym: CLEAR.

O-Factor numbers can be integrated with publicly reported financial and other data to estimate the extent to which opacity adds to the cost of capital, increases the cost of ongoing operations, and deters foreign direct investment (FDI) from entering a host country.

The Opacity Index is survey-based. Interviews were conducted with four different groups of respondents: chief financial officers (CFOs) based in the countries; equity analysts familiar with the countries; bankers in the countries; and in-country PwC employees. Responses were aggregated and re-expressed by standard statistical procedures to obtain a comprehensive O-Factor score for each country. The norm for the respondent sample was at least 20 CFOs, five bankers, five equity analysts and five PwC employees. In practice, the actual numbers of respondents varied. The survey was conducted during the third and fourth quarters of the year 2000.

The composite O-Factor is calculated by averaging the various components of opacity for each country. The specific formula for computing the O-Factor is:

$$O_i = 1/5 * [C_i + L_i + E_i + A_i + R_i],$$

where 'i' indexes the countries, and each CLEAR component is measured. The composite O-Factor score is a linear transformation of the underlying average survey responses, all of which are weighted equally to avoid subjective bias. The best possible score is zero, corresponding to uniformly and perfectly transparent conditions. The worst possible score is 150, indicating that all respondents identified uniformly, perfectly opaque conditions. The results of this scoring methodology are reported in the table.

The O-Factor scores and related analyses indicate that opacity imposes significant costs on investors – be they individual or corporate – and on countries. Investors assume, in effect, a significant hidden surtax when they commit funds to countries burdened with a high O-Factor. Similarly, countries with a burdensome O-Factor may pay an additional risk premium when they borrow by issuing bonds. And countries with a high O-Factor that seek FDI set up a barrier. Each of these consequences of opacity – the hidden surtax, higher risk premium, and foregone FDI – is for the first time quantitatively estimated in the series of Opacity Index releases.

The concepts and research are still new. Much remains to be undertaken and further refined. However, even where the concept currently runs ahead of quantitative research, there is no lack of useful insights. For example, the April 2001 release introduced the idea of the 'FDI-Transparency Accelerator', which describes the virtuous circle that may develop in emerging market countries when new FDI gives rise to domestic investment, increased management know-how, economic growth and the emergence of a middle class with a stake in a well-ordered, relatively transparent economic environment. In a similar vein, the May release 'Opacity in Latin America' explored the relation between transparency and the emergence of greater economic opportunity for motivated and talented, but undercapitalised, individual entrepreneurs.

The Opacity Index points unmistakably to the benefits of transparency for nations, governments, businesses and the public at large.

Contact: Max Henderson-Begg, PricewaterhouseCoopers
(max.henderson-begg@us.pwcglobal.com),
or see the website: **<http://www.opacityindex.com>**.

---

1   The Opacity Index was conceived by Joel Kurtzman, partner in PricewaterhouseCoopers (PwC), and managed by the PwC team of Carlo di Florio, Max Henderson-Begg and Roger Lipsey. It has been developed with valuable input from PwC experts around the world, and in close cooperation with economists at the Milken Institute and the Brookings Institution.

Scores for O-Factor and components

Country	C	L	E	A	R	O-Factor
Argentina	56	63	68	49	67	61
Brazil	53	59	68	63	62	61
Chile	30	32	52	28	36	36
China	62	100	87	86	100	87
Colombia	48	66	77	55	55	60
Czech Rep.	57	97	62	77	62	71
Ecuador	60	72	78	68	62	68
Egypt	33	52	73	68	64	58
Greece	49	51	76	49	62	57
Guatemala	59	49	80	71	66	65
Hong Kong	25	55	49	53	42	45
Hungary	37	48	53	65	47	50
India	55	68	59	79	58	64
Indonesia	70	86	82	68	69	75
Israel	18	61	70	62	51	53
Italy	28	57	73	26	56	48
Japan	22	72	72	81	53	60
Kenya	60	72	78	72	63	69
Lithuania	46	50	71	59	66	58
Mexico	42	58	57	29	52	48
Pakistan	48	66	81	62	54	62
Peru	46	58	65	61	57	58
Poland	56	61	77	55	72	64
Romania	61	68	77	78	73	71
Russia	78	84	90	81	84	84
Singapore	13	32	42	38	23	29
South Africa	45	53	68	82	50	60
South Korea	48	79	76	90	73	73
Taiwan	45	70	71	56	61	61
Thailand	55	65	70	78	66	67
Turkey	51	72	87	80	81	74
UK	15	40	53	45	38	38
Uruguay	44	56	61	56	49	53
US	25	37	42	25	48	36
Venezuela	53	68	80	50	67	63

Business attitudes to corruption

Control Risks Group

In 1999, Control Risks Group (CRG) commissioned a survey of business attitudes to corruption, which focused on actions taken by companies to avoid corruption and companies' expectations of the impact of the OECD Anti-Bribery Convention.

On behalf of CRG, a market research company (the Industrial Research Bureau) conducted telephone interviews with international business directors of large international companies based on a set questionnaire. The sample was made up of 50 US companies and a further 71 companies from France, Germany, Scandinavia and the UK. The results were published in CRG's *Outlook 2000* report.

The 1999 survey was part of a longer questionnaire on business attitudes to globalisation. Many of the questions were repeated from a survey conducted in 1997. CRG may commission further surveys on the same model in the future.

Overall, the survey showed that international companies are taking corruption more seriously, but they remain sceptical about the prospects for change, despite recent international reforms.

As indicated in table 1, some 39 per cent of companies said that they have been deterred from making an otherwise attractive investment on account of concerns about corruption. This compares with 27 per cent who gave a similar response in a survey conducted in 1997. Corruption emerges as a greater concern than controversies related to human rights, the environment or labour.

Table 1: **Country features that have deterred companies from an otherwise attractive investment (%)**

	European companies	US companies
Corruption	38	40
Human rights abuses	28	13
Environmental problems	34	14
Controversial labour issues	35	16

Companies are responding by introducing codes of conduct that forbid the payment of bribes to secure business (see table 2). Whereas 70.5 per cent of European companies surveyed in 1997 had introduced anti-corruption codes, the 1999 survey reported that 85 per cent had.

Table 2 also indicates that there is a gap both in the US and Europe between declarations of principle and practical measures to curb corruption. Only a minority of companies have anti-corruption training programmes. European companies lag behind their US counterparts in management procedures such as annual declarations by senior executives, hotlines and formal agreements with agents that they will abide by anti-corruption codes.

Table 2: **Anti-corruption measures in companies (%)**

	European companies	US companies
Company codes that forbid bribes to obtain business	85	92
Company codes that forbid 'grease payments'	62	76
Anti-corruption training programmes	23	46
Annual declarations by senior executives that they have abided by anti-corruption codes	34	74
Hotline for reporting corruption	24	56
Formal agreements with agents that they will abide by anti-corruption codes	32	62

The survey demonstrated a general scepticism about the impact of the Anti-Bribery Convention. Only 31 per cent of European respondents and 21 per cent of US respondents said that they are familiar with it. Many of these did not expect the Convention to reduce the level of corruption. These percentages may change in future as governments take action to publicise and implement the Convention.

Similarly, respondents expressed a degree of scepticism about other international companies' compliance with new legal measures inspired by the Convention. Of the top ten OECD exporters, Canadian companies were expected to have the highest levels of compliance, and Korean and Italian companies the lowest (see table 3).

Table 3: **Assessment of other companies' likely standards of compliance, by country of origin**

Ratings for the top OECD exporters (on a scale of 1 to 4)		Ratings for non-OECD countries (on a scale of 1 to 4)	
Canada	1.6	Singapore	2.3
UK	1.7	South Africa	2.6
US	1.8	China	2.9
Netherlands	1.8	India	3.0
Germany	1.9	Brazil	3.1
Belgium/Luxembourg	2.0		
France	2.2		
Japan	2.3		
Italy	2.7		
Korea	2.7		

Four-point rating scale:
1 *Strict compliance*
2 *Generally high standard of compliance with only occasional lapses*
3 *Companies would prefer to comply but will pay bribes if competitors are doing so*
4 *Companies will always pay bribes if it is customary to do so in the host country*

Contact: John Bray, Control Risks Group (john.bray@control-risks.com).

Benchmarking corruption practices: the Sustainability Group Index

SAM Group and Dow Jones

The Dow Jones Sustainability Group Index (DJSGI) is the first global benchmark for sustainability investments. Launched in September 1999 as a partnership between SAM Group and Dow Jones Indexes, it tracks the financial performance of the top 10 per cent of the leading companies in terms of sustainability. These 'sustainability leaders' are creating value by embracing opportunities and managing risks deriving from ongoing economic, environmental and social developments (these are the 'three pillars' of sustainability).[1] More than 26 financial institutions are managing approximately € 1.5 billion (US $1.3 billion) based on the DJSGI.

In the course of 2001 SAM Group and Dow Jones are launching a new European Sustainability Index using the same methodology.

The DJSGI is reviewed annually to ensure that the index composition accurately represents the top 10 per cent of the leading sustainability companies in each industry group. The 2,000 largest capitalised companies of the world are invited to participate in a yearly survey that, together with submitted documentation, policies and reports, company interviews, media screens and publicly available information, is used as an information source for the assessment. Once the companies are selected, they are continuously reviewed and monitored throughout the year.

The ways in which corporations deal with corruption and bribery issues were considered important assessment criteria for the DJSGI from the outset. Companies' involvement in corruption and bribery cases is monitored by means of an extensive media screening procedure, covering up to 1,000 global and regional media sources.

Some 600 companies were analysed for the year 2000 assessment for the DJSGI. Results are presented here for a sample of 350 companies that not only responded to the survey, but also provided supporting documentation. Respondents were from 64 different industry groups and 27 countries. A surprisingly high share of those companies (about 85 per cent) answered that 'corporate codes of conduct concerning corruption and bribery valid for all employees' were in place.

Table 1 shows the type of specific issue covered by these corporate codes of conduct. A majority prohibit employees from offering items of value to government officials and include guidelines concerning gifts and entertainment. In approximately 45 per cent of cases, the same codes are also applied to third parties operating in the name of the company.

Table 1: **Issues covered in corporate codes of conduct (%)**

Employee prohibited to offer items of value to government officials	74
Guidelines concerning gifts and entertainment, travel expenses	89
The above codes also apply to third-parties operating in the name of the company	45
No answer or not known	4

Note: Based on a sample of 297 corporate codes of conduct.

The share of companies prohibiting employees to offer items of value to government officials varies according to the companies' country of origin. Table 2 shows that US companies lead the way in considering corruption an important issue and including it in their corporate codes of conduct. European companies on average lag behind Australia, Canada, Japan and the US. The fact that an increasing number of South American companies (compared to last year) are explicitly excluding corruption practices should be seen as a very positive development, even if their share is still comparatively low in table 2.

Table 2: **Share of companies prohibiting employees to offer items of value to government officials as part of their corporate code of conduct, by country (%)**

Australia	65
Canada	78
Europe	56
Japan	66
South America	50
US	82

Note: Based on a sample of 350 companies.

A slightly different picture emerges from table 3, which shows the share of companies with compliance systems in place to check that codes are implemented. US and Australian companies lead the way, while European and Japanese companies have much lower implementation levels.

Table 3: **Share of companies with a system in place to check compliance with their corporate code of conduct regularly, by country (%)**

Australia	71
Canada	61
Europe	45
Japan	48
South America	33
US	74

Note: Based on a sample of 350 companies.

Contact: Ivo Knoepfel, Head of Rating and Index Research,
SAM Research (ivo@sam-group.com).

1 Economic criteria assessed for the DJSGI include: strategic planning; organisational development practices; intellectual capital management; IT management; quality management; corporate codes of conduct (with a focus on corruption); and risk and crisis management. Environmental criteria include: environmental policies and governance; environmental management systems; environmental performance; environmental, health and safety reporting; and environmental profit and loss accounting. Social criteria include: social policies and governance; human rights practices; standards for suppliers; stakeholder involvement; occupational health and safety; reporting on social issues and community programmes; and remuneration of employees.

Company programmes for resisting corrupt practices

The Conference Board

Company Programmes for Resisting Corrupt Practices: A Global Study was written as part of The Conference Board's work to identify and describe standards for global business practice. It addressed the perception that corrupt practices are a cause for concern among businesses. By surveying diverse medium to large-sized companies in all major industries, the report provided a comparative study of best practices used by companies in tackling corruption and the formulation, implementation and monitoring for effectiveness of business conduct codes.

The project, carried out by The Conference Board, was launched with a grant from the John D. and Catherine T. MacArthur Foundation. The survey questionnaire, devised with assistance from Belgian, Canadian, French, UK and US working-group sponsoring companies, reflected a diversity of North American and European views regarding benchmarks for best practices. Working group discussions, interviews and a survey of 151 companies worldwide (25 per cent from the US, 34 per cent from Western Europe and 41 per cent from outside of North America and Western Europe) focused on company efforts to resist corrupt practices. The final report, published in 2000, included questionnaires returned between January and June 2000.

The working group held meetings in Washington and Paris to facilitate an exchange of views between business, NGO, academic and governmental leaders regarding the best approaches for cutting off corruption's supply-side. In addition to fieldwork, The Conference Board convened seminars and discussions with interested parties in Buenos Aires, Cairo and Tel Aviv. Survey data, interviews and information gathered from these meetings formed the basis for the report.

The report shows a high level of CEO and senior executive commitment to tackling corruption and a range of well-articulated statements, policies and operating procedures. Management responsibility for these efforts is acknowledged and resources are allocated for compliance.

With regard to the reasons cited as the most important for developing anti-corruption statements or programmes (see figure), there is little difference between industries or regions on most points. Companies believe that their anti-corruption statements and programmes are not simply a response to brand equity

Reason cited as most important for developing anti-corruption statement/programme (%)

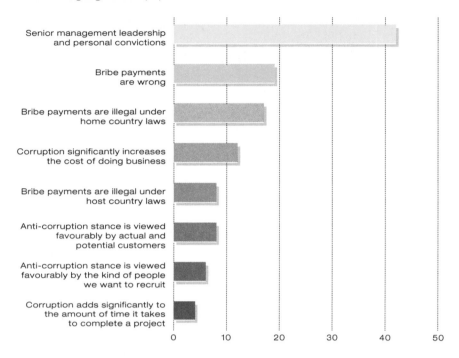

Note: Survey of 146 companies.

concerns, increased costs or legal requirements. Even compliance ranks well behind 'management leadership and conviction' as a reason for positing a serious anti-corruption effort.

Contact: Ronald E. Berenbeim, The Conference Board
(ronald.berenbeim@conference-board.org).

Corruption and the Globalization Index

A.T. Kearney and Foreign Policy *magazine*

Critics of globalisation have long argued that an inevitable rise in corruption is among the ill effects of opening national borders to greater trade and investment flows. Recent results from the A.T. Kearney/*Foreign Policy* magazine Globalization Index™ cast doubt upon this interpretation.

In fact, a comparison of Globalization Index rankings with the results of Transparency International's Corruption Perceptions Index (CPI) suggests that economic, social and technological integration is associated with perceptions of cleaner government. Business leaders and international experts alike perceive public office-holders to be remarkably 'clean' in countries that have achieved high levels of globalisation, while perceptions of public corruption appear higher in the least globalised countries (see figure). This relationship holds true not only for advanced economies but also emerging markets, with global countries like Chile, Israel, Hungary and Malaysia showing fewer signs of corruption than their less global neighbours.

These results merely suggest that countries that have integrated most deeply into world markets have also managed to develop political, social and legal institutions that deter corruption. No causal linkage is implied. As the Globalization Index project continues, future research will seek to clarify the social impact of globalisation, including its effect on corruption levels. Of chief concern is whether countries that globalise rapidly are more likely to witness rising corruption than countries that undergo more gradual integration with the outside world.

The Globalization Index is a statistical gauge designed to measure composite levels of integration in 50 key advanced economies and emerging markets. The index encompasses traditional measures of economic globalisation, including international trade levels, income payments and receipts, the inflow and outflow of foreign direct investment, the inflow and outflow of portfolio capital, and the convergence of domestic and world prices. The index also assesses the globalisation of personal contact through international travel and tourism, international telephone traffic, and transfer payments and receipts. It examines technological integration through indicators for internet users, the number of internet hosts, and the number of secure internet servers.

The Globalization Index is a joint research initiative of *Foreign Policy* magazine and the Global Business Policy Council, a strategic service of the management consultancy firm A.T. Kearney.

Correlation of the Globalization Index with the CPI

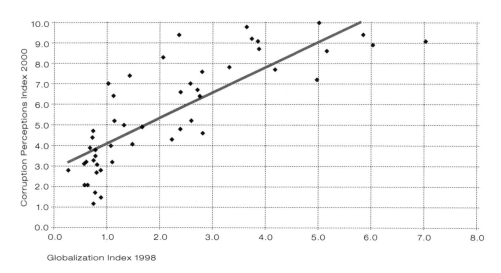

Globalization Index 1998

Note: Corruption-globalisation correlation = 0.84.

Contact: Jay Scheerer, A.T. Kearney
(jay.scheerer@atkearney.com).

Why is fighting corruption so crucial for embracing globalisation?

Shang-Jin Wei (Brookings Institution and Harvard University)

What does corruption have to do with globalisation? Research reveals an intimate linkage between the two. Corruption may hinder a country's ability to absorb the beneficial side of globalisation, by reducing foreign direct investment (FDI). Corruption may also make a country more vulnerable to the risks of globalisation by increasing the likelihood of a currency crisis.[1]

This research has been presented in a series of articles and books, some still forthcoming.[2]

Corruption reduces the benefits of globalisation

International direct investment has been expanding rapidly. In 1999, sales of foreign affiliates of multinational firms were US $14 trillion, nearly twice as high as global exports of goods and services. A small number of countries in the industrial world receive about two thirds of this investment. FDI is especially important for developing countries, as a source of scarce capital and an important conduit for the transfer of technological and managerial know-how.

Corruption, however, is a major impediment to the economic progress of such countries. For international investors, the need to pay bribes and deal with official extortion is equivalent to facing an extra tax. Some foreign firms may obtain business as a result of the bribes they pay. But for every dollar of business that these firms obtain, the country loses hundreds of dollars of potential foreign investment (see figure 1). Research indicates that an increase in host country corruption from a low level, such as that in Singapore, to a higher level, as in Mexico, has the same negative effect on inward FDI as raising the corporate tax rate by 50 percentage points. It is important to note that, while corruption is like a tax on firms, it generates no tax revenue for government. If anything, corruption typically erodes the domestic tax base. Developing countries are eager to attract FDI by offering generous tax benefits to foreign firms. This research suggests that reducing corruption could in fact be more effective in achieving this objective, without sacrificing government revenues.

Figure 1: **Corruption reduces the benefit of globalisation**

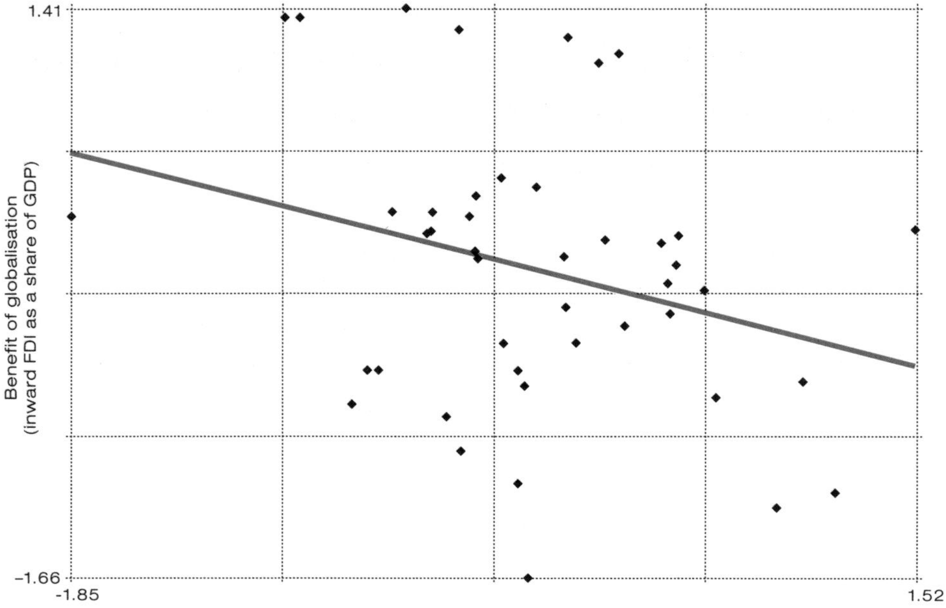

Corruption (as measured by *Global Competitiveness Report / World Development Report*)

Note: Partial correlation based on a regression of log (FDI/GDP) on corruption, tax rate, FDI incentives, FDI restrictions, log (GDP per capita) and exchange rate volatility. Source: Author's calculation.

Corruption raises globalisation's risks

Corruption can affect a country's exposure to the risks of globalisation by impacting on the composition of its capital inflows. Corruption tilts capital inflows towards less stable forms, raising the likelihood of a currency crisis.

International capital flows consist of FDI, foreign bank borrowing, portfolio investment and official debt to other governments or inter-governmental institutions. They are not equivalent in terms of the associated risks for recipient countries. Bank lending and portfolio investment may be less stable than direct investment, because they are often subject to the whims of investors. Using data on FDI and loans as a share of GDP for all emerging market economies for which data is available, the standard deviation of these variables over the period from 1980–96 was computed as a measure of volatility. Foreign bank lending to developing countries was found to be about twice as volatile as FDI.

There are two reasons why a high level of corruption may result in a higher proportion of capital inflows being in less stable forms. First, given that international direct investors are more likely to have repeated interactions with local officials (for permits, taxes and health inspections) than international banks, one would expect local corruption to be more detrimental to FDI than to other forms of capital flows. Along the same lines, direct investment involves greater sunk costs than bank loans or portfolio investment. Once an investment is made, corrupt local officials, knowing that the investment cannot easily be liquidated, may threaten to raise obstacles to the investment's success unless they are paid a bribe. Hence, direct investors find themselves in a weaker bargaining position than international banks. This *ex post* disadvantage of FDI tends to make international direct investors more cautious, *ex ante*, than lenders in a corrupt host country.

Second, under the current international financial architecture, international creditors are more likely than international direct investors to be bailed out in a time of crisis. During the 1994–95 'tequila crisis' and the more recent Asian currency crises, the IMF, the World Bank and the G7 countries mobilised large amounts of funding for the affected countries to prevent or minimise potentially massive defaults on bank loans. By now an international bailout of bank loans in the event of severe crisis is embedded firmly in market expectations. (In addition, many developing country governments implicitly or explicitly guarantee loans to the country's private sector.) No comparable examples of international assistance packages exist for the recovery of nationalised or extorted assets of foreign direct investors, except for a modest amount of insurance from the World Bank's Multilateral Investment Guarantee Agency, which is expensive to acquire. This difference makes banks more willing than direct investors to do business with corrupt countries, further distorting the composition of capital flows.

For example, New Zealand and Singapore are perceived to have relatively low corruption and relatively low loan/FDI and portfolio investment/FDI ratios. Conversely, Uruguay and Thailand are perceived to have relatively high corruption and also relatively high loan/FDI and portfolio investment/FDI ratios.

More formal statistical analyses on the composition of capital inflows, based on bilateral FDI and bank lending for all countries for which such data are available, and controlling for other possible determinants of capital inflows (see figure 2), confirmed the above conjecture. More corrupt countries tend to rely on the types of capital inflows (for example foreign bank borrowing) that are more volatile than FDI and more likely to be reversed in the event of unfavourable news about the country in question, or even about a different developing country.

A number of research papers have pointed out that a higher foreign borrowing/FDI ratio is associated with a greater chance of a currency or financial crisis for developing countries. This research suggests a particular channel through which severe domestic corruption could raise the likelihood of such crises.

Figure 2: **Corruption increases the risk associated with globalisation**

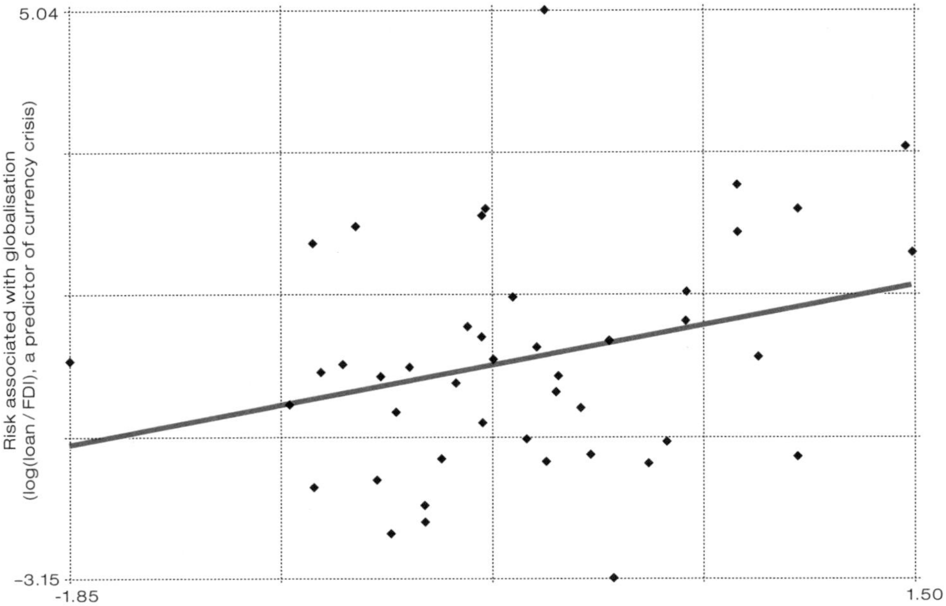

Corruption (as measured by *Global Competitiveness Report / World Development Report*)

Note: Partial correlation based on a regression of log (loan/FDI) on corruption, tax rate, log (GDP per capita), and exchange rate volatility. Source: Author's calculation.

In sum, fighting corruption is crucial for economic development. This is particularly true in a globalising world economy. The gap between countries that manage to control corruption and those that do not is widening. More benefits of globalisation will go to the first group. At the same time, the risks of globalisation, such as a volatile international capital flow, will pose a greater threat to the second group of countries.

Contact: Shang-Jin Wei, New Century Chair in International Economics at the Brookings Institution and Research Fellow at Harvard University's Center for International Development (swei@brook.edu).

1 The author would like to thank Rachel Rubinfeld, Yi Wu and Mike Prosser for their help in preparing this contribution.
2 Shang-Jin Wei, 'Local Corruption and Global Capital Flows,' Brookings Papers on Economic Activity, 2000; Shang-Jin Wei, *Corruption and Globalization* (Washington: Brookings Institution, forthcoming); Beata Smarzynska and Shang-Jin Wei, 'Corruption and the Composition of Foreign Direct Investment: Firm-level Evidence,' National Bureau of Economic Research (NBER) Working Paper No. 7969, 2000; Shang-Jin Wei and Yi Wu, 'Negative Alchemy? Corruption, Composition of Capital Flows, and Currency Crises,' NBER Working Paper No. 8187, 2001.

Are you being served? Political accountability and quality of government

Alícia Adserà (University of Illinois at Chicago), Carles Boix (University of Chicago), and Mark Payne (Inter-American Development Bank)

The research explored the causes of cross-national variation in levels of corruption and effective governance, focusing particularly on links between corruption and different aspects of political accountability.

As measures of the level of corruption, the research employed three different data sets. The first consisted of a sample of around 120 countries in the late 1990s, for which an extensive battery of governance indicators (on corruption, government efficiency, and so on) was developed by Kaufmann, Kraay and Zoido-Lobatón at the World Bank.[1] The second was a panel data set of about 100 countries for the period 1980–95, with information on corruption and quality of government performance, developed by the Political Risk Services Group. The third data set measured the number of public officials in different states in the US convicted for violating laws against public corruption from 1977–95.

Using econometric techniques to analyse the three data sets, the research showed that low corruption levels and good governance are a function of the extent to which citizens can hold political officials accountable for their actions. More precisely, the extent to which politicians engage in rent-seeking behaviour and other corrupt practices declines with: the presence of free and regular elections, which allow citizens to discipline politicians; the degree of information of citizens (measured through the frequency of newspaper readership), which curbs the opportunities politicians may have to engage in political corruption and mismanagement; and the involvement of citizens in politics (measured through electoral turnout).

According to the findings, the combined effect of the level of newspaper readership, the existence of democratic elections, the level of per capita income and the degree of political instability together explain over 80 per cent of the variance in the level of corruption. Figure 1 shows the strong negative correlation between corruption and press readership. Figure 2 then shows the negative correlation between corruption and electoral turnout for those countries where there are free elections.

Figure 1: **Level of corruption and newspaper circulation in 1997–98**

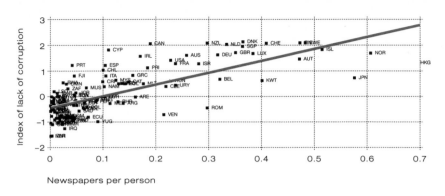

Figure 2: **Level of corruption and turnout in democratic regimes in 1997–98**

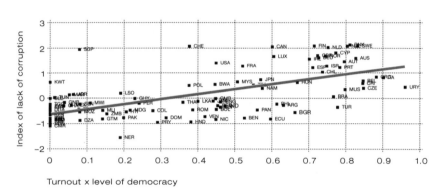

The combined impact of newspaper readership and democratic elections is marked, though complex. On the one hand, the level of corruption does not change in the absence of newspaper readership, and actually worsens in authoritarian regimes with high levels of newspaper readership (relative to authoritarian regimes with populations that do not read the press). On the other hand, the combination of a vibrant press and democratic elections cuts down corruption sharply. Moving from an authoritarian regime (with or without newspaper readership) to a democratic regime with high newspaper circulation reduces the level of corruption by a whole standard deviation in the sample, other things being equal.

Similarly, the higher the level of political mobilisation in a democratic country, as measured by electoral turnout, the lower the level of corruption. Other things being equal, the level of corruption declines by about half a standard deviation in the sample when one moves from a country where only 50 per cent of the population votes to a country where everybody votes.

These results are robust to the use of the following controls: per capita income; social capital; the structure of the legal system; the level of ethnic fragmentation and conflict; variations in the type of constitutional framework; and religious values.

Although the research focused on the mechanisms through which political accountability reduces corruption, it also generated estimates of the influence of other factors. Political stability, economic development and, to an extent, the degree of financial openness (as measured through the extent of capital controls) reduce the extent of corruption. On the other hand, no association was found between corruption and the type of legal structure, different constitutional structures (federal, presidential or electoral), the size of the public sector, or the extent of trade openness.

The research is presented in full in Alícia Adserà, Carles Boix and Mark Payne, 'Are You Being Served? Political Accountability and Quality of Government,' Inter-American Development Bank Research Department Working Paper No. 438, December 2000.

Contact: Alícia Adserà (adsera@uic.edu),
Carles Boix (cboix@midway.uchicago.edu),
or Mark Payne (markpa@iadb.org).

1 Daniel Kaufmann, Aart Kraay and Pablo Zoido-Lobatón, 'Aggregating Governance Indicators,' World Bank Working Paper No. 2195, 1999.

Bureaucracies and perceptions of corruption: survey evidence from Africa

Julius Court (United Nations University)

Despite increasing evidence that disparities in bureaucratic performance help explain differences in economic outcomes around the world, key questions remain to be answered adequately. In what ways does bureaucratic structure vary? What organisational and incentive structures affect bureaucratic performance the most? How can bureaucratic structures be improved?

Drawing on the assessments of senior bureaucrats (usually around five), this survey generated systematic information on bureaucratic structure and performance in 20 African countries. It focused on policy formulation, recruitment and careers, salaries and relationships with the private sector. Conducted in 1998, the survey provided the first systematic data on such structural issues in the region. It also expanded the existing global data set on bureaucratic structure and performance, which now includes 50 countries globally.[1]

While any conclusions must remain tentative given the methodology, it is worth drawing attention to a number of issues. Reflecting much of the literature, the findings highlighted significant challenges for many of the countries in the survey: from lack of 'ownership', to high levels of corruption, to weak service delivery. They also pointed to a greater degree of variation than is usually acknowledged, with Botswana, Mauritius and Tunisia, for example, scoring well. The substantial improvement in bureaucratic structures in Botswana, Eritrea and Tanzania indicate potential sources for policy lessons.

The survey asked how common it is for private firms to pay irregular 'additional payments' (bribes or tips) to get things done. Figure 1 shows a great degree of disparity across the region. In Namibia bureaucrats believed that such payments are virtually 'non-existent'. In a quarter of the sampled countries such payments were 'seldom' the case. In contrast, in Kenya, Nigeria and Togo, such payments were perceived to be 'mostly' needed to get things done.

The survey also investigated the proportion tips and bribes added to civil servants' salaries over the last 20 years. Figure 2 shows that overall the proportion of salaries coming from such payments seems to have increased during this time. Again, the diversity in performance is marked: in Botswana, Mauritius,

Figure 1: **The degree to which firms needed to provide corrupt payments to operate in Africa, 1998**

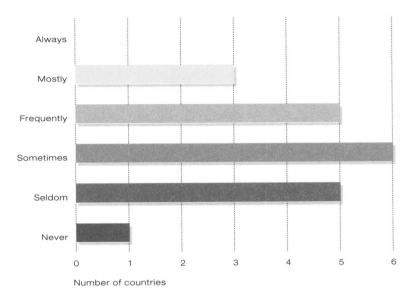

Namibia and Tunisia, firms' bribes add very little to civil service salaries. The situation has improved in some previously troubled countries, such as Eritrea, providing important cases for further investigation. At the other end of the spectrum bribes were thought to double bureaucrats' salaries in Kenya and Nigeria.

The table presents the empirical relationships between bureaucratic structure variables and bureaucratic performance, after controlling for GDP.

Given methodological limitations, the findings must be seen as indicative rather than conclusive in any way. However, better performance is associated with the following characteristics:

- Higher civil service salaries (in proportion to private sector levels)
- Greater influence of core economic agencies in formulating new policies
- Greater job security for top civil servants when political leadership changes
- Greater opportunity for meaningful career development in the civil service.

Interestingly, the movement of officials between the civil service and the private sector seems to have a negative impact on bureaucratic performance.

Figure 2: **Amount corruption adds to bureaucrats' salaries in Africa**

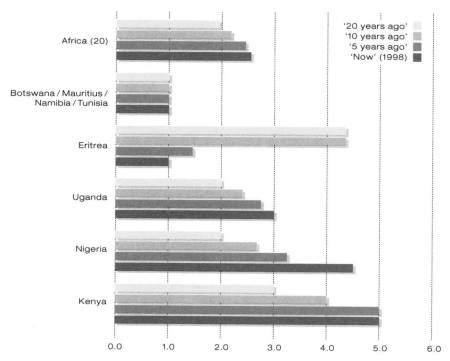

Note: 1 = 'no tips and bribes'; 2 = 'tips and bribes add to base salaries up to 10%'; 3 = 'between 10–50%'; 4 = 'between 50-100%'; 5 = 'tips and bribes add more than 100% to base salaries'.

Statistical associations between structure and performance indicators

	Bureaucratic quality	Consultation	Less corruption	Efficiency	Implementation
(i) Relative wage		**		*	***
(ii) Agency power	**				
(iii) Autonomy	*		*		
(iv) Career opportunity				**	
(v) Public-private movement	* (-)	* (–)			** (–)

*Note on level of significance: * = low significance (10%); ** = medium significance (5%); *** = high significance (1%); (-) = inverse relationship*

This United Nations University (UNU) research project was undertaken by Julius Court (UNU) and Petra Kristen and Beatrice Weder (University of Basel), with the assistance of the African Economic Research Consortium (AERC). Depending on the availability of additional funding, the survey may be repeated in 2002.

The project website contains the findings and data as well as the questionnaire and other documents used for the data collection: <http://www.unu.edu/hq/academic/Pg_area4/b-structure.html>.

Contact: Julius Court, UNU (court@hq.unu.edu).

1   P. Evans and J. Rauch, 'Bureaucratic Structure and Bureaucratic Performance in Less Developed Countries,' *Journal of Public Economics*, No. 75, January 2000.

Corruption and the 2001 Environmental Sustainability Index

Marc A. Levy (Columbia University)

Early this year the 2001 Environmental Sustainability Index (ESI) was released at the World Economic Forum (WEF) Annual Meeting in Davos, Switzerland. As pointed out in a report accompanying the ESI, researchers found a striking correlation between the level of corruption and environmental outcomes: the higher the level of corruption in a country, the lower the level of environmental sustainability.

The ESI was the result of a partnership involving the WEF Global Leaders for Tomorrow (GLT) Environment Task Force, the Yale Center for Environmental Law and Policy, and the Center for International Earth Science Information Network (CIESIN) at Columbia University.[1]

The ESI was created to help address the critical need to be able to measure national levels of environmental sustainability. Many governments purport to seek environmental sustainability as a policy objective, but it is difficult to track actual performance. The lack of concrete measures hinders the ability of policymakers and citizens to set meaningful priorities, understand trade-offs, or identify areas of success or failure.

The ESI was constructed using a methodology intended to make it relevant to the broader set of activities underway to measure sustainability in a manner that was transparent and reproducible. Environmental sustainability was defined as the ability to produce high levels of performance in a lasting manner on indicators that range across five areas:

- State of environmental systems, such as air, soil, ecosystems and water
- Stresses on those systems, in the form of pollution and exploitation levels
- Human vulnerability to environmental change, in the form of loss of food resources or exposure to environmental diseases
- Social and institutional capacity to cope with environmental challenges
- Ability to respond to the demands of global stewardship by cooperating in collective efforts to conserve international environmental resources such as the atmosphere.

A total of 22 indicators were identified across these five core 'components' of environmental sustainability. These indicators, in turn, were measured using a total of 67 variables drawn from a wide range of data sources.

The ESI contains information on 122 countries. The three highest-ranking countries in the ESI are Finland, Norway and Canada. The three lowest are Haiti, Saudi Arabia and Burundi. Although high-ranking countries have higher levels of per capita income than low-ranking countries, per capita income does not explain everything. Many countries have ESI values that are far higher or far lower than the values of countries with similar levels of per capita income.

Corruption figures in the ESI in two ways. First, it constitutes one of the variables within the 'social and institutional capacity' component. It was chosen because of a growing recognition that corruption is incompatible with sound environmental management, due to the distortion it introduces into the policy-making process. The variable used in the 2001 ESI is the corruption measure found in the World Bank's Aggregated Governance Indicators data set.

Second, though just one of 67 variables that make up the ESI, corruption has the highest correlation with the overall ESI, with a correlation coefficient of -0.75. What is striking is not just this overall level of correlation, but the fact that the corruption measure is correlated strongly with many other more specific measures within the ESI, including air quality, water quality, population growth, environmental health, availability of environmental information, and energy efficiency.

Correlations between level of corruption and environmental sustainability indicators

Indicator	Correlation with corruption
Social and institutional capacity: science and technology	−0.73
Global stewardship: international commitment	−0.67
Capacity for debate	−0.62
Air quality	−0.53
Basic human sustenance	−0.53
Environmental health	−0.52
Environmental information	−0.51
Reducing population pressure	−0.49
Water quality	−0.46
Global stewardship: global–scale funding/participation	−0.44
Eco-efficiency	−0.18

Note: All correlations are significant at 0.05 level or greater.

This was largely unexpected. Though some level of correlation with the ESI was expected because of the governance indicators that the ESI includes, the correlation was not expected to be as high as it is, nor were significant correlations expected with so many direct measures of environmental conditions. The table shows the 11 indicators out of 21 (not counting the indicator that includes corruption as a measure) that have significant negative correlations with levels of corruption.

The conclusion is inescapable: if levels of corruption have a strong measurable correlation with a wide range of factors that comprise environmental sustainability, then corruption deserves a stronger role on the environmental sustainability agenda.

This suggests a number of further questions relevant to current policy debates. First, to what extent does corruption explain the deviation in environmental performance among countries that are otherwise comparable? Initial analysis of the ESI data suggests that corruption measures are useful in this regard. Second, what are the mechanisms by which corruption contributes to poor environmental outcomes? Does it stifle innovation, generate inappropriate policy choices, limit information on environmental conditions, contribute to poor management or increase incentives to engage in unsustainable use of natural resources? Third, in terms of policy interventions, is it necessary to target the root sources of corruption within a political system, or are there intermediate strategies that can help reduce corruption's impact on the environment? The ESI data by itself does not answer these questions, but it provides a basis for testing propositions using empirical measures.

The full ESI report, as well as a spreadsheet containing the data, can be found at the website <**http://www.ciesin.columbia.edu/indicators/ESI/**>.

Contact: Marc A. Levy (marc.levy@ciesin.columbia.edu).

1 Daniel C. Esty at Yale was overall project director and Marc A. Levy at Columbia directed the work at CIESIN. Kim Samuel-Johnson chaired the GLT Task Force. A Pilot ESI was released in 2000, and a number of changes were implemented for the 2001 ESI based on the commentaries and criticisms received.

A culture of corruption?

William Miller (University of Glasgow), Åse Grødeland (Norwegian Institute of Urban and Regional Research) and Tatyana Koshechkina (GfK-GB)

This study focused on the treatment of citizens by low-level officials in four post-communist countries: Bulgaria, the Czech Republic, Ukraine and Slovakia. This citizen-centred approach excluded high-level corruption from its scope of study, but it included far more than low-level corruption. It set bribe giving in the context of other strategies citizens use to influence officials. And it set bribe taking in the context of other faults of street-level bureaucrats. Experiences and behaviour were investigated as well as perceptions.

The findings are based on 26 focus-group discussions (with 187 participants) and 136 in-depth interviews, followed by representative surveys of 6,050 citizens and 1,307 officials during 1996–98. Fieldwork covered all regions and included both rural and urban areas.[1]

Large numbers of citizens confessed that they have personally used contacts, presents and bribes recently, though they use other strategies even more in an attempt to influence officials (table 1). Attempted extortion by officials stimulates the use of bribes, but it stimulates argument almost as much. When faced by incompetent or lazy officials, the public responds more with argument than bribes.

Table 1: **The public's use of presents and bribes to influence officials 'in the last few years' (%)**

	All	Czech Republic	Slovakia	Bulgaria	Ukraine
Public alleges that, at least rarely, officials made 'unnecessary problems' in order to get a bribe	54	44	56	48	67
Public confesses that they themselves offered...					
'... a small present'	42	23	56	33	57
'... money or an expensive present'	24	11	31	19	36

Extortion by officials and citizens' personal values both have an independent impact on the use of bribes (figure 1). Condemnation stiffens resistance to extortion, even if many of those who condemn bribes still submit to it. But the ability of citizens' values to stiffen resistance to extortion varies and seems exceptionally ineffective in Ukraine.

Figure 1: **Impact of values and extortion on bribe giving**

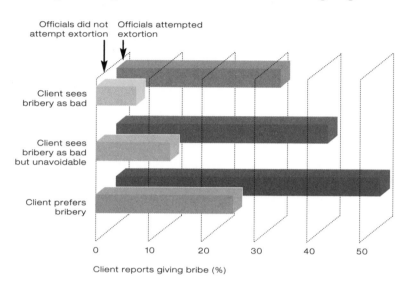

A majority of officials confessed they have recently accepted at least a small present from a client. Up to a quarter in some countries said they were willing to accept 'money or an expensive present', though far fewer confessed to having done so recently. However, such confessions vary sharply across different types of official. The bargaining power of officials vis-à-vis their clients has a much greater impact on actual bribe taking than do inadequate salaries (figure 2).

The most popular reform options were 'stricter controls and penalties' or 'better salaries'. Yet the analysis highlights the corruptibility of both citizens (in the face of extortion) and officials (in the face of temptation). The authors therefore put more weight than either the public or officials themselves on reforms that target situations rather than people.

Significantly, both the public and officials believed reform was possible if their government made 'a strong and sincere effort'. Unfortunately, except in Bulgaria, very large majorities thought their government was not doing so. One consequence is widespread public support for international pressure to be applied to reduce corruption (table 2).

Figure 2: **Bribe taking – willingness and behaviour**

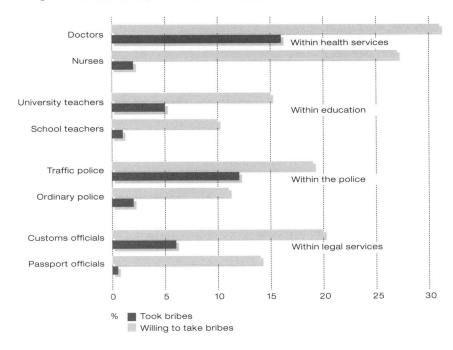

Table 2: **Public perspectives on cutting corruption (%)**

	All	Czech Republic	Slovakia	Bulgaria	Ukraine
It is possible to cut corruption among low-level officials	83	82	81	88	80
The government is really trying	24	18	22	41	18
International pressure is a good way	68	68	59	78	68

The full report is *A Culture of Corruption? Coping with Government in Post-Communist Europe* (Budapest: Central European University Press, 2001).

Contact: William Miller (w.l.miller@socsci.gla.ac.uk).

1 The fieldwork was carried out by OPW Prague, MVK of Bratislava, CSD Sofia and GfK-USM Kyiv, directed by Ladislav Koppl, Pavel Haulik, Alexander Stoyanov and Tatyana Koshechkina.

Corruption data from the Global Barometer Survey Network

The Global Barometer Survey Network links institutes involved in an ongoing programme of sample surveys of mass attitudes and behaviour in more than 50 countries of post-communist Europe, Latin America, Africa and East Asia. Since 1991, more than 200 surveys have been conducted by social scientists in universities and independent research institutes, funded by multiple national and international scientific institutions and foundations. Further information on the Global Barometer Survey Network as a whole is available at the website: <http://www.globalbarometer.org>.

Each survey covers a wide variety of political, social, economic and demographic topics including: the experience that people have of getting things done by breaking laws, bending rules or paying bribes; crime and insecurity; trust in institutions; and the perception of corruption in national governments. The project is divided regionally:

New Europe Barometer, launched in 1991, covers 21 post-communist countries and regions: Armenia, Belarus, Bulgaria, Croatia, Czech Republic, Estonia, eastern Germany, Georgia, Hungary, Kazakhstan, Kyrgyzstan, Latvia, Lithuania, Moldova, Poland, Romania, Russia, Serbia, Slovakia, Slovenia and Ukraine: <http://www.cspp.strath.ac.uk>.

Latinobarómetro, launched in 1995, covers 17 countries: Argentina, Bolivia, Brazil, Chile, Colombia, Costa Rica, Ecuador, El Salvador, Guatemala, Honduras, Mexico, Nicaragua, Panama, Paraguay, Peru, Uruguay and Venezuela: <http://www.latinobarometro.org>.

Afrobarometer, launched in 1999, currently covers 12 countries: Botswana, Ghana, Lesotho, Malawi, Mali, Namibia, Nigeria, South Africa, Tanzania, Uganda, Zambia and Zimbabwe: <http://www.afrobarometer.org>.

East Asia Barometer launched surveys in China, Hong Kong, Indonesia, Japan, Korea, Philippines, Taiwan and Thailand in 2001. The results will be available in early 2002.

Findings from research by Afrobarometer, New Europe Barometer and Latinobarómetro follow.

Assessing corruption in Southern Africa through the eyes of Southern Africans

Robert Mattes (University of Cape Town and Institute for Democracy in South Africa) and Michael Bratton (Michigan State University)

Is corruption endemic to African politics? The cross-national research project Afrobarometer tried to find out. A common set of questions on corruption was asked in surveys of random, nationally representative samples of voting-age populations in seven Southern African countries between July 1999 and July 2000. Trained enumerators conducted face-to-face interviews in local languages with 13,000 respondents across the region.[1]

The surveys found that popular perceptions of government corruption are extraordinarily high in some Southern African countries (see table 1). In Zimbabwe, more than two thirds (69 per cent) said that all or most government officials are involved in corruption. One half of Zambians and South Africans also shared this view. But there are important differences across the region. Only 28 per cent in Lesotho and 20 per cent in Namibia had this negative perception.

Table 1 also indicates that citizens make distinctions between corruption in different levels of government. Across the seven countries, local government officials and parliamentarians are seen as less corrupt than national government officials and civil servants. While 30 per cent in Lesotho said that all or most civil servants are corrupt, just 11 per cent said this of local government officials. These differences can also be seen in Malawi and Zimbabwe to a lesser degree. Only in South Africa and Namibia do citizens appear to hold a relatively undifferentiated view of corruption.

Perceptions of corruption are only tenuously linked to actual experience. The surveys found that while perceptions of corruption are quite high, actual experience is much lower (see table 2). People were asked whether in the past year they had been forced to pay a bribe, give a gift or perform a favour in order to get various government services.

At their least extreme, average perceptions of government corruption were four times higher than average actual experience (in Namibia). At their most extreme, perceptions were 40 times higher (in Botswana). Whatever their size, these discrepancies suggest that perceptions of corruption could be based on news media reports of a small number of high-profile incidents. Or they may stem from having heard about friends' or neighbours' experiences.

Actual experience of corruption varies widely across the seven countries. An average of 12 per cent of Zimbabweans said they had been asked for a bribe or a favour in order to get government assistance in housing, land, employment or

Table 1: **Perceptions of government corruption (%)**

	Zimbabwe	South Africa	Zambia	Malawi	Botswana	Lesotho	Namibia
National government officials	69	50	51	43	32	28	20
Civil servants, or those who work in government offices and ministries	65	50	50	46	32	30	24
People in parliament	63	45	40	31	29	20	19
Local government officials	51	46	42	n/a	20	11	17
Average across types of government	62	48	46	40	28	22	20

Question asked: 'How many ... do you think are involved in corruption?' Shown are the percentage who answered 'all', 'almost all' or 'most of them'.

Table 2: **Personal experience of government corruption (%)**

	Zimbabwe	Namibia	South Africa	Zambia	Malawi	Lesotho	Botswana
A job	10	3	2	5	5	6	1
A government maintenance payment, pension payment or loan	13	4	2	3	4	2	1
Electricity or water	11	7	7	3	3	1	<1
Housing or land	14	8	4	3	3	2	1
Average experience with corruption	12	6	4	4	3	3	1

Question asked: 'In the past year, have you or anyone in your family had to pay money to government officials (besides rates or taxes), give them a gift, or do them a favour, in order to get the following?' Shown are the percentage who answered 'often', 'a few times', or 'once or twice'.

basic services in the past year. Yet in Botswana, where international visitors encounter anti-corruption posters even before they get past customs, only 1 per cent said they had faced such demands from government officials.

In four countries (Botswana, Lesotho, Malawi and Zambia), citizens are most prone to victimisation when seeking employment. Government administration of housing and land distribution offers the greatest potential for corruption in Namibia and, importantly, Zimbabwe. In South Africa, citizens are most at risk

Table 3: **Corruption as most important problem? (%)**

	South Africa	Malawi	Zimbabwe	Botswana	Zambia	Lesotho	Namibia
Corruption	10	5	4	3	2	2	2

Question asked: 'What are the most important problems facing this country that government ought to address?' Up to three answers were accepted. Shown is the percentage who included corruption.

when trying to obtain electricity and water, which lie at the core of that country's ambitious Reconstruction and Development Programme.

One should not overestimate the present political impact of these percep-tions. In only one country, South Africa, did as many as one in ten rate corruption as a significant national issue requiring government intervention (see table 3).

Finally, while significant numbers of Southern Africans perceived or had experienced corruption under an elected government, they did not associate cor-ruption with the establishment of democracy. On average, 39 per cent across the seven countries said there was more corruption under their present government than there was under its colonial, apartheid, one-party or military predecessors, whereas 46 per cent said the situation was the same or better (table 4). When asked to say in their own words what democracy meant to them, negligible proportions (less than half a percentage point) spontaneously associated it with corruption.

Table 4: **Comparing the extent of corruption today and under the former regime (%)**

	Zimbabwe	Malawi	South Africa	Zambia	Namibia	Lesotho	Botswana
More corrupt	56	50	44	44	26	25	22
The same	13	13	25	17	21	17	13
Less corrupt	19	29	27	27	41	36	22
Don't know	10	7	4	11	10	21	34

Question asked: 'You have told us how you feel about the effectiveness of the way government performs its job, its interest in what you think, corruption, and your trust in government. But how does this compare to the government that this country had under British colonialism /white minority rule/UNIP one-party government/MCP one-party government/military government/South African rule/apartheid? Is government today more, about the same or less corrupt?'

Contact: Michael Bratton (mbratton@msu.edu) or Robert Mattes (rmattes@humanities.uct.ac.za).

New Europe Barometer

Richard Rose (University of Strathclyde)

New Europe Barometer surveys are nationwide representative samples of the adult population in countries in Central and Eastern Europe and the former Soviet Union. Face to face interviews are conducted with an average of 1,000 respondents per country, except in Russia where the samples are normally 2,000. All interviews are conducted by trained interviewers from established national research institutes.

Survey results show that citizens in transition countries do not expect government to operate efficiently or effectively, yet very few feel helpless or passive in the face of bureaucrats unwilling to act on their requests. A variety of strategies can be adopted.

The readiness to pay bribes or use other tactics differs between countries. As table 5 (with findings from 1998) shows, Russians and Ukrainians are far more likely to think of paying a bribe or using connections to get a house than Czechs, who reject these tactics in favour of the market, or pushing officials harder. Only a limited minority in the three countries felt they could do nothing.

Table 5: **Readiness to pay bribes or use other tactics (%)**

	Russia	Ukraine	Czech Republic
Pay bribe	25	21	4
Use connections	24	13	9
Make up story	6	n/a	n/a
Write a letter	n/a	10	24
Buy a house	31	29	47
Nothing can be done	14	27	16

Question asked: 'What should a family do to get a government-subsidised flat, even if not entitled to it according to the rules?'

Whereas paying a bribe can be considered as recognition of the power of the state, doing what you want regardless of government reflects a 'scoff law' mentality. When the New Russia Barometer asked a series of questions about paying tax in the year 2000, 56 per cent said that there was no need to pay taxes since the government would never find out; 27 per cent believed that if the government did find out about tax evasion, a bribe would enable one to continue avoiding payment; and only 17 per cent felt that the tax laws were enforced.

Perceptions about the prevalence of corruption, and whether it has increased or decreased, vary across the countries, as table 6 shows.

Table 6: **Comparing the extent of corruption today and under the former regime (%)**

	Corruption has increased	Corruption is same	Corruption is less
Ukraine	87	11	1
FR Yugoslavia	81	17	2
Slovakia	81	15	4
Hungary	77	20	2
Russia	73	23	4
Bulgaria	71	25	3
Czech Republic	70	24	5
Belarus	70	25	5
Croatia	66	28	6
Romania	58	28	14
Slovenia	58	28	14
Poland	52	37	12

Question asked: 'By comparison with the former communist regime, would you say that the level of corruption and taking bribes has increased?'
Source: New Europe Barometer 1998 (except for Russia results, New Russia Barometer 2000).

Meanwhile, the coin of corruption is changing. In the communist system, power in the party was an important influence in the allocation of goods and services outside the rule of law. Many members of the old communist *nomenklatura* adapted to the market economy by exchanging their party card for dollars and deutschmarks as the currency of influence.

The New Russia Barometer asked two related questions about this in 2000. In answer to the proposition 'some people say that in Soviet times, to get anything done by a public agency, you had to know people in the party', 68 per cent agreed, while 32 per cent disagreed. In response to the statement 'some people say that nowadays to get anything done by a public agency you need to pay money on the side', 90 per cent agreed, while 10 per cent disagreed. Table 7 combines Russians' answers to the two questions.

Table 7: **Comparing the nature of corruption today and under the former regime in Russia (%)**

Party was the old currency of influence	Money is now the currency of influence	%
Agree	Agree	63
Disagree	Agree	27
Agree	Disagree	5
Disagree	Disagree	5

Contact: Richard Rose (i.m.rogerson@cspp.strath.ac.uk).

Assessing perceptions of corruption in Latin America

Marta Lagos (Latinobarómetro)

How have perceptions of corruption, its increase or decrease and its importance as a problem changed in recent years in South and Central America? Latinobarómetro is an annual 17-country survey, undertaken yearly by the NGO Corporación Latinobarómetro, based in Santiago, Chile.[2] There are approximately 1,000 respondents in each national representative sample.

As table 8 shows, in 2000 more than 90 per cent of respondents in Honduras, Nicaragua and Paraguay said that corruption had 'increased a lot' over the previous year. At the lower end of the ranking, less than 60 per cent of the population said this in Mexico, Peru and Venezuela.

The level of debate and traditional occurrence of corruption, along with the objective experience of corruption, have an impact on the extent to which corruption has been seen to increase. Mexico, for instance, where corruption has long been recognised as a problem, ranks only fifteenth out of the 17 countries in terms of perceptions of increasing corruption. Meanwhile Argentina, where corruption is seen as a more recent phenomenon, receives one of the highest rankings. In every country in the region, respondents have reported an annual increase in corruption each year since the surveys began. Indeed, as the final column in table 8 shows, only in Mexico, Panama, Uruguay and Venezuela is the increasing corruption perceived to have slowed down more than marginally over the period from 1996 to 2000. In other countries, the rate of increase has either stayed the same or risen, the largest rises being in Nicaragua and Brazil.

Table 9 presents perceptions of how serious corruption is as a problem. In 2000, the highest proportions of respondents seeing corruption to be a 'very seri-

Table 8: **Perception of change in the level of corruption (%)**

	1996 Corruption increased...		1997 Corruption increased...		1998 Corruption increased...		2000 Corruption increased...		Change: 1996 'increase' to 2000 'increase'
	a lot	a little	a lot	a little	a lot	a little	a lot	a little	
Argentina	87	5	92	5	90	3	87	5	0
Bolivia	74	11	84	10	73	12	83	8	+6
Brazil	64	16	81	6	83	7	85	5	+10
Chile	51	21	62	18	54	18	60	15	+3
Colombia	76	12	89	6	83	5	80	9	+1
Costa Rica	84	8	92	5	89	6	89	5	+2
Ecuador	84	9	93	4	85	7	87	5	−1
El Salvador	70	11	67	19	84	6	72	14	+5
Guatemala	67	8	55	17	77	10	63	13	+1
Honduras	85	4	89	5	77	8	91	4	+6
Mexico	76	12	56	22	58	21	56	19	−13
Nicaragua	79	5	84	7	91	5	92	2	+10
Panama	75	13	66	17	76	11	72	11	−5
Paraguay	84	8	92	2	89	2	92	2	+2
Peru	48	20	73	13	69	14	56	18	+6
Uruguay	73	16	76	17	72	18	62	20	−7
Venezuela	93	1	94	3	94	2	54	11	−29
South America & Mexico	74	12	81	10	77	10	72	11	−3
Central America	77	8	75	12	82	8	80	8	+3
Latin America	75	11	79	10	79	10	75	10	−1

Question asked: 'With regard to the following list of issues, do you think they have 'increased a lot' or 'a little'; or 'decreased a lot' or 'a little'; or 'remained the same' in the last 12 months?'

ous' problem were found in Honduras, Nicaragua and Paraguay. While corruption was seen to be a 'very serious' problem by the majority of respondents in all countries in the region, the lowest proportions of respondents who stated this were found in Chile, Mexico and Uruguay.

The final column of table 9 records changes between 1997 and 2000 in perceptions of corruption as a 'serious' or 'very serious' problem. In no country in the region was there a fall of more than two percentage points in this perception over this period. The largest increase was in Guatemala, which saw a 30 percentage point increase in the perception of corruption as a 'very serious' problem.

Table 9: **Perception of corruption as a problem (%)**

	1997		1998		2000		Change 1997–2000 in 'serious' and 'very serious' combined
	Very serious	Serious	Very serious	Serious	Very serious	Serious	
Argentina	88	11	86	13	90	8	−1
Bolivia	67	30	61	34	81	15	−1
Brazil	73	22	74	21	84	11	0
Chile	65	28	51	37	68	23	−2
Colombia	87	12	82	16	88	9	−2
Costa Rica	82	16	73	20	90	8	0
Ecuador	74	21	69	26	85	12	+2
El Salvador	55	37	60	36	79	18	+5
Guatemala	54	29	58	34	84	12	+13
Honduras	77	20	80	18	92	7	+2
Mexico	47	38	50	38	61	23	−1
Nicaragua	80	17	85	14	93	6	+2
Panama	68	27	68	29	81	15	−1
Paraguay	77	17	84	11	91	7	+4
Peru	66	29	60	35	75	21	+1
Uruguay	57	39	60	35	69	27	0
Venezuela	79	16	89	10	84	13	+2
South America & Mexico	71	24	69	25	79	16	0
Central America	69	24	70	25	86	11	+4
Latin America	70	24	70	25	82	14	+2

Question asked: 'Thinking about the problem of corruption in [country] today, would you say that the problem is 'very serious', 'serious', 'not very serious' or 'not at all serious'?'

Contact: Marta Lagos (mlagos@latinobarometro.org).

1 The surveys in these countries were originally known as the Southern African Democracy Barometer. The authors gratefully acknowledge the support of USAID, particularly its Regional Centre for Southern Africa and its South Africa mission.
2 Funding of the project began with an initial grant from the European Community in 1995, and technical expertise from Eurobarometer. Funding now comes from multiple sources. Access to the data is by purchase, with a four-year lag before public release.